Building Magic
Disney's Overseas Theme Parks

William Silvester

BearManor Media

Albany, Georgia

Building Magic: Disney's Overseas Theme Parks
Copyright © 2016 William Silvester. All Rights Reserved.

No part of this book may be reproduced in any form or by any means, electronic, mechanical, digital, photocopying or recording, except for the inclusion in a review, without permission in writing from the the publisher.

Building Magic: Disney's Overseas Theme Parks is not authorized by, endorsed by or associated with The Walt Disney Company or any of its sponsors or affiliates. References to Disney copyrighted characters and trademarks or any other company copyrights or trademarks are solely for purposes of information, editorial commentary and history under the Fair Use Doctrine. Cover illustrations and brochure scans are copyright The Walt Disney Company and are from the author's collection.

For more about the author go to: williamsilvester.weebly.com

Published in the USA by
BearManor Media
P.O. Box 71426
Albany, GA 31708
www.BearManorMedia.com

Softcover Edition
ISBN-10: 1593939728
ISBN-13: 978-1-59393-972-4

Printed in the United States of America

Table of Contents

Introduction   vii

PART I – TOKYO DISNEYLAND   xiii

Chapter One – Urayasu   1

Chapter Two – OLC and WDP   15

Chapter Three – Building a Park   23

Chapter Four – Opening Tokyo Disneyland   35

Chapter Five – "Kingdom of Dreams and Magic"   59

Chapter Six – Tokyo DisneySea   87

Chapter Seven – "A Whole New World . . ."   99

PART II – DISNEYLAND PARIS   121

Chapter One – Marne-la-Vallée   123

Chapter Two – Euro Disneyland   139

Chapter Three – "When the Dream Becomes Reality"   157

Chapter Four – The Tragic Kingdom   183

Chapter Five – Disneyland Paris   199

Chapter Six – Walt Disney Studios Park   219

PART III – HONG KONG DISNEYLAND   235

Chapter One – Penny's Bay   237

Chapter Two – World's Smallest Disneyland   257

Chapter Three – "The Happiest Land Of Fortune"   271

PART IV – SHANGHAI DISNEYLAND   297

Chapter One – Pudong   299

Chapter Two – "Authentically Disney and Distinctly Chinese"   315

Chapter Three – Unveiling the Magic   333

Epilogue   357

Bibliography   367

Index   379

About the Author   399

List of Maps

Tokyo Disneyland	34
Tokyo DisneySea	98
Disneyland Paris	138
Walt Disney Studio Park	218
Hong Kong Disneyland	256
Shanghai Disneyland	314

Introduction

"... the sun never sets on a Disney theme park..."
Michael Eisner, CEO, The Walt Disney Company

WALT DISNEY FIRST STARTED THINKING about a Mickey Mouse Park in the 1930s, when he would take his daughters, Diane and Sharon, to ride the merry-go-round while he sat on a bench eating peanuts. Walt later told an interviewer, "I felt that there should be something built, some kind of family park where parents and children could have fun together." His first steps towards his park came when he built a railway layout in his backyard in Holmby Hills, named the engine *Lilly Belle* after his wife, designed the landscape, and invited friends and neighbors over for rides around the 2,600 feet of track. Over the years the idea evolved from a small park next to the Disney Studio in Burbank that would have rides for the kids and a place for his train. His ideas soon outgrew that space, so his plans moved on to a plot of orange groves and walnut trees outside of the city of Anaheim. It was a struggle to get funding, as few people could fathom the concept that Walt was pitching. He envisioned more than the typical amusement park of the day; his park would be clean, safe, and organized. Walt recruited imaginative men from inside his own studio and put them to work on his Disney Land project. When his work took him to Europe he would explore the parks there, having an affinity for Copenhagen's Tivoli Gardens. Whenever he could, he visited amusements parks to see what they were doing right and particularly what they were doing wrong. He found that parks needed a single entrance with a single draw into the park, which he envisioned as a fairy tale castle. Food and entertainment had to be not just good but exceptional. It had to be clean and the employees had to be knowledgeable and polite.

Walt hired the Stanford Research Institute to give him a feasible price for his park, and they came up with $11 million. Now all he had to do was raise the money. His own company, Walt Disney Productions, was still recovering from the losses incurred during the Second World War. Feature animation was expensive and there was little money to spare for Walt's dream. Finally, in the early 1950s, the ABC television network asked him to do a TV show; Walt agreed, got his funding, and the perfect vehicle for advertising his new park, Disneyland. The Stanford people had concluded that the population of California would expand towards Orange County, and it was there, near the sleepy town of Anaheim, that Walt should build his park.

Ground was broken in July 1954, and construction, berm building, tree planting, river dredging, train track laying, and all the other myriad projects involved in building the world's first theme park got underway. Inevitably, problems arose, such as when the water for the Rivers of America drained into the sandy soil and the banks had to be lined with clay, and a color-blind bulldozer driver pushed down the trees marked with a green ribbon to be saved because he could not tell the difference. By opening day, costs had soared to over $17 million, but Walt Disney had his dream fulfilled, and his idea of a "theme park," rather than a simple amusement park, was a success.

Introduction

With the opening of Disneyland in July 1955 and its subsequent success, requests came in from all over the world from companies wanting to build similar theme parks. Walt wasn't sure that he wanted another Disneyland, and after his death his executives concentrated on the construction of his last theme park dream, Walt Disney World (WDW). The Magic Kingdom in Florida was completed in 1971 before any serious consideration was given to similar theme parks around the world. It was during the expansion of Walt Disney World with the building of the Experimental Prototype Community of Tomorrow (EPCOT), which opened on October 1, 1982, that plans for a foreign park finally came to fruition.

This is the story of the overseas Disney theme parks, how they are the same as the prototypes in America and how they differ. Why they were built where they are, who wanted them constructed, and the problems that were faced in the building of these magical places. Did the parks spread Americanism or did they adjust to adopt the culture of the country they were in?

In Japan, some referred to the forthcoming Disney theme park as "The Black Ship," for it was reminiscent of the black ships of Commodore Perry who sailed into Tokyo Harbor in the mid-1800s and forced the Japanese to open their doors to foreign trade. In France, reporters called the park a "cultural Chernobyl" or "The Tragic Kingdom" for the French media feared the impact of American consumerism on their way of life. Conversely, in the United States, the Disney theme parks in Orlando and Anaheim bear the names "The Magic Kingdom" and "The Happiest Place on Earth," and the overseas parks one day hope to earn those names.

The first Disney theme park outside of the United States opened near Tokyo, Japan in 1983, and expanded to include a second park, Tokyo DisneySea in 2001. The second was erected in 1992, just outside Paris, France under the name Euro Disneyland, changed its name to Disneyland Paris a few years later, and added a second venue, Walt Disney Studios Park, in 2002. The third, and smallest, opened as Hong Kong Disneyland in 2005, and a fourth was constructed in Shanghai, China, and opened in mid-June, 2016.

All faced problems and controversy in their early days, but now it appears that they have been warmly embraced by the people who attend them and the corporations that support them.

Countless hours have been spent reading documents, browsing through websites, perusing books, newspapers, and magazines, and watching endless videos of varying quality, in an effort to present a balanced, detailed story of the overseas Disney theme parks. Following is as unbiased an account as a Disney fan can write. Chapters begin with the background story of each park, from preconception to opening day, and then conclude with a tour of the park, pointing out what is there, what is new, what is different, and in some cases, what is coming, to give readers as in depth a look at the parks as can be obtained without actually going there. In many cases the author presupposes that the reader has some familiarity with American Disney theme parks. This book also answers the oft asked and burning question, "If I've been to Disneyland and Walt Disney World, is it worth my while going to the overseas parks?"

In the case of conversions, lineal to metric or foreign currency to U.S. dollars, the author usually notes the conversion once and then leaves it up to the reader to decide if they need to know that much detail by using only one version in future references.

It should be noted that Japanese and Chinese names are used here in Western order, that is, first name before last name in reverse of Asian tradition which is last name, or family name, first. Company names are Anglicized and Romanised.

Frequently Used Abbreviations

DCA – Disney's California Adventure
DLP – Disneyland Paris
EDL – Euro Disneyland
HKD – Hong Kong Disneyland
OLC – Oriental Land Company
SAR – Special Administrative Region
SDL – Shanghai Disneyland
SSG – Shanghai Shendi Group
TDL – Tokyo Disneyland
TDR – Tokyo Disney Resort
TDS – Tokyo DisneySea
WDC – Walt Disney Company
WDI – Walt Disney Imagineering
WDP – Walt Disney Productions
WDS – Walt Disney Studio Park
WDW – Walt Disney World

PART I
TOKYO DISNEYLAND

Chapter One
Urayasu

FOR MANY GENERATIONS the old fishing village of Urayasu lay serenely in a landscape largely dominated by water. It had been built on the tidal flats of north Tokyo Bay near the border of Chiba prefecture, only 10 miles (16 kilometers) from the center of the Japanese capital city of Tokyo. Urayasu was proclaimed a village in 1889 and a town in 1909. For generations the people of Urayasu had harvested the clear, shallow, fertile waters off the coast for fish, crustaceans, and other produce of the sea. Though badly damaged by bombing during the Second World War, and suffering the loss of many residents, the village survived and was rebuilt.

In 1958, Honshu Paper constructed a mill on the Edo River near where it emptied into Tokyo Bay. The subsequent waste and effluent from the mill drifted into the bay and settled in the shallow waters along the shore. In a very short time the clear blue waters near Urayasu turned black and the sea life beneath was destroyed.

Desperate, the fishermen appealed to the National Diet, Tokyo Metropolitan Government, and Honshu Paper. In response to the petitions, Honshu Paper was ordered by the government to shut down the Edogawa plant to preserve the small part of the Urayasu habitat that survived. Honshu Paper paid lip service to the order but continued business as usual, deciding that the government was too pro-business and weak to do anything to enforce the order. They were right but they reckoned without the fishermen.

A group of eight hundred fishermen and their supporters marched on the capital to hold demonstrations outside the Tokyo Metropolitan Building and the National Diet. After a loud protest they obtained copies of the government documents ordering Honshu Paper to cease operations and marched to the company factory in Tokyo.

Upon arriving at the factory, the group's leaders attempted to present the orders to the factory officials but were denied access to the building. Regardless, the eight hundred protestors forced their way into the building and occupied it. The situation deteriorated quickly after that. Honshu Paper contacted the police, who soon arrived in full riot gear. The fishermen refused to leave and the police decided to forcibly evict them. In the violent clash that followed, eight fishermen were arrested and 105 people received varying degrees of injury.

Until that time, the fishermen's complaints had been overlooked by the press, but the battle at the Honshu Paper factory received extensive national attention. When the reasons for the protest became known, public opinion was solidly behind the fishermen, and angry citizens sent the Diet scrambling when they demanded to know how such a thing could be permitted to happen.

Though too late for Urayasu, the Diet quickly pushed forward the first water quality control legislation in Japanese history under the title of "Law for the Preservation of Water Quality in Public Water Areas." This led to increased interest by the average citizen in the government's environmental policies and, before long, to challenge it through the opposition parties, the courts, and local governments.

By the 1960s, Urayasu was facing another devastating crisis as the fishing industry continued to rapidly decline due to industrial pollution wiping out fishing grounds in the delta of the Edo River. In addition, land reclamation projects were shrinking shellfish harvesting areas by filling in the lands covered in shallow water to further expand industrial development. This reclamation had an enormous impact of the marine life and people of the area. The fishing, shellfish, and seaweed industry, upon which some 15,000 households around Tokyo Bay had depended, was devastated. By the end of the century that number would be reduced to around 2,300.

As these dismal events were transpiring, an incident took place in Tokyo that in time would have a tremendous effect on the region. On July 11, 1960, the president of Keisei Electric Rail Co., Ltd., (*Keisei Dentetsu* in Japanese) Chiharu Kawasaki, and the president of Mitsui Fudosan Co. Ltd., (*Mitsui Fudōsan*) Hideo Edo, formed a new company they called the Oriental Land Co., Ltd. Their prospectus of 1959 stated that their new company would "like to reclaim the sea off Urayasu to develop commercial and residential areas, as well as a large-scale recreational facility, so as to contribute to the nation's culture, health, and welfare." The fledgling company established their three employees with an equal number of desks in a corner office on the fifth floor of the Keisei Electric Railway's main office building in Ueno, Tokyo. So utilitarian were they that they shared a telephone with the Equity Division of Keisei Electric Railway and the company telephone operator handled their calls. The three employees were Chiharu Kawasaki, an office lady, and an executive ready for retirement.

Chiharu Kawasaki wanted to be an artist, but when he graduated from Tokyo University in 1933, he became a banker and would remain so until after the world war. In 1945, a friend from university and then president of Keisei Electric Railway Co., Ltd. persuaded him to join his railroad company.

Kawasaki agreed, found the challenge suited him, and within eight years had become president of the company. He continued with his painting and developed a love for roses which, curiously, would lead to Tokyo Disneyland.

Whenever he traveled aboard, to Europe or America, he would seek out varieties of roses, and "when I saw a good rose I bought it immediately," and entered it in the annual Keisei Gardening rose competition. Such was his passion for roses that he wanted to build a rose park. At the time the Japanese rail system was tied to department stores (*depato*) and amusement parks which the railway companies created themselves in outlying areas and then constructed a rail line and station to take people to it. Kawasaki wanted to expand on that concept with a better park than the uninspired and low budget parks that were usually built. When Kawasaki became president of Keisei the company already had an amusement park they called Yazu Park, which had opened in 1925. Kawasaki took advantage of these holdings to build his world class rose park, but he was not satisfied with the overall quality of the park and dreamed of something better. Like the people at Disney with whom he would later deal, Kawasaki insisted on quality; had he been otherwise, his rose garden, in which there was no profit, would never have been built.

"When I would go to America to visit rose gardens (prior to the formation of OLC) I would also visit amusement and theme parks. Disneyland was the best. Japan didn't have a park like Disneyland, but I thought that the Japanese people are going to want one. I believed if we made a park just like Disneyland it would succeed. Up to that time, building parks was just part of developing railways. I was doubtful about whether building parks like that was the right thing to do. I was very impressed by Disneyland. I started thinking about building a park like it," Kawasaki was quoted as saying in Marc Borrelli's article *Land of the Rising Mickey*.

The original purpose behind the reclamation project came about in the early 1950s when the Chiba Prefecture government recognized that "there was an imbalance between work and leisure activities in Japan." The idea was to reclaim the shallow lands in Tokyo Bay and use them for residential, commercial, and recreational facilities. The Oriental Land Company was one of a number of companies formed to take advantage of the offers of land from the prefecture.

Once the Japanese government had given its blessing to the Oriental Land Company to proceed in their reclamation project, negotiations were started with the two fisherman's cooperatives in Urayasu. The main problem they faced were the demands from the fishermen for compensation for the loss of livelihood caused by the land reclamation, a highly contentious issue. Into the breach stepped Masatomo Takahashi.

The negotiator had been born on September 4, 1913, in Fukushima, Japan. After attending Tokyo Imperial University, Takahashi graduated with a law degree in 1939 and shortly afterwards joined Riken Heavy Industries Company until he was drafted to serve in the army during World War II. He was sent to Shanghai, China and later the island of New Guinea where he acted as an Army interpreter. When the war was over he returned home and took employment as the Executive Managing Director with Kenzai Co., working his way up to the company presidency.

Hideo Edo, a former classmate of Takahashi, arranged for him to meet Kawasaki at the Keisei Railway headquarters. Their initial conversation is said to have gone something like this: "So you're Takahashi. Edo told me about you. I heard you can drink a lot. Drink a lot and don't worry about money." These were apparently sought after qualities for the man he wanted to negotiate with the fishermen. Not long after, Kawasaki held a welcoming party for Takahashi and during the course of the evening put on a slide show featuring his last trip to Disneyland. "I want to do this in the future," he told him.

Years later Takahashi admitted that when he heard that, he thought "What is he thinking?" The completion of the land reclamation was years off, he still hadn't convinced the fishermen to give up their land, he had no interest in Disney, and as far as he was concerned, once the reclamation was done, he would move on to something else.

Takahashi joined the real estate development firm Oriental Land

Company as its senior Executive Managing Director in 1961, which made him responsible for negotiating land reclamation deals with the Urayasu fishermen.

Those in the know expected the negotiations to take several years, but Takahashi was not one to wait around for results to happen. He insisted on frequent face-to-face talks with the fishermen in his efforts to persuade them to reach an agreement. He met them where they felt most comfortable, in the local bars, and drank along with the best of them. He knew the issues, knew that the fishermen were upset about the loss of their ancestral fishing grounds which resulted in the loss of their livelihoods as well. The law, both customary and administrative, stated that various Japanese communities held sea tenure over specific areas. These rights were administered by and belonged to the fisheries cooperatives.

Takahashi knew that he had to have total consensus with the fishermen. He also knew this would not be easy as the smaller groups were not allied with the large cooperatives and those groups were often at odds with each other. In the bars, Takahashi singled out the various leaders and worked to convince them that OLC's plans were in their best interest. Fortunately, he could speak their language, hold his liquor, and understand the hard lives they led. The more he worked with the fishermen, the more determined he became to make the negotiation successful. Not only did he pour OLC money into it but his own as well, ultimately selling his home to finance some of the expenses that OLC could not. It has been estimated that in the first month of negotiations he added 800,000 yen (approximately $60,000) to his expense account mostly on parties and liquor. The reason being that the fishermen were not satisfied with cheap booze; they wanted the good stuff and to dine in high class restaurants when they talked. Little *sake* cups were soon dispensed with and tea cups were filled with alcohol. Takahashi later admitted that on more than one occasion he had to excuse himself, make his unsteady way to the washroom, vomit, and then return to continue "negotiations." His strategy was to sway the various leaders and have them, in turn, convince their followers. Slowly, he won them over.

The result of the negotiations was that the cooperatives settled in six months, agreeing to give up part of their fishing rights in 1962 and the rest by 1971. In exchange they would receive rights to some of the reclaimed lands as well as a substantial cash settlement from the prefecture government and the developers. OLC gave each fisherman 500,000 yen ($40,000) and 100 *tsubo* (330.5 square meters) of land.

Generations past of Urayasu fishermen had extensive connections with the seafood trade in Tokyo, both retail and wholesale. They often sold fish door to door in Tokyo and sold them to fishmongers who sold them at the Tsukiji auctions. Though the reclamation put an end to the shellfish trade, it also provided the fishermen with new capital to expand their fishing business.

Some out of work fishermen found work with the wholesalers, gained experience, and went into the wholesale trade themselves becoming some of Tsukiji's most prosperous dealers in the world's largest seafood market.

At about the same time as the negotiations were going on other events with far reaching consequences for Urayasu were also transpiring. A fledgling commercial presence had been established in the Japanese market when Walt Disney Productions founded a local subsidiary in 1959. Disney had already begun releasing movies to the Japanese populace again, reopening the market closed tightly by the Second World War starting with *Snow White and the Seven Dwarfs* in September 1950, *Song of the South* in October 1951, and *Treasure Island* in December of the same year. It was noted by Kosei Ono in a *Look Japan* article that attending theaters in Japan in those days "became part of the schooling . . . a whole theatre would be reserved for the party of children."

The first Mickey Mouse cartoon in Japan, *The Opry House*, had been released in September 1929, mere months after being released in the United States. The charming mouse had the same effect on Japanese viewers as American and soon became very popular amongst moviegoers. The Disney movies were subtitled in Japanese but that did little to detract from the shorts as most of them required little dialogue to convey the story. Once America started applying embargoes on Japan for its aggressions against China in the 1930s, Disney and all other American films were banned.

After the war Disney came back with its shorts and feature films and *Mickey Kids*, a Japanized version of the *Disneyland* television show hosted by Walt Disney and dubbed in Japanese. Later, the show was broadcast under the name *Walt Disney Presents*, and like many American shows of the era, became very popular, particularly amongst the younger generation. The results of children in the 1950s and 1960s watching the Disney shows would have a profound effect upon Tokyo Disneyland many years later. The children who had watched the shows were now parents with fond memories of Disney and a desire to share those memories with their children.

As the Japanese networks began broadcasting more and more home grown shows the allure of the American shows diminished, though the effects of the Disney programs was securely internalized in the Japanese. The effect of Disney animation on the uniquely Japanese animation styles known as manga and anime should not be underestimated. Early Japanese characters often had pie-eyes in imitation of the American cartoons. Osamu Tezuka, considered by some to be the Walt Disney of Japan, admitted that he was influenced by Disney after having watched "*Snow White* fifty times and *Bambi* eighty times."

As a result of the popularity of Disney films and merchandise, Chiharu Kawasaki, as President of OLC, and a big fan of the *Disneyland* TV show, arranged through a friend at Yamiuri Newspaper Company to meet with the Disney brothers. His newspaper contact had previously worked with Walt's brother, Roy Disney, on the contracts to bring the Disney TV show to Japan.

In January 1962, Kawasaki paid a courtesy visit to the Disney Company in Burbank. He hoped to meet with Walt Disney and his top executives, Card Walker and Donn Tatum for a discussion about building a Disney park in Japan. For reasons that can only be speculated on, no one would meet with him.

Though Kawasaki had nothing to do with Nara Dreamland, it has been suggested that the building of that Disneyland knockoff in Japan in 1961 might have soured the Disney executives towards considering a Disneyland in Japan. The entrance to Nara Dreamland is virtually identical to Disneyland with its copy of the Disneyland railway station up on a berm. Once inside and on the main street a replica of Sleeping Beauty Castle is visible, and after strolling around one would see a reproduction of the Matterhorn (called Bobsleigh) complete with a skyway passing through it, a figure eight tracked monorail, and an Autopia-style attraction. Some non-Disney rides included Aska, a wooden roller coaster, Screw Coaster, a steel coaster, a couple of kid sized roller coasters, a Jungle Cruise type ride, a carousel, and a log flume. There were no Disney characters but Nara Dreamland had its own mascots, Ran-chan and Dori-chan, dressed as bear-skin wearing guards. (Surprisingly, Nara Dreamland managed to remain open until 2006 before finally giving in to competition and shutting down. It was never demolished and remains a derelict, neglected ghost-park to this day.)

Regardless of his initial reception, Kawasaki persisted and eventually a lower level executive was assigned to hear him out. Kawasaki explained his plan, but would not receive an answer until much later when he was told that they might consider his proposal once the land reclamation project was complete. As it had not even started yet, that was a reasonable reply.

That was apparently good enough for Kawasaki. When he returned to Japan he had a new perspective on what OLC required regarding the reclaimed land. They had already been granted land by the government, which could be taken back if not used within a certain time period, but Kawasaki was of the opinion they needed more. He sent Takahashi to the Chiba Prefecture to request one million *tsubo* (330 hectares) of reclaimed land to be used for the recreational area. The prefecture was not impressed and noted that even "Disneyland in Los Angeles is only 90,000 *tsubo* (30 hectares)." In the end OLC was granted 750,000 *tsubo* (250 hectares).

Kawasaki explained to Takahashi that he wanted the extra land around the park for the same reason Walt Disney had wanted the vast expanses of land in Florida for Walt Disney World. "By the time the (Disney) company wanted to build a few hotels close to the park as the business was booming, all the adjacent lands had been bought up by others. I don't want to see the same thing happen to us."

A few months later, in July 1962, OLC and the Chiba prefecture concluded an "Agreement on Urayasu District Reclamation and Land Sales." With the fishermen in agreement and the Chiba prefectural government on side, the Urayasu offshore reclamation project could proceed.

Oriental Land began reclamation work in 1964. Though some difficulties were encountered work progressed at a steady pace and by 1966, the Benten, Higashino, Imaigawa, Tekko-dori, and Tomioka areas had been completed. Phase two of the project involving Kairaku, Mihama, and Irifune areas began nine months later and was finished in 1969. The last area, Maihama, was completed in 1970. As the lands were being reclaimed, construction began on commercial and residential sites and OLC began looking for a suitable recreational facility that they planned to locate in the Maihama area.

A minor political scandal transpired with OLC over the area's development. It seems there were improper application procedures and rumored attempts by Mitsui board members to influence the ruling Liberal Democratic Party to change land usage restrictions in the reclaimed areas. In November 1967, a Diet member from the Kōmeitō party publicly denounced the Ministry of Construction and accused a number of companies, including Mitsui Real Estate, Oriental Land Company, Asahi Real Estate, and Keisei Railway of reclaiming land without permission. Blame was transferred to Chiba Prefecture for not having followed the correct application procedures laid out by the Ministry of Construction, which in turn promised "a strict investigation."

A long delay now followed as the red tape was untangled. The land known as Area C contained many hectares necessary for OLC's plans for the park and it was at the center of the investigation. It was not until a new Minister of Construction had assumed the post by March 1969 that permission to continue was granted. To OLC's detriment, however, he had decided to remove 77.5 hectares from the originally designated landfill site. As it transpired, the land removed was within the area designated by OLC for its park. This necessitated five years of continuous lobbying by OLC until the Ministry finally agreed to an additional landfill in 1974 under the stipulation that it "be used as a green tract of land."

The initial master plan for what they intended to be "the best recreational facility in Asia" was unique and had little resemblance to what would eventually be built. It was called the "Oriental Land (Recreational Facility) Basic Plan." The concept review began shortly after the reclamation work first began, was subjected to numerous revisions, and was finally approved by Chiba Prefecture in 1974. "Wonderful People and Their World" was the theme of the proposal that would consist of hotels, an auditorium, a fashion square, and a themed play land. Research into theme parks around the world was undertaken as teams went to Europe and North America. In May 1972 the research team visited Disneyland and Walt Disney World, the latter having just opened some six months previous. Noburu Kamisawa, later Managing Director of Tokyo Disneyland, was there at the time and later recalled, "It was like another world . . . the philosophy of heart . . . smiles . . . taught by Walt Disney himself – this is what we wanted to bring to Japan." According to the Oriental Land website, "Through this process, the dream of bringing Disneyland to Japan began to gain momentum."

At about the same time, Disney corporate management had instructed Frank Stanek, WED Enterprises' Director of Research and Planning, to look into the possibility of constructing an overseas version of Disneyland in Europe or Japan. This he did, basing his research on how receptive a country was to the Disney brand, travel patterns, cultural characteristics and growth, and economic stability of the areas in question. When he submitted his summary memo to the company in early 1973 he concluded that while Japan and Europe both had potential and could support a Disneyland project, "Japan offers the highest potential for success, even though it may be more difficult to execute."

Frank Stanek was born in Stamford, Connecticut on July 8, 1940. Here he attended the Holy Name of Jesus parochial school and the St. Basil's Preparatory School before moving with his family to Anaheim, California in

1959. A year later he enrolled at the California State University in Fullerton in their Business Administration Program. Like many students he worked part time at Disneyland, starting out as a short order cook and later attaining an industrial engineer position. His Disney employers were so impressed with his work that they asked him to graduate a semester early and come to work for them as Financial Controller for the "It's a Small World" project they were working on for Pepsi-Cola's exhibit at the 1964 New York World's Fair. Stanek was happy to oblige, and according to Marty Sklar in his book *Dream It! Do It!* "he learned things one day before he had to teach them to someone else, which proved to be a first step to an incredibly successful career at Disney."

As he was beginning his second summer in New York, Roy Disney recalled him to California to take control of the WED Enterprises (now Walt Disney Imagineering) business planning function. His position made him responsible for all the new Disney projects such as Mineral King Ski Resort and Walt Disney World. The former did not come to fruition, but Walt Disney World was a full time project eventually leading Stanek into leadership of the Walt Disney World Project Control Office.

Proclaimed the world's largest private construction site, Walt Disney World was like a jigsaw puzzle with components coming in from all over the United States, from the delicate computer controlled audio-animatronic versions of Disneyland's favorite attractions to massive monorail beams manufactured in Washington state. Frank acted like an orchestra's conductor blending and melding a medley of components using creative imagination and technical know-how, what Walt called "Imagineering." He also made sure there was plenty "of Coors Beer and Mexican food to keep the California 'expats' motivated."

The Magic Kingdom in Walt Disney World opened on October 1, 1971 with twenty-three attractions of which twenty were replicas of attractions in Disneyland and three were unique to WDW. The lands were also replicated with Main Street, Fantasyland, Adventureland, Frontierland, and

Tomorrowland. Liberty Square was added as an exclusive Magic Kingdom area.

With the launch successful, Stanek did not rest on his laurels but continued to work on plans to expand and enhance the Disney World experience. Thirteen major attractions were in the works as well as a campground, hotels, and restaurants. Back in California work continued towards developing Mineral King Ski Resort, Golden Oak Ranch, and EPCOT Center, the Experimental Prototype Community of Tomorrow. In time, Frank's business development experience resulted in him becoming the Executive Project Manager for EPCOT, and eventually he volunteered to head the overall development process for Tokyo Disneyland.

Exactly when the metaphor of "the black ship" was applied to the negotiations surrounding Tokyo Disneyland is a matter of conjecture. In fact, the phrase has a number of meanings, though it initially referred to the black hulled ships of Commodore Matthew Perry sailing into Tokyo harbor with the intention, at gun point, of forcing the Japanese to open their doors to foreign influence. In his book *Riding the Black Ship*, Aviad E. Raz states "The black ship is a historical symbol, an ideological façade, a ride, and a hyperbole . . . a journey for real among many imaginaries."

It was Disney's Japanese amusement park competition who first used the term regarding Walt Disney Productions' inroads into their territory. In an effort to shine a bad light on WDP's presence, they referred to the Disney theme park as "a smoke screen of infantile happiness and false consciousness" and the early negotiators as "the shock troops of American capitalism." What they failed to realize, and what OLC had planned from the beginning, was that Tokyo Disneyland would be seen from the perspective of "an American in Japan and a Japanese view of America."

Chapter Two
OLC and WDP

HAVING SECURED THE LAND and made the decision to build a recreation facility, Oriental Land Company began looking around to find the best way to proceed. Initially the park was to be called "Oriental Land," and from 1972 to 1973 teams were sent to Europe and North America to study their leisure and recreational facilities. OLC came to the conclusion that the ideal choice for their purposes was a recreation of Disneyland.

In February 1974, a letter was sent to Walt Disney Productions with a formal request for Disney executives to visit Japan. To back up the request OLC President Kawasaki flew to Burbank in June to visit the studio. He met with top Disney management to explain OLC's plans for a Disneyland in Urayasu and again extended the invitation for the Disney executives to visit Japan. Upon returning to Tokyo, Kawasaki had the "Oriental Land Feasibility Study Report 1974" drawn up and sent to Walt Disney Productions in July. The report explained what OLC had in mind and emphasized the suitability of the Urayasu reclaimed land, emphasizing its position close to metropolitan Tokyo.

A drop in attendance at Walt Disney World due to the 1974 energy crisis caused Disney to hesitate about negotiating a deal with OLC. The "oil shock" as it was called in Japan also had an effect on OLC, and the ensuing financial difficulties necessitated that Kawasaki focus his full attention on Keisei Railway affairs. In addition, a second group, the Mitsubishi Company, had also expressed an interest in a deal with WDP. After much deliberation, Disney executives finally agreed to visit Japan in December 1974. The team consisted of Disney President Card Walker, Dick Nunis (Vice-President of Park Operations), Donn Tatum (CEO Walt Disney Productions), Orlando Ferrante (Vice-President of Administration and Production), Imagineer John Hench, and Corporate Lawyer, Ron Cayo. Their first stop was at the Mitsubishi site at the foot of Mount Fuji. At first glance it appeared to be the perfect place to build a theme park, situated as it was at the base of Japan's most famous and iconic natural feature. After a tour of the site they were informed, for reasons unknown, that Mitsubishi had "changed its mind" and the site was no longer available.

On the fourth day of the month, the Disney executives met with OLC in the Imperial Hotel. The OLC executives had done a thorough study and their presentation was comprehensive with market data, aerial photographs, Japanese stock market values, and the notation that the site was virtually in the heart of Japan. Commercial and residential projects were already well underway and the site earmarked for the theme park was within one hour of a population of almost thirty million people.

With the end of the presentation, one of the few luxury limousines in Japan at the time took the Disney executives on a tour of the Urayasu site.

After having a look around at ground level the OLC and WDP executives boarded three helicopters for an aerial view of the site. The OLC later reported, "They could see how the site was located adjacent to the Tokyo Metropolitan area with the sea and rivers surrounding it on three sides, which gave it an out-of-the-ordinary quality. We explained how appropriate the proposed site for Disneyland would be, and pointed out its special features. The Disney executives were particularly impressed by the view from the air."

The executives met again on December 6, at which time the Disney delegation expressed a desire to further pursue the possibility of building a Disney theme park in partnership with the Oriental Land Company. A "Basic Agreement" was drawn up, and the years of passion and hard work of Kawasaki's Japanese company to build a leisure facility were finally beginning to come to fruition.

There was still some dissent on both sides. Disney was in the midst of building EPCOT and it was proving a much greater drain on resources than had been anticipated. Roy E. Disney, Walt's nephew, and a member of the Board of Directors, was against the project, feeling that Walt Disney Productions was becoming more of a real estate company than a movie company.

Card Walker wanted to retire but before he did he wanted to fulfill Walt's dream of EPCOT.

The new park was his main focus, and so the movie side of the company languished, much to Roy's chagrin. Mitsui representatives, from a real estate point of view, still thought the land should be used for housing. They could not see how it was possible to make a profit from the enterprise, and they knew that if the theme park idea did not succeed, the deal with Chiba prefecture allowed them to make a profit by selling the land. In his book *Success Stories*, Leonard Koren suggested that "Ron Cayo thought that Mitsui was just waiting for the deal to collapse."

With an agreement in hand, OLC began a study on the best way to build and operate the Disney theme park. The first phase began in January 1975 and nine months later, in the "Oriental Disneyland Concept" document,

OLC and the Disney company agreed that the Urayasu area would serve quite well for building the park. This led to Disney producing a site development plan based on that document.

Representatives of the two companies continued to meet on a regular basis as they ironed out the terms for beginning the second phase. The "Oriental Disneyland Project" finally entered the concrete design stage in June 1976. Stanek and Cayo, the corporate lawyer, had spent almost a year working on a letter of intent that was signed in July. Now began another year of deliberations on the Second Phase. At a cost of one million dollars, financed by OLC, another study went forward to take a closer look at construction conditions, the feasibility of the site, and the market, as well as projected attendance figures.

At the same time, negotiations on business terms were in the planning stages and despite occasional tense moments moved forward reasonably smoothly. Both sides were determined to see the park work and spent countless hours in meetings to make it so.

One of the problems faced by the two companies was agreeing on attendance numbers. OLC felt that 17 million guests in the first year was not an unrealistic figure. WDP, on the other hand, based on what was happening at Walt Disney World, suggested that 10 million was more likely. In addition, Stanek felt that a park could not be built "with that kind of visitor capacity, due to both costs and time required." The lower number was "a number we knew was achievable" based on Disney World having reached that result when it opened in 1971.

As 1977 dawned, negotiations were still progressing. Stanek likened the project to "a bottle floating in the ocean," as various issues and personalities involved in the agreement "moved forward and backward." At times it even seemed that talks would break down completely. Even the Japanese media "were unanimous in predicting the project's failure."

There were three main problems. Firstly, Disney was not willing to invest as much in the project as OLC would like. They had another major project in Florida with EPCOT Center, and though Card Walker had committed to an overseas theme park, he was determined it would be on Disney's terms. He was reluctant to proceed as he felt that all incoming capital should go towards financing EPCOT.

In his book *Dream It! Do It!*, Marty Sklar suggested that Walker's attitude towards the Japanese was "compounded" by "his World War II experience." Having served as a flight deck officer on USS *Bunker Hill*, an American aircraft carrier, during the *kamikaze* attacks in the spring of 1945, he was in the thick of the battle. As luck would have it, when one of the suicide pilots crashed into the deck of *Bunker Hill*, he was on a five day leave. Over three hundred officers and men were killed, including the officer who was serving in Walker's place; he never forgot it.

The second stumbling block was that the negotiators could not agree on the percentage of fees Disney would be paid, and thirdly OLC was very wary of the cost burden that would eventually fall to them. OLC failed to understand why Disney could be so positive about the success of Tokyo Disneyland but not be willing to invest in it. This question was also posed by Japanese banks. Was it too risky a project? Should they lend money to finance a plan that Disney seemed unwilling to invest in? A compromise was finally reached when Disney agreed to the option of investing two and a half million dollars for a 10% share of ownership in the theme park. The banks felt more secure with the possibility that Disney could invest in the future, and a deal could now be made. As it happened, Disney never did exercise the option and due to that omission, according to Stanek, "left over $600 million on the table."

The name of the park was officially proclaimed "Tokyo Disneyland" (*Tōkyō dizuniirando*) in March and by September 1977, WED was ready with a presentation. "During the last week of September," the 1977 Walt Disney Productions Annual Report stated, "Representatives of the Company made a comprehensive presentation to Mitsui Real Estate Development Co., Ltd., Oriental Land Co., Ltd., and Keisei Electric Railway Co., Ltd. in Tokyo covering the results of the phase II work performed by WED Enterprises in close liason (sic) with the Japanese interests.

"This year-long effort, the expense of which was borne by the Japanese, covered planning, conceptual design, preliminary engineering, preliminary construction, fabrication and installation estimates, operational planning, organizational development planning and marketing and promotional guidelines. This work also developed the areas in which additional information and input will be forthcoming from the Japanese groups covering essential information available to them and based upon their knowledge and information of conditions in their country."

The report went on to detail how OLC had recently reorganized so that the company could "appraise the entire project on its own initiative" so that "the Japanese and our Company will be in a position to make a decision as to whether the project will go forward."

Delays in the construction of the Tokyo Bay Expressway had pushed the completion date into the future, and "start of construction for the new Keiyo Line Railroad is indefinite at this time. Assuming a favorable decision to proceed, it would therefore appear that the project could not open to the public before 1982."

To add to the problems negotiators faced, OLC President Kawasaki, a strong supporter of the Disneyland project, resigned. This led to internal problems within the Keisei portion of the company and forced the Mitsui Real Estate section to pick up the ball. Being a conventional, conservative company with no knowledge of theme parks, Keisei was less than enthusiastic about the project and as mentioned earlier, would prefer the land be used in other ways or sold for profit. They had built the thirty-six story Kasumigaseki building, Tokyo's first skyscraper, and expanded to build more high rises but knew little about entertainment facilities.

In addition, construction costs for the park had climbed from fifty billion yen to one hundred and twenty billion, and financing was becoming more and more difficult to obtain. The new OLC President, Masatomo Takahashi stepped into the breach as talks were on the verge of breaking down again. He met directly with the Chiba Prefecture Governor, convincing him to assist in changing the status of the reclaimed land. Chiba's Governor was a supporter of the theme park, as he knew it would draw new business into his prefecture. Over 300 hectares of land, previously designated as green tract and for leisure facilities was designated for "business and dwellings." In addition it now became possible for OLC to sell some of the real estate which was valued at over 200 billion yen. The Governor's support and pulling of various strings also resulted in the mortgage value of the land being increased and thus allowed the banks to safely approve loans.

By March 1980, OLC had completed its part of the residential development in the reclaimed area when the last of 6,500 homes were completed. The ultimate goal was the creation of a residential city capable of housing 70,000 people by 1982, a goal that was completed ahead of schedule.

Determined to see the park project through and, according to some media reports, to enable him to make his mark on Japan, Takahashi got the parties back together in an effort to jump the last hurdle facing agreement. Ron Cayo had been instructed by Card Walker to insist that 10% of admissions and 5% of revenue from food and merchandise would go to WDP. Takahashi, reminding Cayo that "amusement is a tough business," offered 5% of each. Cayo did not budge, and eventually Takahashi consented with the stipulation that the deal included "licensing and ongoing advice and expertise." It was a good deal for both sides, at the time, for revenue in the first year reached 20 million dollars.

A small hurdle from the Ministry of Finance appeared when it was noted that the foreign rights licensing agreement in Japan was for only twenty years. The Disney company asked for that to be extended to fifty years and in the end settled for forty-five.

Finally, on April 30, 1979, President Takahashi of OLC and Card Walker of WDP met in the Disney Studios in Burbank, California. The basic agreement, "Contract on Construction and Operations of Tokyo Disneyland," regarding the construction, design, and operation of Tokyo Disneyland was signed. OLC guaranteed the land on which the park would be built, would look after financing, and oversee construction while the Disney Company would offer technical assistance and advice and provide the master plan and design of the park. Five years of tenacious negotiations had led to achieving the biggest step towards the final goal.

Now it was up to OLC to secure final financing for the project. Despite their hopes, raising the construction funds to the amount of several hundred billion yen (one billion yen equals about 8.3 million US dollars in today's money) still did not proceed smoothly. First, OLC re-approached Chiba Prefecture "to position the Tokyo Disneyland business as a strong pillar for the prefectural government." Next, in April, with the support and presence of the vice-governor of Chiba, Takeshi Numata, a business trip was arranged to the Industrial Bank of Japan where they "were warmly welcomed." Appeals were also made to numerous other institutions for support of the Tokyo Disneyland project, and in time a co-financing group was organized in August 1980 by twenty-two of them. A foothold had been achieved and a major milestone reached in the move towards building a Disneyland in Japan.

Now that the first basic contract for the construction of Tokyo Disneyland had been signed, "Japanese engineers and architects flocked to California to tour Disneyland and prepare to construct the new operating dreamland in Tokyo."

Chapter Three
Building a Park

THE FIRST CONTINGENT OF TOKYO DISNEYLAND trainees departed Japan for Disneyland in Anaheim, California in January 1980. There were only nine management employees to begin with, but they were slated to be the Park Operations key personnel. Amongst these were Noboru Kamisawa and Yasuo Okuyama, later Executive Director of TDL Employee Relations. Okuyama said at the time, "Our greatest responsibility will be to get the ideas of the Disney traditions and philosophies across to future Tokyo Disneyland employees who will never have the chance to see Disneyland." Before long, more trainees arrived in California and would spend the next year learning every detail of what there was to know about operating a Disney theme park. From 1980 to 1982 over eighty OLC employees took part in the on-the-job training.

Over time about 150 people would receive the comprehensive training which covered everything from the history of the Disney Company to business overviews to technical knowledge. During the 30th anniversary celebration of the park, it was stated that "the passion and enthusiasm of those trainees have been handed down successfully to the 300,000 cast members who have been involved with Tokyo Disney Resort so far."

The training program had been devised by Van Arsdale France, who has been credited with beginning the process long used for training new employees in the "Disney Way." France started working for Disney in 1955 and before long had created the University of Disneyland training center. Using Walt's own philosophy for the parks as the basis to creating happiness, he encouraged smiling faces on cast members and insisted that all guests be treated as important.

France was still working for Disney in 1980, though he had been offered a retirement package and turned it down. He was later presented with the challenge of working with the orientation training team by Jim Cora, Managing Director for Operations for Tokyo Disneyland. In his autobiography *Window on Main Street*, France stated "Some of us at Disneyland were not enthused about this new Disneyland in Japan. After all, Walt had said there would be only ONE Disneyland." Regardless, he threw himself into the project with enthusiasm and devised an extensive international training program.

Jim Cora had been with Disney since 1957 when he was hired part-time to work on various attractions in Disneyland. It was while he was working the Matterhorn bobsleds that Walt Disney asked him if he was interested in training. He was told that Van France was just starting the Disney University and needed some more guys. Cora was interested and before long was moving up in the organization.

By 1971 he was deeply involved in Walt Disney World's leadership training program, and he assisted in opening the park. In 1974 he was one of the production directors in Disneyland, redesigning the park operating organization and being responsible for Tomorrowland and Fantasyland. When work began on Tokyo Disneyland, Cora was appointed Managing Director of Operations, responsible for all management and operational training.

All aspects of the Disney Company were open to the trainees. Not only did they learn how things were done in Disneyland and Walt Disney World, but they also received extensive training at the Disney Studio, WED Enterprises (the design and development part of the Disney Company, now known as Walt Disney Imagineering or WDI), and MAPO (the manufacturing area of WED founded with the profits of MAry POppins). Through observation, keeping journals, and actually working at the jobs they would eventually supervise, the Japanese cast members became proficient at "doing things Disney" to the extent that France later confessed "they may know more about Disneyland than we do."

It had occurred to France as he noticed the trainees becoming friends with their counterparts in America that it might be beneficial to all involved if the training program was slated towards the Japanese way of looking at things. Thus thinking, he studied Japanese literature, history, culture, and traditions with the intention of adapting the training program. When Disneyland head, Dick Nunis, heard about that, he took France aside and told him that one of the first things the Oriental Land Company executives had stressed to him was "Don't Japanese it up!" OLC wanted Tokyo's Disneyland to be just like the one in California.

Dick Nunis began training cast members for Disneyland before the park even opened in 1955. He had heard about Walt's dream for a theme park from his class mate, Disney's son-in-law, Ron Miller. Like Ron, he had a football scholarship to the University of Southern California. Needing a summer job, he applied at Disneyland and was hired by Van France to work on the newly developing orientation and training program.

Before long Nunis was an Attractions Supervisor, and he developed standard operating procedures for all the Disneyland attractions. In 1961 he became Director of Park Operations and assisted in working on the very hush-hush "Project X" later revealed as Walt Disney World. He went on to chair the Parks Operations Committee, and in 1968 he was Vice-President of Operations. When the Magic Kingdom opened at Walt Disney World in 1971, Nunis was appointed Executive Vice-President of Walt Disney World and Disneyland. He had served twenty-five years with the Disney organization when in 1980, he was named President of the Outdoor Recreation Division, which included Walt Disney World, EPCOT Center, and, later, the Disney-MGM Studios Theme Park. Dick Nunis was a natural to be involved in the planning and organization of Tokyo Disneyland.

The second part of the program was aimed at introducing the orientation training to Japan. Working on a plan similar to the one France and Nunis had originally designed for Disneyland in the mid 1950s, Van France and Jim Cora gathered a team of "bright, young men and women" to work with and learn from. The difference between then and now was that they had a wealth of experience and state of the art equipment to draw on.

France had first thought that his job was to chart the course and let the younger team members take over when they went to Japan. Dick Nunis had other ideas when at a planning meeting he asked France if he had a passport. He had noted that "The average age of the top executives of the OLC is sixty-seven, and you'll be our 'ancient one.'" France's name tag had the title "O.F. Number One" which either meant "Old Friend" or "Old Fart" depending on one's preference. Age and youth were to be blended to the mutual advantage of the team.

Once the group was equipped with a dazzling array of visual aids, handbooks, cards, and a wealth of knowledge, they set out for Tokyo. France had prepared his orientation program and Bob "Bubba" Allen headed the audio-visual training group with his key players, Debbie Brown, Tom Carr, Chris Donovan, and Steve Kaspar.

Allen and Kaspar went first "to plan the presentation" followed by Van France, Dick Nunis, Jim Cora, and Jim Pasilla. The first presentation to the OLC executives took place in what France described as "rather sterile-looking quarters in a Mitsui office building. The Japanese executives were seated according to status, with the most senior men in the center front seats."

Fortunately, the presenters had already been warned "that they might be stone faced but they would listen." Nunis was skilled at speaking through an interpreter and began the presentation with a historical overview followed by motivational information. France then stepped forward and, using virtually the same techniques he had used in the pre-opening days of Disneyland in 1955, gave his presentation.

The seminar went well but Dick Nunis felt he still had a couple of things he wanted to stress to the OLC officials. He had his opportunity at a reception held on the presenters' last night in Tokyo. It was a formal but friendly gathering at Mitsui Mansion, and after the OLC execs had given their speeches, Nunis stood up. He wanted to respond to one speech maker in particular, a key executive who stressed the need for control and cost cutting. Asking his interpreter, Harry, to translate his words exactly, Dick spoke clearly, slowly, and with a smile, expounding the philosophy that Walt Disney himself had taught him many years before. He wanted to make certain that the people at OLC were well aware that Walt Disney Productions' tradition "was one of quality regardless of cost."

The next day, Nunis, Cora, and France were given a tour of the prospective Tokyo Disneyland site at Urayasu. It was completely undeveloped, with only a sign indicating where the center-piece castle would be built. Afterwards, Nunis, Cora, France, and Allen went out for a farewell dinner just before boarding their plane for the flight back to Los Angeles.

Meanwhile, back in Chiba Prefecture, the construction plans were approved by the prefecture on November 28, 1980. The site dedication and ground breaking ceremony was held on December 3 following a press conference attended by some 250 reporters with high expectations for the new enterprise. Walt Disney Productions Chairman of the Board Card Walker and Oriental Land Company Chairman Masatomo Takahashi, along with other executives, took part in the Shinto purification ceremony known as *Kiri-Nusa-San Mai*, involving the waving of sacred leaves to formally initiate the project with salt and rice to cleanse the land. The Shinto priests were garbed in the traditional *jōe* and a peaked hat called a *tate-eboshi* and carried a ceremonial wand or *shaku*. The two chairmen also broke the soil in a traditional Shinto ground breaking ceremony, followed by a Shinto priest throwing confetti like pieces of paper, wishing safety during construction. Before the year was over planting and civil engineering work had begun.

The Japanese cast members who had been training in Disneyland began to arrive back in Japan as early as 1981. Following them, over time, came some 200 members of the Disney team, recruited from Disneyland, Walt Disney Imagineering in California, and Walt Disney World in Florida. They would stay in Japan from six months to five years and consisted of Division Directors, Operations Working Leads (responsible for the day to day workings within the park), and assorted Imagineers. Training continued in Japan as an estimated 6,000 cast members had to be ready for opening day. The teams were led by Jim Cora and Ron Pogue, whose job it was the make certain that the two nationalities worked side by side towards the common goal of having Tokyo Disneyland ready on time. "We had to teach them to think beyond the moment, to foresee potential problems and work out solutions before the problem occurred," Pogue explained.

The construction of Tokyo Disneyland began in earnest in January 1981. It did not take long before the 100 billion yen budget began to look overly optimistic and costs ballooned to an eventual 180 billion yen. Regardless, Takahashi refused to compromise, insisting they "create the real thing." According to the OLC website, "The staff members and Disney poured their knowledge, strength, and total energy into the construction of the Park."

A few small glitches in construction plans soon became apparent when planners went to use the original diagrams and blueprints for attractions and buildings from Disneyland and found that some modifications had to be made to suit the new site. In addition, Japanese construction laws and safety regulations differed in some respects from American, particularly in regards to earthquake proofing.

Over the next two years over 3,000 construction workers were at work on the site. Carpenters, painters, electricians, landscapers, sound men, mechanical engineers, and designers by the score were involved in the project. The painters used around 6,000 vivid colors when putting the finishing touches on the buildings and attractions. WDP personnel remained on site to supervise daily operations and to ascertain that Disney's high standards were maintained.

Maintenance Chief Bob Penfield later commented, "The Japanese are easy to work with. They really get in there and get it done. They're good at electrical and sound, machinery and animation." There was one thing that they had to be taught, according to Penfield: "They don't practice preventive maintenance. When something breaks they replace it. They don't do repair checks."

Tokyo Disneyland would be one-and-a-half times the size of Disneyland in Anaheim. Located on a peninsula at the juncture of the Edo River and Tokyo Bay, the theme park would cover 114.31 acres, with the service area, parking area, and roads entailing another 87.3 acres for a total of 201.61 acres. On opening day the parking area would have room for 8,404 vehicles.

Special attention was paid to the berm around the park, with materials being selected for cold hardiness and salt tolerance to protect the landscaping due to the sometimes harsh winters in Japan and the proximity to the ocean. In addition to winter snow, there was rain to contend with as well as the occassional typhoon. To protect the foliage in the area that would house the Jungle Cruise, gas heaters and a spraying system were installed. A giant glass roof in latticed Victorian design was built over World Bazaar. Restaurants were primarily indoors and overhangs were installed to protect guests in the open areas.

An estimated 300,000 trees were planted throughout the park with an additional 5,000 flowers and shrubs arranged to make up the Mickey Mouse face at the entrance.

Whereas Disneyland and Walt Disney World's Magic Kingdom both have trains circumnavigating the entire park, this would not be the case in Tokyo Disneyland. The curtailing of this system was due to Japanese bureaucracy. The Western River Railroad was constructed to travel only around Westernland and part of Adventureland because the Transportation Department of Japan has strigent rules when dealing with railroads. To run a train to more than one station would require licences, inspections, and supervision from the department. Neither Disney nor OLC wanted to deal with that, and by traveling to and stopping at only one station it was deemed a ride and not a train. In addition, it has been suggested that "the elevation of the tracks at various point ... would have allowed guests to catch glimpses of the surrounding Chiba area ..." spoiling the fantasy of their visit to the park.

In October 1981, the first fifteen corporate sponsors were chosen. When the park opened there would be eighteen sponsors. This system was one adopted by Walt when Disneyland was struggling for funding. It is designed for corporations to put their names forward on various facilities within the park. It gave them an opportunity to promote their own businesses alongside the internationally known Disney name. The name of the business is displayed on the attraction or facility that they sponsor, giving them advertising and promotion within the theme park. They are also permitted to use Disney images and logos on their advertising outside of the park. Some of the first sponsors included Japan Airlines (Starjets), Fuji Photo Film (Magic Carpet 'Round the World), Coca-Cola (Space Mountain), K. Hattori & Co. (New Century Clock Shop), House Food Industrial Co. (Country Bear Jamboree), and Bridgestone Tire (Grand Circuit Raceway).

The company headquarters of OLC had moved from the Nihonbashi area of Tokyo to Urayasu City in Chiba Prefecture in late 1981. Takahashi gave a speech to the employees of the time stressing that "Most important to this business is to be in line with the public interest and to make our guests happy. We must have that attitude to make this business a success. Just having the money and the facilities is not enough. We must put heart and soul into it as well. Sincerity, not academics or eloquence, is the key to moving the hearts of people. We must not just repeat what we receive from Disney. I am convinced that we must contribute to the cultural exchange between Japan and U.S.A."

In September the top of Cinderella's castle was laid, making the structure an exact repeat of the one built in the Magic Kingdom at Walt Disney World and towering to 51 meters over the park. (Depending on how it is measured, the castle at WDW is 58 meters tall.)

At the same time, the costumes for cast members, park operating manuals, and assorted other material essential for a smooth running operation were being prepared. TDL contains the largest working wardrobe in Japan with 275 different types of costumes amounting to some 216,000 individual pieces.

The widespread hiring of cast members began in May 1982 when the Tokyo Disneyland Employment Center was established with the formidable task of hiring 3,000 employees. Only Japanese people were interviewed for jobs in the park, as all foreigners were contract employees from Disneyland and Walt Disney World. The hiring of so many people was made even more difficult due to the lack of an efficient transportation system to the park site making commuting difficult.

Walt Disney Attractions Japan, a subsidiary of Walt Disney Parks and Resorts, was also founded at this time with the purpose of operating as a liaison with OLC. In cooperation with Disney Imagineering they would develop ideas for attractions within the park with an eye on future development. They also acted as Receiver of Finances through licensing, assessed that the park was meeting Disney standards and specifications, advertised the new park through American media, and approved OLC's use of Disney artistic properties.

Jim Cora was promoted to Vice-President of Walt Disney Productions Japan, Ltd. Having moved to Japan he oversaw Disney's operational and design standards and provided support and advice to OLC. After the successful opening of the park, Cora returned to California to become Vice-President of Disneyland International in 1983.

EPCOT Center opened on October 1, 1982. All of the directors were there for the opening ceremonies except for Roy E. Disney. As the company's largest stockholder, he was dismayed that so much money had been spent on the project. Originally budgeted at $400 million, by opening day the costs had spiralled out of control up to $1.2 billion, triple the original projection, and it wasn't finished. The GE-sponsored Horizons pavilion was not scheduled to open until the next year, and Living Seas, sponsored by United Technologies, was not expected for two years. Couple that with the $100 million needed to start up the Disney Channel and the bottom line was looking bleak.

Regardless, TDL went ahead. In November 1982, the opening date was announced. The construction of TDL was finally completed in March 1983, some twenty-eight months after the initial ground breaking ceremony. A construction completion ceremony was held and intensive training now began as cast members trained on the actual attractions in preparation for the grand opening. "Day by day, the expectations and nervousness of cast and staff increased," the official OLC site proclaimed.

By opening day TDL had hired 6,700 cast members of whom 1,400 were full time and 5,300 part time. In addition, there were about 300 frontline American cast members and thirty Imagineers and advisors backstage. These were hired by OLC as contract employees, and many were provided with apartments in Chiba City. The initial contracts were for six months, but many extended these despite the sixteen hours days some of them worked.

"Premiere Days," an unannounced trial opening, was held for the local population during March in order to give the new cast members a chance to hone their skills while there were only a relatively small number of guests in the park. It took a while to get the staffing levels correct; sometimes there were too many people on and not enough guests and at other times the opposite problem happened. Pogue commented, "In Japan there are rigid schedules and work locations, governed by individual employment contracts. This made it literally inconceivable to switch someone even from shop to shop. They had to learn to modify the system to meet the needs of the operation."

There were a few other problems looming on the horizon. There were no hotels in the immediate area, though some were in various degrees of planning. The freeway exit to the park was six months behind schedule, and the new train line was not expected to be completed until 1987. The other main travel option at the time was a shuttle bus travelling the 3.8 kilometers (2.4 miles) through busy downtown Tokyo.

The TDL Guide Book given out at the park contained specific directions about getting to the park by subway: "Take Tozai Line to Urayasu Station (15 minutes from Nihonbashi Station, 10 minutes from Nishi-Funabashi Station) then 15 minutes by direct bus to Tokyo Disneyland Transportation Center." If the bus was your choice then: "A direct bus is available at the North Exit on the Yaesu side of Tokyo Station." For those who wanted to drive: "Take Wangan Highway, exit at 'Kasai Ramp' (#008) or 'Urayasu Ramp,' and follow the Tokyo Disneyland access signs."

A large parking area was provided in front of the park entrance. Here buses, motorcycles, and cars could be parked for a fee (¥700 for cars) in Mickey, Donald, Goofy, and Pinocchio areas.

Expectations for a successful first year were high. With more than thirty-five million people located only a ninety minute train ride from TDL and over 117 million people living on the California sized island, Disney President Ron Miller proclaimed that when added to the popularity of Mickey Mouse and the other Disney characters, the park's financial success was guaranteed.

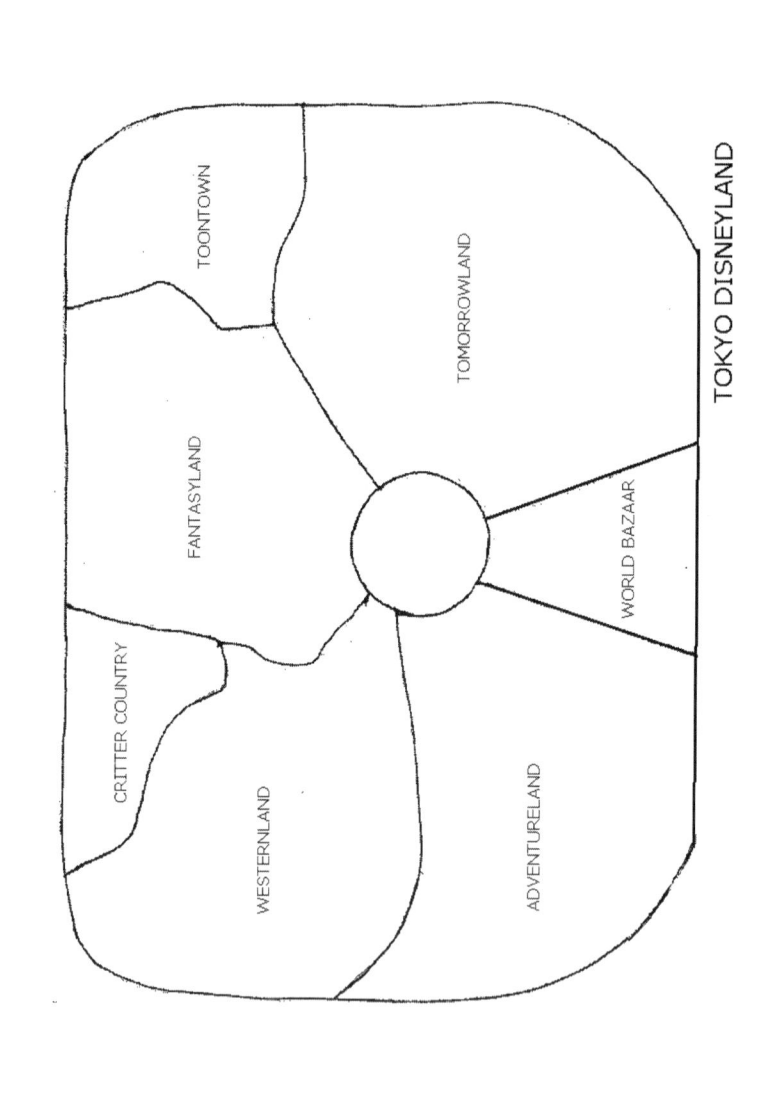

TOKYO DISNEYLAND

TOONTOWN
TOMORROWLAND
FANTASYLAND
WORLD BAZAAR
CRITTER COUNTRY
WESTERNLAND
ADVENTURELAND

Chapter Four
Opening Tokyo Disneyland

Tokyo Disneyland's Grand Opening Celebration Ceremony was held undercover in World Bazaar on a drizzly Sunday, April 15, 1983. The afternoon ceremony began with a medley of Disney classics performed by a 200-member choir backed by a 150-piece symphony orchestra. In the audience were executives from the Disney Company, Disneyland, and Walt Disney World, as well as special guests from government and industry. Among the honorees was Takeo Fukuda, former Prime Minister of Japan, and the MC was a well-known TV personality. Card Walker, Chairman of the Board at Walt Disney Productions, and his wife sat beside Masatomo

Takahashi, President of OLC, and his wife. This was to be Walker's final duty as Chairman of WDP; he would retire when he returned to California, turning the reins over to Ray Watson and Ron Miller. The main reason he had retained his position as chair was to be in Tokyo when his pet project was completed.

Mickey, Donald, and Goofy escorted the three Disney ambassadors to the stage for their greetings. The Ambassadors were "Emissaries of Goodwill" for the parks as well media representatives and official hosts. The program was initiated by Walt Disney in 1965 when he selected Julie Reihm as the first ambassador. At this ceremony they were Yaeko Terasaki (TDL), Mindy Wilson (DLD), and Cynthia Pleasant (WDW), and the girls offered greetings to Takahashi and Walker and congratulations from Shinzō Abe, Minister of Foreign Affairs, and Mr. Satoyama, Minister of Education.

To the tune of "How Do You Do and Shake Hands" (from *Alice in Wonderland*), a procession of characters and children of WDP Japan employees entered to shake hands with invited guests and add their happiness to the ceremony. The voices of children from Japan, America, and other nations joined in with the girls' choir from Seisen International School and the boys' choir of St. Mary's International School to sing "It's a Small World."

Doves were released to fly over Cinderella Castle to the tolling of bells to symbolize the hopes and dreams and efforts of all of those who created Tokyo Disneyland. Then thousands of white, blue, and purple balloons were released into the skies above Cinderella Castle and floated over the entire theme park as the choir sang "When You Wish Upon a Star."

Card Walker then spoke from a platform set up in World Bazaar, giving a very Walt-like speech: "To all of you who come to this happy place, welcome. Here you will discover enchanted lands of Fantasy and Adventure, Yesterday and Tomorrow. May Tokyo Disneyland be an eternal source of joy, laughter, inspiration, and imagination to the people of the world, and may this magical kingdom be an enduring symbol of the spirit of cooperation and friendship between the great nations of Japan and the United States of America."

Takahashi then addressed the guests: "We are just beginning at Tokyo

Disneyland. There is still much work ahead of us, creating new dreams and bringing them to reality. On this day, April 15, 1983, I declare the opening of Tokyo Disneyland!" Before the gates opened, Takahashi and Walker cut the tape with Mickey Mouse and other Disney characters looking on. The Main Entrance gates were opened and approximately 3,000 invited guests, who had been waiting for the opening, entered the Park

Frank Stanek told a reporter in a pre-opening interview, "They know their own culture and they know their own country so well that they really don't believe anyone can do it as good as they know it already and I think to a certain extent they are exactly right so why try to mingle the two."

Despite these words there was some "mingling of the two," as some differences between the California Park and the Tokyo Park were very obvious. First was the glass canopy over World Bazaar, the TDL version of Main Street, USA, and there was cover against the elements over many of the queue areas. The Japanese language was incorporated into show dialogue and sign graphics, and some of the restaurant menus reflected Japanese food preferences though hot dogs and hamburgers were more popular. Popcorn was initially frowned upon because the Japanese do not generally walk about while eating. Some wanted alcohol served, and others thought guests should be permitted to bring their own food into the park. The Disney officials insisted that things be done as originally planned, the same way as in Disneyland, no alcohol, no tobacco, no food brought into the park. Before long OLC executives had to admit that the Disney people were right; the Japanese people accepted it as the way it should be done. They wanted the Japanese people to feel like they were taking a foreign vacation when they went to TDL. Guests hear American (albeit Disney) music continuously playing, American and Japanese voices are heard over the public address systems, and there are real live Americans amongst the cast members, all designed to make the Japanese guests feel like they are in a foreign land.

Despite the restrictions against food, people still brought their traditional mats in with them. Half an hour before a parade was to begin, the mats came out and the guests would sit along the parade route, often snacking on the riceballs (*onigiri*) they had brought with them. Unlike Westerners, those who wanted a better view would remove their shoes before standing on a bench. For the most part, the new rules were accepted and abided by.

Another quintessential Japanese symbol is the vending machine, with Japan being the world's largest market for the devices. These were banned from the park as being "too Japan" and therefore detracting from the American feel of TDL. Another reason was that the machines were too impersonal and did not encourage interaction between guests and cast members. Thirdly, it reduced the amount of garbage.

"It's the Disney culture, not the U.S., that's easily translated," Pogue said later. "Even sumo wrestlers, dressed in their traditional *ukata* came . . . wear Mickey Mouse ears and eat popcorn."

For the first time a reservation system was set up in an attempt to prevent overcrowding. Nearly two million Japanese made reservations to the park through mid-October 1983. The down side of the system was that the highly popular advance sales and the lack of press coverage once the park was open led people to believe that TDL was sold out. Jim Cora launched a publicity program to spread the word that "There are tickets available for every operating day."

There were a number of different ticket packages available such as the "Big 10 Ticket Book," which was for general admission and offered a choice of ten attractions (1– A, 1 – B, 2 – C, 3 – D, and 3 – E tickets); or the "Tokyo Disneyland Passport," "an all-inclusive ticket good for general admission and use of all attractions;" a "Guided Tour" including general admission, four attractions on the tour and one ticket for any attraction; "Starlight," good for general admission and any five attractions; "General Admission" for admission "and all free shows, entertainment and attractions." Also, individual tickets could be purchased at the ticket booths in the individual lands. Prices ranged from ¥100 for A-ticket attractions to ¥400 for E-ticket. The most popular rides were the E-ticket rides and consisted of Pirates of the Caribbean, Jungle Cruise,

Mark Twain, It's a Small World, Haunted Mansion, Space Mountain, and Magic Journeys.

TDL is amongst the cleanest of the Disney theme parks as "the highly trained custodial staff takes a near-fanatical approach to cleanliness." The park holds an annual "Custodial Section Sweeping Contest" where skills are tested in the sweeping up of popcorn, cigarette butts, and other debris, as well as the competitors courtesy in answering guests' questions. A local TV station televises the event.

Officials at Tokyo Disneyland never doubted that their park would be a success, but opening week was not to be believed. Not only had more than 150,000 beaming Japanese braved an April storm to meet Mickey, Donald, and the rest of the Disney gang, but it appeared that a lot more than 150,000 were leaving. "We were puzzled, of course," the unflappable Jim Cora said, "but we finally traced it to the turnstiles. Japanese aren't very familiar with them, it turns out, and a lot of youngsters and many older people were passing through uncounted."

When the park first opened it contained five lands: World Bazaar, Fantasyland, Westernland, Tomorrowland, and Adventureland.

After passing through the turnstiles, admiring the floral Mickey Mouse head and taking the obligatory photos, guests could stop at Main Street House for general information, purchase tickets for the Guided Tour, or utilize a storage locker. There is also an entrance to the Emporium here. Restrooms were also available, though apparently the signage on them caused some confusion. According to Yasuhisa Kano in *The True Story of Tokyo Disneyland*, guests would sometimes confuse the English wording "Restrooms" for *resuto*, which is a Japanese version of restaurant.

Guests then entered World Bazaar, the TDL answer to Main Street, USA in Disneyland. The main difference being that while Main Street represents America before the turn of the century, World Bazaar is designed to reflect America after the turn of the century. Whereas Disneyland has a train station, city hall, fire hall, and horse drawn conveyances, World Bazaar has none of these and is more like a glass covered mall. Its main purpose is to provide numerous different shops in which Japanese guests can carry out their tradition of buying gifts for those still at home. Known as *omiyage*, it is a Japanese custom to buy gifts for friends, neighbors, and co-workers whenever someone travels somewhere. It is necessary that these gifts have something to associate them with where they were purchased; thus all TDL merchandise is marked "Tokyo Disneyland."

The name "World Bazaar" originated in the early planning stages when the Imagineers wanted to do something different for the main entry. They thought to do away with "Main Street, USA" and have an international shopping center filled with exotic shops from various places around the world. It would be a smaller version of World Showcase in EPCOT Center in Florida. OLC executives vetoed the idea; they wanted it just like Disneyland. As a result only the name, World Bazaar, remained on opening day, the only part of the idea that OLC liked.

The covering over World Bazaar consists of glass inserts framed in metal permitting sunlight into the area. The one disadvantage is that while plenty of light comes in, noise is not able to get out, and voices bounce around inside the structure.

It is interesting to note that the forced perspective used on Main Street in the American theme parks was not utilized when building TDL. The Victorian themed buildings lining the World Bazaar area are full size and many include a public second floor instead of a façade or storage area like the U.S. parks. There are no curbs along the streets; the sidewalks and roadway are the same height though there is the illusion of difference as they are painted different colors and made of varying materials.

All of the signs in the park are in English first with smaller Japanese letters underneath in keeping with the OLC desire for an American style park. Though English is taught in school many Japanese do not speak the language, so the additional lettering is necessary.

As in the U.S. parks, there were some problems between the characters and guests as, according to *Look Japan* magazine, "It's a headache to the strolling costumed characters that visitors inevitably touch and pull Mickey Mouse so much that the man inside the suit becomes exhausted."

The following tour of Tokyo Disneyland is based on how the park was in the first weeks it was open in 1983. Later additions or changes are sometimes mentioned but most will be covered in greater detail later. Upon entering the park, guests are facing south towards Cinderella Castle, unlike Disneyland which faces north; thus east is to the left and west is to the right.

As the guests hurry through World Bazaar on their way to their favorite attraction the cast members from the shops will often step outside, wave to passersby, and practice the "Disney smile" learned in orientation. First thing in the morning is usually not the time most guests linger in World Bazaar, though there are three attractions and a number of restaurants. The attractions include a Penny Arcade with a number of old time games, the Main Street Cinema showing vintage Disney shorts, and transportation facilities including a fire engine and horseless carriage.

While the American parks have a short street crossing the main thoroughfare, World Bazaar's Center Street actually goes somewhere, offering guests a shortcut to Adventureland to the east and Tomorrowland to the west. Going straight up Main Street takes one to The Hub. Yes, it is called Main Street even though the area is designated World Bazaar.

On the east side of the street is the Camera Shop opposite Main Street Cinema. The Confectionary sits on the east corner of Main and Center Streets with the Magic Shop and House of Greetings on the way to Adventureland. Subject to numerous expansions over the years to follow, the Confectionary proved to be one of the most profitable stores on a square footage basis, exceeding $100 million in revenue annually. On the west side of Center Street is the Toy Kingdom, The Storybook Store, and Uptown Boutique on the way to Tomorrowland. Continuing up Main Street on the east one finds Victoria's Jewelry Box, Disney & Co., and Silhouette Studio with many souvenirs unique to TDL. The artists working in Silhouette Studio (called The Shadow Box in WDW) are contract employees from America employed by Arribas Brothers Company. On the west side of Main Street is Towne

Clothiers where one can find the latest in Disney apparel and the New Century Clock Shop.

There are a number of full-service restaurants in World Bazaar. When the park first opened, hamburgers and hotdogs were the main fare, but over time more Japanese cuisine has been introduced. Restaurant Hokusai is on the second floor of World Bazaar on upper west Main Street and utilizes Japanese motifs in its design, and some tables offer a superb view of The Hub and Cinderella Castle. This restaurant was opened later in the year due to pressure from older guests who wanted traditional Japanese food. Younger guests preferred American cuisine because "We can eat Japanese anytime."

The Eastside Café, on the Adventureland end of Center Street, has an early 20th century atmosphere and its menu boasts meat and pasta dishes. Contrary to the standard design, Center Street Coffeehouse, on the Tomorrowland end of Center Street, one of the few breakfast places, is decorated in an Art Deco style from the 1920s instead of the Victorian era. At the end of Main Street are places for light snacks such as Ice Cream Cones, Ice Cream Parlor, Refreshments Corner, and Citrus House.

Having passed through World Bazaar, guests enter The Hub which in TDL is in two parts. The first is a courtyard like area called Plaza Terrace which will eventually contain the Walt and Mickey "Partners" statue seen in the other parks. In addition there are two dedication plaques with Card Walker's opening day speech in English and Japanese, benches, and an area for the Disneyland band to perform. This is also the hopping off spot for the fire engine and horseless carriage. The Omnibus also loads here but it only makes a five-minute circuit of the plaza. The TDL Hub, also called the Plaza, is larger than its U.S. counterparts but serves the same purpose, that of directing guests to the various lands. To many Japanese, used to close quarters and crowded conditions, the spacious hub was a major enhancement, and the enlarged area has proven extremely popular. Imagineer Marty Sklar noted that it also allowed for "a changeable venue for special seasonal shows that can perform before large numbers of guests, with the castle as a backdrop."

Two restaurants face onto The Hub. Curiously these buildings are not considered to be in The Hub or World Bazaar despite their turn-of-the-century architecture. Crystal Palace, "an elegantly themed Victorian buffeteria" is almost identical to its twin in Walt Disney World and is, according to the guidebook, in Adventureland and Plaza Pavilion, "a turn of the century buffeteria" copy of the one in Disneyland, and is in Westernland.

There are two ways to enter Adventureland, one from Center Street in World Bazaar and the other under the traditional Adventureland sign from The Hub. Unlike Disneyland where Adventureland and New Orleans Square are considered two separate lands, in TDL they are a combination of the two. In fact the New Orleans section does not have its own designation; it is just a part of the overall Adventureland. This may be because, though the architecture is virtually identical, it is considerably smaller than the Disneyland version and does not contain a train station, Haunted Mansion, or French Market Restaurant.

Entering Adventureland from The Hub, the first attraction is the Enchanted Tiki Room. As it can get a bit chilly waiting around for the show to start, heated lava rocks have been placed strategically around the patio. When the park first opened the original 1963 Disneyland show was presented with the soundtrack in Japanese. The show was changed in 1999 to a presentation, again in Japanese, called *Get the Fever*, which replaced the original host birds (José, Michael, Pierre, and Fritz) with Las Vegas lounge birds (Danno, Scats, Buddy, and Lava, the first female host bird). The story was similar but with Lava singing "Fever" to the Tiki Gods. A third version, *Stitch's Aloha E Komo Mai*, was introduced in July 2008, six months after *Get the Fever* closed. Presented in Japanese and featuring the alien, Stitch, from the feature film, *Lilo and Stitch* (2002), the plot was changed to having Stitch disrupt the show until he is permitted to join in the production. It is amusing to note that the sign on the outside of the attraction which read "The Enchanted Tiki Room" has the word "Tiki" crossed out and "Stitch" painted in yellow beside it as if the little, blue alien had done it himself. Other bits of yellow graffiti were also added along with a figure of Stitch on top of the sign.

Across the tracks and over a bridge is a combination attraction and restaurant in the form of the Polynesian Terrace Restaurant. Here a fifty minute Polynesian musical extravaganza is performed. Originally, there was only one live dinner show with no entertainment during lunch. The show features a live band, singers, and a number of beautiful and talented Hawaiian dancers who are actually from Hawaii. Mickey, Minnie and other Disney characters also participate. A lunch show was added later with Lilo and Stitch throwing a luau for the Disney characters. The shows are so popular that guests will line up at the entrance before the park opens and then make a mad dash for the nearby reservations kiosk in Adventureland.

Following the wide path deeper into Adventureland, the next attraction is the Western River Railroad sponsored by Tomy Kogyo Co. Inc. and Tomy Company Inc. The railway shares a loading facility with the Jungle Cruise with the Western River Railroad on the top floor. The queues are protected from the elements by a roof over most of the line area. As mentioned in the previous chapter, the railroad does not encircle the entire park and has only one station in order that it remain a ride and not public transportation subject to Japanese government administration.

Only a portion of the ride is in Adventureland as the tracks skirt the Jungle Cruise and guests can see the boats and some animatronic wildlife. Therefore, the rest of the ride will be mentioned later in the Westernland portion of this chapter.

It should be mentioned that the TDL railroad is a narrower gauge than the other Disney versions and now has four 2-4-0 steam locomotives. In keeping with the name of the railroad, the locomotives are named after western American rivers. Three of these have been in operation since the park opened: *Colorado* (#53), *Missouri* (#28), and *Rio Grande* (#25). *Mississippi* (#20) was brought on line in October 1991 with slightly different design elements. The engines were built by Kyosan Sangyo Co. Ltd. in 5/8th scale.

Sharing facilities with Western River Railroad is the fabled, exotic, classic Jungle Cruise. The first thing anyone who has been to an American Disney park will notice is that this Jungle Cruise goes in the opposite direction from the U.S. versions. The scenes are the same and according to the TDL guidebook, in this E-ticket attraction you will "Ride an adventure boat down the rivers of the world."

The gas heaters that were installed to protect the lush vegetation from the cold when the attraction was built have attracted a number of different species of birds to make Jungle Cruise's jungle their home. When some of the birds take wing, guests should know that it is not a new development in animatronics but "real ducks, pheasants, owls, starlings and magpies."

The main difference in the Jungle Cruise is that the traditionally male skippers on the boats in the TDL attraction deliver their spiels in Japanese. Generally the spiel is the same for all the skippers, with very little of the personalized adlibbing that happens in the U.S. parks. For the most part this is fine, as most of the puns used by American skippers simply do not translate well into Japanese, so a new spiel had to be written that was different from but similar to the American spiel. One example, given in *Riding the Black Ship*, refers to a game the animals are playing: "To the right, the gorilla and crocodile are playing 'paper, scissors, stone.' What happened between them? Gorilla made a paper, alligator made scissors with his mouth. But the alligator cannot beat the gorilla for long, because he can only make scissors." In addition, the magical, mystical Schweitzer Falls have been renamed *Shubaitzuwa* in the spiel.

After the Jungle Cruise comes a cluster of shops in buildings reminiscent of a colonial Spanish design. According to the guidebook, Chiba Traders offers "special products from China prefecture craftsmen;" Tropic Toppers (later Safari Trading Company) sells "Polynesian straw hats and colorful, decorated hats;" Tiki Tropic Shop features an "exotic mix of Polynesian clothing and gifts;" and Adventureland Bazaar specializes in "arts and crafts, baskets and clothing, primarily from South America and Mexico. Cigarettes and rain goods are available."

The Adventureland Stage (later renamed Theater Orleans) is next. In this small amphitheater, Mickey and Friends perform a high energy show with songs, comedy, and dance, usually with a Latin America theme.

Behind the Adventureland Stage where guests enter a New Orleans

Square themed area is La Petite Parfumerie, where one can buy "a wide selection of the finest perfumes and soaps from around the world." Passing through an archway, guests next encounter Lafitte's Pirate Chest where "gold and silver jewelry and decorative gifts" are available. To the east is Le Gourmet with "unique kitchen utensils, cookware and decorative accessories." To the west is the Blue Bayou Restaurant, which is virtually identical to the one in Disneyland where you can "dine in the serenity of New Orleans twilight," and Blackbeard's Portrait Deck where guests can have their portraits taken "in a realistic pirate setting." Next is The Golden Galleon with "gifts, toys and jewelry presented in a pirate setting."

At the end of the block, guests can buy dessert crepes or fast food entrees at Café Orleans or across the street find tropical fruit drinks at Royal Street Veranda. If none of those appeal there are sandwiches, soft drinks, and soup available at The Gazebo across the way. Most of these are very similar to, if not exact copies, of the U.S. counterparts.

All of this leads up to Pirates of the Caribbean, the showpiece attraction of Adventureland. Marty Sklar and his Imagineers knew that the Japanese wanted a carbon copy of the WDW attraction in Tokyo. That seemed simple enough at first glance, but it did not take long for problems to appear. First, there was no New Orleans Square in TDL, so that area had to be incorporated into one of the lands. In the Magic Kingdom in Florida a new façade had been created with a Caribbean flavor but it was decided to preserve the original Disneyland New Orleans motif, including the Blue Bayou Restaurant in TDL. But where to put it? As New Orleans, with its mixture of French, Spanish, American, Cajun, and Creole influences was an exotic port of call to the Japanese, Adventureland was the obvious choice.

The second problem the Imagineers encountered was that the water table in Tokyo was much higher than Anaheim, though lower than Florida's. In WDW they had solved this by having only one drop in the waterfall instead of the two drops that are in Disneyland, thereby not going as deep into the ground. This worked and added to the thrill as it is a longer drop, but it necessitated the removal of the scene showing the skeletal pirate captain reading in bed. After that it was virtually identical to its Anaheim counterpart.

The entrance to Pirates of the Caribbean is somewhat different from the U.S. versions as the often inclement weather necessitated more of an indoor queue area. This was solved by the addition of an ornate Grand Foyer. Guests are able to explore the lobby while they wait, viewing paintings of ships, battles, pirates, maps and the portraits of, presumably, the gentleman and his lady whose house this is. A few other objects are scattered about in anticipation of the nautical adventure to come.

Thereafter it is the same, though the boarding at Lafitte's Landing presented a bit of a challenge. The Japanese do not want to step where people will be sitting, as they consider the bottoms of their shoes to be dirty. Therefore they are inclined to step down to the floor of the boat instead of onto the seat as most guests do in the States, making boarding a slightly more difficult and slower process.

Another small problem was the translation problems from English to Japanese. Initially it worked well until it came to phrases like "Dead men tell no tales," which translated literally to "There is no mouth on a dead person." The latter phrase did not have the impact or meaning of the former, so a solution was required. The problem was solved by using both languages. The beginning spiel was done in Japanese, but once down the waterfall it all becomes English. "Dead men tell no tales" reverberates through the caverns in English, the audio-animatronic figures speak in English, and the song "Yo Ho, Yo Ho" is song in English. Japanese is not heard again until guests are advised to watch their step as they come off the escalator at the end of the attraction.

There is no Frontierland in TDL as the word "frontier" does not translate well in Japanese, nor is it an adequate term for the Japanese view of the American "Old West." Instead Westernland is used for the next area.

Leaving Adventureland, the first thing guests encounter is the Old West town. To the west, the backside of the Plaza Pavilion which fronts on The Hub contains Pecos Bill Café and Slue Foot Sue's Diamond Horseshoe. The first serves meat pies and beverages; the second is a reservations required restaurant with the "Diamond Horseshoe Revue" Old West floor show. In Disneyland it is called the Golden Horseshoe with the show the Golden Horseshoe Revue. The interior of the Diamond Horseshoe in Westernland is almost identical to the one in the Magic Kingdom in Florida. The TDL version presents "a rollicking revue from the days of the wild west. Features high-stepping dancers in a rip-roaring can-can routine."

One problem that has been commented on by guests is the proximity of Westernland to Fantasyland and the fact that there is practically no division. Snow White's grotto can actually be seen from the Diamond Horseshoe, though hopefully in time the trees in the area will grow enough to shield the grotto and thereby resolve the issue.

Across the street is the Old West town section. The buildings are similar to the U.S. versions, with a Trading Post featuring Old West hand crafts and Indian arts and crafts; Westernland Picture Gallery where "family-style portraits are taken in authentic Western dress;" General Store where guests can purchase "snacks, candies and coffee from the frontier age of America;" and Western Wear offering Western style clothes.

This is also the home of the popular Country Bear Theater, where "hometown bears perform hillbilly classics." While the dialogue and many of the songs are in Japanese, our ursine friends are now bilingual, as several of the songs are sung in English. Other than the language differences, the show is the same as the American version.

Next to the Country Bears is the Mile Long Bar for snacks and beverages and the Hungry Bear Restaurant "specializing in beef and curry dishes."

As in the U.S. parks, the Westernland Shootin' Gallery is one of the few attractions not included in the passport and must be paid for separately. The gallery is in an old time saloon and shooters are armed with Winchesters that fire lasers at various targets.

The Western River Railroad continues its journey from Adventureland and into Westernland near this area having passed by a caboose on a siding and a railway station with a sign proclaiming it to be Stillwater Junction.

The cast member has a continuous spiel throughout the ride, in Japanese, pointing out the various forms of wildlife seen from the train as they pass through the wilderness. The train passes by a native American teepee village with animatronic inhabitants working at various chores or just standing and waving to the guests. As the tracks travel closer to the river, Tom Sawyer Island Rafts and Davy Crockett Explorer Canoes can been seen as well as the fabled Mark Twain Riverboat. It is interesting to note that the Davy Crockett canoes are limited to only six, as more than that "would make them subject to the laws that regulate subways and trains."

Leaving the backwoods, the train crosses a lengthy trestle skirting the Rivers of America and eventually enters a tunnel to transport guests back to prehistoric times through the same Primeval World diorama found in Disneyland. Once out of the tunnel the train glides into the Adventureland station for the end of the ride.

While on the train passing by the Rivers of America, guests caught glimpses of Tom Sawyer Island. As in Disneyland, the only way to get to the island is on Tom Sawyer Island Rafts. Once there, guests will find that this island differs slightly, as one blog writer stated, "Instead of being located in the middle of the Mississippi River, this island is more likely to be found in the middle of the Colorado River." The island itself is very similar to its U.S. counterparts of the day, though shaped quite differently, with a myriad of areas for kids to run about and explore, including caves, a barrel bridge, suspension bridge, and Fort Sam Clemens (Mark Twain's real name), called Fort Wilderness in Disneyland. Guests can go inside the fort, where there are restrooms and The Canteen for snacks, and visit Castle Rock Ridge, Teeter-Totter Rock, and Tom Sawyer Treehouse.

Some of the sights on the island can, as in the U.S. parks, only be seen from *Mark Twain*, an exact copy of the one in Disneyland, as she sails around the Rivers of America. Assorted animals, a burning cabin, and the Indian village on the west side of the island are not accessible by land. According to the map of the island this is because the "Terms of treaty prohibit entry."

Leaving Westernland, guests now enter the magical realms of Fantasyland across the drawbridge and into Cinderella Castle. An exact replica of the castle in the Magic Kingdom, this fifty-one meter structure initially did not have any attractions inside and simply served as a gateway to the rest of Fantasyland. The main walkway is decorated with a mosaic of pictures from the Cinderella story. It is said that when Dorothea Redmond designed the mural she used fellow Disney artists for inspiration, and so John Hench and Herb Ryman appear as pages in the scene where Cinderella tries on the glass slipper.

The interior buildings were designed after the old-style Disneyland façades with medieval tournament tent fronts. In the row of buildings to the east, guests will find two attractions, Peter Pan's Flight and Snow White's Adventure. There are also two shops, Fantasy Gifts with Disney themed toys and The AristoCats with more of the same, including clothing and records and two restaurants, Troubadour Tavern with ice cream treats and Captain Hook's Gallery where pizza can be found.

Snow White's Adventure (called Snow White's Scary Adventure in Disneyland) still has a sign outside warning of the terrors within for young children. The dark ride is a mixture of the two U.S. versions with emphasis on the WDW attraction. After boarding the mine cars the guests move into the Evil Queen's dungeon, then through the forest of grabbing trees, as Snow White did when running from the huntsman. They then pass through the dwarf's cottage while they are singing "The Dwarf's Yodel Song" (in Japanese as is all the dialogue), then outside to see the witch again, through the dwarf's diamond mine, back towards the cottage, and then the finale with the dwarfs and witch on the lightning illuminated cliff.

Snow White's grotto, which is located behind this attraction on the Westernland side, is a duplication of the one in Disneyland. The anonymous sculptor who donated the figures to Walt Disney made the mistake of making Snow White the same size as the dwarfs, a problem that was rectified by the use of forced perspective and putting Snow White at the top of the hill. When the figures were sculpted for TDL, they thought they would correct the mistake and make Snow White taller. In the end it was decided to replicate the Disneyland version and leave the princess the same size.

Peter Pan's Flight is similar to the one in WDW with the main difference being the dialogue is in Japanese. Guests get into the flying ships in much the same manner as they clamber into the Haunted Mansion's doom buggies, thus speeding up the loading procedure, as compared to the Disneyland ride where the ships stop to let people get in.

"Fly high in the Fantasyland sky," the guidebook says about Dumbo, The Flying Elephant ride located in front of the Haunted Mansion. The Dumbo rides in all of the parks are virtually identical: sixteen Dumbos slowly spinning counter-clockwise on articulated arms. As he did originally in Disneyland, Timothy Q. Mouse stands atop a disco ball holding a training whip. There is an extra Dumbo on the ground in all the parks for photo ops, though the one in Tokyo differs slightly in that Timothy is riding in Dumbo's hat and the pachyderm holds a "magic" feather in his trunk.

After Dumbo comes the Haunted Mansion. Most Westerners will think it peculiar that this attraction is in Fantasyland, but the reasoning is simple. Firstly, there was the problem of where to put the mansion, as there was only a small New Orleans area (where the mansion is in Disneyland) in Adventureland and no Liberty Square (as in the Magic Kingdom) at all. Making it part of Main Street in the World Bazaar or incorporating it into Westernland were considered but it did not seem appropriate. In the end it was Japanese culture that decided where the mansion should be placed. Ghost houses had been popular amusements in Japan for centuries, but ghost stories are regarded more as fantasy or fairy tales, so Fantasyland seemed the right place.

The mansion in TDL is a copy of the one in WDW though some think it appears a little more derelict than the original. Unlike the mansion in Disneyland with its distinctive ante-bellum southern flair in keeping with the New Orleans area in which it was built, the WDW mansion is more in keeping with the Liberty Square area where it resides in its Dutch Gothic pre-revolution style. This style was thought to provide a smoother transition between Westernland and Fantasyland.

The name plaque over the entrance is unique to TDL, as are the two griffin statues guarding the entrance. At night their eyes glow red. The family burial plot tombstones are arranged slightly differently, and the graveyard is located in the front of the mansion instead of around to the side as in WDW. There is an additional derelict stone crypt and a secret part of the mansion not seen elsewhere. An outdoor queue goes to the east of the mansion and provides little in the way of diversion as it eventually meanders through a covered area and into the mansion. Guests now enter the famous stretching rooms, where they are introduced to the attraction's "Ghost Host." In Disneyland's Haunted Mansion the room is an elevator and goes down to the next level as the pictures stretch, but in TDL and WDW the ceiling rises while the guests remain on the same level. Inside there is one effect unique to TDL, in the corridor of doors one door has a face pushing out of it. The narration is done in Japanese but the characters in the vignettes, such as Madame Leota, speak in English. Francis Xavier Atencio, also known as X Atencio, a former animator and Imagineer, supervised the recordings for the Haunted mansion in TDL. At the end of the ride, with the strains of "Grim Grinning Ghosts" in their heads, guests exit through a mausoleum.

When this attraction first opened the lines were very short, as the exterior of the building did nothing to suggest to guests what was inside, so they passed it by for more exciting attractions. In time popularity grew as the word was spread as to what to expect inside.

Guests can then stop for an ice cream at Alpine Haus before proceeding to Cinderella's Golden Carousel, where "in a kaleidoscope of color, ninety hand painted horses whirl to the tunes from a calliope." The carousel is a replica of the one in WDW which was originally built by the Philadelphia Toboggan Company in 1917 and restored for use in the park.

The TDL version of It's a Small World is a carbon copy of the Disneyland façade though it is more colorful and is set in vast, brightly decorated halls. The entrance is to the east of the clock tower, it has indoor boarding similar to WDW, and the boarding area features a 360-degree mural of world landmarks. The Japan section is larger than any of the other Small World versions; the final room is much smaller and the song is sung in Japanese.

To the west of Small World is Four Corners Food Faire, one of only four places to eat in Fantasyland. It features fried chicken and croquettes and was later renamed Small World Restaurant.

On the west side of Cinderella Castle is the second half of the interior structures with the old style Disneyland façades of medieval tournament tent fronts. Here guests will find four shops: Tinkerbell Toy Shop, where guests can purchase "Disney character dolls and clothing . . . toys and dolls from around the world;" The Mad Hatter for novelty hats; the Fuji Photo Film-hosted Fantasyland Camera Shop; and Pleasure Island Candies, "a fantasy of packaged chocolates, nuts and candies."

There are two attractions featured here; first, The Mickey Mouse Revue which was originally an E-ticket attraction in the Magic Kingdom in Florida. It was an indoor stage show featuring audio-animatronic Disney characters with Mickey Mouse conducting the orchestra. The show closed in The Magic Kingdom on September 14, 1980 and was put into storage to await resurrection in TDL on Opening Day. The show was rebuilt in the same way with the only difference being the Japanese rendition of the songs. Some of the eleven songs included "Heigh Ho," "Who's Afraid of the Big Bad Wolf," "All in the Golden Afternoon," and "Zip-a-Dee-Doo-Dah" performed by Minnie, Daisy, Pluto, Goofy, Huey, Dewey, Louie, Mad Hatter, Winnie the Pooh, Dumbo, and Baloo to name a few of the twenty-four characters.

The second attraction is Pinocchio's Daring Journey, one of the few dark rides to open in an overseas park before a U.S. park. It had been decided in 1976 to remove the Mickey Mouse Club Theater from Disneyland and replace it with a Pinocchio dark ride. The renovation took some time, however, and for one reason or another it was put into storage until it was finally brought out during the refurbishment of Disneyland's Fantasyland in 1983. In the meantime, TDL was under construction, and it was decided to build the Pinocchio ride there as well. When TDL opened in April 1983, Pinocchio's

Daring Journey opened with it, six weeks ahead of the same attraction in Disneyland. The show is the same with the exception of the Japanese dialogue. It is the first attraction in any of the parks to use holographic illusions, as with the mirror in the Pleasure Island scene.

Leaving Fantasyland, guests can take a three and a half minute ride to Tomorrowland on the Skyway. Unlike Disneyland, the Skyway does not traverse any mountains but does provide an aerial view of the park in colorful gondolas. At the end of the ride is the Skyway Station Shop, where a selection of Disney souvenirs can be purchased.

Below the Skyway cables is the entrance to TDL's version of Disneyland's Autopia. Called the Grand Circuit Raceway and presented by Bridgestone, guests can "take the challenge of an exciting race as you drive your own formula car through the twisting curves of the world's most famous racetracks." The 0.4 mile track is a vague figure eight configuration, and a grandstand has been provided for spectators to watch the gas powered cars accelerate to seven miles per hour and "speed" past lush foliage, around bends and under a bridge to Victory Circle. As the Japanese drive on the east side of the road, the steering wheels in these cars are on the right. Unlike in the U.S., the Japanese do not use the vehicles like bumper cars, and collisions are rare. The course includes backdrops showing famous speedways around the world. It has remained virtually unchanged since opening day.

Across from the speedway sits StarJets. Unlike Disneyland where guests load at ground level, here an elevator takes them to a loading platform and one can "pilot your own rocket" for less than a minute. The attraction is the original Disneyland version, as the jets were shipped over to provide guests with this great view of the park.

Nearby are two of the four refreshments areas in Tomorrowland, the first, Space Place Food Port, an "outdoor stand offering sandwiches and soft drinks." The second is Tomorrowland Terrace (identical to Cosmic Ray's Starlight Café at WDW), offering fast-food service and sponsored by Coca-Cola (Japan) Company. In the same building is The Starcade with "the ultimate in contemporary and futuristic arcade games." At the other end was

The Eternal Sea, a film that explored man's relationship with the sea shown in 120° format on five screens. It was replaced by *Magic Journeys*, "a spectacular 70mm 3-D film fantasy as seen through the imagination of a child," in 1985 and by Michael Jackson's *Captain EO* in 1987.

Magic Journeys had previously been shown since opening day at EPCOT in the Magic Eye Theater and since 1984 in Disneyland, first on the outdoor Space Stage and later in the Magic Eye Theater, and like the TDL version, it was replaced by *Captain EO*.

Between the last two attractions is The SpacePort with "futuristic and contemporary ceramic and glass gifts,"

The Space Mountain attraction in TDL is the first Space Mountain to be in a park on opening day. It is an almost exact replica of Disneyland's Space Mountain as it opened in 1977, smaller in diameter than WDW's by 100 feet. They have the same shape and dimensions and the same interior. Minor variances include some different effects such as "the tractor beam light on the second lift hill changed during the climb, and the re-entry effect was a blue hexagonal pattern."

Across from Space Mountain and flanking the entrance way to Tomorrowland is a second building containing a Circle Vision 360 Theater. The first film shown there was *Magic Carpet 'Round the World*, a twenty-one-minute Circle Vision presentation that took guests on a tour of the world. The film was first shown in Disneyland and WDW, and when it arrived in TDL it received new footage of North America and Europe. According to a Disney press release, more than thirty-seven hours of film were edited to create the movie. The soundtrack was in 12-track stereo and featured a 24-voice chorus and 56-piece orchestra that included folk instruments. In 1984, the film *American Journeys* was shown as a replacement.

Nearby is Character Corner for "Disney character toys, clothes and souvenirs," The Lunching Pad (I wonder if the Japanese understand the pun) for a quick snack of milk shakes and meat pies, and the Plaza Restaurant featuring hamburgers and fried chicken.

The last attraction to visit in Tokyo Disneyland is unique to this park. It is called "Meet the World" and is presented by National Panasonic. Legendary Disney Imagineers Herbert Ryman, Claude Coats, and Marty Sklar were all involved in the Meet the Worlds project even though Ryman had retired in 1971. The songwriting Sherman Brothers, of *Mary Poppins* (1964) and *The Jungle Book* (1967) fame, were brought in to write music and lyrics for the attraction. OLC had requested them specifically, having sent a note to Marty Sklar asking "If the people who wrote 'It's a Small World' are still alive could you find out if they are available?" Robert and Richard Sherman assured Marty that they were indeed still alive and available, and they began work on the Meet the World attraction.

According to the guidebook, guests will "revolve on a carousel through time and relive Japan's fascinating encounters with other cultures." The theater holds about 150 people and is entered through a round anteroom. There is an arched ceiling and a multitude of clocks showing the time in various cities around the world, along with television screens showing sightseeing tours of those cities. The cast members are dressed in traditional Japanese clothing, the only place in TDL where women wear kimonos, as this is a show for and about the Japanese. The spiel is in Japanese but there are English translator phones in the last rows.

Matsushita Electric was the initial sponsor of Meet the World, and as they subsidized the attraction it was one of the few free attractions available while the park used ride tickets.

The rotating theater is similar to the one in Disneyland and Walt Disney World that held the Carousel of Progress attraction. In Tokyo, however, the theater works in the opposite way in that the audience is in the rotating part in the center with the stages moving around them, whereas in the Carousel of Progress the stage moved in the center and the audience sat on the outside.

Meet the World was designed by WED Imagineer Claude Coats, a long time Disney animator who was also responsible for major designs in all of the theme parks, including Pirates of the Caribbean, World of Motion, and Toad's Wild Ride. The animatronics were constructed at the shops in WDW at the same time as attractions at EPCOT were underway. According to one of his Imagineer informants for the book *Riding the Black Ship*, Aviad Raz quoted him as saying, "That show was originally designed for EPCOT. But they shipped it here instead. They modified it here, of course." That statement is confirmed in the pre-opening book *Walt Disney's EPCOT Center*, where it is stated, "The Florida version will be substantially the same as the Tokyo show, although there will be a few changes, if only in phraseology." That book also contains a number of pre-production sketches and paintings of what was planned. The attraction having been intended for EPCOT explains why there was an English translation of the spiel which does not exist in any other TDL attraction.

Before going to Tokyo the over thirty audio-animatronics were shipped to the WED facility in North Hollywood for programming and integration. By the time the show was set up in Tokyo the figures were supported by fifteen pieces of equipment, including "three proscenium filled perforated scrim/screens" and two large rear projection screens. The theme song was scored by the Sherman Brothers and Blaine Gibson did the sculpting for all of the figures except the three *Meiji* figures who introduce the show, which were done in Glendale by a Toho Studios sculptor.

A crane and two children open the show as they discuss the creation of Japan. The crane takes them back through time to the ancient Jōmon people, then on to Prince Shōtoku and the constitution, Buddhism, and Japanese writing. The next stop is Tanegashima and the arrival of Portuguese traders, the introduction of firearms and Christianity, followed by the isolationist policy of Sakoku until the arrival of the U.S. Navy and Commodore Perry's "black ships." The ruling power begins to change Japanese policy from peace to war and Japan's "dark days" begin, though Japan's part in World War II is noticeably underemphasized. The crane hastens to inform everyone that these days are over and the modern accomplishments that close the show is the true "Spirit of Japan." The closing song, "We Meet the World with Love," has been seen by some to suggest that the black ships have become love boats.

Some of Disney's management had concerns about how the "dark days" were glossed over and how this would be perceived by U.S. visitors, particularly veterans of the war. In addition, according to Raz's Imagineer informant, "The spiel is full of mistakes and nobody bothered to correct it . . . believe me it's an embarrassment for everyone." Whether or not that is true is open to interpretation, as Raz goes on to explain that "the historical narrative of Meet the World, however, is too reminiscent of other Japanese accounts of Japan's history" and is similar to "a concise historical narrative recently presented in another popular medium, the *Virtual Times* (the internet edition of the *Japan Times*)."

The Tokyo Disneyland Parade began on opening day and the Night of 1000 Stars spectacular was held that night. The Fantasy in the Sky fireworks show began on April 23 and one month later, on May 23, TDL welcomed its one millionth visitor. On August 13 the Tokyo park welcomed 94,378 guests, breaking Disneyland's single day attendance record that had stood for twenty-eight years. Less than a year after that, on April 2, 1984, the ten millionth guest walked through the gates. The new park also had a great effect on Urayasu as land values appreciated more rapidly than anywhere else in Japan.

Chapter Five
"Kingdom of Dreams and Magic"

It did not take long before the Oriental Land Company was planning to expand Tokyo Disneyland, now promoted as the "Kingdom of Dreams and Magic." According to the OLC website, "In October 1983, just a few months after the opening of Tokyo Disneyland, we began making plans for new facilities and attractions as stated in our First Plan for New Capital Investment. This became our primary master plan which was used as a basis for our negotiations with The Walt Disney Company and Chiba Prefecture. Although the service industry was not an established category at the time, and the company had not even begun to consider a second theme park, Mr. Takahashi had a vision of how the service industry and Tokyo Disney Resort might be in future."

One of the first new attractions, imported from Disneyland, was the Main Street Electrical Parade, renamed Tokyo Disneyland Electrical Parade. First running in Disneyland in 1972, the TDL parade debuted on March 9, 1985 and would run for ten years. Excepting for the name it was identical to the U.S. version, though the floats were not necessarily in the same order, and any "To Honor America" floats were omitted. The main attraction of the parade is the use of millions of colorful electric lights on the floats and Disney characters. The theme song is a version of Perrey and Kingsley's 1967 tune "Baroque Hoedown" arranged by Don Dorsey. The parade route began at the Haunted Mansion, skirted Westernland and Adventureland, went through the Plaza, and ended past Tomorrowland.

Sponsored by Unisys, the original Electrical Parade ended in June 1995 but was revised and changed to Tokyo Disneyland Electrical Parade: DreamLights, in June 2001 and runs to the present day. It included a new soundtrack focusing more on orchestral music rather than electronic, though still retaining the original "Baroque Hoedown." New floats, based on more current films such as *Aladdin* (1992), *Finding Nemo* (2003), and *Toy Story* (1995) were added to the more traditional ones. A Christmas version of DreamLights was introduced in 2007 and includes the same floats but with the characters in holiday garb and more Christmas carols and seasonal dialogue. Since that time the parade has been updated twice more, once in 2011 and again on July 10, 2015. It had originally been scheduled to premiere on July 9 with a number of refurbished floats and a new *Tangled* (2010) addition, but was postponed to the next night due to rain.

To accommodate the continual rise in attendance, "The Tokyo Disneyland Official Hotel Program (currently the Tokyo Disney Resort Official Hotel Program) was implemented in 1986 with the first hotel, the Sunroute Plaza Tokyo, opening on July 20 of the same year. Over the next four years, more Official Hotels opened one after the other. In addition to the Official Hotels,

Disney Hotels, owned and operated by our company, were opened starting in 2000. Today, there are three Disney Hotels and six Official Hotels within Tokyo Disney Resort."

Cinderella Castle Mystery Tour was one of the first additions after the opening of the park. Constructed to exactly replicate the castle in WDW, Cinderella Castle has gained a few differences over the years. Unlike the castle in WDW, King Stefan's Banquet Hall restaurant was not installed in TDL; instead there is a shop named The Glass Slipper where "artisans demonstrate glass cutting, glass blowing, porcelain painting and damascene (inlaid gold)." Some of the artisans were imported from America and their art includes replicas of Cinderella's glass slippers as well as other themed souvenirs. Just past the elaborate mosaic murals depicting scenes from *Cinderella* (1950) are entrances to the utility tunnels that enable people, products, and services to move unseen backstage.

Beginning on July 11, 1986, an attraction unique to TDL for being a walkthrough attraction and for being one of the few to use characters from *The Black Cauldron* (1985) debuted as Cinderella Castle Mystery Tour. This "D" ticket attraction has turned the castle into a haven for Disney villains. "Can you conquer the forces of the Disney villains in the Castle?" the guide book asks.

When each group of about twenty guests first enter the castle, they are told that they will be taking a tour of the various parts of the castle such as the gallery, ball room, dining room, and tower with a cast member as a guide. "*Konnichi wa.*" she greets them, and then takes them to the gallery where there are paintings of various Disney heroes and heroines hanging on the walls. Not long after the guide starts praising these heroes, the Magic Mirror appears and takes exception to the guide's remarks and insists that no hero is complete without a villain. Having said that, the heroes' portraits transform into their respective villains: Cinderella becomes Lady Tremaine, Pinocchio turns into Stromboli, Aurora into Maleficent, Taran into the Horned King, and Snow White becomes the Wicked Witch. The illusion is controlled by the tour guide at the control panel where everything is labeled in English.

Apparently it had been manufactured in the U.S. and shipped over to Japan.

The mirror challenges the guests to confront the forces of evil, and they are led down a dark staircase and through a dungeon area where the evil Queen's laboratory is set up. Here a magic potion is brewing, bats flitter about, a raven ceaselessly caws from atop a skull, and the shadow of the evil Queen is on the wall. The guests walk on, passing mummified ghosts, skeletons, suits of armor, and a swinging pendulum axe.

Abruptly, Chernabog, from *Fantasia* (1940), appears in footage from the film as he summons the spirits from Bald Mountain. As they move along, guests catch glimpses of Maleficent's goons peeking from behind cover before she starts sending lightning bolts down upon them from her Forbidden Mountain Castle.

Further down the dark passages, a talking skull warns guests of dangers ahead as they enter a cavern filled with treasure and guarded by a sleeping dragon. The dragon, apparently the prototype for the behemoth that would later appear in the dungeon of the Euro Disneyland castle, awakens, but the guests manage to escape in an elevator up into the castle.

In the next area the guests are confronted by the Horned King with the Black Cauldron. The guide explains that "The Horned King, the evil lord, used the black cauldron to manipulate and control the soldiers of death. Then the courageous and pure-minded hero, Taran, deprived the power of the great kiln using his sword of light." The guests then move into the next room where "The Black Cauldron is waiting to swallow you whole!"

One of the guests, usually a brave child, is selected to wield the Sword of Light and defeat the Horned King. The guide then presents the hero with a medal for bravery in a special ceremony, and the tour is over as the guests pass a sign with the message "Good Conquers Evil," the only English in the attraction.

Cinderella Castle mystery Tour is unique to TDL. Aviad Raz, in his book *Riding the Black Ship*, suggests that the attraction was built to compete with other theme parks in Japan, most of whom have a ghost house, a very popular amusement in that country. Japanese literature contains a wide variety of demons and ghouls and has done so for hundreds of years, so a villain-filled tour would not be out of keeping with what is already familiar to the Japanese. The official explanation from an American Imagineer working at TDL was that as most of the tour was underground, then the idea of a dungeon tour was obvious.

As for the tour being unique to TDL, that has been explained by John Van Maanen in his article *Displacing Disney* in which he asserts, "It is hard to imagine a similar attraction working in either Disneyland or WDW. Not only would group discipline be lacking such as to ensure that all members of the tour would start and end together, but selecting a sword bearer ... would likely prove to be a considerable test for the tour guides when meeting with the characteristic American chorus of 'Me, Me, Me' coming from children and adults alike."

As the guides never know what the groups will be composed of from one tour to the next, sometimes all adults, sometimes mostly children, or perhaps all teenagers, they have more leniencies in their spiels than most of the cast members. The spiel for adults, for example, would be less theatrical than that for mostly children. Unlike some of the attractions where the spiel moves along mechanically with the ride, the Mystery Tour moves at the pace of the guide.

By 1986, OLC's company balance began to show a profit "and the accumulated loss was cleared in just four years from the Park's opening." With the park now in the black it was time to develop "the Second Plan for New Capital Investment. The time frame covered in this plan was positioned as a 'growth period' for the Park to further enhance attendance, and major attractions were scheduled to be newly introduced."

First on the list was Big Thunder Mountain. The original Big Thunder Mountain Railroad opened in Disneyland in September 1979 and was an immediate hit. Construction soon followed on a larger version at WDW which became, at 197 feet, the tallest mountain in Florida when it opened in September 1980. According to Jason Surrell's *The Disney Mountains*, the mountains in Disneyland are based mainly on those seen by Imagineer

Tony Baxter at Bryce Canyon National Park, Utah, while the WDW and TDL mountains are modeled after Monument Valley, Arizona. The two inspirational sites are often reversed in articles about Big Thunder.

According to the Tokyo Disney Resort Site, "It's a few decades after the big gold rush. The rush now is from the mine trains that careen at high speed through the old, abandoned gold mine. You're headed straight for the rocky side of the mountain or going down fast at a tilt . . . You'll be screaming with the thrills!"

The mountain was constructed near the Westernland Shootin' Gallery and the queue winds its way up into the mountain, at times affording a bird's eye view of parts of Westernland. The line is under cover as it enters a tool shed / train station then proceeds down stairs to a further queue, eventually coming to the loading area. Embarking is fast and efficient with each train having five cars able to accommodate thirty guests.

Opening in Westernland on July 4, 1987, the attraction contains elements of both the WDW and the Disneyland versions as well as some quirks of its own. One example is the name; the word Railroad was dropped in the TDL version possibly due to Japanese railroad restrictions and regulations. The Florida ride passes through the Old West town of Tumbleweed after the second drop and a sharp right turn, while the TDL version goes left and into an underground cave as in the Disneyland version. The end segment differs as well with a 180-degree left turn of the track before a tunnel exit, the boneyard scene, and the final braking after a sharp right-hand turn and into the station and loading area. Accommodation also had to be made for the Western River Railroad tracks to pass by the mountain providing the best views of the Big Thunder attractions buttes, valleys, tracks, and assorted paraphernalia. Just before entering the prehistoric diorama area, the train goes through a tunnel under the queue, which accounts for the queue moving up and down.

One of the few fried chicken places in Japan (outside of KFC) was opened to provide sustenance to Big Thunder Mountain riders. Lucky Nugget Café is hidden to the right side of Big Thunder Mountain overlooking the Rivers of America close to the Lucky Nugget Stage, which once had live Country and Western shows.

To celebrate TDL's fifth anniversary in 1988, a new daytime parade was introduced. Disney Classics on Parade replaced the original parade from opening day and would run until 1991. Outside the park a Mickey Mouse-shaped hot air balloon floated to sixteen different cities around Japan in a "Flying Mickey Friendship Tour" to attract attention to the park and celebrate Mickey's sixtieth birthday.

The tactics seemed to work as park attendance reached a record high of 13.38 million guests. So confident was OLC in increasing revenues and attendance that on April 15 they held a press conference to announce a second theme park to be called Tokyo DisneySea.

Celebrating the fifth anniversary was easier for guests now after JR Keiyo Line train service opened Maihama Station in December 1988, within easy walking distance of TDL's main entrance. Until then the closest station was the Urayasu Station on Tokyo Metro's Tozai Line which connected to a bus service about twenty minutes ride from the park. Recognizing the importance of the Maihama Station, Mickey Mouse put in an appearance at the grand opening.

OLC's website announced a momentous honor on November 3, 1989, when "the autumn recipients of the Medals of Honor were announced and our chairman ... Masatomo Takahashi, received the Blue Ribbon Medal for 'his great contribution to the public as a member of the private sector;' and with the development of Tokyo Disneyland, which achieved an attendance figure of more than 10 million people from the first year of its opening, created a model case for large-scale leisure development by becoming a major source of domestic leisure expenditure as well as a major destination for international tourism, thereby greatly influencing the Japanese leisure industry."

The attraction listed next in OLC's Second Plan was Star Tours, scheduled to open in 1989 in a park-like area next to the Meet the World attraction. This simulator-based ride takes place shortly after the events of *Star Wars V: The Empire Strikes Back* (1980). Guests are taken on a tour of the forest moon of Endor but through various accidents end up in the middle of a battle against a Death Star. Hydraulic motion-base cabins simulate the Starspeeder in motion while a 70mm film is projected onto a screen at the front of the cabin to simulate the view the tourists have of the action. The movie shown was the same in all the theme parks. The TDL version has six motion bases compared to only four in the original Disneyland Star Tours adventure. The exterior and queue areas in TDL and Disneyland are both Tomorrowland space-port based, while the area in WDW is inspired by an Ewok village on Endor.

After exiting the ride vehicle, guests move through the space terminal and into the attraction's gift shop, Cosmic Encounter, where they can purchase "Star Wars toys, novelties and other gift items."

In conjunction with the new Star Tours attraction, a counter service restaurant, Pan Galactic Pizza Port, was opened across from it. As the name suggests, pizza is the main item on the menu and the restaurant was constructed around a giant, animated pizza-making machine (PZ-5000) run by a colorful alien named Tony Solaroni from the Spumoni galaxy. Every few minutes there may be a futuristic Pizza Port television commercial, the pizza making machine might go ballistic, or a phone call might come in from Tony's equally-alien wife, all of which are displayed on the televisions above Tony's head.

The idea for the Pizza Port came about after Disney Imagineers Steve Kirk and Kevin Rafferty started looking for "some environment" for the alien maquettes Kirk had designed. They knew that OLC was looking for a restaurant idea to complement the new Star Tours attraction, and so they approached the Imagineer's Director of Design for TDL, Yoshi Akiyama, who liked the concept. Kirk and Rafferty then started work on "a delightfully funny multi-media show" involving the aliens and their "intergalactic pizza making and delivery service." In time more people became involved, from video specialists, sound effects technicians, and the entire audio-visual department, to produce "live action video and backgrounds." To mesh the realistic aliens of Star Tours with the cartoonish aliens in the Pizza Port, another character, Officer Zzyxx, a "part realistic and part cartoon" security guard, was created. Zzyxx is located at the end of the second floor exit from Star Tours and he welcomes guests back to Earth before they head either left into Tomorrowland or right to the Pizza Port.

On April 2, 2012, Star Tours closed in Tokyo Disneyland for a total refurbishment. Thirteen months later, as part of TDL's thirtieth anniversary celebrations, it reopened as Star Tours: The Adventure Continues. As the Publicity Department of OLC described it, "The main feature of the revamped attraction is that guests can enjoy the thrills of a new and unpredictable experience with every ride. The ride is comprised of several scenes, each with multiple scenarios for each scene that are selected at random. This means that guests never know what they will encounter out of the more than fifty possible story combinations for every ride. The attraction will also feature 3-D images for the first time, allowing guests to feel like they've truly entered into the world of the Star Wars film series." Darth Vader and a group of Storm Troopers attended the opening, along with Jedi Mickey and Princess Leia Minnie.

Star Tours: The Adventures Continues takes place between *Star Wars III: Revenge of the Sith* (2005) and *Star Wars IV: A New Hope* (1977), as droids R2-D2 and C-3PO attempt to safely return a rebel spy to the Rebel Alliance. The seamless use of 3-D brings characters, locales, and effects to life like never before.

To celebrate TDL's fifth anniversary in 1988, a new daytime parade was introduced. Disney Classics on Parade replaced the original parade from opening day and would run until 1991. Showbase 2000, a covered amphitheater next to Space Mountain in Tomorrowland, began live stage shows with "One Man's Dream" in 1988. The show would run until 1995 before being changed. The theme of the shows is similar, focusing on the history of Disney movies and characters with song and dance and spectacular special effects. Subsequent shows were "Feel the Magic" (1995-1999), "Once Upon a Mouse" (1999-2004), and "One Man's Dream II: The Magic Lives On" (2004 to date).

TDL tested the waters with a one-day Hallowe'en event in 1999. It proved very popular and has since evolved into a series of parades and shows throughout September and October. Around the same time, the city of Kawasaki held a Hallowe'en costume parade, which has become a major draw for cosplay fans.

Businesses in Japan had tried to bring Hallowe'en to their country in the 1980s in the wake of the success of Christmas and Valentine's Day. Unlike the other Western imports with their serenity and romance, Hallowe'en was darker and not as readily accepted. But as cosplay grew more popular so did dressing up for Hallowe'en.

The main difference between the way the Japanese celebrated Hallowe'en and Western culture is that "sexy" and "cool" costumes vastly outnumber the "scary" ones, with Mickey Mouse or anime characters being far more popular than vampires, ghosts, or goblins. The idea of trick-or-treat at private homes has not caught on either; though a shopping mall in Yokohama has advertised that some businesses will be giving out candy, the event is more of an excuse to dress up and have fun rather than be scary.

Three new hotels opened in the vicinity of TDL: Sheraton Grande Tokyo Bay Hotel and Towers (later changed to Sheraton Grande Tokyo Bay Hotel) in April, and in July, Tokyo Bay Hilton (later Hilton Tokyo Bay) and Dai-ichi Hotel Tokyo Bay (presently Hotel Okura Tokyo Bay), all Tokyo Disney Resort Official Hotels.

Not all was rosy, however; a minor controversy occurred when, according to an article in *Japan Times*, a show with "three clowns in monkey costumes with colorful Filipino outer attire performing Filipino dances" was removed "following a request from the Philippine Embassy in Tokyo, signed by Consul Erlinda Gavino." The show was replaced by Chip 'n' Dale.

Attendance continued to rise and records continued to be broken even after the high of the fifth anniversary celebrations. By the end of the 1991 fiscal year, the annual attendance had surpassed sixteen million, with TDL welcoming its 100 millionth guest.

In the spring of 1992 TDL presented the Disney World Fair, "celebrating the fact that there is now a Disney Theme Park in all major areas of the world." Merchandise from each park was available. In the fall, the Mickey Mouse Carnival presented the Party Gras Parade with related entertainment and booths.

An economic boom in Japan was partly responsible for increased park attendance during the Second Plan period. OLC stated, "With that in mind, we expanded what was supposed to be a single attraction into an entire new themed land. Splash Mountain was turned into the focal attraction of Critter Country."

The new land was to be situated behind Westernland with access next to the Haunted Mansion. The first eight months were spent moving the railroad to accommodate the attraction and adhere to the "strict structural regulations necessitated by the Park's location on landfill."

The area was built to have the same scenes as Disneyland and with an almost identical layout. In Splash Mountain a meandering river takes guests through the story of "Brer Rabbit Leaves Home," highlighted with dark ride sections and a roller coaster-style track. From the caverns of Brer Rabbit's Laughin' Place, the log in which the guests sit travels through what was a Tar Baby segment in the film but now a bee hive sequence, ending with Brer Fox tossing Brer Rabbit into the Briar Patch, which translates to a fifty-six foot drop for the guests. The log then floats down the river and into the "Zip-a-Dee-Doo-Dah" finale.

The Splash Mountain attraction had greater significance to Japanese guests than American ones, for though the story takes place in the States and the Uncle Remus books are a part of American culture, the film *Song of the South* (1946) is not available on home video as readily as it is in Japan.

The main difference between TDL and WDW's version of Splash Mountain is that due to TDL version being on the opposite side of the river, it is a mirror image. In addition, there are some different secondary characters, some of the scenes are in a different order, TDL does not have a mill structure on the second lift, and the Slippin' Falls drop is an interior one, with the only outside drop being the final one.

Though it took Imagineers over eighty hours to synchronize each figure and months of testing, the TDL workers did not have to reprogram the characters to forget their America Sings tunes, as the characters were new and not repurposed as in Disneyland. When they were done each character worked on a forty-five second loop of dialogue and movement before restarting for the next log full of guests.

As in America, the main instruments heard in Splash Mountain were fiddles, harmonicas, and banjos. The vocal renditions, however, are quite different, with the songs in a different order and the backup and chorus in different harmonies. All of the lyrics are sung in Japanese with the exception of "Everybody's Got a Laughin' Place," which is in English. A dramatic, instrumental track called "Burrow's Lament" is heard that was originally recorded for Disneyland but never used.

According to Show Producer Joe Lanzisero, "We used brighter, punchier colors to communicate, due to the abundance of cloudy days in Japan." Different materials were used for the trees and props than in either of the other Splashes.

Splash Mountain officially opened on October 1, 1992. The first difference a guest familiar with the Disneyland version would note is that, as the Japanese are not as at ease with sitting in a row virtually in someone else's lap, the logs have side by side seating. When it was discovered that this method enabled faster loading times, WDW also adopted the side by side seating system for their Splash Mountain. Statistics indicate that while Disneyland's Splash Mountain capacity is 1,700 to 1,800 guests per hour, the new mountains can accommodate 2,400 guests per hour. Japan's stringent safety code also required the log to have an internal steel frame and a lap bar which made for larger logs, which meant that the turning radii throughout the attraction had to be adjusted to allow the logs to make the turns. The ripple effect came into play as now there was more room between the loops so more show had to be added. Another requirement was for green and white emergency exit signs throughout the attraction, which needed some imaginative thinking on the part of the Imagineers to camouflage them so as not to detract from the show.

Splash Mountain itself is ninety feet high compared to the eighty-seven feet in the American parks, which allows for a forty-five degree, sixty foot drop into the Briar Patch instead of the fifty-two foot, forty degree drop found in the States. This drop posed another problem for Imagineers with guests likely to get wet. In Anaheim and Florida the climate results in "the bigger the splash, the better." But unlike Disneyland or WDW which are warm or hot for most of the year, in TDL it can get quite cold during the winter months, and getting wet is not an attractive alternative when it is cold. In addition, many Japanese guests tend to dress up to visit the park and would not appreciate getting soaked. These differences resulted in a decrease in the log speed and shallower water at the bottom of the last plunge to minimize the splash.

The only other attraction in Critter Country was previously in Westernland. Formerly known as Davy Crockett's Explorer Canoes, it was relocated during the railroad renovation and renamed Beaver Brother's Explorer Canoes. Costumes were changed to reflect the new name, but the idea of paddling around the Rivers of America remained the same.

Unlike Critter Country in Disneyland, which was renamed from Bear Country to accommodate Splash Mountain, the reverse was true in TDL, where Critter Country was specifically created to complement Splash Mountain. Though the critters are not always visible, signs of their passing are all over the ground. On closer inspection a pattern emerges. The squirrel's footprints lead from the critter's dwelling to Grandma Sara's Kitchen, and tracks around a mailbox show that twitterpated squirrels had been chasing each other around. Another set of tracks leads to the entrance to Splash Mountain.

Naturally the new land would require somewhere for hungry guests to eat and shop. A counter service restaurant called Grandma Sara's Kitchen was installed adjacent to the Haunted Mansion, "offering chicken au gratin, salads and desserts in a cozy, critter cavern." In addition a little counter stand called Rackety's Racoon Saloon was tucked in at the back of Critter Country and offers "chili dogs, churros, soft serve ice cream and beverages." It is situated close to Beaver Brothers Canoes and offers a refreshing break after all that paddling.

Nearby is a non-tech, high concept hand washing machine that could almost be termed an attraction. As cleanliness is very important to the Japanese, these machines are a delight as they dispense Mickey shaped puffs of cleaner. The machine has its own cast member attendant, skilled at producing the sudsy Mickey, towels to dry off, and a sign proclaiming "Clean Hands, Happy Faces!"

Also new to Adventureland were China Voyager Restaurant, "a buffeteria with indoor and outdoor seating featuring a Chinese menu," and Boiler Room Barbeque "themed to a castaway setting and offering chicken, pork or beef with vegetables on skewers." Japanese guests were gradually requesting more rice-based dishes instead of the Western-style food offered when the park first opened. One exception was churros, which had become so popular that "we opened a wagon featuring them."

For the first time in TDL, the Country Bear Jamboree was given a themed makeover to the Country Bear Christmas Show which partly attributed to breaking the attendance record for that month.

Hoot and Holler Hideout is located close to Splash Mountain and is apparently "the critter kids' old hideout" converted to a shop in 1994 "offering critter design stationery, woodcrafts and apparel." Not far away is Splashdown Photos, where your expression as you plunge down the ninety-foot drop is captured and made available for sale.

In addition to a great interest in anything from the American West, Japanese guests also have a passion for the American 1950s. As a result, the Southside Haberdashery in World Bazaar became the Be Bop Hop, a 1950s apparel shop. To satisfy guest's character-based shopping needs, a hundred square meters of space were added to Disney & Co. "We can't build new facilities fast enough to handle the increase in attendance," Tom Turley, Director of Operations for Walt Disney Attractions Japan, is quoted as saying. One way to deal with that was with more entertainment and shows changing from daytime revues to night time extravaganzas. The Diamond Horseshoe presents its famous revue during the day and a dinner theater show, the Hoop-De-Do-Revue, at night. In Adventureland the Polynesian Terrace presents Aloha Mickey during the day and the Golden Island Revue at night. Tomorrowland Terrace features live bands with American singers in daylight hours and Roger Rabbit's Dancin' Time Warp when darkness falls. There are as many as twenty-six different entertainment experiences per day available to guests. This includes the Tokyo Disneyland Electrical Parade and Cinderellabration, which includes a stop for a royal wedding in front of the castle.

By TDL's tenth anniversary in 1993, some 125 million visitors had passed through the turnstiles, almost the total population of Japan. As a result of this success, small theme parks were popping up all over the country, everything from Gluck Kingdom in Tokachi City to Universal Studios in Osaka. TDL had more visitors than all the others combined, with a 16.3 million attendance total in the tenth year.

Circlevision in Tomorrowland was given a new show in the form of *Visionarium* in April 1993. Similar to the WDW show, where it was called *The Timekeeper*, it was the first 3-D Circlevision presentation that had an actual story and plot and not just a series of landscapes. The pre-show was decorated with a large stain glass mural picturing numerous famous visionaries and inventors. There was also a number of models such as a twenty foot rendering of Da Vinci's heliocentric solar system and the submarine *Nautilus* from Disney's version of Jules Verne's *20,000 Leagues Under the Sea* (1954). The main focus of the film was how the work of Jules Verne and H.G. Wells changed history.

A new nighttime parade, Disney's Fantillusion, replaced Tokyo Disneyland Electrical Parade on July 21, 1995. Specifically created for TDL, it was developed by creative talents from all four Disney parks with the storyline loosely based on that of Fantasmic, with the musical score done by the same composer as well. The team began developing the basic creative direction and story line in 1993 with the objective to "produce nighttime entertainment that would challenge the entire idea of a parade." Actual construction began in Japan in August 1994 with the usual fiber optics, mini lights, and strobes as well as, for the first time, light-emitting diodes (LEDs) and black light painting and ultraviolet light. Another first is the use of a computer controlled digital audio system to synchronize the movement and special effects.

To condense the story, the thirty-one parade floats and 160 cast members were divided into three acts beginning with Mickey, Tinker Bell, Flora, Fauna, and Merriweather bringing "the gift of Disney light." Naturally the Disney villains, Maleficent, Jafar, and Ursula, must appear to "take the light and make it night" until thwarted by the Disney heroes who "turn the dark back into light".

Having been designed for TDL's parade route, the show was able to stop at specific locations, do their performance so all guests could see, and then carry on to the next "show stop."

This popular show ran for six years, ending on May 15, 2001, with a final Sayonara Disney's Fantillusion show. The plan was to send the floats to Disneyland Paris (DLP), but they were improperly stored and the harsh conditions of a Tokyo winter damaged many of them before they were packaged up and shipped to Europe. Those not bought by DLP were believed to have been destroyed.

Aladdin's Great Adventure also arrived in 1994, playing from April 29 to November 14 at the Castle Forecourt Theatre, as the motion picture comes to life with "amazing special effects." After the show, guests could wander into Adventureland and walk "through the streets of Agrabah, find refreshments at Abu's Oasis," or get your picture taken with the Aladdin stars at Genie's Photo Magic.

By this time, TDL's shops had strong competition, not just from outsiders but from the Disney Stores. Though often selling the same merchandise, they had different suppliers and different operators. There were twenty-seven Disney stores in Japan by 1995 doing ¥7 billion in sales.

TDL's first winter event, Alice's Wonderland Party, started 1995 off with an interactive tea party, stage show, and parade. Another parade, Mickey Mania, also debuted that year with specially themed merchandise. June saw the Japan premiere of *Pocahantas* (1995) in Showbase Theater 2000 drawing capacity crowds. *Fiesta Tropical* was the newest show in 1996, with an unusual blend of Spanish lyrics, American performers, and a Japanese audience. The mix of beats, dances, and color got an unexpected reaction from the usually subdued guests when the music started for the trendy "La Macarena," and "the entire audience is ready to join in." In World Bazaar, two new shops opened, The Disney Collection selling artwork and cels and Movie Premiere Showcase with merchandise from the latest Disney films.

The next major renovation for TDL was the addition of Toontown. Following the success of *Who Framed Roger Rabbit* (1998), Toontowns were discovered in a number of the Disney theme parks. A team of Imagineers was sent from California to Japan. The Toontown in TDL opened on April 15, 1996, an exact mirror image replica of Mickey's Toontown in Disneyland. Toontown was constructed on the former site of a portion of the Grand Circuit Raceway, with the entrance near the Star Jets ride on the boundary of Tomorrowland and Fantasyland.

Under the "Welcome to Toontown" sign and to the right is Toon Park, a play area for small children or a rest area for tired parents. The ground is soft and spongy to keep the little ones from injury. Not far away is Goofy's Drink Stand, a self-explanatory refreshment booth that is a lead-in to Goofy's Bounce House, the best place for kids to bounce and jump on cushioned walls and floors. This attraction was later converted to Goofy's Paint 'n' Play, where eight children at a time can help Goofy redecorate "using the Toontone Splat Master paint applicators" on the walls and furniture..

Donald's Boat, *Miss Daisy*, looms up after Goofy's house, and here again kids are encouraged to play with whatever they can reach which includes steering the boat, talking on an intercom, or ringing the ship's bell.

The first ride in Toontown is Gadget's Go Coaster, based on the character Gadget Hackwrench from the TV show *Chip 'n' Dale Rescue Rangers*. The eight car train takes less than a minute to go around the track made of salvaged materials, over a hill, and through a pond.

Chip 'n' Dale's Treehouse is a walkthrough attraction in a big oak tree next to Gadget's Go Coaster and features numerous and ingenious uses for acorns.

Mickey's Trailer, a snack bar, stands next to Mickey's House and the Meet Mickey attraction, where guests can wander through Mickey's home, meet the famous mouse, pose for pictures, and check out his bedroom, living room, kitchen, and backyard. Right next door is Minnie's House, but unlike her famous boyfriend she rarely makes an appearance there.

Before hopping on the Jolly Trolley next to Mickey's Fountain, guests can stop at Daisy's Snack Wagon for some refreshments. The Jolly Trolley bumps and pitches back and forth as it makes its way to downtown Toontown. Of interest here is that as the trolley is moving, three cast members become involved. One drives the trolley, a second walks in front, clearing the way, and a third walks behind to make sure nobody tries to climb onto the moving vehicle. The trolley stopped running on a rainy day in 2009 and was stationed outside of the Trolley Barn, where it continues to sit with its key moving but otherwise immobile.

Huey, Dewey, and Louie's Good Time Café makes up restaurant row, where "Our Food is Simply Ducky" and guests can purchase Mickey Pizzas or Donald Burgers and other fast food items. Nearby City Hall is sandwiched between a bank and a courthouse and a school as well as other municipal buildings. There are a few other restaurants that have appeared that do not have a counterpart in Disneyland. They are Dinghy Drinks (shaped like a rowboat on a trailer), Out of Bounds Ice Cream (looks like a golf cart), Toon Pop (a covered wagon), Pop-Lot-Popcorn (resembles a car), and Toontone Treats (a food truck), none of which really require an explanation as to what they sell.

At the far end of Toontown is the major attraction for the area, Roger Rabbit's Car Toon Spin. Entered through the Cab Co., it is run by Lenny the Cab, Benny's twin cousin, who takes guests on a whirlwind dark ride through a China Shop (run by a bull), the Toontown Power House, and the Gag Factory, narrowly escaping the Dip-Mobile. The attraction is the same as the one in Disneyland with the only obvious difference being two guests per car in TDL compared to three in Disneyland.

On the way to the exit, guests pass the Gag Factory where gags are manufactured in a giant Gag-O-Matic machine. A television showing Roger Rabbit cartoons was initially installed but was later removed. Next, and connected to the Gag Factory, is the Five and Dime where "hilarious gifts and Disney merchandise" is available.

Known as *Honey, I Shrunk the Audience* in Disneyland and WDW, this 3-D movie is exactly the same in TDL with the exception of the name change to *MicroAdventure* and the soundtrack dialogue being dubbed in Japanese. The show replaced *Captain EO* in 1997 and ran until May 2010, when it was in turn replaced by *Captain EO Tribute*.

The 1997 winter show, "Christmas Fantasy," saw a fifty foot Christmas tree, angel-costumed young guests singing "Silent Night," and restaurants offering holiday fare. Two years later, Disney's "Christmas Town," a castle show with Mickey and Friends was offered along with a 166-person Christmas parade led by Santa and the usual Christmas tree in World Bazaar.

Rumors were floating around about a major upgrade to Tomorrowland. In addition to redecorating, a new area to be called Sci-Fi City was said to be in the works. According to Shaun Finnie in *The Disneylands That Never Were*, there were to be two new attractions, "the Sci-Fi Zoo, a combined audio-animatronic walk through and theatre show, and Rockit Bikes . . . motorcycle versions of Disneyland's . . . highly temperamental Rocket Rods." The expansion never happened; instead OLC began focusing on the new theme park, Tokyo DisneySea.

By the time TDL celebrated its fifteenth anniversary in 1998, it had achieved another record for high annual attendance figures, topping 17.46 million.

Over the preceding years most of the Disney theme parks had begun closing their Skyway attractions. Disneyland's closed in 1994 and TDL followed suit on November 3, 1998. In time the Tomorrowland Station was remodeled to accommodate Stellar Sweets, a candy store, and the Fantasyland Station was demolished to be replaced by a new and unique to TDL attraction, Pooh's Hunny Hunt.

This tribute to Winnie the Pooh is a dark ride which apparently had a budget of $130 million to invest in the new trackless ride technology. Instead of the previous technology of having a wire imbedded in the floor, this attraction utilizes a range of sensors and a local positioning system (LPS) to control the vehicles. Limitless variations are possible, which makes every trip through the attraction different. Construction would take almost two years but the end result, when it opened on September 4, 2000, held the longest wait times in the park.

The entrance is shaped like a huge storybook with the queue line passing by pages of the book telling parts of the story until guests board the five seat honey pots. After a short video in which Pooh is given a balloon by Christopher Robin, the honey pot enters a blustery day scene where guests see characters in various windy situations. The next scene is dark and begins to bounce along with Tigger's song and dance routine. Pooh's house follows and the bear is seen sleeping with his balloon, which grows and morphs into a heffalump, leading to the next dream scene. Whirling heffalumps and woozzles fill the air in Pooh's dream as honey pots and disco balls dance in circles. The vehicle exits through a heffalump's trunk and moves backwards down a tunnel with creatures projected on the walls. The guests are reunited with Pooh, who is eating his fill of honey, and exit through a closed storybook.

On July 7, 2000, a new four floor shopping mall, Ikspiari, opened outside the resort. The Japanese equivalent of Anaheim's Downtown Disney, it contains dining, shopping, and entertainment. The complex is operated by Ikspiari Co. Ltd., a subsidiary of Oriental Land Company.

To compete with the Disney stores, a new merchandise outlet was opened outside TDL in March 2001 near Maihama Station called Bon Voyage. According to the Disney Resort site, "you'll find the grandest selection of Disney merchandise available under one roof anywhere in Japan. Bon Voyage welcomes visitors to the Resort as they begin their journey and bids them farewell as they set off on their return."

It took until July 27, 2001 for TDL to get a monorail. Disney Resort Line is managed by Maihama Resort Line Co., Ltd. The single track, five kilometer circuit has four stations themed to their area: Resort Gateway Station, Tokyo Disneyland Station, Bayside Station (near the parking lot), and later, Tokyo DisneySea Station. The straddle type monorail trains have strap handles and windows shaped like Mickey Mouse and come with a multitude of colored stripes: green, purple, blue, yellow, and peach. Each train pulls six cars and can carry 537 passengers.

An accident occurred on December 5, 2003, when a car derailed in Space Mountain. Fortunately, no one was injured, but the ride was closed for two months while an investigation was carried out by OLC. It was determined that an axle had failed because its diameter was smaller than specifications required. Seventeen park officials received reprimands and the attraction was reopened in February 2003.

Another new attraction that opened on April 15, 2004 was Buzz Lightyear's Astro Blasters. Identical to its Disneyland counterpart, it is different from the WDW version which had been operating on a different track system from its Anaheim cousin. It also had a weapons upgrade that allowed greater flexibility when shooting with the laser guns on a retractable cord, instead of being attached to the vehicle as in WDW.

Meet the World, which had been one of the initial opening day attractions, closed on June 30, 2002. Sponsored by Matsushita Electric, it was one of the few free attractions under the ride ticket system. Konosuke Matsushita died in 1989, and the company later shifted its sponsorship over to Star Tours. Japan Airlines then took over Meet the World sponsorship. The building remained unused as an attraction until it was demolished in the summer of 2006 to make way for Monsters, Inc. Ride and Go Seek.

This dark ride attraction can be found at the entrance to Tomorrowland as the Scare Factory seen in the film. The slogan has changed from "We scare because we care" to "It's laughter we're after." When inside, guests are shown an instructional video, narrated by Mike Wazowski, on flashlight tag, before being sent on their way in a security vehicle. Sulley has brought Boo to Monstropolis to encourage her to join in the flashlight games. Randall has also returned and is after Boo to capture her scream. The ride turns dark and flashlights come on activating various objects and characters as they are caught in the light. It is now a search for Boo as guests see various characters on the same mission. The vehicle leaves the factory and goes out onto the streets of Monstropolis where more characters from the film are seen. Randall almost catches Boo in a dark alley, but Sulley arrives from a manhole beneath Boo and lifts her into the air. Harryhausen's Sushi Restaurant is next, where Boo pops in and out and guests can use their flashlights to dunk Celia in a tank of water. The vehicles are then back on the streets and tagging more monsters before re-entering the factory, where guests see Randall about to catch Boo again. The lights come back on and Sulley and Mike effect a rescue, sending Randall onto a conveyor belt to be cubed. The ride ends in the Monsters Inc. Company Store where pictures of the guests on the ride can be seen.

Cinderella's Castle Mystery Tour closed on April 5, 2006 to be replaced by Cinderella's Fairy Tale Hall, still inside the castle, on April 15, 2011. This is a walkthrough attraction because according to the TDL website, "Cinderella and Prince Charming have opened Cinderella Castle to Guests even while they are away. Cinderella wished to share the story of the magical way that she became a princess. Guests are welcome to wander through the castle to view paintings, dioramas, and other artworks that follow her story." The murals show Cinderella's progression from little girl, to servant, to princess, and the diorama shows her clothes being magically transformed from rags to a beautiful gown. The Grand Hall has displays of the glass slipper, a throne, and special paintings that, when hit with a photographer's flash, reveal a magical message.

Until 2006, TDL's Space Mountain was identical to Disneyland's in every way with a few architectural elements. Closed for refurbishment, it reopened on April 28, 2007 with a more futuristic theme, including a sleeker spaceship in the main queue area. It has the same track with a new show featuring a new space port, new and darker effects (some unique to TDL), and a hyper speed tunnel at the end of the ride. Another change made in 2006 was the painting of Cinderella Castle to make it different from the one in WDW. The rooftops received a different shade of blue, the white stone walls and the turrets have a tan-pink hue, and the trims were painted gold.

A new daytime parade began in 2006, Disney Dreams On Parade: Moving On, featuring Disney characters from the latest films and following the Twentieth Anniversary Parade titled Disney Dreams On Parade. Speculation has it that the short run of that parade may have been due to an accident on January 8, 2008, when a portion of the Buzz Lightyear float collapsed and a steel pillar (estimated at 660 pounds) fell near some park guests. No one was injured, but the parade was canceled until safety checks were completed. It only ran for two years and was replaced by the Twenty-fifth Anniversary parade, Jubilation, which in turn was replaced in 2013 by Happiness Is Here, the Thirtieth Anniversary parade.

In the same month, a fire is reported to have broken out in the Swiss Family Treehouse.

Due to a prompt evacuation, no one was injured and firefighters had the fire out in an hour.

Oriental Land Company held a ground breaking ceremony on February 14, 2006, at the site of the seven-hundred-room Tokyo Disneyland Hotel, set to open in 2008. In the traditional Shinto style ground breaking ceremony, OLC Chairman Toshio Kagami broke a pile of dirt, wishing for safety as construction progresses. A Shinto priest threw confetti-like pieces of paper in a purification ritual and priests waved sacred leaves. After the Shinto ceremony was concluded, Mickey Mouse, in dark blue coveralls and a hard hat, greeted the guests attending the ceremony. He was soon joined by Donald, Goofy, and Chip 'n' Dale. The hotel opened on July 8, 2008 as part of TDL's Twenty-fifth Anniversary celebrations. The hotel has a Victorian theme like its counterparts in Paris and Hong Kong and is located near the entrance.

It was the earthquake and tsunami on March 11, 2011 that caused the most damage in the park. The magnitude 9.0 earthquake caused TDL to be shut down in the middle of the day. Many people were staking out their spots to watch the parade when the quake began. Videos posted online show the ground shaking, water splashing out of fountains, and people barely managing to stay on their feet. Water gushed onto the parking areas, not from the tsunami but, as later officially stated, liquefaction of the ground that was created from landfill. Cast members promptly moved the parade route, marking stanchions to permit people to move about. There were no injuries amongst guests or cast members at first but an estimated twenty thousand to thirty thousand of the 69,000 people in the park that day spent the night inside the theme parks or hotels when the public transportation system shut down.

New York Post Travel Editor David Landsel was in the resort at the time and reported that all of the people in the park "ended up outside on the ground waiting for shaking to stop."

He recounted that the shaking continued on and off for hours but despite the concern people felt, some of "our neighbors here in the café are groups of schoolgirls eager to practice English. Lots of laughs." Cast members kept people out of the buildings until it could be determined if they were safe. Disney also stepped up with offers of "seaweed rice and chocolates . . . tea and cookies."

As darkness fell, guests were informed that they could leave the park if they wished to do so as some buses were now running. The trains were down as was the monorail system which had some damage to the beams. The crowds remained calm throughout the ordeal as they were given safety instructions and kept informed of happenings over the park loudspeaker system. Raincoats, blankets, and heaters were provided to those required to stay in the park due to safety concerns. Cast members served up a warm breakfast in the morning which was most welcome after camping overnight in thirty degree temperatures. "What a bizarre (and wonderful) place to be trapped!" Landsel concluded.

First reports indicated that there were no injuries but later Disney indicated that a few people had minor damage or anxiety problems. By noon the next day, all guests had left the park and the gates were closed behind them. Subsequent official park operational calendars indicated the parks would be closed until March 21 as damage was assessed and repairs made to attractions and infrastructure.

Electric power, gas, and water were found to be operational though not at full capacity. There were patches of buckled pavement and flooding along the monorail beams and into the parking lot. Damage appeared to be minimal, but the parks remained closed due to the lack of transportation; people were best kept away from the recovering area until it was stabilized.

Blackout issues continued for some time afterwards.

While TDL was recovering, the surrounding area of Urayasu's 100,000 residents were still without running water. Garbage collection, sewage, water, and gas services were all disrupted. Though two hundred miles from the earthquake's epicenter, Urayasu was not out of the danger zone. There was no tsunami damage, no crumpled buildings, but the landfill on which the town was built was subject to liquefaction, and gurgling ooze came out of any cracks it could find as the violent shaking turned the ground to mud. Streets warped, houses tilted, utility poles sank, and manhole covers were pushed three feet into the air. In TDL the parking lot buckled and rippled and Urayasu began sinking. A resident of Urayasu commented, "Even when the water went away, the mud stayed for a week." Mayor Hideki Matsuzaki, in the emergency town center, noted that "as much as 85% of the town had been submerged in mud."

Hundreds of people left their uninhabitable homes, some taking advantage of reduced rates at the Disneyland hotels and the use of their hot springs baths. The parking lot was quickly repaired, but due to the energy shortage, the park would remain closed.

OLC had estimated that the park would stay closed for at least ten days to allow a full, thorough inspection and for any required maintenance to be carried out. One of the casualties was in the It's a Small World attraction, where set pieces for the seasonal "It's a Small World Holiday" were damaged so that the overlay could not be done that year. In the end, TDL was closed for almost a month, not opening again until April 15. On that day, ¥300 ($4.00) for each guest entering TDL was donated to the Japanese Red Cross. Guests had started lining up at 6:30 that morning, and when they entered the park at 8:00 they were greeted by Mickey, Minnie, and a number of other happy Disney characters. Mickey did an impromptu dance minutes before opening, to the delight of the fans.

While some Japanese people refrained from celebrations out of respect for the 13,500 people killed by the earthquake and subsequent tsunami, others felt that it was just as important to enjoy life and relieve stress by returning to normalcy as quickly as possible. Others felt that by getting out and spending money the economy would recover faster. The public relations manager for OLC, Hiroshi Suzuki, said "visitors were so elated when they saw Mickey and the other characters," he wished he could bring that kind of happiness to all people in Japan.

After effects of the earthquake still produced problems even after TDL opened. Power shortages limited lighting and air conditioning and caused a prolonged shutdown of Big Thunder Mountain. Operating hours were shortened to conserve energy. The Tokyo Disneyland Hotel and the Disney Ambassador had also been affected and stayed closed until the park opened. It was estimated that the closures, the first in the park's history, cost over $400 million in profits.

Shoplifting is enough of a problem in TDL that *The China Post* reported on it in an August 2015 article: "According to the Taipei Economic and Cultural Representative Office in Japan from May 2013 to June this year, seventeen Taiwanese had been caught red-handed while shoplifting. The office said that most of those caught were young women between the ages of twenty and forty, while the first man was arrested this year. The Bureau of Consular Affairs stated that one female tourist had purchased merchandise worth more than 300,000 Japanese yen in the gift store, but still stole an accessory worth 10,000 yen." The article went on to state "that although there are no theft-proof gates at the gift stores, customers are still under the watch of clerks and security. People who are found leaving without paying, will "immediately be tailed, stopped and reported to the police ..."

Admission price increases in 2015 were not popular, but it was announced that some of that revenue would be going towards further expansion and new attractions. ¥3 billion has been earmarked for a new character meet-and-greet area similar to Mickey's House in Toontown. but this time the focus will be on the Disney ducks. Huey, Dewey, and Louie's Junior Woodchucks organization will be the focus of the new attraction. As an outdoors and conservationist group, it is only proper to have the new attraction modeled after a Junior Woodchucks campground. A new lodge-like restaurant with a Junior Woodchucks theme will replace the present Lucky Nugget Café. The two-story structure will have indoor and outdoor seating, with the latter having a campfire space and views of the Rivers of America. Both are expected to be completed by the end of 2016.

Alice in Wonderland (1950) and *Beauty and the Beast* (1991) are also slated for TDL and are projected to almost double the size of Fantasyland as that area is overhauled and spills into Tomorrowland's Grand Circuit Raceway, guest parking, and backstage. This aggressive expansion involves the "overall redevelopment of Fantasyland with multiple major attractions, shops, restaurants and other facilities." A new parking lot has already been completed on the other side of Shuto Expressway. Concept art shows a walkthrough garden maze for Alice that looks very similar to the one in Disneyland Paris, an idea once proposed for WDW but later rejected. Concept art for *Beauty and the Beast* (1991) includes Beast's castle approached by a Gothic style bridge. There are definite similarities between the TDS expansion and the New Fantasyland in WDW's Magic Kingdom, though the TDL version may be much grander. Both developments are targeted for a 2018 opening.

TDL's profit figure in 2014 was almost on par with the 2013 figure of ¥114.4 billion. This was attributed to the thirtieth anniversary celebrations and particularly to the events featuring the characters from the hit film, *Frozen* (2013). Anna and Elsa's Frozen Parade ran from mid-January to March and was so popular that admittance had to be restricted on some days in February, usually one of the slowest months of the year. Another attraction planned for July will feature Lilo and Stitch and is expected to further increase turnout.

The winter season of 2016 will be celebrated with Anna and Elsa's Frozen Fantasy with the return of the show on January 12. "It will run through March 18 and also includes the Frozen Fantasy Parade with Kristoff, Hans, and the Trolls." Cinderella Castle supports the *Frozen* (2013) theme with Anna and Elsa's Winter Greeting, which includes the nighttime event "Once Upon a Time: Special Winter Edition which features scenes from *Frozen* in Japanese."

OLC announced at the end of October 2015 that an update to their Star Tours: The Adventures Continue will include a segment based on the film *Star Wars: The Force Awakens* (2015) in early February 2016. "Guests will meet new characters and go on an adventure to an iconic world from the film." Merchandise themed to the new film will go on sale in December and for a limited time, tickets purchased through Disney's eTicket online system and Day Pass Tickets for the monorail will have a Star Wars theme.

A fourth Tokyo Disney themed hotel, to be called the Tokyo Disney Celebration Hotel – Wish, will be taking the place of the existing Palm Terrace and Fountain Terrace Hotels about fifteen minutes by free shuttle from TDL. The first phase will open in June 2016 and the second, to be called Tokyo Disneyland Celebration Hotel – Discover, in the autumn. The two hotels will have 702 Tokyo Disneyland and DisneySea themed rooms. The developer, Milial Resort Hotels, and Disney hope that the new hotel will relieve the pressure on the existing accommodations, which are operating at 90% annual occupancy.

Chapter Six
Tokyo DisneySea

TOKYO DISNEYLAND HAD ALWAYS BEEN only the beginning; like Disneyland it would never be completed. The "Oriental Land Basic Project (leisure facilities)" plan of 1974 contained OLC's original concept for the future of all of the reclaimed land near Urayasu. Shortly after the opening of TDL in 1983, specific project planning began in coordination with the Walt Disney company and "in 1984, the 'Tokyo Disney World Framework' was determined and the two companies started work on the joint development." Concepts for a second theme park and adjacent facilities were outlined in the "Land for an

Amusement Park Project," formulated in 1985. The entire Maihama area was to be developed into "a high-quality entertainment area" that was "a globally recognized leisure-recreation destination."

On April 15, 1988, Masatomo Takahashi, President of Oriental Land Company, held a press conference at Showbase 2000 for the fifth anniversary of Tokyo Disneyland. He was expected to summarize the outstanding success of the theme park in Urayasu, but he went on to announce the construction plans for a second, as yet unnamed, Disney theme park. This was nothing new to those in the know at OLC, for according to the OLC website, "We started looking into the idea of creating a second theme park soon after the opening of Tokyo Disneyland. In October 1983, at the same time plans were being made for the future development of Tokyo Disneyland, deliberations were also underway on the development of the area around the Park."

In California, Michael Eisner had recently taken control of what was now called The Walt Disney Company (WDC), and as with everything else to do with the company, he had his own ideas on what should be done in the new Tokyo park. OLC reported, "Discussions were repeatedly held with The Walt Disney Company and Chiba Prefecture, and by 1987, a significant amount of time was being spent on evaluating the idea of a second theme park; among them was a joint research conducted with Disney on what the public reception would be toward a second park." The "Maihama Area Monorail Business Feasibility Research Project Team" was set up by OLC in 1988 in order to add a monorail to the new project.

Eisner was partial to two ideas; the one he liked most and according to Mary Sklar "did mount an all-out effort to convince OLC's chairman" was similar to the under construction theme park in Orlando, Disney-MGM Studio. Soon after taking up the reins as CEO for Disney, Eisner put a team of Disney Imagineers to work creating two new pavilions for Future World at EPCOT. Led by Randy Bright and Marty Sklar, the brainstorming sessions that followed produced Wonders of Life and The Great Movie Ride. The latter would have been positioned between The Land and Journey Into Imagination pavilions. The original idea was for a three-part experience with emphasis on movies, television, and radio. A great-moments-in-movies ride through, a stage show of a TV studio, and a feature about radio's importance in storytelling were to be the main parts of the attraction. Eisner, however, saw great potential in the movie ride idea and suggested that instead of it being built in an existing park, it should have a park all its own with Hollywood and show business themes. At about the same time, Disney and Metro-Goldwyn-Mayer had entered into a licensing agreement that gave Disney use of the MGM logo for what would become Disney-MGM Studios theme park. The idea grew and evolved rapidly until the three experiences originally planned had become The Great Movie Ride, Superstar Television, and Monster Sound Show. What Eisner liked most about the concept was that it followed an idea Walt Disney had had about bringing people into the studio to see how things really worked behind the scenes. The concept was deeply rooted in the Company's past. Disney-MGM Studios opened on May 1, 1989, the third theme park in Walt Disney World, and proved immensely popular from the beginning.

Building on that, Eisner attempted to persuade OLC that a similar park was the way to go in expanding Tokyo Disneyland. Plans were discussed for what was to be called "Disney Hollywood Studio Theme Park at Tokyo Disneyland," and at first progressed smoothly. According to the OLC website, "In developing a second theme park, we were searching for a plan that would create a new market by providing a completely different experience from Tokyo Disneyland and that is suited to the Japanese people, making them want to return to it again and again." In time OLC began to think that a Hollywood Studio was not the answer, as the movie industry in Japan did not have the glamor it did in America. OLC thought that "The second theme park should have a marketability independent from TDL. It should not be the second park simply to catch the guests overflowing from TDL. Unless it provides an experience entirely different from that offered by TDL, there is little meaning for building it." OLC told Disney, "We would like to make up our minds after seeing it in the U.S." They thought that Eisner's idea was "too dangerous" and that they would lose money, they wanted something safer, more conventional, Aviad Raz reported.

The main stumbling block in negotiations was defining exactly what role Disney would take in the park. Did they want to license the project or be a participating partner in a joint venture? Eisner preferred the former.

By 1991 the entire concept came under reconsideration. A meeting was held in Tokyo in September with the top executives from both companies in attendance. OLC announced it was not interested in the Disney Hollywood idea. The Disney execs were disappointed, though they must have seen it coming. Frank Wells, President of the Disney Company, reportedly said, "Was our effort the Myth of Sisyphus after all?"

OLC now started looking at another project Disney was working on, Port Disney in Long Beach, California. When the Disney Company bought the Disneyland Hotel upon the death of the owner and friend of Walt Disney, John Wrather, it came with interests in Long Beach along with other assets which were quickly sold off. Eisner set his Imagineers to work on what they could do with the Long Beach property, and before long they came up with a resort they called Port Disney. The project was to include a port for cruise ships, retail stores, hotels, and a marine themed park called Disney Sea. Also belonging to Disney in the Long Beach area was the recently purchased *Queen Mary* cruise ship, slated as a Disney Hotel for Port Disney guests to stay in, and *The Spruce Goose*, an aircraft originally belonging to Howard Hughes.

The goal of the park, according to *Port Disney News* (the one and only edition, published in 1991), "is to sensitize millions of visitors each year to the enormous challenges and opportunities of our seas—our most precious resource—in a setting that encourages play and fantasy." David Malmuth, project director and Vice-President with Disney Development Company went on to say, "Basically, we want people to have fun. We also want our guests to directly experience the sea, to wonder about it, to ask questions and to have a memorable time."

This was more like what OLC had in mind. To complement their Disney Land they wanted a Disney Sea. "After further consideration, a new theme based on the idea of the 'seven seas' was born in 1992. Upon further negotiations, ideas for this second theme park gradually began to emerge in more detail. This became the basis of what we know of today as Tokyo DisneySea Park." President of OLC Toshio Kagami stated, "We also had a strong attachment to the theme concerning the sea. Japan is an island country surrounded by sea. Historically speaking, cultures were brought to Japan across the seas. The Japanese have a strong love of the sea; you may call it our home."

So, negotiations continued until the "Development of Park Environs Plan" was finally concluded in 1994. The plan envisioned a "themed city" offering twenty-first century recreation and an elegant Golden Age of Hollywood-themed hotel. OLC's business structure was reorganized the following year with two objectives: "One was to ensure that we would be able to make important contributions to Tokyo Disney Resort in the future. And the other was to bring to fruition the new facilities outlined in our uniquely developed large-scale business projects which also entailed high expectations for the future of the company."

These objectives would be realized with the launching of five projects: "construction of a Second Theme Park, development of the Maihama Station Area, start of the hotel business, introduction of a new transportation system, and listing the company on the stock exchange." A new corporate philosophy was enacted through "OLC 2010 VISION," which outlined what the company hoped to achieve by 2010.

The new park was officially announced at a news conference in Japan by Michael Eisner in November 1995. The basic concept was put forward and the name, though still a working title, would be DisneySea. The "Tokyo DisneySea Park Development, Construction and Operations Contract" was signed in April 1996 by OLC and WDC along with the "Tokyo DisneySea Hotel Development, Construction and Operation Contract." The basic plan was finished and written down in a draft as the "Tokyo DisneySea Project." OLC stated, "With the completion of this plan, we were finally able to announce the outline of Tokyo DisneySea Park to the general public on

November 26. On the day following the announcement, a variety of media took up the news under the title of 'new sea-themed park to open' together with illustrations of the Park. After nearly 10 years, 'the public was finally able to learn what this new Park would look like when completed.'"

The planning department at OLC was made up primarily of corporate elites who had studied in business schools in the States. They were instructed to work out a plan that WDC would accept. Though the Americans wanted the same licensing agreement as they had at TDL, the Japanese wanted to "issue preferred stock (annual dividend 5%) in an amount equivalent to 20% of the total funds of US$3.4 billion required for the project, 30% of which is to be purchased by WD."

Disney, on the other hand, did not want to take any risks, just reap the benefits through licensing fees, a position that did not sit well with the Japanese. WDC wanted a 10% licensing fee, which the OLC board rejected.

As negotiations continued, worldwide economic conditions deteriorated. Many within OLC management, the major shareholders and money lenders, were beginning to question if this was the right time for such a massive undertaking. Profitability was uncertain and some thought the risk too high. WDC saw it differently and urged OLC to aggressively increase its investment. It was not until May of 1997 that a basic agreement was concluded between OLC and WDC for the new theme park and hotel.

The summer of 1997 brought more pressure to bear on the OLC executives than they had ever had. They knew that Disney's support and insightful advice had enabled them to achieve the success they now enjoyed. They also knew Disney would continue to play hardball with the negotiations. New analyses were ordered from the planning department to examine various sales growth projections, interest rate levels, and profitability ratios from every angle.

Still, the two companies remained in disagreement as to the next course of action, and their relationship deteriorated. In August of 1997, it reached its lowest point. OLC top management had gone to California to try and smooth Disney's ruffled feathers. As they sat down to a dinner hosted by

WDC, a spokesman addressed Takahashi saying, "Mr. Chairman, our president in furious. There is no point in any discussions. We have to ask you to go back to Tokyo."

The response from the Japanese was immediate: "Since we are paying a royalty in excess of ¥6 billion (US$50.84 million) each year, we can hardly agree to a plan to do it under the same conditions. It is quite unfair if the U.S. side is to take no risks, use the land free with no financial burden, but collect the royalty. We don't want that."

WDC did not agree; they had long felt that they had ended up with a bad bargain after the TDL negotiations. Their bywords for these talks had been "Never repeat the mistake of Tokyo Disneyland."

A financial analysis from OLC's planning department now became top priority. More meetings were held, both with WDC and internally with shareholders, as the results of the analysis and shareholders' wants sometimes clashed. Finally a decision was reached; management decided to go ahead with TDS with the licensing mode and the board agreed. The two sides were finally reunited, Disney with its know-how, OLC with its huge chunk of land.

The final decision was not made until November 1997 when the official name, Tokyo DisneySea, was confirmed. Matasomo Takahashi had this to say: "We are often asked about the cause of success of this project that brought a revolution into the leisure industry in Japan. We believe it is because it was a combination of Walt Disney's genius idea … family entertainment that makes 'families and friends unite across age, sex and nationality,' with the delicate service of the Japanese people." He then quoted the late Frank Wells, at one time the Walt Disney Company President, who said, "The Japanese operation is doing better than ours. There's nothing more we can teach them. Rather, we are learning from them."

Relations between the two companies changed overnight. Confrontation was out; cooperation between two indispensable partners was in. The president of OLC, Toshio Kagami, reportedly said, "Our relation with Disney was originally that of a master and a servant but it changed to one of equality as OLC grew and also with the growth of OLC's capabilities and experiences, so that we were able to discuss more freely. A continuation of hard edged negotiations changed to more agreeable discussions as we mutually grew to realize that both sides are indispensable partners to the other side. We came to a common understanding that disrupting negotiation is the worst kind of negotiation."

Some of the initial ideas for Port Disney's theme park included "Pirate Island" to bolster public interest in the *Pirates of the Caribbean* (2003) movie in production at the time; "Oceania," a giant aquarium with a tidal exchange with the ocean; "Shark Cage Encounter," which is self-explanatory; "Fleets of Fantasy" would include an Egyptian galley and a Chinese junk; "Heroes Harbor," where myths and legends come to life; "Lost City of Atlantis," a boat ride through the lost city; and "Mysterious Island," a simulator-based attraction involving Captain Nemo's submarine and a giant squid.

Port Disney was never built, mainly due to rising costs, estimated at over $3 billion, the unavailability of enough land to house all the ideas, and local opposition particularly from the California Coastal Commission. Instead, Disney turned towards another doomed project, the Westcot expansion of Disneyland, and OLC scooped up many of the ideas from DisneySea.

Michael Eisner had lost interest in what TDL was doing when his movie studio idea was quashed, and the Imagineering design team led by Senior Vice-President Steve Kirk had an open path to create a new genre in Disney parks. One of their first ideas was to use the Euro Disneyland approach of having a Disneyland Hotel as the entrance to the park. Guests would enter the park by walking under the southern European-style hotel called Miracosta and once they were inside, the back of the hotel could serve as a background for live performances on the Mediterranean Harbor. Other ideas included a Mermaid Lagoon, Mysterious Island with an erupting Mount Prometheus volcano, Lost River Delta, and the Arabian Coast.

The question soon became could Steve Kirk and Jim Thomas (Senior Vice-President for Tokyo Resort Development) convince OLC to spend the kind of money necessary to not only build the park but make it look as good as or better than TDL? The answer, according to Marty Sklar's educated guess, was that "the OLC executives responsible for the project were not going to 'lose face' when Tokyo DisneySea (TDS) was compared to Tokyo Disneyland."

The negotiations had, as with TDL, raised cultural concerns and brought up differences between Japan and America. A minor example was the logo for TDS. Disney thought a lighthouse would be perfect, as to Americans it symbolized "a beacon of a safe return for the adventurous seafarers." To the Japanese, however, "a lighthouse brings up images of melancholy and loneliness," so would not be appropriate for a Disney park. In time the parties agreed that a new symbol with the Earth as the water planet would be more fitting for a park themed to the sea. They called it the aquasphere, and it stands at the entrance to the park.

The luxury liner, SS *Columbia*, that was to be docked at American Waterfront was the subject of heated discussion for a time. The Japanese thought it was much too large and construction costs were too high. The Americans had in mind a ship about the size of RMS *Queen Mary* that had been in the original plans for Port Disney. In the end the Imagineers won out, and a magnificent 140-meter-long ship was built. Though nowhere near the 310 meters of *Queen Mary*, there is some resemblance and she is still an impressive sight.

The ground breaking ceremony was held on site on October 22, 1998, when ninety members of both WDC and OLC gathered to stick hoes in the ground to signify the commencement of construction work. The usual Shinto ceremonies were held to grant safety to the workers, and afterwards a joint press conference was held nearby. Michael Eisner and Toshio Kagami gave further details on their plans for DisneySea and announced that the new name of Tokyo Disney Resort (TDR) would encompass not only the two parks but also a shopping complex and the hotels. Steve Kirk, Walt Disney Imagineering Executive Designer for TDS, later remarked, "After five years of designing and redesigning, it's great that all we have to do now is build it."

Masatomo Takahashi was inducted as a Disney Legend in the same year, at which time Roy E. Disney, then Vice-Chair of WDC, said of him:

"Masatomo's vision and desire to bring the joys of a Disney park to Tokyo were instrumental to the establishment and continuing success of Tokyo Disneyland. Thanks to Masatomo, for years to come, families around the Asia-Pacific region will experience the delights of Disney and its magical theme parks." Regrettably, Masatomo Takahashi passed away on January 31, 2000, before the opening of Tokyo DisneySea.

As construction continued on TDS, both Ikspiari and Disney Ambassador Hotel began operations on July 7, 2000. A water-pouring ceremony was held in January 2001 as water was poured into the TDS waterway. In March, it was announced that the official opening day for TDS would be September 4. The Disney Resort Line Monorail opened on July 27, 2001, encircling TDR and linking all of the major resort destinations. In August, a ceremony was held to celebrate the completion of the new park which had not been without difficulties. At one point a number of contractors had refused to bid on construction work. They claimed that to build it according to specifications would be technically too difficult, as much of the high-tech engineering was to be hidden. A way was found around the problem and the contractors were back to work.

The 176-acre park opened on schedule. At a press conference held on opening day, Michael Eisner praised the OLC and announced that "There is no third park plan in Japan yet, but we would work with OLC if there would be one." The project had cost ¥335 billion, was completed on schedule, and was the only Disney theme park of its kind in the world.

The gates opened at 8:00 on September 4, 2001, and the Grand Opening Ceremony took place on a gilded barge in Mediterranean Harbor near the entrance to the park. The numerous guests in attendance may have seen a similarity to the opening ceremonies of TDL as a light rain fell on the dignitaries. Present on the barge were Mickey and Minnie Mouse, resplendent in nautical garb; Toshio Kagami, President of OLC and his wife; Michael Eisner, Chair of WDC; Roy. E. Disney, Vice-Chair of WDC and Chair of Disney Feature Animation; and Tokyo Disneyland Resort Ambassador, Satoko Shiyanagi.

Kagami spoke first, welcoming guests and briefly describing the new park. He spoke in Japanese, which was translated into English when he finished each sentence. Michael Eisner was next, and he commented in an aside to Mickey as he adjusted the microphone before speaking, "Roy Disney and I are thrilled to be here with you in your beautiful country and experience the warmth of your hospitality." Eisner then concluded by reading the wording from a plaque that overlooks the harbor: "Welcome one and all to a world where Adventure and Imagination set sail. Tokyo DisneySea is dedicated to the spirit of exploration that lives in each of us. Here we chart a course for Adventure, Romance, Discovery and Fun and journey to exotic and fanciful Ports of Call. May Tokyo DisneySea inspire the hearts and minds of all of us who share the water planet, Earth." Mickey and Minnie clapped as his words were translated into Japanese, and at the same time, the skies partially cleared and sun shone down on the barge where the ceremony was being held "as if the sky was also celebrating this dream-come-true moment."

Roy Disney, Walt's nephew, was next to speak, and he began by comparing TDL to Disneyland and commenting on the huge part OLC played in making the parks possible. "I can think of two people in particular who would have been thrilled with this park which has risen next to a park they would have found very familiar. Of course I refer to Walt and Roy Disney. They would both have loved to be with us here today but in a very real way, I believe they are."

Toshio Kagami returned to the mic with the opening proclamation: "Now, the time has come to sail out to the sea of adventure and imagination with you." Fireworks filled the skies across the bay as Mount Prometheus erupted in a dazzling display of pyrotechnics and TDS was officially open. The barge with the dignitaries on it sailed out into the harbor to the strains of a DisneySea theme song as a couple of other ships filled with Disney characters joined in for a sail past and waved at the guests assembled on the shores.

TDS set a world record by being the first theme park to reach the 10 millionth guest total in only 307 days after its grand opening.

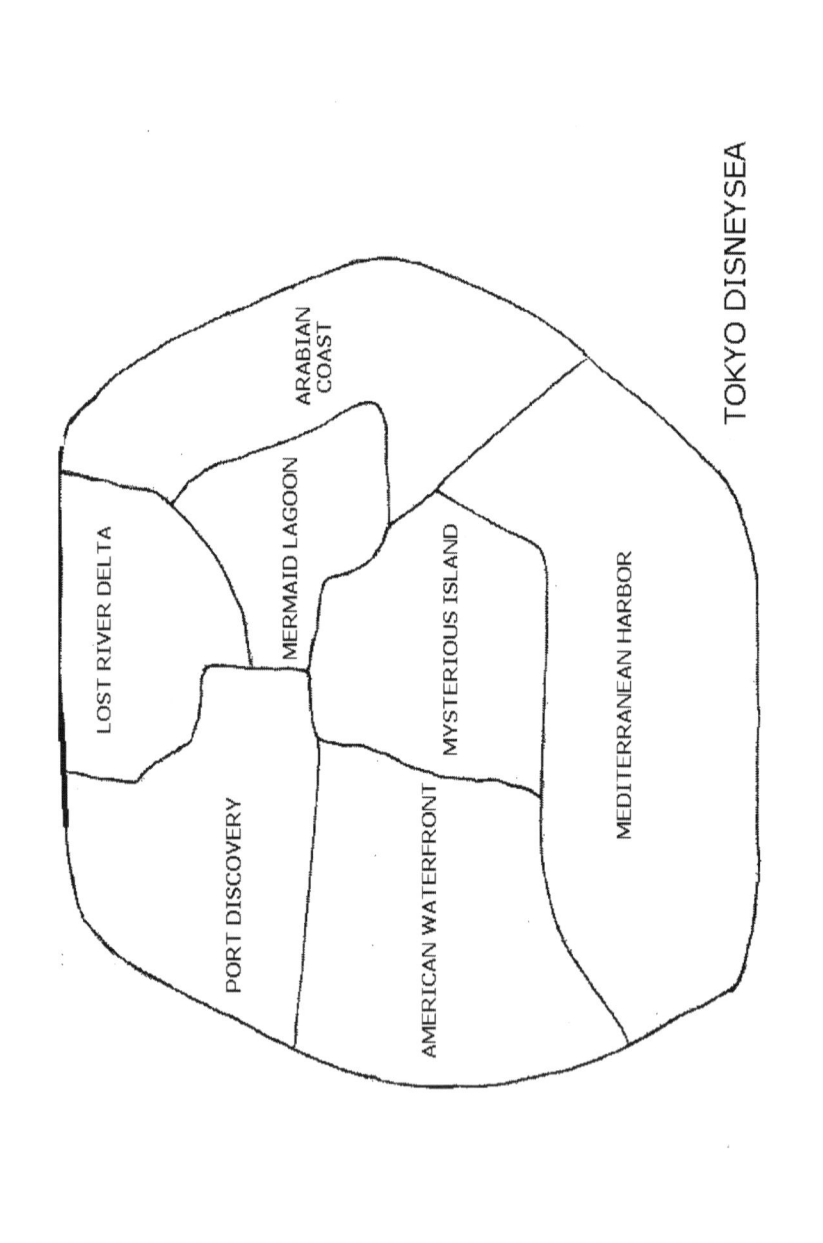

TOKYO DISNEYSEA

- ARABIAN COAST
- LOST RIVER DELTA
- MERMAID LAGOON
- MYSTERIOUS ISLAND
- MEDITERRANEAN HARBOR
- PORT DISCOVERY
- AMERICAN WATERFRONT

Chapter Seven
"A Whole New World..."

Now, let's take the grand tour of Tokyo DisneySea, as it was in 2015.

After passing through the turnstiles the first thing guests come across is a 14 ton, 26.5 foot diameter globe of the Earth seemingly balanced on a fountain of water. This is the symbol of TDS, the DisneySea AquaSphere centered in the DisneySea Plaza, where its very presence prepares guests for the amazing adventure ahead. The water surrounding the globe has been slowed down to defy gravity so that it clings to the sphere all the way to the bottom and creates "a rippling ocean under its seven continents and eighty islands."

From there guests pass under the Hotel MiraCosta (Italian for "view of the coast") and enter TDS. Here they find seven unique lands or 'ports of call'—Mediterranean Harbor, American Waterfront, Lost River Delta, Port Discovery, Mermaid Lagoon, Arabian Coast, and Mysterious Island.

In keeping with the hotel overlooking it, Mediterranean Harbor has an Italian seaport theme and unlike the other Disney theme parks with a Main Street or World Bazaar leading into the park, the harbor is a large V shape. To the right is a path to Mysterious Island and to the left American Waterfront.

Upon entering the park the merchandising begins. Three shops, Valentina's Sweets, Emporio, with "the park's largest selection of merchandise," and Galleria Disney, featuring "Duffy merchandise and more," tempt the guests. Most will wait until they are leaving to visit these areas and continue on. There are numerous shops and restaurants in this area built into the architecture as full-scale reproductions of buildings in the Italian cities of Portofino and Venice. Continuing to the right, there are Piccalo Mercato, a wagon with items that light up, Mama's Biscotti Bakery, and Café Portofino, a buffeteria serving "pasta rotisserie chicken and more." Further on, guests discover Miramore, a wagon selling cold weather gear in case one came unprepared; Bella Minni Collections, "with accessories and other items;" Il Postino Stationery; and Zambini Brothers Ristorante, with "pasta, pizza and more."

Here also is the first attraction, DisneySea Transit Steamer Line, sidewheel steamers that take guests on a leisurely voyage from Mediterranean Harbor around the entire park. This is the TDS answer to a railroad around the park, as it stops in American Waterfront and Lost River Delta and then returns to Mediterranean Harbor. The colorful boats are replicas of steamers that flourished on American lakes and rivers in the late 19th and early 20th centuries. Low decks facilitate easy boarding and the open sides allow guests easy views of the diverse scenery.

There are three docks along the TDS waterway following the clockwise voyage of the steamers. The first, in Mediterranean Harbor, is themed to a turn-of-the-century South American port. The second, at American

Waterfront, is reminiscent of a tranquil Cape Cod fishing village. The third, at Lost River Delta, is a Central America, Caribbean Coast, a 1930s-themed, two-story dock made of rusty galvanized iron, old wood, and a thatched roof. From here the steamer returns to Mediterranean Harbor. The round trip takes about twenty minutes.

The boats do not run while shows are being set up or performed, and from opening day until April 22, 2004, the show in Mediterranean Harbor was *DisneySea Symphony*. Other shows followed, such as *Porto Paradiso Water Carnival*, *BraviSEAmo*, *The Legend of Mythica*, *Fantasmic*, and *Be Magical*, with *Crystal Wishes Journey* slated for 2016.

Returning to MiraCosta to finish the tour of Mediterranean Harbor, guests cannot help but notice how the hotel contributes to the illusion of an actual city. The hotel itself is part of the "façade" and as a functioning building, guests in the rooms can be seen on the terraces and balconies enjoying the view of the harbor as they would in a real city. To the left of the entrance, guests will find the Splendido wagon, offering "fun caps and hair bands," Figaro's Clothiers, Merchant of Venice Confections, Venetian Carnival Market, Villa Donaldo Home Shop, and Gondolier Snacks. Lido Isle, on the left shore of Mediterranean Harbor, would become the showplace for the lively and festive shows. Not far away is another pizza place, Ristorante di Canaletto, Barnacle Bill's sausage wagon, and the second attraction, Venetian Goldolas managed by two charismatic gondoliers. The ride takes sixteen guests at a time on an eleven minute tour of the Palazzo Canals to Mediterranean Harbor and back, serenaded part way by the gondoliers.

Halfway across the bridge to Fortress Explorations is another cold weather shop, Rimenbranze. The Fortress is on the opposite side of Mediterranean Harbor from the hotel. "Walk through the fortress and galleon and explore on your own. See exhibitions on the study of the planets and the earth's rotation, operate cannons, and various nautical instruments, and more," the guidemap beckons.

Fortress Explorations is built into the cooled lava that flows from Mount Prometheus. The four story fortress features ten individual exhibits within its many domes and towers. Amongst them are: a recreation of Leonardo Da Vinci's Flying Machine, a three-story pendulum, a hall containing a remote-controlled game where guests can pilot antique sailing ships, and an ancient dark chamber camera *obscura*. A recording station is accessed by a stone bridge within Mount Prometheus, where the volcano's activity is recorded and tracked.

In the citadel's main golden dome is a giant Chamber of Planets. Here guests "can create the planets' orbit using enormous ancient cranks and cogs." The sailing ship *Renaissance* is docked outside at harbor's edge and "a courtyard of crates and interactive exhibits" encourages hands-on discovery. Leonardo's Challenge is a Japanese language quest where guests can "follow the clues on the map to complete your mission."

There is a table service restaurant called Magellan's in the fortress as well as Magellan's Lounge (inside Magellan's) for "appetizers and cocktails," and if only a light snack is desired, there is Refrescoes.

Guests now have to retrace their steps across the bridge to visit American Waterfront on the west side of the park. This port of call is themed to the United States' northeastern seaboard in the early part of the 20th century. There are two areas, Old Cape Cod and New York. Running beside the bridge is the elevated electric trolley known as the DisneySea Electric Railway, a 2'6" (762 mm) gauge that takes guests in two open cars to Port Discovery and back, where they get an opportunity to see parts of the park one would not normally see. On the way to the railway, guests will pass Steamboat Mickey's apparel shop, McDuck's Department Store, New York Deli, and Delancey Catering's hot dog wagon. Just past the railway station is Japan Airlines' Broadway Music Theater, and after passing Slinky Dog's Gift Trolley, guests arrive at Toy Story Mania, a show so popular that in its opening months guests sometimes waited up to eight hours to get inside.

Toy Story Mania is located in a new Coney Island-inspired area of Cape Cod called Toyville Trolley Park, unlike the American *Toy Story* versions which are presented as taking place in Andy's bedroom. Inspired by the *Toy Story* films, this 4-D, interactive attraction is Imagineering's most technologically advanced. It opened on July 9, 2012 and requires guests to wear 3-D glasses as their spinning vehicles pass through classic carnival games and the guests shoot at assorted targets. In addition, there are mini-games in shops adjacent to the attraction.

Moving north, the ominous presence of the Tower of Terror looms over head. Unlike its American counterparts, this hotel is built of red brick and has a Gothic appearance. It does not have the Twilight Zone theme, as Japanese guests are not as familiar with the old TV show and OLC did not want to pay the royalties CBS demanded. Tower of Terror opened as Hotel Hightower on September 22, 2006 as part of the fifth anniversary celebrations.

The backstory is naturally different, placing the scene in 1912 New York sometime after the hotel's owner, Harrison Hightower III, explorer and adventurer, mysteriously disappeared on New Year's Eve 1899. All that was found of him after the elevator he was riding in crashed several stories was a mysterious statue of Shiriki Utundu, which Hightower had found in remote Africa. Sharp-eyed guests will note photos of Hightower claiming artifacts from the site of the Raging Spirits attraction in Lost River Delta. After being closed for one hundred years, "the New York City Preservation Society has finished restoring the infamous hotel, and started giving tours to the public. But what happens when you take the elevator to the top floor?" The abundance of artifacts in the pre-show rooms makes guests want to take their time getting to the elevator, as there is so much to take in, even more than in the American versions.

In front of the Tower of Terror is Waterfront Park, which serves a variety of purposes. Here character meet-and-greets are held, as well as other forms of entertainment, and the annual Christmas tree is often set up here. Nearby is Tower of Terror Memorabilia where guests can purchase "souvenir photos of your experience and Tower of Terror merchandise." There is also the Sailing Day Buffet in case the attraction made you hungry.

Before heading over to the cruise ship docked nearby, guests often take a tour of New York City on the Big City Vehicles. The idea is similar to the vehicles running up and down Main Street in Disneyland, with the difference that the vehicles are early 20th century instead of late 19th century, "right when automobiles began to take over from horse-drawn carriages. High end for the time, these vehicles are extra fancy." There are a number of different modes of transport, including a police wagon, delivery truck, an open-top town car, and others.

SS *Columbia* represents the iconic steamships of the era and is not a recreation of any particular vessel. The funnels display the Cunard Line's color and the ship is similar to RMS *Queen Mary*, which was once owned by Disney and was to be the centerpiece of Port Disney in Long Beach, a plan that never came to fruition. There is a stage on the dock for live entertainment, using the ship as a backdrop. *A Table is Waiting* is the current show put on by Mickey and Friends who have just returned from a world cruise "and they've brought back treats from many different countries. Mickey has invited Guests to the Dockside Stage, which is set up to look like a giant dining table, where that famous host, Lumiere, is waiting."

Once on board, guests can explore the ship and take in a view of the park from the upper decks. SS *Columbia* Dining Room (on Deck B) offers table service, and a la carte and full-course meals are available, along with atmosphere music from a pianist. For those who prefer a lighter snack, the Teddy Roosevelt Lounge serves "sandwiches, cocktails and draft beer." Menus are in Japanese only but every detail in the restaurant from the ship's name on the plates on up is designed with dining on the high seas in mind.

Despite the tug parked off the bow of *Columbia*, the ship does not move from its moorings.

Turtle Talk With Crush is one of the few imports from the U.S. parks to be found in TDS. It first opened in EPCOT and Disney's California Adventure in Anaheim before going to TDS in October 2009. It is located in *Columbia's* Undersea Observatory, a theater-style attraction, where guests can see and converse with Crush the sea turtle through an underwater window as if he is "swimming happily through the open seas."

Leaving *Columbia*, guests can cross a bridge near where a second dock for the DisneySea Transit Steamer Line is located and enter the Cape Cod portion of the land. Here is Aunt Peg's Village Store, with Duffy merchandise, Cape Cod Cookoff, counter service with hamburgers and a show, and the Cape Cod Confectionery next door with "sweets and drinks themed to Duffy."

Copper-domed Port Discovery is "the center for weather control in this futuristic marina located across the horizons of time." Considered by some to be the Tomorrowland of TDS, it incorporates some of the planned but never built aspects of Discovery Bay in Euro Disneyland. There are three attractions located here after passing the Seaside Snacks wagon. The first one guests come across is Aquatopia, which is reminiscent of the Mad Hatter's Teacup ride on water. The three person watercraft spins and twirls in unexpected directions, and there is a possibility of getting wet from spurting water and a waterfall. The ride uses the same LPS trackless technology used in TDL's Pooh's Hunny Hunt attraction.

Leaving Aquatopia, there are a few shops and restaurants, such as Discovery Gifts, where cold weather gear is available; Horizon Bay Restaurant, a buffeteria for Disney character dining; and the pastry wagon called Breezeway Bites. The Port Discovery terminus of the overhead electric railway that connects with American Waterfront is located nearby, and just before the next attraction is Skywatcher Souvenirs, a wagon offering hats and hairbands.

Stormrider is a Star Tours-style flight simulator attraction located inside the Center for Weather Control building at the top end of Port Discovery. Imagineer David Edminster reports that "The attraction was 100% mocked up in a remote hanger outside of Los Angeles" under WDI supervision, "then completely disassembled and shipped to Japan where it was reconstructed." The building is reminiscent of a Victorian-era laboratory with its mechanical devices and copper roofs. Inside is the "Storm Diffusion Device which can diffuse storms when detonated inside the center of a powerful storm." Guests are seated just in time as a huge storm just happens to be approaching. Naturally, all does not go as planned, as guests attempt to deliver and detonate "the fuse," a storm dissipating device. With 122 seats, the vehicles (The Stormrider) are three times larger than in Star Tours, making them amongst the largest moving theaters in the world. Events are explained in Japanese with English subtitles on the LCD screen.

Heading north, guests approach Lost River Delta which is dominated by the ruins of an ancient Aztec pyramid and attached temple. There are two bridges across the waterway to this port of call as well as access to the DisneySea Steamer Line wharf. To the left after crossing a bridge are Mickey and Friends Greeting Trails, which opened on April 28, 2011. Here guests can explore trails through the Lost River Delta and discover Mickey, Minnie, or Goofy at the end of the trail as they research plants and insects or study the ancient ruins.

Scattered about are the usual shops and restaurants. Peddlers' Outpost, a wagon with light-up items, Lookout Traders for cold weather gear, and Expedition Photo Archives, where guests can retrieve pictures taken in the Indiana Jones Attraction. Places to eat include two wagons, Expedition Eats with "Yucatan sausage rolls," as well as counter service at Yucatan Base Camp Grill specializing in "smoked pork and chicken," and Lost River Cookhouse serving "smoked chicken legs."

Having explored the port of call, it is time for the attractions. Indiana Jones Adventure: Temple of the Crystal Skull is very similar to the Disneyland Indiana Jones attraction, with the Forbidden Eye being replaced by a Crystal Skull as guardian of temple secrets. As Asian jungles are not overly exotic to Asians, this adventure takes place in an unknown region of Mexico circa 1930s. The concept is the same, that of guests taking turbulent, high speed military transport vehicles through a perilous lost temple.

The attraction debuted with the opening of the park in 2001 before the film, *Indiana Jones and the Kingdom of the Crystal Skull* (2008), was released, so there is no connection between the two other than general location. Scenarios are different and even the Crystal Skull's appearance is not the same. Outside the pyramid is a wealth of detail, a seaplane (C-3PO is its designation) is tied up nearby, and a tent encampment for the workers has been set up. Passing that, guests go over a wooden bridge and into the temple itself where they see stone reliefs, catwalks, and scaffolding going every which way. The floor becomes littered with skeletons and the walls decorated with Mexican inspired frescoes. The initial entrance room is large but soon dwindles down in size as the queue moves through a series of intricately-themed chambers: areas overgrown with jungle foliage, derelict bridges, moss covered rock, carved statues, all lit by sun beams penetrating through cracks in the ceiling above. Atop the scaffolding a crystal skull warns guests not to proceed, but the warning is ignored and guests enter smaller chambers passing a large gold medallion, a map of the chambers, and venture into dark catacombs lit only by sculpted faces back-lit with red light. Just before the loading area is reached, a black and white film presentation is played with the host, Paco, speaking in Japanese with a Mexican accent, telling guests to keep their hands, feet, and other body parts inside the cars at all times.

As the vehicles pull up to the loading area it appears identical to the Disneyland version. There are a few minor changes, mainly in keeping with the Crystal Skull theme. In Disneyland there are three paths guests can be sent down; in TDS there is only one. Once inside, the eyes of Mara and warnings about her eyes are absent; instead the crystal skull that guests try to sneak past starts to glow and shoots out beams from its eyes.

The track layout is the same as in Disneyland, though when we meet Indy trying to keep some doors closed, he speaks in Japanese. Proceeding along with the John Williams score reverberating off the walls, guests will notice another crystal skull instead; Mara and the brilliant red and orange hues have been toned down to blue and green in keeping with the Fountain of Youth theme.

Next comes a chamber filled with skeletons and assorted bones, followed by the bug chamber with insects that are much more convincing than the ones in Disneyland. Moving across a bridge, there is a burst of smoke but no fire effects as guests are hit by a spinning vortex and a massive skull shoots beams of green and blue from its eyes. The vehicle guns it across the swaying bridge and behind the skull.

"Snakes, why did it have to be snakes" is next in Disneyland, but instead of snakes in TDS there is a fully animated dragon that lunges at the guests as the vehicles pitch down to be assaulted by another crystal skull. The next chamber is filled with skeletal remains but with none of the pyrotechnic displays from Disneyland. What would be the rat room in Disneyland has been converted to a long hallway with a large stone face with its mouth gaping. Accelerating towards the face, a huge smoke ring puffs out of the mouth. The vehicle plows through and stops again before a long dark chamber which has three-dimensional walls, unlike the painted flat ones in Disneyland. The jeep moves again and darts seem to whizz over the guests heads. The finale is the same as Disneyland, with Indy hanging and yelling (in Japanese) as the giant stone ball careens towards the vehicle just as it drops down to safety and the final scene of Indy saying goodbye.

Overall the ride has been judged to be smoother than the Disneyland version, perhaps due partly to the fact that the TDS Indy ride has electromagnetic components instead of the hydraulics used in Anaheim.

On the far right side of Lost River Delta is the Raging Spirits attraction. Designed by Disney Imagineering and opened in July 2005, this roller coaster-style ride has the same track layout as Indiana Jones et le Temple du Péril in Disneyland Paris which debuted in 1993. Though the backstory has to do with explorers in the jungle, they obviously do not have the expertise of Indiana Jones. The explorers stumbled upon a five-thousand-year-old temple with two altars, one for the water god, one for the fire god. The altars were in ruins so the explorers decided to put them back together, which would have been fine except for they put the water god's head on backwards so it faced the fire god. This upset the gods, and fire and water spewed all about as a result of their anger. The roller coaster speeds around corners, upside down and through mists of water in architecture similar to preliminary artwork done for Kuzco's palace in *The Emperor's New Groove* (2000).

The first case of a guest being injured on an attraction at TDS happened on Raging Spirits. At the end of May 2012, a man attempted to get out of the coaster train while it was moving. Apparently he had become alarmed when the restraining bar did not come down and he decided to get back on the loading platform as the car started to move. His leg was caught and he was dragged about six feet (two meters), injuring his right leg. Subsequent police investigations revealed that the bar being still up was a result of "an employee temporarily unlocking the car's safety bars after finding a restraint on an empty seat to still be up. Following this, the bar on the man's seat also unlocked, and as he failed to press down on the bar before the train started to move, the restraint did not deploy." The attraction was suspended until the safety of the ride was confirmed.

On the opposite side of the river, bordering on Mermaid Lagoon, is an abandoned aircraft hanger, partially reclaimed by the jungle, called Hanger Stage, where for entertainment there is a live stage show called *Mystic Rhythms*. In a lively corner full of Latin music, and between Miguel's El Dorado Cantina with tortillas and tacos and Lost River Outfitters, is the Saludos Amigos Greeting dock. Here pictures can be taken with one of the Disney characters (usually Donald Duck) in Latin American garb, though "this greeting may not be available due to weather conditions or Park attendance levels." Before heading off to the next port of call, guests can stop at Tropic Al's for "a tortilla confection."

Looking at a map of Tokyo DisneySea, guests will see that Arabian Coast is located at the top right of the park. This port of call is themed after the popular Disney movie, *Aladdin* (1992), and features an exotic Arabian harbor with an "enchanted world from *1001 Arabian Nights*."

Entering from the top from Lost River Delta, the first attraction is Jasmine's Flying Carpets. This ride is similar to the Dumbo ride in the other theme parks, but guests ride on a carpet over Jasmine's garden rather than on elephant. The carpets can hold four and guests are able to guide their vehicle "up and down or tilt it forward and backward, as if flying your own magical carpet."

Sindbad's Storybook Voyage is in a fortress-like building and was originally called Sindbad's Seven Voyages, and features the titular adventurer and his tiger cub Chandu. *Disney Magazine* described it as "Pirates of the Caribbean meets It's a Small World," and it is based on the stories of Sindbad from *1001 Arabian Nights*. The extra "d" in Sindbad comes from the 1888 Sir

Francis Burton translation of the story. The boat ride meanders amongst 163 audio animatronics figures, people, and animals (more than any other Disney attraction), and with the exception of a fifteen-foot-tall giant, all figures are less than three feet tall. The figures are also amongst the most advanced of Disney animatronics and have a full range of movement. In addition to regular folk, belly dancers, and such, they include eel people, a huge, swooping Rukh bird, an island that turns out to be a whale, and a bunch of Monkey People. The music for the attraction was written by Disney songwriter Alan Menken.

On the waterfront nearby is a Japanese language only meet-and-greet featuring Stitch in Arabic garb. Continuing on is a churro wagon called Open Sesame and Sultan's Oasis, serving snacks and ice cream. Close by is Abu's Bazaar, where guests can try their skill at two different games and win a prize for a price not included in park admission.

The open spaces of Agrabah Marketplace sprawls over the last third of Arabian Coast, and one shop has a "demonstration and sales of glass items and magic tricks." A counter service restaurant, Casbah Food Court, has "curries served with rice and naan" for Middle-eastern, Japanese, and Indian tastes.

The Magic Lamp Theater show begins with a five-minute preamble featuring a turbaned cobra giving the background story, which ends with the appearance of the Genie and his granting a wish to Shaban to become the world's greatest magician. Switch to live-action, and Shaban starts his magic show by performing a trick with Assim, often a female cast member "volunteer." Guests now put on their 3-D glasses as Genie appears and makes a number of transformations, such as a bunny and a woman (dressed like Jessica Rabbit) as Shaban uses his second wish. Genie tries to persuade Shaban to use his last wish but he vanishes, so Genie puts Assim on his magic carpet and pulls her inside the screen. He then turns her into a poor boy resembling Aladdin and they soar away on the magic carpet, even going under guests' seats, to end the show. The lead animator of the computer graphic Genie sequence in this production was Eric Goldberg, who animated the Genie in the original *Aladdin* film.

The last attraction is Caravan Carousel, which is unique to Disney parks in two ways. First, it is a two-story carousel with a 190 person capacity. Secondly, it features characters and animals inspired by the *Arabian Nights* stories "including camels, elephants, griffins, even the Genie from *Aladdin*. Illustrated panels on the upper level depict scenes from the stories."

Often referred to as TDS's Fantasyland, Mermaid Lagoon is surrounded by Lost River Delta, Arabian Coast, and Mysterious Island. "Mermaid Lagoon is really a surprise attraction because you can't see the bulk of it from outside," said Disney Imagineer David Mumford. Crossing over the waterway and moving to the right, guests first encounter Flounder's Flying Fish Coaster. According to *Disney Magazine*, "When King Triton decided to open his undersea kingdom to humans, he asked his subjects to come up with fun things to make us two-legged strangers welcome. Flounder thought it would be cool to soar up and out of the water like a flying fish."

The closest existing attraction is The Barnstormer in the Magic Kingdom at WDW, which Imagineers modified to a flying fish theme. The ride is meant for younger children and only lasts about one minute.

Across from the coaster is a Little Mermaid-themed shop called Mermaid Memories and the attraction Scuttle's Scooters, in which young guests sit in a two-seater hermit crab and ride in a circle under Scuttle's watchful eye. Sea Turtle Souvenirs is close by, selling "fun caps and hairbands."

The Palace of Triton's seashell façade entrance to Triton's Kingdom is the main feature of Mermaid Lagoon. Most of this area is inside and "underwater." Shops inside include The Sleepy Whale Shoppe that is entered through a whale's wide open mouth for "Ariel items and confectionery," Mermaid Treasures, and Kiss de Girl Fashions. Sebastian's Calypso Kitchen features hot sandwiches and pizza, and remarkably is the only place for snacks in this port of call.

Having successfully navigated past the shops on the right, the first attraction is Blowfish Balloon Race, where young guests clamber into colorful gondolas carried by puffed up blowfish and spin around in a circle. The ride is similar to Flik's Flyers in DCA.

After that exciting spin, it is time to relax in Mermaid Lagoon Theater. The original show was *Under the Sea*, a recreation of *The Little Mermaid* story through live actors, audio-animatronics, and puppets. It was recently replaced by *King Triton's Concert*, described by the TDR website as "An unprecedented musical show of dynamic performances! A musical concert is about to start in the kingdom under the sea but Ariel, the star of the show, is nowhere to be found … Enjoy this new show with music, visuals, and dynamic performances!"

After the show, young guests can proceed to Jumpin' Jellyfish where they gently float up and drop down amongst jellyfish on ocean currents in a parachute-like seashell. There is a similar outdoor version in DCA, a child-sized version of the Maliboomer.

For those liking a little more excitement in their rides, there's The Whirlpool, an undersea version of the Disneyland favorite, Mad Hatter's Teacups. Young guests sit in one of only six whirling kelp cups for a brief spin.

Ariel's Playground is a combination playground and extensive walkthrough of various scenes from the movie. Young guests can "climb through a fishing net, explore a secret, treasure filled cave" in "a playground full of fun and games that's perfect for kids who want to explore Ariel's incredible world." Exploration maps are handed out by cast members.

Before leaving Mermaid Lagoon, guests can stop at Ariel's Greeting Grotto that opened in 2006 for photographs with the famous mermaid and pick them up at Grotto Photos and Gifts along with other mermaid merchandise.

Mysterious Island is the smallest of the ports of call and is situated in the smoldering caldera of Mount Prometheus. Named after the Jules Verne novel of the same name, it is themed towards the books of the celebrated author. Guests enter the secret base of Captain Nemo and see his submarine *Nautilus* moored in a small lake. Some of the features of this port of call were to be used in the original Discovery Mountain plan for Disneyland Paris, another Jules Verne tribute.

Mount Prometheus is the largest man-made structure that the Imagineers have built to date. It is made up of some 750,000 square feet of rock soaring 189 feet into the air. Inside are ten three-thousand-pound rocket burners capable of shooting fifty foot flames and submerged cannons firing high powered bursts of over thirty thousand gallons of water. Mount Prometheus "erupts" about once an hour with an ominous rumble and impressive spewing of flames.

The area has only one shop, Nautilus Gifts, and three places to eat, Vulcania Restaurant with Chinese cuisine, Nautilus Galley for takeout snacks, and a Refreshment Station wagon with pork buns.

Interestingly, Mysterious Island is not an island at all though it has that appearance from a distance. The attraction show buildings are built into the side of Mount Prometheus, which is the main feature of TDS and which stands as tall as Cinderella Castle in neighboring TDL. In keeping with the Jules Verne theme, the architecture is Victorian and the volcano fortress is called Vulcania. It should be noted that the volcano is "active," and occasional bursts of fire escape from the summit and steam vents from the sides, contributing to the lack of vegetation.

There are two attractions here, arguably amongst the most popular in TDS. Journey to the Center of the Earth is based on a book by Jules Verne and was first designed as a freefall ride for Discovery Mountain in Euro Disneyland that was never built. The reimagined version in TDS is based more on Disneyland's Rocket Rods and EPCOT's Test Track technology. Music for this attraction was composed by Norman "Buddy" Baker, who was responsible for the scores of a number of Disney films.

Guests travel through the caverns of Nemo's base and board elevators ("Terravators") to descend down the bore hole to the base station below, to which Nemo has bored using a huge drilling machine. Here they learn of an imminent volcanic eruption which is not being monitored, as the man responsible is on a tea break. Despite the warnings, guests clamber into steam-powered mine vehicles and ride through a cavern of glowing crystals and a forest of giant mushrooms and insect/amphibian creatures. Before long, the vehicle stops due to a cave in and takes an alternate route into a cavern filled with giant egg sacks and out into a subterranean sea to be narrowly missed by a lightning strike. Forced into the active volcano, guests then encounter the huge lava monster (almost 20 feet tall) who resides there but escape to safety riding on a fast-moving wave of lava back to the surface traveling from slow to 40 mph in seconds.

Imagineer David Edminster noted that because of her size, the lava monster "required our Imagineers to look for industrial application components...that are robust enough to operate thirteen hours a day without failing." Though the monster has only twenty-four animation functions, she "is one of the most complex in the Disney pantheon."

20,000 Leagues Under the Sea is a submarine-style dark ride based on the Jules Verne novel and 1954 Walt Disney movie of the same name. Unlike the submarine rides in Disneyland and WDW that can be seen to travel in water, these vehicles are suspended from an overhead track. The water illusion is created by double-paned portholes (which the Imagineers call "bubble windows") that contain the water and bubbles and are unique to this attraction. The action is performed on dry land with sets, projections, murals, props, and animated figures.

The vehicle used to carry guests is a 157-Neptune submarine that carries six passengers.

After passing through the queue and seeing Nemo's offices, equipment, and miscellaneous diving gear, guests enter the mini-subs where each two seats has its own viewing porthole. There is also a hand-operated joystick that controls searchlights on the front of the vessel so guests can look at whatever terrors they want to see. Searching for ancient Atlantis, the submarine descends into colorful underwater grottos, the ruins of an ancient civilization, a threatening giant squid that is repulsed by electric charges from the subs hull, into the graveyard of ships called Kraken Reef, and then sails through the dangers and mysteries of Lucifer's Trench.

Leaving Mysterious Island, guests walk around Mediterranean Harbor to exit the park. Now is the time they usually stop at the multitude of shops near the entrance/exit.

*　*　*

In 2002, the Themed Entertainment Association presented TDL with the Thea Award for design, construction and concept of the theme park at El Capitan Theatre in Hollywood, California. A second award was presented in 2009 for the show *Legend of Mythica*.

Attendance at the theme parks has climbed steadily since the opening. In 2003, TDL celebrated its twentieth anniversary with the theme of "Dreams." During this period, the combined annual attendance for both parks surpassed the twenty-five million mark for the first time. The first half year attendance for 2010 was just shy of thirteen million guests. It dropped to around eleven million in 2011, mainly due to the earthquake and tsunami that ravaged Japan, but was back to thirteen-and-a-quarter million the next year, peaking at 15,359,000 in 2013. Due to "the high number of rainy days and extremely high temperature during the summer" of 2015, as well as a raise in entrance prices for the second year in a row, combined attendance at the two parks only reached 14,372,000. In all, as of April 2015, the two parks have drawn 630.39 million visitors since they opened.

As more shows and attractions are added to the resort, it has also become necessary to expand facilities and develop new infrastructure outside of the parks. With the opening of TDS, more guests tended to stay longer and in order to accommodate them, more hotels were built under the "'Tokyo Disney Resort Good Neighbor Hotel' (from 2001) and the 'Tokyo Disney Resort Partner Hotel' (from 2005) programs," enabling guests to choose accommodations according to their wants and budget requirements. To date there are twenty-eight hotels surrounding TDR, along with a Welcome Center opened in July 2001adjacent to JR Maihama Station. The Disney Resort Cruiser, with Mickey shaped windows, was established at the same time to shuttle guests from the hotels to the parks.

Tokyo Disney Resort's Twenty-fifth Anniversary Celebration was held in 2008 at TDR beginning on April 15 and continuing for a year. Festivities were held under the slogan Magical Dreams 25 "Unlock Your Dreams," a program wherein twenty-five guests would win the dream of having TDS all to themselves. The 705-room Tokyo Disneyland Hotel also opened that year as the largest Disney hotel in Japan.

The same year saw OLC President Toshio Kagami inducted as a Disney legend at the same ceremony in Burbank as Roy E. Disney, Walt's nephew.

Entertainment at the resort was also expanded with the addition of Cirque du Soleil Theatre Tokyo to provide a spectacle unlike any other in the parks. It took a year of negotiations between OLC and the theater group before an agreement was finally reached in 2005 and then two years for the construction of the resident theater. *Zed* premiered on October 1, 2008. The show was inspired by the Tarot and its Arcana, the lead character based on the Fool and his journey to unite the two mythical groups of the people of sky and earth. Due to the earthquake and tsunami of 2011, the shows of March and April were canceled, but the cast and crew continued to train in Macao. They returned to reopen the show in April after safety concerns in the theater had been addressed, but due "to the business environment that arose from impacts of the 2011 earthquake," the show was permanently canceled as of December 31, 2011.

The earthquake of March 11, 2011 occurred at 2:50 pm during the *Legend of Mythica* show in Mediterranean Harbor. Before long it was announced that "Due to unforeseen circumstances we must cancel the remainder of the show." Water sloshed about in the harbor but there was no damage to the structures. All of the attractions were stopped and guests inside were hastily evacuated by cast members. An announcement on loudspeaker system said, "Please be assured that the park has been designed with earthquake safety in mind." Aftershocks throughout the afternoon caused people still in the park to stop and crouch or sit down as the ground shook beneath them. As if that was not enough, it started to rain around 4:45, so people moved out of the open areas and under whatever cover they could find as they awaited instructions from cast members. Half an hour later, some people were tired of waiting, a cold wind was blowing in from the ocean, and guests were making their way to the exits. As darkness fell, more people were seeking shelter inside the buildings. Cast members passed out blankets, drinks, and snacks, and people waited until they could be safely evacuated.

The earthquake also resulted in the closing of the MiraCosta until April 28, when the rest of the park reopened. The planned debuts of Fantasmic and Mickey and Friends Greeting Trails were able to go ahead as planned despite limited lighting and power shortages. Other TDS Tenth Anniversary Celebrations were postponed as restoration work continued and three electric power generators were installed.

Mickey & Duffy's Spring Voyage ran from March 18 to June 30, 2013, and told the story of Duffy and Mickey as they traveled around the resort celebrating springtime. The characters hopped aboard a boat from Cape Cod and visited Mediterranean Harbor, American Waterfront, and the Arabian Coast. At each resort stop, Duffy, Mickey, and other springtime characters performed in mini-shows for guests.

Duffy the Disney Bear celebrated his tenth anniversary with Journeys with Duffy. Duffy's best pal Shellie May helped him host Sweet Duffy, which featured fun confections. There was also a new show, Come Join Your Friends, which welcomed Duffy's new friend Gelatoni to the Mediterranean Harbor.

The Duffy phenomenon did not gain the same degree of popularity in America as it did in Japan. In the States, he is generally regarded as a "thinly veiled merchandising ploy" and largely ignored. Duffy was first introduced as Mickey's teddy bear in the early 2000s, but it was not until 2005 that Disney and OLC gave him a backstory and a more prominent position in Tokyo DisneySea. He was refreshed in 2010 and given friends: Shellie May, his girlfriend; Tippy Blue, his mail-bird; and Gelatoni, his artist-cat friend. Whereas he just appeared in the parks in the U.S., he actually has a home in Cape Cod in TDS and is beloved by the Japanese guests, who refer to him as "The Bear of Happiness and Luck."

In June 2015, OLC's publicity department announced that TDS will celebrate its fifteenth anniversary with "The Year of Wishes" from April 15, 2016 to March 17, 2017. OLC said that "During the anniversary, Guests will find that their wishes will shine even brighter . . . During the event, crystals of various colors symbolizing individual wishes will decorate the Park. The crystals will even sparkle on the Disney characters' costumes and merchandise, creating an atmosphere of hope and dreams throughout the Park."

Crystal Wishes Journey was a new show presented at Mediterranean Harbor, where "The Disney characters, each with their own wish, will appear in this show that celebrates the start of the Guests' journeys of adventure, sparkling with hope." There has also been a new version of "Big Band Beat," the popular show presented at the Broadway Music Theatre, since July 2006, with new music, costumes, and scenes. Finally, a new musical that incorporates projection mapping, a technique that projects images that fit building and structural contours, premiered at the Hangar Stage in Lost River Delta in mid-2016. The TDS Hotel MiraCosta also celebrated its fifteenth anniversary in 2016. "Besides the festive decorations around the hotel interior, the hotel will offer special menus at the restaurants and the lounge."

All this was coming about despite the reports from *Japan Times* that by the end of the 2015 fiscal year, Tokyo Disneyland Resort's attendance had dropped by 1.18 million. OLC blamed it on an unusually hot summer and was confident figures would return to normal levels by the next year.

OLC has announced that further in the future, the Stormrider attraction in Port Discovery will be replaced by a Finding Nemo-themed ride in 2017. "The attraction will blend visuals and motion systems together to take you on a submarine ride, that 'shrinks' to the size of a fish, to explore the underwater world from the same point of view as Nemo and Dory." Production staff that worked on the Pixar film, *Finding Dory*, will be involved in creating visuals for the attraction.

At the same time, a new port of call will be built behind Lost River Delta to accommodate a Scandinavia port themed around Disney's hit movie *Frozen* and Nordic cultures. Concept art shows large scale designs for the port town of Arendelle as well as Elsa and Anna's castle. There will also be "development of multiple major attractions, shops, restaurants and other facilities." OLC is reportedly planning to spend ¥500 billion (US$4.13 billion) expanding and adding new areas in both parks before TDL's fortieth anniversary in 2023, with some ready by 2020 and the Tokyo Olympic Games.

"Our story is not finished yet, as Oriental Land Co., Ltd. and Tokyo Disney Resort will continue to keep on growing and expanding," OLC says. "As we move on to take on new challenges for the next 25, 50, and 100 years, we will continue to strive to create even more 'happiness' for our Guests."

PART I I
DISNEYLAND PARIS

Chapter One
Marne-La-Vallée

THE PRIMARY DIFFERENCE BETWEEN building a theme park in Europe and building one in Japan was that the Japanese knew what they wanted and they knew where they wanted it to be. This was not the case in Europe. Before anything could be done, a suitable area had to be found somewhere on the continent. On the surface, it appeared that establishing a park in Europe would not be difficult. Disney films had always done well in Europe, oft times better than in the United States, and Europeans were already very familiar with Disney merchandise and entertainment. The French, for example, were not that far behind the Americans in visiting the cinema and being enthralled with Mickey Mouse in the new sensation of sound cartoons, *Willie, le bateau à vapeur* (*Steamboat Willie*) when it arrived in 1929.

Roy O. Disney established a presence for the company in the late 1920s and early 1930s as the Mickey Mouse craze spread across the United States and into Europe. He hired representatives in a number of countries to establish the company and backed them up with lawyers watching out for copyright infringements. The latter had their hands full. On one memorable occasion when Roy had visited Germany, he had come across a local fair selling hundreds of pirated Mickey Mouse items. He promptly sent the company's London-based lawyer, Bill Levy, to pay the largest German manufacturer a visit. When told he would be sued, the German proclaimed that "There are a thousand others around here doing it." Levy told him that he was aware of that but he was the biggest, and if he would agree to purchase a license for the Mickey Mouse goods, they could take down the others together. The manufacturer agreed, and the ensuing court cases led to some 1,500 defendants agreeing to stop making the knock-offs and apply for a proper license to avoid being sued. The victory was short lived, as the excitement over Mickey Mouse was quashed when Adolf Hitler came to power and proclaimed that German youth must wear the swastika and not an image of Mickey Mouse.

The rest of Europe continued to be enthralled by Disney, as the Mickey Mouse, Donald Duck, and Silly Symphony shorts were followed by *Snow White and the Seven Dwarfs*. The popular fairy tale spread from theater to theater across Europe throughout 1938. Roy had previously arranged for the film to be dubbed in French, Dutch, Czech, Italian, Swedish, Danish, Polish, and even Hindustani and Arabic. The excitement was not to last. A year later, Walt Disney Productions lost 45% of its income when the European market collapsed with the beginning of the Second World War.

The only new appearances of Disney characters in occupied Europe for some time would be on insignia designed by Disney for the Allied military and naval forces and on the occasional nose of an Allied aircraft. For six years, Disney was denied a presence in continental Europe with the exception of neutral Spain, Sweden, Switzerland, and Portugal. *Snow White and the Seven Dwarfs* was first released in Madrid and Barcelona in 1941, and *Pinocchio* had been seen in Portugal the previous year. The story of the little wooden puppet would not be seen in Germany until 1951.

Roy returned to Europe after the war to try to reorganize and put back together the pieces of the company left after the destruction of the Second World War. He hoped to visit the European offices, meet with representatives, and generally restructure operations. He would be there for three months, returning in SS *Liberté* from Le Havre to New York on December 14, 1951. After that Roy and his wife, Edna, would often spend six weeks, once or twice a year, in Europe, touring and visiting Disney representatives and their families.

The postwar depression did little to rebuild Disney's fortunes in Europe. Though *Pinocchio*, *Fantasia*, and *Bambi* were popular, the box office receipts could not leave the country where the films were playing due to government restrictions imposed to protect the local economy. That left Disney with the option of waiting until restrictions were relaxed to access the money or spend the money in the country where it was made in the production of live action films. Walt liked the latter idea, as he later recalled, "When I came to Hollywood I was fed up with cartoons . . . I tried to get into the live-action end of the business." Fortunately for the animation industry, he was unable to do so and returned to cartoons. Now, a new opportunity presented itself of which he was able to take advantage, and in 1949 he sailed to England with his wife and daughters and began production on his version of Robert Lewis Stevenson's *Treasure Island*. Finishing a film in three months, compared to the three years needed for an animated film, appealed to Walt, and he returned to England three years in a row to spend more of the frozen funds.

Meanwhile, in France, Disney's first postwar merchandising offices had been established in Paris. Armand Bigle struggled to run the business out of the apartment he shared with his wife, Betty, and their daughter. They lived in half and used the rest for promoting Disney. Bigle brought back the Mickey Mouse magazine and began distributing it throughout Europe. He ran into some trouble when manufacturers wanted to know how much Disney would pay them to put Disney characters on their merchandise. Bigle told them that it did not work that way, and before long he was able to convince them to pay Disney for the right, as it aided their sales.

As time passed and Disney became a larger presence in Europe, thoughts about a Disneyland park came to the fore. Disney CEO Card Walker had made the suggestion as early as 1976 and discussions continued off and on over the following years. Though the Oriental Land Company of Japan brought forward proposals as early as 1974, Walker was leery of overseas expansion on any terms but his own, and negotiations dragged on for many years. Finally, an agreement was reached and work could begin of Tokyo Disneyland. Thoughts of a park in Europe had been temporarily shelved as the company concentrated on building EPCOT and negotiating for Tokyo Disneyland. Construction plans were approved, and the site dedication and ground breaking ceremony was held by the end of 1980. The construction of Tokyo Disneyland began in earnest in January 1981, and Grand Opening Celebration Ceremony was held undercover in World Bazaar on a drizzly Sunday in April, 1983. By mid-August, the Tokyo park had welcomed over 94,000 guests, breaking Disneyland's single day attendance record that had stood for twenty-eight years. Less than a year after that, on April 2, 1984, the ten millionth guest walked through the gates.

"We knew then that we had to go to Europe," Dick Nunis is quoted as saying.

Heady with the success of Tokyo Disneyland, Disney sent executives out to search for sites in France, Germany, Italy, Portugal, Spain, and the United Kingdom. At one point, over 1,200 sites were under consideration as potential locations for the next Disneyland. The Disney executives had little doubt that Europeans would flock to a Disneyland nearby, for it was already known that some two million Europeans visited the U.S. parks every year. Disney was not so conceited as to believe that the only reason these people crossed the Atlantic was to visit their parks, but they were confident that the magical kingdoms were part of the draw. During the 1980s, Los Angeles and

Orlando ranked as two of the top three American destinations for Europeans. Tourists were spending over a billion dollars on Disney merchandise. One quarter of all Disney salable items such as Donald Duck t-shirts, Mickey Mouse dolls, and Cinderella coloring books went to Europe.

Disney executives joyfully envisioned placing one of their parks in the center of some 370 million people in a smaller geographic area than what held the 250 million Americans. Coupling that with a high standard of living, government-mandated four to five week holidays, and Disney's solid reputation, it quickly became apparent that the venture would have a high chance of success.

During the tumultuous days of 1984, when the Disney company was being besieged by Wall Street mercenaries and corporate raiders, thoughts of a European theme park were the furthest from the minds of Disney executives. Disney president Ron Miller had experience in running parks and making movies but knew little about corporate takeovers. As the sharks began to circle, the Disney directors attempted desperate measures to ward off the attack. They were only partially successful. The company takeover by outsiders was thwarted but Ron Miller was ousted in favor of Michael Eisner and Frank Wells.

With the company seemingly back on secure footing once again, the executives charged with working on the European park approached Eisner and Wells with their proposals. Michael was surprised to learn that there were two groups working on the same project. "Each group approached us as though they were the only ones working on a European park," he later wrote. "Not only was this wasteful, it was odd. We combined the groups immediately."

Eisner and Wells immediately saw the enormous potential of a European park. Not only would it bring in increased revenue as a theme park but it would also serve as a basis for the expansion of merchandise sales, the Disney Channel, and theatrical releases.

The job of paring down the 1,200 possible sites to a more manageable number was left to Dick Nunis, Jim Cora, and Chuck Cobb. They began with deleting the sites in Great Britain and Italy due mainly to the lack of a large enough area of flat land. The largest in Britain was only three hundred acres outside of London and Italy's was disrupted with mountain ranges. Disney had nothing against mountains, in fact they are rather fond of them, but they preferred to make their own. Not long after, Germany was scratched off the list, as it was found that most Germans preferred to take their vacations in other countries.

Large tracts of available land were not the only criteria. Other factors to be taken into consideration were climate, accessibility, the stability of the government, a large labor force, a strong tourist base, and willingness of the locals to negotiate.

Dick Nunis and Jim Cora gave their first presentation to Michael Eisner and Frank Wells in the late fall of 1984. The number of sites had dwindled rapidly over the ensuing months until only locations in France and Spain remained. Of these, the area around Alicante on the Mediterranean coast of Spain appeared the most promising due to its having a climate similar to Florida, where Walt Disney World prospered, a rapidly growing population, and one of the busiest airports in Spain. Another promising Spanish site was further up the coast at Barcelona. This city shares a similar climate with Alicante but is larger and possesses an airport, thriving seaport, and railway hub. In France, the sites had been whittled down to Toulon, also on the Mediterranean coast, and the French capital city of Paris. When the presentation was over, Wells told them to start negotiations with both countries to "see if you can get us a deal."

Further investigation led to the elimination of two more prospects by March 1986, Alicante due to the unpredictable and notorious Mistral winds, and Toulon when it was discovered that a thick layer of bedrock lay just under the soil that would make excavation difficult and extremely costly. That left just Barcelona and Marne-la-Vallée, just east of Paris.

Both countries had advantages. Spain was a frontrunner due to its sunny and mild climate, Barcelona's proximity to transportation hubs, and a government that could be very flexible in negotiations. France on the other hand had the huge advantage of a central location with more than 50 million people within a two hour drive and as many as 310 million only a two hour flight away.

The disadvantages of both countries were also strong factors. Spain did not have a nationwide road network, its trains ran on a different gauge than the rest of Europe, and it was off the beaten path. France was lacking in mild climatic conditions and often had rain and snow. Regardless, Spain's problems were harder to overcome, Paris was a ready-made tourist destination in its own right, and Tokyo Disneyland had already shown that the parks could be weather proofed.

The French negotiators had taken Cora on a tour of the area they had selected for the park. He was not impressed. For reasons unknown, they had taken him on a scenic tour of the countryside, where he later complained, "You couldn't see anything but cornfields around for miles." The next day, he flew over the area in a helicopter and from that vantage he could easily see the potential of the site. Marne-la-Vallée was about 32 kilometers (20 miles) east from downtown Paris and on the A-4, a main highway running from Paris to Strasbourg.

Still, neither country was about to give up bidding for the attraction. They both rolled out the red carpet and offered The Walt Disney Company numerous sweeteners such as free land, tax breaks, expanded transportation networks, and financing deals. Spain's minister of tourism and transport declared, "We want to obtain Disneyland at any price." The park was a once in a lifetime opportunity with the obvious perks of increased employment, particularly while the park was under construction, and the influx of additional tourist dollars to stimulate the economy. At first Nunis and Cora favored the Spanish site, primarily because the Spanish were easier to negotiate with and Spain had weather more conducive to a year round theme park. Eisner, on the other hand, favored France. He was familiar with Paris, having spent many vacations there in his youth. He felt that its central location was key to making it the best choice, and the fact that the city itself was a year-round tourist destination. The fact that he had received a threat of violence from the

Basque separatist movement should the park be built in Spain "did not make me feel especially welcome" but did little to influence his decision.

The less than perfect weather was dismissed as not being an important factor; after all, Tokyo had similar weather and TDL was thriving. Eisner's main concern was the lack of stations in Marne-la-Vallée for the Paris Metro to bring guests from Paris and France's high-speed train service, the *Train à Grande Vitesse* (TGV), to bring in people from the rest of Europe. He told Nunis to make certain that those items were on the negotiating table.

In the end it was Paris that won out. The main reason was the old real estate dictum of "location, location, location." Spain was not centrally located in Europe and it was estimated that while a park in sunny Barcelona would attract over six million guests in the first year, a similar projection for Paris estimated between twelve and sixteen million tourists.

Once the host country had been decided, it now became a matter of how to get the best deal to justify building the resort. Eisner made it clear that he would still walk away from the table if he was not satisfied with what the French government offered. France's Socialist prime minister, Laurent Fabius, was well aware that the ball was in his court, and he could not afford to lose the project to Spain.

Dick Nunis led the Disney negotiating team and by mid-December 1985, the beginnings of a deal were drawn up. Eisner insisted that Disney retain management control as they had in Tokyo, thus ensuring a substantial profit share. The French agreed to sell land around Marne-la-Vallée at its farmland value rather than at the commercial price it would soon command. Disney ended up with 4,481 acres at a fraction of market value, at only $5000 an acre. In addition, they had first right of refusal to another ten thousand acres surrounding the site to prevent "parasitic hotel and leisure developments from springing up and restricting future development." The government also offered a loan of $700 million at below market interest rates, agreed to improvements on the A-4 highway, finance the extension of the Metro, and (by 1994) extend the TGV from Marne-la-Vallée to Geneva, Brussels, and eventually to link with the then under construction Eurotunnel to Britain.

Eisner flew into Paris on December 16. His first stop was a meeting with the producers of the film *Trois Hommes et un Couffin*, which he would rename *Three Men and a Baby*, once he had the rights for Touchstone. Later that night, despite feeling some jetlag, he met with his negotiating team at his hotel to iron out any last details. As there were still a few issues yet to be resolved, Eisner and his team decided that only a letter in intent would be signed when they met with the French the next day.

At a press conference, Eisner outlined the Disney Company's ambitious plans. Not only did they intend to build a Magic Kingdom theme park, to be known as Euro Disneyland (EDL), but also enough hotels to hold five thousand rooms, convention facilities, golf courses, campgrounds, dining facilities, shops, a residential complex, and office facilities. Disney would receive royalties and a management fee. Investors from France and elsewhere in Europe were welcome.

Initially, the prominent French newspapers supported the deal. *Le Matin* featured Mickey dancing across the front page, while *Libération* added mouse ears to its logo for the day. *Time* magazine noted that "no one ever seemed to have anything against Mickey Mouse."

Now the negotiations could begin in earnest. Eisner and his team expected the final deal would be signed within three months, it took more than a year. Numerous government agencies became involved in the process along with their substantial red-tape. Half-way through negotiations, a French federal election was called and Fabius and his Socialist government were voted out.

Fortunately, the new conservative government was sympathetic to the Disney cause. Disney executives had made certain of that. As soon as the election was called, Dick Nunis and his team were scheduling a meeting with the mayor of Paris, Jacques Chirac, the front runner as the next premier of France. The very fact that the project would go a long way towards reducing unemployment in France had Chirac on side. After the election, Chirac was no less enthusiastic than his predecessor and even took further steps to make negotiations easier.

With an estimated expense of over $2 billion at stake, Eisner was determined to get the best deal possible. Frank Wells took on the main role of overlooking negotiations, and Joe Shapiro became chief negotiator and corporate counsel in Paris. Shapiro was new to the Disney Company, having been lured away from the Los Angeles law office of Donovan, Leisure, Newton, and Irvine by Michael Eisner. He was known for his aggressiveness in upholding the Disney copyright and for wearing a Mickey Mouse tie when he appeared in court.

Wells and Shapiro worked tirelessly to get what Disney wanted. The best deal was not always good enough and they would always push for more. Wells would sometimes phone Shapiro in the middle of the night, paying no attention to time zones, demanding that they could not proceed with the project "if you don't do better on this point." Joe would go back to the table and up the ante until Wells was satisfied. Finally, on March 24, 1987, Eisner and Wells flew back to Paris to meet with Prime Minister Jacques Chirac and sign the completed deal.

The next step was to arrange the financing. French law stated that foreign investors could not own a majority interest in a company. Eisner assigned Gary Wilson, newly hired by the Disney Company as Executive Vice-President of Finance, Strategy, and Development, to advance a strategy. Before long, Wilson came up with a plan to sell shares to the public and still maintain control and 49% ownership of Euro Disney. The same terms adopted for TDL regarding royalties and revenue percentages also applied for EDL. The Disney Company would invest $100 million, but the majority of funding would come from private investors and financial institutions.

With the passing of time, however, the initial excitement the French had over the emergence of the new park began to fade. As the government granted ever more concessions, a number of French magazines began running "gloom and doom" stories about the disastrous effects the park would have on France. One likened Mickey to a Godzilla-like monster hovering over Paris, about to destroy everything in his way. Left Bank intellectuals feared the destruction of French culture under an invasion of American imperialism.

Small carnival operators saw their demise, as they felt they would be unable to compete with Disney. They also feared the environmental impact as people flooded into the district with their exhaust-spewing cars, litter, and related contaminates.

Farmers, villagers, and woodcutters feared losing their land and livelihoods, particularly those residing in Marne-la-Vallée and the surrounding villages. Many families had lived on the land for generations and felt a profound loss, not only because the land was to become an American amusement park but because they felt betrayed by their own government for selling them out. In addition to the village of Marne-la-Vallée, there was also Bailly-Romainvillirs, Chessy, Coupvray, Magny-le-Hongre, and Serris containing the homes and businesses of over five thousand people.

The residents had not been consulted by the government or even kept informed as negotiations progressed. When the deal was made, they expected, even "demanded total and immediate cooperation with efforts to accommodate Disney." The villagers were informed that their land would be purchased, or if necessary, seized "under the law of eminent domain." Naturally, such heavy-handedness invoked hostility towards the government and by extension, the Disney Company.

The locals were determined to fight back, knowing it would not be an easy battle. To protect their interests, they formed *L'Association des Opposants au Project Eurodisneyland* (Association of People Opposing the Euro Disneyland Project) in May 1986. Its ranks quickly swelled to over one thousand members. The question of expropriation was foremost in their minds. They could understand if the land was to be used for military purposes or a power station or even a railway right of way, but a commercial theme park was outrageous. The Association also wanted assurances that those who became unemployed because of the deal would be retrained, that taxes would not be raised to build roads or extend the rail lines.

In addition, the towns closest to the site formed the *Syndicat d'Agglomeration Nouvelle des Portes de la Brie (SAN)* to protect themselves "against the impending flood of tourists and other delinquents." The head of

SAN, Charles Boetto, went on to stress that they did not want to be "the city of Disney parks" but rather "a city that welcomes Disney parks." The main concern of one of the local mayors was that the towns would become known as Mickeyville and "he would refuse to serve as the elected official" of any such town. Other mayors tried to be more optimistic about the future, as they knew full well that it would be impossible to block the progress of the park. The mayor of Bailly-Romainvilliers, Michel Colombe, stated that "We prefer to get maximum benefit from an operation that, in any case, will be imposed." Jean-Claude Thoenig, an expert of local politics, mused that development of the area was just a matter of time and that even if the park failed, it would still provide an infrastructure that would be beneficial to the locals.

The villages could, all going well, expect large financial benefits from the park. The weekly publication, *Quotidien de Maire*, stated that each was in line for 83 million francs ($16.5 million) in property taxes in the first five years of operation. In addition, another 170 million francs ($34 million) could be expected from a business tax based on eleven million visitors a year. How that would work out, time would tell, as there was no guarantee the number would be met.

The new French government appointed former ambassador to Mexico, Jean-Rene Bernard, to act as chief negotiator to facilitate smoother talks. He first met with the Disney team at the seventeenth century Chateau de Vaux-le-Vicomte in Maincy, southeast of Paris. The parties agreed that the earlier letter of intent was meaningless and that a new, more specific proposal was required to go forward.

Over the next few months negotiations swung back and forth, sometimes tottering on the brink of disaster, but on July 11, 1986, only four months after the election, a deal was struck and approved by the government with a 112 to 20 vote in favor. The Communist Party members were the only opposition, on the grounds that the money could be better spent elsewhere.

With a deal in place, serious work could now begin on designing and selling the park. Eisner appointed Robert Fitzpatrick as president of Euro Disney in March 1987. He was a natural choice, as he spoke fluent French, was married to a French woman, and had a degree in medieval French literature. In addition, he had served as president of the Disney founded California Institute of the Arts, a city councilman for Baltimore, director of the 1984 Olympic Arts Festival, and dean of students at Johns Hopkins University.

Two weeks later, on March 24, Eisner and Chirac met at Hôtel Matignon, where the final $7.5 billion contract was signed. Also invited were numerous right-wing pro-businessmen from the area to display regional support.

The primary concern of the Disney Company was not to make the same mistakes they had made with Tokyo Disneyland. They wanted more than a small percentage of admission fees, licensing fees, and merchandise sales. With that in mind, two French owner companies were formed, Euro Disney SNC, to oversee the park for the first twenty years, and Euro Disney SCA to take over after that. The French officials were not pleased with that and countered by limiting Disney's shares to less than half, or 49% of the total. The Walt Disney Company complied, as their profits were not restricted to that but also included admissions, souvenirs, and food in the same percentage as with TDL. In addition, though they only owned a little less than half of the company, they had 100% control of operation and development. It was a sweet deal for Disney. The French government provided a $960 million loan with another $1.6 billion in floating rate loans from assorted banks, and some $400 million came "from special partnerships formed to buy properties and lease them back." The $400 million cost of supplying the park with water, electricity, and other services was also borne by the French government. Disney in turn only had to put up $250 million for its 49% share of the equity and operation of the park.

The French government saw the huge benefits the park would bring in reducing unemployment. *The New York Times* estimated that the park would create thirty thousand jobs for construction, another thirty thousand in off-site services, and twelve thousand jobs within the park itself. Compared to the 150,000 jobs created by TDL, these figures were considered to be low. In addition, tourist revenues were expected to rise by at least 10%. The first European cast members were hired in June 1987.

Over the time it took to garner a deal between the government and WDC, opposition to the park began to make itself heard. Sidney Sheinberg, President of MCA, referred to Mickey as a "Ravenous Rat" but at the same time unveiled his plans for a Universal Studios theme park in Europe. The disgruntled locals could do little more than put up protest signs and write anti-Disney graffiti on public buildings. In *Mickey-sur-Marne: Une Culture Conquerante*, Martha Zuber wrote about posters with Mickey in a Michael Jackson crotch grabbing pose; a sad Mickey reading a "Stay Home, Mickey" sign; and Uncle Scrooge (called Picsou in France) proclaiming, "I don't give a damn for the locals. I buy land, I buy villages. I buy the residents, I buy everything." The latter resulted in some people referring to EDL as Euro Picsouland.

The intellectual "elite" denounced the park as "a black stain on the soul of France" and referred to it as "the fifty-first state." A *New York Times* article quoted writer Alain Finkielkraut as describing EDL as "a terrifying giant's step toward world homogenization" as he feared the crushing of the imaginations of France's youth. There were more of the same from disgruntled writers of various ilk and political leanings, but the one that most captured the imagination and was the subject of repeated quotes was theater director, Ariane Mnouchkine, who coined the term "cultural Chernobyl."

Mnouchkine's quote was all the more damaging, as she was a friend of EDL president Robert Fitzpatrick and had not long before returned from an enjoyable visit to Disneyland in California where she had posed with Mickey Mouse. It seems as if she felt guilty about having enjoyed "having had fun at a place designed by American capitalists."

Despite the rhetoric, public opinion polls came out with a much louder voice. It was proclaimed that over 86 percent of people in France favored the park, something Disney executives suspected all along but were relieved to have confirmed. In a press release, Fitzpatrick was quoted as stating, "In France, more than the United States, there's a small group, an arts mafia, who sees everything popular, anything American as endangering French culture." Another wrote that French culture must be "disturbingly fragile" if it could be crushed by a Mouse.

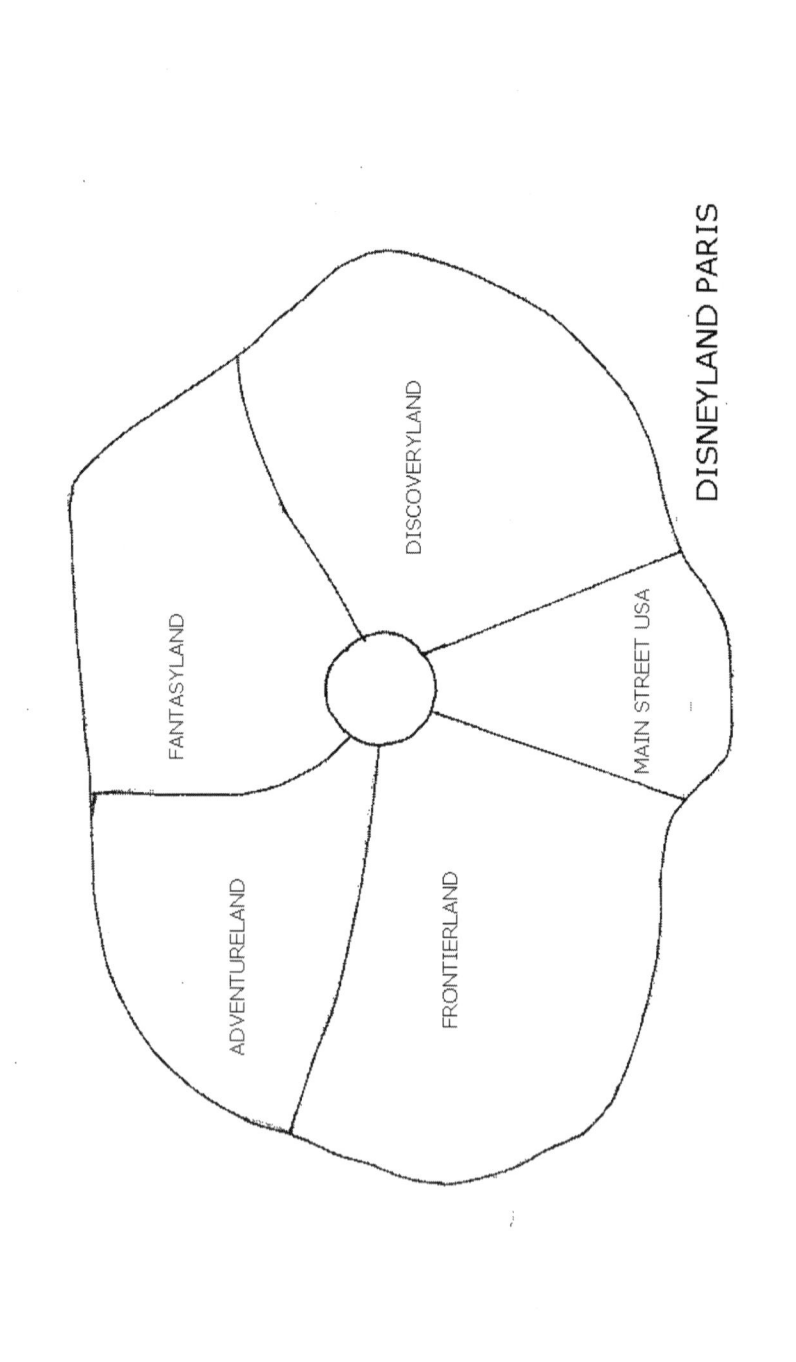

DISNEYLAND PARIS

- FANTASYLAND
- DISCOVERYLAND
- MAIN STREET USA
- FRONTIERLAND
- ADVENTURELAND

Chapter Two
Euro Disneyland

THE FRENCH GOVERNMENT DID NOT WANT a carbon copy reproduction of Disneyland, California. EDL was to be "strikingly original" and have "its own continental flavor and identity." They did not want to provide ammunition for cultural critics to snipe at the new park due to excessive Americanism. France's chief negotiator, Jean-René Bernard, insisted that Disney respect "European and French culture."

Tony Baxter, best known for his design of Splash Mountain in Disneyland, was the Imagineering Executive in charge of design. Michael Eisner described him as "a grown-up with a kid's unfettered enthusiasm." Baxter had been with Disney since 1965, when he was hired to work in Disneyland as an ice cream scooper and popcorn seller. His creative imagination was soon noticed by WED Enterprises (later Walt Disney Imagineering), and his first major project with them was on Big Thunder Mountain Railroad. When it came time to design Euro Disneyland, he had already worked on redesigning Disneyland's Fantasyland in 1983, Star Tours in 1987, and Splash Mountain, scheduled to open in 1989.

Some of the Disney executives thought that it would be a simple matter to transport the successful ideas used in Tokyo to Paris, but Baxter disagreed. He believed EDL needed to be unique, as he noted that they would be "competing with the great art and architecture of Europe."

Fortunately, Michael Eisner agreed with him, but unfortunately, he felt that as the Japanese wanted an American version of the park, so in time would the Europeans, despite their comments to the contrary. Eisner wrote that this meant "fast food instead of smoky bistros, Coca-Cola and lemonade in preference to wine, animated movies rather than film noir." He had no intention of removing all Americanisms from EDL. Main Street, USA would remain in name as well as content and so would the ever-popular Frontierland with its American Wild West theme. (Similar to TDL, the area was to be known as Westernland until changed to Frontierland in early 1989.) He felt that to not do so would be tantamount to removing the "Disney" from Euro Disney. What was required was a balance between old and new world cultures. Baxter did not want to overdo the America theme, nor did they want to Europeanize the park "with the redundancy of bringing Europe to Europe."

Over the ensuing months, the creative groups met repeatedly to discuss every aspect of the park, "from architecture to ashtrays." Here was an opportunity to improve on what had been done before as well as expand into new ideas. Not a single detail went unnoticed. Attractions, entertainment, stores, and restaurants would all be under intense scrutiny and demanding of new and original ideas. There was an entirely new generation of Imagineers working on designing the park specifically for Europeans. As in Japan, local talent was recruited as well as personnel from almost every branch of the Walt Disney Company.

Euro Disneyland would be built in the same design as the earlier parks, consisting of four lands around a central plaza. Main Street, USA would have a decidedly American/Victorian theme to seem more like a foreign town to European visitors. Frontierland would be themed to the gold rush days of the American Southwest and contain Phantom Manor and Big Thunder Mountain. In Adventureland, guests would visit the realms of the Arabian Nights, with onion-domed buildings and "mysterious nooks and charming shops." Adventure Isle would feature Disney's pirate films, *Treasure Island* (1950) and *Swiss Family Robinson* (1960), adjacent to the Pirates of the Caribbean attraction. The castle in Fantasyland was inspired by the artist who influenced the artwork in *Sleeping Beauty* and the characters would be familiar to Europeans, as most of the fairy tales originated in Europe. Even It's a Small World would have a European difference, as guests would also "travel" to the United States, which does not happen in the Disneyland version. The most distinctive land was Discoveryland, which would replace the Tomorrowland of other parks. Here the concept had been changed to one of "paying homage to the great futurists and visionaries of the past" such as H.G. Wells, Jules Verne, and Leonardo da Vinci. Science fantasy was to be acknowledged with George Lucas' Star Tours and Michael Jackson in *Captain EO*.

One of the earliest problems under scrutiny was the Main Street, USA portion. Baxter wanted to do something "more uniquely American," so his design team put forward plans for a 1920s-style street from Chicago or New York, complete with jazz clubs, Keystone Kops, and the occasional speakeasy. When the idea was presented to Eisner, he thought it was too violent and glorified gangsters, not the sort of thing Disney wanted to promote. The designers went back to the drawing board and instead presented a modification of a Victorian theme which Eisner approved.

Baxter had noticed that the French "demanded more depth and sophistication," so he encouraged his designers to put more detail into everything they did. The materials they wanted to use for Main Street would extend to actual wooden and brick fronts and real gas in the lamps, rather than fiberglass and flickering electric bulbs.

Imagineer Marty Sklar told the story of how Frank Wells had been on a tour of Main Street as it was being built and when he walked into one of the arcades noticed that there was a decided lack of detail. Wells immediately pulled Eddie Sotto, the principal designer of Main Street, aside, and comparing the arcade to the "Black Hole of Calcutta," made it known that he expected much better. After Sotto had explained what he had in mind, he could see that Wells was not convinced, but he "was willing to fund any gilding those lilies would require." Taking him at his word and reminding him later of the conversation, Sotto set about making the arcades "as elegant as the rest of the street." Wells went even further and had eight architects flown in to work on adding millions of dollars worth of moldings and ornamentation to the areas. In Sotto's mind, it was the right thing to do, investing early on saved making major enhancements later.

Unlike TDL where a covering was installed over the entire Main Street area, in EDL it was decided to install some thirty-five fireplaces throughout the resort for warmth and covered arcades running the length of the street to keep guests dry. While touring Europe for inspiration and research, Tony Baxter had noticed that "most places have an extended entrance before guests are asked for an admission fee." As a result, Center Court was incorporated into the design, which in turn led to what was originally called the Magic Kingdom Hotel. The ticket booths were sheltered inside the hotel and a moving sidewalk, covered by a colorful canopy, carried dry guests to the park from the parking area.

Another of the major problems the designers faced was designing a showcase castle for a country where castles abounded. Baxter insisted they needed "something that can stand on its own" and not a recreation of part of a German castle, as was done in Disneyland, or a French chateau that inspired Cinderella Castle in WDW and TDL. The answer was to base the castle on what had already been done in films such as *Snow White and the*

Seven Dwarfs and *Sleeping Beauty* with a little bit of inspiration from Mont Saint Michel. To make it even more special, this castle would have a dungeon with a fire-breathing dragon in residence. Imagineer John Hench, an artist with an extraordinary sense of color who had worked with Walt Disney, was called upon to pick just the right shade of pink for the castle. Before he was satisfied, the model they had built to represent the castle had been repainted three times. In the end, the EDL castle ended up costing millions of dollars more than the one in TDL.

In the summer of 1988, Michael Eisner and his wife, Jane, rented an apartment in Paris. They planned to stay for a month each year as the park was being built. Frank Wells was also a frequent visitor to the site, and the two men took the opportunity to not only oversee progress of the park but also to expand other business interests in Europe, devise their television strategy, and "solve our preconstruction Euro Disneyland over budget items."

Eisner took French classes each morning and on weekends set about recruiting new executives for the park. He began traveling around Europe with Jane, scoping out the competition, visiting theme parks to get a feel for what worked in Europe and what did not. Tivoli Gardens in Copenhagen, Denmark, also praised by Walt Disney when he visited it, was high on Eisner's list of favorites. What impressed him most about the successful ones was the landscaping and the attention to detail. Most of the others were of little consequence as far as competition was concerned, as few of them managed more than 2 million visitors a year and they were usually day trips from locals. This helped convince Eisner that EDL would have to have some place for visitors to stay for more than one day. EDL should be a vacation destination.

Another problem had arisen that required Eisner's attention. Bob Fitzpatrick, formerly of CalArts in California, had been hired to run the show at Euro Disney. Under him was Jim Cora, an expert on everything to do with the parks, but also "blunt, no-nonsense, and so defiantly American that he refused to learn more than a few words of French during his seven years in Paris," Eisner wrote. The pair could not be more different; though their skills were decidedly complementary, they did not like each other, causing no little friction for which Eisner had to run interference.

Even before construction began the park was running over budget by $300 million, a situation Eisner described as "unacceptable, and we are chopping, re-drawing and getting our act together." As Disney employees and construction workers moved into the area to start work on the project in August 1988, the population more than tripled and the villages lost a considerable amount of land. Ground breaking of the five thousand acres began amongst the fields of sugar beets and hay and had been scheduled to ramp up for the fall, but an unusually wet late summer and fall had caused much of the work to be postponed until the spring of 1989. Eisner preferred the new date, as warmer, drier weather would be more conducive to producing a TV special that he had in mind for his new Sunday night TV show. The show was never made, as NBC canceled *The Magical World of Disney* in May 1990 due to poor ratings.

The recruiting of corporate sponsors, who according to *Disney News*, "wish to showcase their image and expertise with the magical Disney touch," began in earnest. The first major addition came in September when the French car maker, Renault, announced their sponsorship with a showcase window on the Champs-Elysees featuring Mickey Mouse. Renault was scheduled to present a 360-degree film in French titled *Le Visionarium* in Discoveryland.

In December, *Banque Nationale de Paris* signed on to sponsor Orbitron, another Discoveryland attraction, while Europcar would present the Main Street vehicles. Kodak would come on board in April to present *Cine Magique* featuring *Captain EO* in Discoveryland.

With the coming of spring in 1989, work intensified on the site. The berms were completed and festooned with an estimated 52,000 trees and shrubs of various shapes, sizes, and types. Work began on dredging out waterways and digging underground facilities for the larger attractions. By May, the number of newly-hired cast members reached two hundred, of whom 186 were European. As was the case with the TDL new hires, they were sent to America to learn their skills on the job and to be immersed in the

"Disney Way" at Disney University. The first expressway interchange opened in July, and work began on grading the east entrance highway.

As revenues and attendance at Disneyland and Walt Disney World continued to grow, Team Disney became more enthusiastic about the prospects of the Paris Park. To boost interest amongst potential investors, Disney invited "several hundred European bankers and stockbrokers to Orlando to experience Walt Disney World for themselves." They arrived in the summer of 1989, not long after the opening of the latest theme park in Florida, Disney-MGM Studios. Impressed by the crowd sizes and the quality of the attractions, they "returned to Europe singing our praises." The reaction made Eisner all the more determined that they must "not undersell the Disney brand as the company has done in the past."

Despite the controversies, the official launch of Disney stock went ahead. WDC controlled 49% of Euro Disney SCA and planned to sell the other 51% to investors. As the French government required that the stocks would be first offered to the European community to prevent American investors from promptly taking control, WDC announced on September 12, 1989 that they would make some 86 million shares available to European markets. These were to be distributed around the continent by first offering half on the Paris Bourse, the rest through London and Brussels at $11.30 per share. In conjunction with the announcement, WDC launched a massive ad campaign consisting of a European road show tour through ten nations and advertisements in all the major newspapers and television networks, resplendent with Mickey Mouse and his entourage in all their magical glory. Details of the forthcoming attractions included the iconic Disney castles, Pirates of the Caribbean, and a myriad of fairy tale characters from Snow White and her dwarfs to the latest Disney release, *The Little Mermaid*.

In London, Disney characters put in an appearance at the Broadgate complex as the $1.2 billion in shares were launched on October 5. It had more the appearance of a celebration than a stock exchange. The situation at the Paris Bourse began in a similar fashion but soon became something quite different. As Michael Eisner stood on the stage and looked down at the Disney characters in the crowd, he noticed that there were more Mickeys than should have been in one place. Ten youthful members of the Communist Party had donned cheap Mickey Mouse masks and were jeering their protests and waving signs stating "Mickey Go Home" amongst other things. Before long they were hurtling things somewhat heavier than taunts, as flour, eggs, and tomato sauce pelted the people on the stage. In his book *Work in Progress*, Eisner described the event after he arrived in a car, driven by Mickey Mouse, with other members of the Disney team:

"Confident and in a great mood, I emerged from the car smiling. Then I walked up to make a short speech from the steps of the exchange, still confident, still smiling. Suddenly objects started flying through the air towards me. When I looked out at the crowd, I suddenly realized that we were in the midst of a demonstration, apparently by critics of the deal the government had made with us for the park. Gary Wilson had an egg thrown at him, I rushed through my talk, and we all ran off the stage, no longer smiling or confident." He later added that he now "had a sense of what it was like to be a politician during a campaign."

What bothered Eisner the most about the affair was not the abuse but the fact that the media focused on that small portion of the incident. As it spread around the world, news reporters reminded their audiences of the minority opposition to the park rather than the majority support. In addition, they initially excluded what he considered the more important story, that by the end of the day the price of the stock had jumped from $11.30 to $16 a share. Within days the nearly 86 million shares would be sold out, some reaching $30 each. That, more than any poll, indicated the European willingness and enthusiasm to accept the Disney Park. Disney executives acknowledged that all publicity was good publicity, those against the deal were too late to protest, the deal was made and could not be undone. As one professor from Collège de France remarked, "The more one shouts now, the more one raises the decibels of publicity for Disney, the more one serves it."

The enthusiastic response to the Disney stocks began to make the Disney executives wonder if perhaps they had not thought big enough.

Robert Fitzpatrick was not trying to be funny when he said, "My biggest fear is that we will be too successful." Accordingly, they raised the amount of their investments, made plans to increase the number of attractions initially planned, and moved the opening day of the proposed second park (a version of Florida's Disney-MGM Studio) up to 1994.

The biggest regret Walt Disney had about Disneyland was the fact that he did not have enough money to buy up the land surrounding the park and thereby build his own hotels to accommodate his guests. He made certain that would not be a problem when he starting buying land in Florida for his proposed Disney World theme park, and after his passing, his successors made plenty of land around the overseas parks a priority. Michael Eisner had brought Gary Wilson on board in 1985 as Executive Vice-President of Finance, Strategy, and Development. He described him as "a very astute thinker, with a rare capacity to analyze the value of any potential deal." Wilson was a strong voice in deciding on how many hotels would be on the resort property, advocating "a large enough number . . . that other operators would be discouraged from competing with us." They decided that they needed at least five hotels with a total of 5,200 rooms when the park opened. As Disney planned to expand the resort to include another park modeled after Disney-MGM Studio in Orlando as well as other amenities, Wilson felt they should build the hotels now rather than later, as by then "it would be much more expensive and disruptive."

Eisner agreed and the situation seemed to be well in hand until he and Bob Stern, who was designing projects for WDW, went to see Wing Chao, Disney's in-house architect. Stern looked at Chao's plans for Euro Disney hotels with obvious dismay. "It looks like an American subdivision in the French countryside," he complained. Chao agreed but pointed out that it was still in the early design stages. Stern countered that it would be too difficult to make changes once the plan was presented to the French government; the changes had to be made before then.

Coincidentally, a number of famous architects were planning a dinner and get together at a Venice Beach restaurant, hosted by *Architectural Digest* editor Elizabeth McMillan. Bob Stern had been invited, and Chao suggested he put it to them to gather that night and discuss the plans for EDL. The architects agreed and McMillan graciously gave up her dinner plans.

For five hours, the architects huddled together at one of the Imagineering warehouses in Glendale to critique the plans and munch on Chinese food. After much discussion, they decided to meet again in Stern's office in New York two weeks later. By the time Eisner and Wells arrived the next day, they had redesigned the entire site plan. The next step was to design the hotels themselves, and for this, Eisner suggested a competition. The world's best and brightest architects were challenged to come up with designs in three weeks. The competition received tremendous support, and despite the fact that Eisner already had a basic idea of what he wanted, he received and reviewed numerous proposals. Many of the ideas were "very stark, modernist . . . mostly abstract, cool, stylized," while Eisner was looking for "romance, whimsy and drama."

The first hotel design commission was awarded to Bob Stern for his Cheyenne Hotel based on an Old West gold rush town to be complete with a dance hall and log fort. The second went to Michael Graves' concept of a Manhattan skyline to be named Hotel New York and feature a seasonal ice skating rink. The third was an adobe pueblo village designed by Antione Predock, leaning heavily for inspiration on the monuments of the American Southwest, to be called Hotel Santa Fe.

The last two designs were more of a problem, as Eisner wanted at least one of them to be the product of a European, preferably French, architect. In time the choice was Antione Grumbach, who designed the Sequoia Lodge, "set in a wooded riverside haven . . . reminiscent of the American National Parks." Lastly, the Magic Kingdom Hotel, soon renamed the Disneyland Hotel, was the idea of Tony Baxter and Eddie Sotto, who suggested a Victorian design hotel as a grand façade to the park. Frank Wells feared that people hanging their bathing suits and underwear out the window would ruin the view, and Baxter and Bob Venturi almost came to blows arguing over whether or not the hotel would block the guests' view of Sleeping Beauty Castle. In the end, Baxter won out when he submitted a model and computer graphics to support his argument.

Two more lodging areas were later added to the plans to round out the hotel space. Newport Bay Club, designed by Bob Stern, had a nautical theme "in the grand tradition of New England coastal resorts." Lastly, Camp Davy Crockett, a campground in a quiet, wooded area, with "fully equipped cabins," was approved and was the first completed in order to house early employees working on the site. Additionally, the hotel district was to have its own entertainment center for guests to visit after the park closed for the night. Festival Disney was to be designed by Frank Gehry and would include thousands of glittering lights, themed boutiques with souvenir memorabilia, bars, and a myriad of dining options including a New York diner, American steakhouse, and California bar and grill. Entertainment would be available nightly in the form of Buffalo Bill's Wild West Show.

It was not long before problems started arising on the construction site. Mickey Steinberg, who had been with Disney only since 1988 and was now Executive Vice-President of Imagineering under Marty Sklar, was asked to look into how things were progressing. He reported back to Frank Wells with the terse words "You are headed for one of the biggest failures I've ever seen in construction. Unless something changes, you're never going to get finished on time." As Steinberg had worked overseeing the construction of hotels for over twenty-seven years, Wells listened to what he had to say.

Steinberg explained that the problem lay in the fact that Disney had hired construction managers to oversee the site when they should have hired project managers. The latter oversaw the entire project and could make trade-offs and compromises where necessary, something that was not and could not be done by construction managers. Steinberg's analysis of the problem concluded that an addition $150 million was required to finish the project. In addition, he recommended that the project managers come from within the ranks of Disney's Imagineers in Glendale, as they were "the only ones who had the expertise we need to get this park built." Eisner and Wells agreed, and Steinberg proceeded to do whatever was required to have the project finished on budget and on time.

By the spring of 1990, three more sponsors had come on board. Nestlé would have location outlets throughout the park, Coca-Cola agreed to sponsor Café Hyperion in Discoveryland and Casey's Corner on Main Street, and Phillips would present Videopolis in Discoveryland. The first façades of the Disneyland Hotel were up by April, and it was on track to be completed up to the fourth floor by August. The number of cast members hired had swollen to 770, of whom 610 were Europeans speaking at least two languages. In July, Disney welcomed its one thousandth cast member. One hundred twenty thousand trees and shrubs had been planted in the campground and three hundred thousand cubic meters of topsoil had been stocked to be used for horticultural purposes.

On September 1, 1990, the casting center was officially opened and recruiting of the remaining thousands of cast members required to maintain the park began in earnest. Some saw this as a potential problem. Guy Sorman, a French economist and author, thought there would be a shortage of service-oriented labor: "Recruiting in France will be extremely difficult. Maybe they'll have to look to the Spanish and Italians, who are more service-oriented than the French."

Euro Disney Human Resources Vice-President, Thor Degelmann, seemed to agree with that assessment but thought the problem lay not with France in general but Paris in particular, and focused recruitment efforts outside the capital. "If we had tried to staff Disney World with New Yorkers, we wouldn't have had the success we've had there, either," he mused.

France Telecom was brought in to install some ten thousand telephone lines throughout the resort, and they also signed up to sponsor It's a Small World in Fantasyland. By the time the Disneyland Hotel was topped in October, the installation of Videopolis, Pirates of the Caribbean, and Big Thunder Mountain had also been initiated. Marty Sklar wrote about the problems involved with the latter concerning the variety of contractors involved. There was "an Italian contractor (steel), a Dutch contractor (ride system), a French contractor (rockwork) and an Irish contractor (electrical)."

Espace Euro Disney, the onsite information center, opened on December 6 on the outskirts of the village of Serris, south of the park site. It was far enough from the site that it would not interfere with construction traffic. Designed by Bob Stern, the preview center had interiors themed to the Sorcerer's Apprentice sequence of Fantasia and was topped by a huge cone-shaped wizard's hat with assorted Disney characters and strip lights on the exterior walls. Stern commented that "when the building was new it literally stopped traffic." The building was designed to advertise the park and give potential visitors a chance to see what the park was really all about. A small prefabricated ticket booth had been installed to collect the 10 franc (US$1.50) adult admission fee. Inside the exhibition hall were myriad concept sketches, costumes, props, and scale models of the attractions. The structure also contained a movie theater, retail store, and just outside in a nearby building, a snack bar with half a dozen tables.

Once visitors had inspected all of the exhibits, which they could do with or without the cast member's spiel, they were directed into a huge theater for a presentation of the film *Euro Disney: Quand l'Imaginaire Devient Réalité* (Euro Disney: When the Dream Becomes Reality).

After the film, guests were guided into the gift shop, which had the same ambience and decor of the Disney Stores of the day and similar merchandise for sale. Tickets and Euro Disney Resort vacation packages were also available despite opening being almost two years in the future. Admission to the park at the time was 200 francs (US$40).

In addition to providing visitors with a look at what was to come, Espace was also designed as a training center where cast members could practice their newly-learned skills in management, admissions, operations, guests services, restaurant, custodial and retail. The center was always over-staffed, as it was required to send as many new hires through the facility as possible, and by the end of 1990 there were 1,300 cast members on the payroll. Disney wanted to show that in the country not known for quality customer service, they were different. It seemed to work, for from the time Espace opened until opening day of the park, some eight hundred thousand visitors wandered through. At the end of the year a celebration was held, attended by Mickey Mouse and Roy E. Disney along with the recently appointed EDL ambassador, Sabine Marcon.

By the summer of 1991 progress was very apparent. The creation of berms, rivers, lakes, and underground facilities had necessitated the moving of over 4 million cubic meters of dirt. According to *Disney News*, "Landscape architects are selecting stock from local or imported species such as birches, pine trees, weeping willows, nut trees, holm oaks, wold cherry trees, bay trees, rhododendrons, maple trees, bamboo trees, redwoods and palm trees." Big Thunder Mountain was rising out of the ground, and more than a third of its tracks had been installed. Videopolis' Hyperion airship, from the 1974 Disney film, *The Island at the Top of the World*, was ready to be put in place on the steel vault constructed for it. Pirates of the Caribbean and Phantom Manor were well underway, and Sleeping Beauty Castle's ground floor was almost complete. Vehicles for the Peter Pan, Snow White, and Pinocchio attractions had been completed, as well as the flight simulators for Star Tours.

Over in the hotel district, most of Hotel Cheyenne's fourteen buildings were nearing completion, and Hotel Santa Fe had half of its rooms finished. Of the 5,200 rooms projected for the site, 3,800 could be recognized. The employee parking lot, designed to accommodate three hundred cars, was already in use. A close look at the site of the golf course would reveal where the lakes, tees, and bunkers would be laid out. A five-kilometer trench had been dug for the new TGV line and some thirty-two kilometers of roads, interchanges, and bridges had been completed.

Meanwhile, across the channel in the United Kingdom, Europe's first Disney Store opened in London on Regent Street on November 3. Given the success that the Disney stores had in the U.S., growing from one store to seventy within three years, it seemed a natural progression and also a fantastic way to increase awareness of the upcoming Euro Disney Resort. The excited crowds that arrived for opening day seemed to confirm their optimism.

The word continued to spread as Euro Disney articles appeared in magazines and newspapers, whether pro or anti-park, the publicity continued to generate interest. Disney characters started appearing in various public places. Mail order catalogues were stuffed with glossy pages of Disney merchandise touting the familiar characters and the new park. The *En Route pour la Magie* tour hauled a huge façade of Sleeping Beauty Castle around Europe. Disney videos had promotional clips for the park before the screenings of such hits as *The Little Mermaid* and *The Rescuers Down Under*. TV spots aimed at promoting EDL were broadcast on some of Europe's largest commercial stations. The Disney Channel increased in popularity and weekly TV shows began airing on other channels, packed with ads for the upcoming park. The TV show *Disney Club* even did a behind-the-scenes show from the still incomplete resort when it was shown in surveys that the Disney park shows were proving to be the most popular. Though on the surface these programs appeared to be half-hour commercials, European networks were clamoring to pay top dollar to broadcast the popular shows.

In the final year before opening, recruiting was ramped up. Two thousand cast members had been signed up by mid-June, mostly to fill management, administration, and clerical positions. A projected total of twelve thousand employees in both on-stage and off-stage positions was expected by opening day in April 1992. Thor Degelmann, Euro Disney Vice-President of Human Resources, acknowledged that the type of people needed must be "capable of grasping the 'Disney way' and imparting the knowledge to others." The first three hundred cast members were sent to WDW for training in programs ranging from two weeks to five months "participating in every aspect of Theme Park and Resort operation." The trainees would start at the bottom as attraction operator then slowly progress to Lead, Supervisor, and by the end, work alongside their counterpart doing the job they would be doing in EDL. Once back in France, they became involved in the installation of their attraction, the writing of manuals, and the development of their own training programs.

People were recruited from all over Europe and from amongst European expatriates living in the States. Sixty interviewers spoke to as many as 750 prospective cast members every day, six days a week. Of these only about 10 percent would be offered employment. With the economic downturn that had recently hit France, Disney could afford to be picky. They also paid 15% above minimum wage at $6.50 an hour and had no problem attracting prospective workers. Still, in an effort to recruit only the best, Disney did not wait for prospects to come to them but launched an extensive ad campaign in newspapers and magazines all over Europe and North America and sent scouts to all the major European Economic Community cities throughout Europe looking for that international flavor. Competition for the much sought after positions became so fierce that one cast member stated it was easier to get a job at the French pavilion at WDW's World Showcase than at EDL. In the end, cast members had been recruited from thirty-five different nations, many of whom had never been to a Disney theme park. Mickey Steinberg wanted it known that the park was built mainly by Europeans: "At one time we had 8,000 people working here, of those, maybe 150 were Americans."

Not all cast members were sent to the States for training. On September 2, 1991, a Euro Disney version of Disney University opened in France with the intention of training some ten thousand cast members. The final four thousand would be going through orientation only a month before opening with four classes a day, seven days a week. Without an actual park to work in, much of the training had to be done with audio-visual aids. A series of manuals was distributed to applicants with such titles as *La Courtoisis Selon Disney* (*Courtesy Disney Style*) and *Le Guide du Cast Member* (*Cast Member Guide*) to provide "unmatchable levels of guest service."

One such manual, *The Euro Disney Look*, caused some controversy with the personal appearance guidelines it set out. Degelmann insisted that Disney required "a conservative, professional look" with "no extremes in dying hair or in makeup" for women and "no facial hair ... no earrings, no exposed tattoos and no jeans" for men. The French labor union, the *Confédération Français Démocratique du Travail*, called the rules repressive and insisted they "infringed upon individual freedom" despite the fact that many French companies also had similar dress codes. Naturally, the international press zealously reported on the "scandal," as their intrigued readers followed the story of "Disney's clean-cut wholesomeness sparking a storm in France." The tempest in a tea cup raged on regardless of the fact that none of the people to whom the jobs were offered refused because of the dress code.

More scandalous fodder for the press came around the same time, when a group of subcontractors working on the site demanded more money due to Disney having altered the projects they were involved in thereby costing them more time and labor. The sum of 850 million francs ($157 million) was demanded in addition to the sum originally agreed upon. Fitzpatrick declined to pay. The press began featuring Disney as the unscrupulous big American corporation lording it over the poor small French workers. In addition, the subcontractors threatened to disrupt the opening ceremonies. Eventually, Euro Disney agreed to pay 60% of the debt and the workers were placated.

The Italian contractor who was working on Fantasyland thought he would like a bigger piece of the pie as well and went to Steinberg to inform him that the job could not possibly be finished on time unless he and his crew were paid a bonus over what had been agreed upon. Steinberg had been told ahead of time what the man was planning, and after consulting the company lawyers, waited until the threat was made and fired them on the spot. He then replaced them with an Irish contractor who, according to Sklar, "turned out to be the best construction worker on the project."

To make certain everything was ready on time, another five hundred executives were imported from WDW during the final five months. Michael Eisner would later write in his book *Work in Progress*, "The miracle was that EDL opened as promised...."

As opening day rapidly approached, the numbers were adding up even more quickly. Future plans, extending to 1997, had a projected cost of between US$2.67 to $2.83 billion (17 to 18 billion French francs). This included the Magic Kingdom itself, a commercial and entertainment area,

5,200 hotel rooms, a golf course, and 570 single family homes. At this time a second phase of the resort, scheduled for 1996, was to include another gated area modeled after Disney-MGM Studio in Orlando, more hotel rooms and golf courses, time share condos, and a shopping mall. The future of Euro Disneyland looked bright on opening day, the sun shone brightly and the crowds came in droves, but dark clouds loomed just below the horizon.

Chapter Three
"When the Dream Becomes Reality"

THE FIRST GUESTS TO EURO DISNEYLAND were invited to come in late March for a practice run. The main sponsors, employees, and their families had an opportunity to enjoy the attractions while some of the cast members practiced their newly-trained skills.

On April 11, 1992, a day before the official opening, a two-hour TV special was filmed and beamed live to twenty-two countries around the world. Attendees included the media, travel agents, suppliers, tour operators, journalists, and anyone else likely to spread the word about the park. The show featured "a cavalcade of celebrities" reflecting the multi-cultural diversity of the park, behind the scenes footage of Imagineering, clips from Disney films in various European languages, and overviews of the lands and their attractions. Roy E. Disney appeared in a clip standing at the side of a country road near a sign proclaiming the town of Isigny-sur-mer. "This is a very sentimental place for me because the roots of my family come right back here to this village of Isigny-sur-mer," Roy said. "It was over nine hundred years ago that Hughes D'Isigny and his son Robert lived here."

Michael Eisner took the opportunity to dedicate the castle in a brief ceremony where he was introduced by Mickey Mouse and the EDL ambassador Sabine Marcon. "Thank you, Sabine, and thank you everyone," he began. "The founder of our company once said 'What I want more than anything else is for Disneyland to be a place where grownups and children can experience together, can enjoy the wonders of life and adventure and come out feeling the better for it.' Well, Walt's dream is also our dream for Euro Disney and so, with young voices from all over Europe we dedicate the *Le Château de la Belle au Bois Dormant* to both the young and the young at heart. To those who believe when you wish upon a star your dreams do come true. Thank you." A choir of children from all parts of Europe then gave a French rendition of *When You Wish Upon A Star* as fireworks burst over the castle.

The choir members were not the only imports from outside of France. The locomotives that circled the park were made in Wales, Adventureland had drums or Tam Tams from Zaire, Frontierland featured a mariachi band from Mexico, buffalo had been flown in from the United States in 747s, and the fairy tales of Fantasyland were from the storybooks of Europe. All of this was purposely shown to emphasize that EDL was "uniting the world under the name of Disney."

But not everyone was thrilled with the new park. Villagers from neighboring Meaux organized a protest against the noise pollution of the expected nightly fireworks. An attempt was made to disrupt the ceremonies when two electrical pylons were damaged by terrorist bombs the previous night in a failed effort to black out the park. Railroad strikers protesting security and staffing problems shut down the RER line between Paris and Marne-la-Vallée-Chessy for twenty-four hours. The police feared a traffic nightmare as thousands of cars converged on the area. It had been speculated by some media reports that as many as ninety thousand cars might be on the roads to the park where only a little more than eleven thousand parking spaces were available. Some reports predicted as many as five hundred thousand people would be on hand for the opening day. Euro Disney hoped they were prepared. For one thing, this was the first time a Disney park had opened with all of its attractions ready and working on the first day.

Fortunately, the massive crowds did not materialize. Apparently, most Frenchmen decided they could wait awhile before attempting the park. Amongst them was France's president, François Mitterand, who stated, "It's just not my cup of tea."

The numbers capped out at just over 20,000, easily accommodated by the new park. Michael Eisner greeted them not long afterwards, standing over the train station entrance to Main Street, USA. He made a brief speech, presented a lifetime pass to the first people to purchase EDL tickets, then climbed into a vintage fire truck and drove to *Le Château de la Belle au Bois Dormant* (Sleeping Beauty Castle). Eisner stood on the ramparts over the drawbridge entrance to the castle with Bob Fitzpatrick, Sabine Marcon, Mickey Mouse, and Roy Disney. Fitzpatrick welcomed the crowd in fluent French, saying "This is the most wonderful park we have ever created...every detail is designed to tell a story." Roy followed that with, "I'm honored to be here today to celebrate with all of you something that even Walt Disney himself never imagined, a Disney theme park and resort in Europe. For my family and me, Disney or D'Isigny have returned to Europe and our best loved characters, some created by Walt, many taken from the pages of European fairy tales now have a magnificent new home in the heart of Europe."

Michael Eisner stepped forward with the official opening speech, beginning by quoting Walt, "To all who come to this happy place, welcome. Once upon a time, a master story teller, Walt Disney, inspired by Europe's best loved tales, used his own special gifts to share them with the world. He envisioned a magic kingdom where these stories would come to life and called it Disneyland. He envisioned a magic kingdom . . . (he appears to have lost his place and started reading the same line again then corrected himself). Now his dreams return to the lands that inspired it. Euro Disneyland is dedicated to the young and the young at heart with the hope that it will be a source of joy and inspiration for all the world." He concluded, in stilted French, *"Je déclare Euro Disneyland officiellement ouvert.* (I declare Euro Disneyland officially open)." The guests who had listened to this opening ceremony applauded politely and proceeded into the park.

The following tour of Euro Disneyland is based on how the park was in the first weeks it was open in 1992. Later additions or changes are sometimes mentioned, but most will be covered in greater detail later.

Like Disneyland and The Magic Kingdom, the first thing Euro Disneyland's guests see, after buying their tickets and passing through the turnstiles under the Disneyland Hotel, is the Main Street Station of the Euro Disneyland Railroad. The traditional plaque above the tunnels under the railroad station has a slightly different wording than that in the other parks due to differing lands. Here it reads, "Here you leave today and enter worlds of history, discovery and ageless fantasy." (*"À partir d'ici, vous quittez le présent et entrez dans le monde de l'histoire, des découvertes et de la fantasie éternelle."*)

Unlike the other parks, EDL's train station has three portals onto Main Street and the floors are covered with English encaustic tiles. Inside, the stained glass windows and poster frames show visitors the attractions in store for them. Passing through the building to the long, covered loading platform, guests can board a train to take a circle tour around the park. The recorded narration is very limited, with warnings in French and English and the music changing to suit as the train ventures into different lands. Unlike Disneyland, where the Grand Canyon Diorama is at the end of the tour, in EDL it is at the beginning. The scenes are basically the same, though the train moves faster and the music from the *Grand Canyon Suite* is not played, nor is the Primeval World section included. Guests can now see the Rivers of the Far

West (known as the Rivers of America in Disneyland and WDW) before the train stops at the Old West-style Frontierland Station, a copy of the original Disneyland station previous to the 1966 remodeling. The first two lands have changed position for EDL, and Adventureland is where Frontierland is in the U.S. parks. According to *Disney News*, this was done so that the Pirates of the Caribbean attraction at the extreme north of the park would blend more readily with Peter Pan's Flight and Captain Hook's pirate ship in adjacent Fantasyland. A teasing glimpse of Pirates of the Caribbean is possible as the train continues through a dark tunnel. The next stop is the brick-faced Fantasyland Station, where the train stops near Alice's Curious Labyrinth and continues on to provide a good view of the exterior waterway of It's a Small World. The futuristic spaceport design of the Discoveryland Station is close to Star Tours and *Ciné Magique*, the last stop before returning to Main Street Station.

Euro Disneyland Railroad has four 4-4-0 steam locomotives, and the cars they pull are themed to the name of the engine. *W.F. Cody*, (#1) aka Buffalo Bill Cody, operated a Wild West Show, and the cars the locomotive pulls bare the names of Western cities, Cheyenne, Denver, Durango, Silverton, and Wichita. *C.K. Holliday*, (#2) was the founder of the Atchinson, Topeka, and Santa Fe Railroad in 1859. The cars have the names of vacation destinations around the U.S.: Atlantic City, Chesapeake, Coney Island, Long Island, and Niagara Falls. Disneyland also has a locomotive named *C.K. Holliday* (#1). *G. Washington*, (#3) the first president of the United States, is painted red, white, and blue, the colors of both France and the U.S., and its cars were named for significant places in his life, Boston, Mt. Vernon, Philadelphia, Valley Forge, and Yorktown. The last locomotive is *Eureka* (#4); its name is from the Ancient Greek for "I have found it" said to have been used by literate California gold miners during the 1849 gold rush. The cars were given the names of California cities, Los Angeles, Monterey, Sacramento, San Diego, and San Francisco.

Back at Main Street, USA, guests will find the basic layout similar to the U.S. parks. One obvious difference is that the Town Square has a large bandstand in the center of it instead of a flag pole. This is a curious addition, because back in 1955 when Disneyland was under construction, a bandstand was erected in Town Square, but Walt Disney had it moved to another location because it obstructed guest's view of Sleeping Beauty Castle at the end of the street. He wanted his visitors to see the castle and thus be drawn towards it and into the park. The bandstand in EDL obstructs that view.

There had been a lot of debate over how to design Main Street. Imagineers felt that this park deserved to be much more than a duplication of Disneyland. Part of the reason was that a purely American Main Street could be misinterpreted by those looking for rampant, culture-destroying Americanism in the park. They scoped out the other parks in the vicinity and found that none of them had anything like Main Street, and so it would be a unique idea in France. Eisner decided to go ahead with the American Main Street by featuring the spirit of America rather than its politics. The Victorian style would be the basis of the architecture with more of a 1920s look than turn of the century, much like in the Magic Kingdom in Florida. A few of the buildings have huge, retro advertising billboards atop them, unlike in any other park. The street was paved with a New York-style red brickwork "to lend sound and texture to an otherwise drab black surface." To add more depth to the street, Imagineers used paintings, shelving, and tilework to brighten up every nook and cranny with as much detail as possible without becoming garish.

To encourage guests to come to the park despite the weather, arcades or covered walkways were constructed on either side of and down the length of the street. The side to the east of Main Street is the Discovery Arcade and to the west, the Liberty Arcade. These provide access to the shops and restaurants and could also be used as a passage during crowded parade times. The Liberty Arcade design traces the history of the Statue of Liberty through drawings and photographs, while the Discovery Arcade entertains guests with scale models, sketches, and mock-ups of various inventions, from flying machines to horseless carriages.

Few of the buildings bear any resemblance to those found in the U.S. parks. City Hall, located to the left of Town Square, is more angular and topped by a taller clock tower said to have been inspired by the tower of the Western Union Telegraph Building in New York. The building, painted in red, white, and blue, serves the same purpose, that of administration and a place where guests can get programs, entertainment schedules, and general information about the park.

To the left of City Hall is the Arboretum, often found in Victorian architecture, designed for growing trees for a variety of purposes, but in the case of EDL to provide a covered walkway from the ticket booths to the covered arcades in rainy weather.

To the right of City Hall is the Storybook Store, with the appearance of a small town library. As the name suggests, a wide selection of books, stationery, records, and tapes can be purchased. (Remember this is the 1990s; today the records and tapes have been replaced by CDs and DVDs.) At the entrance, an audio-animatronic Tigger in a gilded teller's cage will stamp books much as a librarian used to. Disney characters can be seen throughout the store in various book related poses.

On the opposite side of the Town Square, where Disneyland has an Opera House, is Main Street Vehicles sponsored by Europcar. The name has been changed more recently to Main Street Transportation Co. Here guests can board a vintage Omnibus, a fire truck, a 1920s police paddy wagon, or a 1920s limousine for a one-way, leisurely ride down Main Street to Central Plaza. For those who prefer horse-drawn vehicles, the Main Street Streetcar is available. These vehicles are quite different from those in the States, as they are enclosed to protect guests during inclement weather and are apparently inspired by the streetcars seen in the 1969 film *Hello Dolly*. The cars are also more elaborate, and guests face inwards where they can see advertisements of the Main Street businesses. The three streetcars are named *Saratoga, San Francisco*, and *St. Louis*.

Next door to Main Street Vehicles is Ribbons and Bows Hat Store, where anything head- wise from Mouse ears to chapeaus could be purchased.

Today it runs more to general merchandise and is shared by Bixby Brothers baby store.

Moving north of the entrance of Discoveryland Arcade, guests can easily access all of the shops from inside. The first is Town Square Photography, sponsored by Kodak, followed by Silhouette Artist, Boardwalk Candy Palace (Nestlé), and Disney Clothiers Ltd. Here also is Esso's Main Street Motors, an antique car showroom where guests could actually buy the latest model cars and accessories from the turn of the last century. Today it is more of a clothing store, but much of the original "garage style" décor is still visible.

On a little side street (Market Street) are nestled three self-explanatory refreshment stops, The Coffee Grinder (Nescafé), The Ice Cream Company (Nestlé), and Market House Deli, where one can purchase "made to order hot and cold sandwiches, salads and desserts."

Harrington's Fine China and Porcelains, with "exquisite crystal and glassware," and Disneyana Collectibles, for animation cels, lithographs, and "figurines for the collector," are next. At the end of the street are more eateries such as Cookie Kitchen, Cable Car Bake Shop, The Gibson Girl Ice Cream Parlour with "turn of the century ice cream favorites," and Victoria's Home Style Cooking in a 1890s boarding house specializing in "pot pies, salads and desserts." To the east, bordering on Central Plaza is Plaza Garden Restaurant where guests are entertained by a musical ensemble as they dine buffeteria-style in Victorian décor. The building is virtually identical to the Plaza Inn in Disneyland.

Returning to Town Square and proceeding up the west or Liberty Arcade-side of the street, guests first encounter the Emporium, the largest store in the park. Here guests can buy almost anything Disney. There originally was a small room housing another Bixby Brothers shop that catered to adult fashions and accessories which in time was phased out and integrated into the greater Emporium. Another nook that was later integrated into the Emporium was The Toy Chest, "a floor to ceiling treasury of toys, games and dreams come true."

The Harmony Barber Shop (later renamed Dapper Dan's Haircuts) is located on a short side street (Flower Street) about half way down Main Street. EDL and WDW are the only parks to still have operating barber shops. This shop originally had its own barbershop quartet known as the Main Street Quartet. The Dapper Dans was a quartet that was organized in the early days of Disneyland.

Next is Liberty Court, a Statue of Liberty Tableau where guests could "experience firsthand the inauguration of the Statue of Liberty in 1886." Adjacent is Walt's, An American Restaurant serving "regional American cuisine prepared in the style of celebrated American restaurants." The interior is decorated with concept artwork used in designing Disney theme parks. Guests can climb a staircase from the elegant lobby to the first floor, where they will find a number of rooms dedicated to the various lands of the park.

Next are Disney & Co, for "decorative gift items set around a colorful hot-air balloon," and Glass Fantasies, where guests can watch the creation of glass giftware. At the end of the street is Casey's Corner, sponsored by Coca-Cola, themed to baseball and offering such American treats as hot dogs, chili, and soft drinks.

As in all of the Disney Theme Parks, the Central Hub is the center of the park and provides a place for guests to pause and relax between visiting the various lands, which are all accessible from this point.

To the west is Frontierland, designed to cater to European enthusiasm and interest in the American west. The area was originally named Westernland as was done in TDL, but when it was learned that Frontierland "had meaning for continental audiences," it was changed. Hollywood Westerns had long been favorite fare in Europe and there was a popular Western village in the Paris area catering to would-be cowboys. So not only was it to be named Frontierland, but it would become the largest land in the park and be the first land visitors entered from the hub. The main name change was to change the Rivers of America waterway to Rivers of the Far West, and instead of having Tom Sawyer's Island in the middle, EDL placed Big Thunder Mountain in the place of honor. Other differences are also evident, as the terrain was changed from lush green forests to the arid red environment of the American

Southwest to more reflect the scenery Europeans would have seen in John Wayne and Clint Eastwood movies.

Leaving the hub and entering Frontierland, guests walk through open stockade fort gates similar to those in Disneyland. A plaque reads, "The frontier of the Far West was a rugged landscape of great expectations and grand illusions, where dreams rode wild, and simple lives became legends. As you pass through these gates, follow the footsteps of the pioneers . . . and dream. Welcome to FRONTIERLAND".

To the left is The Lucky Nugget Saloon, similar in appearance to the Golden Horseshoe in Disneyland but grander and more elaborate on the inside with deep brown wood panelling. The saloon boasts a "raucous live stage show and a western-flavored bill of fare." The stage show, The Lucky Nugget Revue, stars saloon owner Miss Diamond Lil', Pierre Paradis, her French boyfriend, Charlie McGee, and half a dozen dancers with musical accompaniment from the Lucky Nugget Boys and invariably culminated with the famous Can-Can.

Next to the saloon is Last Chance Café with an outlaw hideout theme for light snacks and Silver Spur Steakhouse with "prime rib and steak prepared over a wood fire in a stylish nineteenth century cattleman's club."

The first attraction guests arrive at is Thunder Mesa Riverboat Landing. This steamboat attraction is unique to EDL, as it features two riverboats, *Mark Twain* (modled after the sternwheeler in Disneyland) and *Molly Brown*, the only side-wheeler in a Disney park, named for the famous *Titanic* survivor. As the boats steam around the center island, a pre-recorded spiel features a conversation between the captain and either Twain or Brown, depending on the boat the guest is on. From the decks, guests see the town of Thunder Mesa as they leave the landing, pass by the landing areas for the Keel Boats and Indian Canoes, see an old settler dozing in his rocking chair in a riverside cabin, spy a family of moose, watch the runway train careen by on Big Thunder Mountain, marvel at a spectacular natural formation, and view the graveyard and exterior of the Phantom Manor before returning to Thunder Mesa landing.

Continuing west, guests next arrive at Phantom Manor, EDL's version of Disneyland's Haunted Mansion. Unlike the haunted establishments in the other parks, Phantom Manor is designed to be part of Frontierland's Western mining town concept. The exterior of the building differs from the other parks, as it is dilapidated to better convey its contents to diverse guests. As in the other parks, stretching elevators take guests to the next level, in this case downwards, and place them in two person doom buggies. The attraction is darker and scarier than its counterparts and has a unique soundtrack. There are ninety-two audio-animatronic characters in Phantom Manor, along with over four hundred show props, fifty-four animated props, and fifty-eight special effects. The original idea was developed by Marc Davis for a WDW attraction that was never built called Western River Expedition, a Pirates of the Caribbean-style ride.

The backstory, as devised by Tony Baxter, tells the tale of all of Frontierland and is about Henry Ravenswood, a settler who struck it rich, founded the Thunder Mesa Mining Company, and thereafter the town of Thunder Mesa (Frontierland). With his riches, he built a Victorian mansion and raised a family, including a daughter, Melanie. As time went by, miners had to dig deeper and deeper into the mountain until they disturbed the Thunderbird who lived within, thereby causing an earthquake that killed Henry and his wife, Martha. Later it was discovered that shortly before the earthquake, on Melanie's wedding day, her suitor, a train engineer, had been lured to the attic and hanged by a mysterious phantom. Melanie was not aware of this, and spent the rest of her days (and thereafter) wandering around in her wedding dress awaiting his return. Her singing voice can still be heard to this day. As the house began to deteriorate, the phantom invited his demonic friends into the manor for an eternal party. Now there is an ongoing battle between Melanie and the phantom as he wants to drag guests into the hereafter, while she tries to save them.

A few notes on variations between the various attractions might be of interest. The Phantom's cackle was done by Vincent Price and is the same as the one he did at the end of Michael Jackson's *Thriller*. Price was also brought in to redo the ghost host's narration for the early scenes, but it was later redone by Gérard Chevalíer when a French version was needed. The stretching room portraits all feature the young bride in some manner of peril as the room sinks and the lightning strike above guests' heads shows the Phantom in the process of hanging her beloved. The endless hallway scene from the Haunted Mansion with a candelabra floating in air is given more meaning here, as the bride is shown fading in and out as she holds the object. The coffin in the conservatory is replaced by a piano, and a ghost plays a version of *Grim Grinning Ghosts*. Disembodied Madame Leota, voiced by Oona Lind, is in a formal sitting room, and her spiel deals more with the bride and the doomed wedding. The Grand Hall scene with ghosts gathered around a table is closer to the original Claude Coats rendering for the Haunted Mansion of a wedding scene. The main difference is the appearance of the bride on a staircase above the room and the arrival of the Phantom with his evil laughter. In this version, all of the ghosts slowly disappear except for the bride. The attic scene is replaced by the bride's boudoir, where she eternally prepares for her wedding under the malevolent gaze of the Phantom. The final cemetery scene is replaced by a "descent into the Underworld," as the Phantom invites guests to join him as their doom buggies plunge backwards into an open grave. Now beneath Boot Hill Cemetery, guests view all manner of apparitions rising from their graves to the tune of *Grim Grinning Ghosts* and emerge in a recreation of Thunder Mesa as a ghost town during the earthquake. In the final scene, the Hitchhiking Ghosts are replaced by the Phantom trying to climb into the doom buggy in a last attempt to keep the guests in the manor. As guests climb out of their doom buggies and depart the building, they enter Boot Hill Cemetery where they find that "nobody on Thunder Mesa seemed to take death too seriously."

Guests now have to backtrack to visit the eastern side of Frontierland. The first attraction is Rustler Roundup Shootin' Gallery, EDL's version of Disneyland's Frontierland Shootin' Gallery. Across the street is Thunder Mesa Mercantile where Tobias Norton & Sons – Frontier Traders sell leather goods, Bonanza Outfitters deal in "Western clothing and Indian-style goods," and Eureka Mining Supplies and Assay Office sell frontier-themed toys and candy. Next door is *Fuente del Oro* (Source of Gold) Restaurant, an adobe cantina specializing in Tex-Mex dishes enjoyed to the accompaniment of strolling mariachis.

The next attraction is Big Thunder Mountain, where the Thunder Mesa Mining Company came into being and where Ravenswood struck it rich. This version is unique to EDL, being situated on an island in the middle of the Rivers of the Far West, where other parks have Tom Sawyer's Island or a version thereof.

The station where guests board the soon-to-be runaway mine train is situated on the mainland. The trains plummet into a dark tunnel that takes them under the Rivers of the Far West and out to the island in the center, where they climb out of the darkness. A waterfall gives the impression that the tunnel is flooding as the train begins its rapid descent and swooping turns. Approaching a mining camp, the train is propelled through a washed out section and onto a rickety trestle, then passes by a series of tableaux featuring donkeys and goats in a mining camp, upwards again and around more curves and onto a broken trestle and a 540-degree counter-clockwise helix, exiting to shoot down a canyon and up a third hill. Miners with dynamite trigger an earthquake which rocks the train and sends it careening towards a tunnel, through a swarm of bats, accelerating as it drops to go under the river again and emerge at the station back on the mainland.

The next attraction on the river bank is River Rogue Keelboats situated at Smuggler's Cove. The two keelboats, modeled after the ones in Disneyland, are *Coyote* and *Racoon* and hold thirty guests. The landing area is next to a cave tableau reminiscent of the pirates' caves in the Disney film, *Davy Crockett and the River Pirates* (1956). Following the same basic route as the paddle wheeler steamboats, the keelboats cruise the Rivers of the Far West for about twenty minutes, giving riders a closer view of the scenery on the shore and providing a commentary (primarily in French) about life on the river. Due to "operational problems," the attraction closed in 2001 but returned in 2007.

The next attraction is Indian Canoes, known as Davy Crockett Explorer

Canoes in Disneyland and WDW and Beaver Brothers Explorer Canoes in TDL when their Critter Country opened. The concept is the same, as guests do the work paddling around Big Thunder Mountain and Wilderness Island and cast members provide instruction and steering. Indian Canoes was short lived, closing in October 1994 allegedly due to overcrowding on the river.

Pueblo Trading Post is located close by, where guests can purchase "Southwestern and American Indian gifts and jewelry," and if they are getting hungry, they can stop at the big red barn housing Cowboy Cookout Barbeque. This counter service restaurant provides "foot-stompin', finger-lickin' fun with ranch-style menu favorites" and live country entertainment. Woodcarver's Workshop is next and self-explanatory, leading up to Cottonwood Creek Ranch Critter Corral, an Old West-style working ranch with small farm animals for children to pet, until it closed in 2006.

EDL's Frontierland combines elements of the Old and New Worlds to make the land more sophisticated than its U.S. counterparts. It reflects the conception that Europeans have of the Old West rather than the historic west.

Due to Frontierland's size, its neighbor, Adventureland, is the smallest of the EDL lands. Knowing this, the Imagineers decided to make this Adventureland different from all the others, and instead of a rain forest jungle setting switched to a more Oriental and Arabian locale. They went to great lengths to "emphasize the special intrigue of the region" and changed the thick trees to desert landscapes, stone fortress walls, and onion-domed architecture. Hence there is no Jungle Cruise, due to the change in theme as well as the difficulty in growing tropical plants in the cold Parisian climate. At one time, Imagineers considered covering the area with a glass dome to protect the plants, but the idea was abandoned.

Cast members were dressed in North African styles as depicted by Hollywood, and the central bazaar was designed as imagined by French colonialists. Here, according to Tony Baxter, "fantasies of paradise can be fulfilled, of living in a tree or climbing the rocks and looking for buried treasure."

"When the Dream Becomes Reality"

The sandstone towers of a desert fortress form the gateway to Adventureland. Inside, over the Adventureland Bazaar, "citadels soar into onion shaped domes each topped with a brass weather vane" shaped like an Arabian Nights character. The design was meant to showcase the movie *Aladdin*, which was still in production at the time. Here guests will find *La Chant des Tam Tams* (Song of Tam Tams), with "a wide range of wicker and rattan baskets;" *Les Trésors de Schéhérazade* (Treasures of Scheherazade), featuring "exotic clothing and accessories;" *La Reine des Serpents* (Queen of Serpents), selling "gifts and decorative items from the far reaches of the globe;" *L'Echoppe d'Aladdin* (Stall of Aladdin), with various styles of jewelry; and *La Girafe Curieuse Tout pour le Safari* (The Curious Giraffe – Everything for the Safari), for "safari clothing and accessories."

Two restaurants, *Aux Epices Enchantées* (Enchanted Spices), sponsored by Maggi and featuring "brochettes, stir-fry and African stews," which became Restaurant Hakuna Matata in May, 1995, and *Café de la Brousse,* for "unusual desserts and mint tea," are situated nearby.

Continuing west, guests enter a more lush, jungle-themed area to find Trader Sam's Jungle Boutique for jewelry, clothing, and accessories, and Explorer's Club for table service meals. This colonial estate-style building is staffed by cast members playing famous European explorers. The Club has a large outdoor dining area overlooking waterfalls and an interior area with audio-animatronic birds similar to the Enchanted Tiki Room in Disneyland. A year after the park opened, the menu was changed to East Asian cuisine with counter service, which necessitated the need to remove some of the trees. In 1995, the name was changed to Colonel Hathi's Pizza Outpost, with the requisite menu alteration and themed to Disney's *The Jungle Book.*

Leaving the Explorer's Club, guests have to backtrack to visit *La Cabane des Robinson*, EDL's answer to Disneyland's Swiss Family Robinson Treehouse, located on the Northern Isle section of Adventure Isle. The treehouse, as in the other parks, is a walkthrough attraction built into in a twenty-seven-meter-tall banyan tree, whose eight hundred thousand vinyl leaves serve as a centerpiece to the land. Guests can leave the treehouse via a rope suspension bridge (*Le Pont Suspendu*) and explore other areas on Adventure Isle. Under the tree is a network of root-filled caves to be explored, known as *Le Ventre de la Terre* (The Belly of the Earth), much like on Tom Sawyer's Island in Disneyland. Not far away, the wrecked ship that brought the Robinsons to the island lays in *La Mer des Bretteurs* (The Brawling Sea). The Southern Island is rockier, much of it built with actual rock purchased from surprised owners, with a small playground called *La Plage des Pirates* (Pirates Beach) near Captain Hook's pirate ship and Skull Rock, remnants of the old Fantasyland in Disneyland. Spyglass Hill dominates the island and is honeycombed with mazes and caves, including one with a treasure inside, and with some themed to Disney's film, *Treasure Island*.

On the east side of the land, past Adventure Isle, guests find *Le Coffre du Capitaine* (Captain's Chest), "a treasure chest of pirate and nautical novelties" next to Blue Lagoon Restaurant, located inside Pirates of the Caribbean as in Disneyland.

The last Adventureland attraction is located in a battle-scarred eighteenth century West Indies Spanish fortress, unlike the pristine El Castillo in WDW. A black flag bearing a white skull and cross bones flutters proudly over the structure, proclaiming to all that "there be pirates here." The Imagineers, led by Tony Baxter, took advantage of the opportunity to reinvent the attraction. Firstly, the water table in Paris is high, so guests would have to go up rather than down as in Disneyland. Not a problem, as that had already been done in TDL and the tall, ominous Spanish fort façade made this easier to accomplish. Next, they reversed the order of events, as they wanted to "save some of the fun and excitement for the end of the show," Baxter said.

Once inside the fortress, the queue winds through the dungeons, hidden treasure, and arsenals. They even catch a glimpse of skeletal remains in the Crew's Quarters, the only time that a major attraction scene has been viewed from the lineup. In time, the guests arrive on the shores of a tropical lagoon. Here they board the waiting bateaux and sail across the tranquil lagoon beneath a clear night sky and full moon. In the distance is a fortress, and along the way the guests pass out of the town, sail by a wrecked pirate ship, where a crab and octopus are arguing over the ship's cargo, and islanders enjoy a meal. The bateaux are then hauled up an old loading dock's cargo ramp and into the upper level of the fort, which has been flooded with water. Here a band of pirates are trying to encourage a dog to bring them the keys he has in his mouth, a scene that occurs near the end of the Disneyland attraction. Guests can see the silhouettes of pirates clambering over the walls to attack the Spanish soldier within. Leaving the flooded fort, the bateaux splash into the sea below and right in the middle of a ship to shore cannon battle and become targets themselves. Escaping the barrage, the bateaux drift into town, where guests see the mayor of the town being dunked in the well as in the other theme park attractions, followed by the "Take a Wench For a Bride" auction scene. The pirates chasing wenches scene now includes a more advanced audio-animatronic pair of pirates in a sword fight where the actual clanging of blades can be heard. Unfortunately, the early versions of the scene often had the figures slicing at each other's bodies and clothing instead of the intended sword play. The figures were removed from the show for a year and a half before they could be programmed to function as intended. The pirates chasing the women are more libidinous, as the pre-politically correct scenes from the first rendition of the attraction were used in EDL.

Sailing into the burning town guests are now serenaded by pirates singing (in English) "Yo, ho, yo, ho, a pirate's life to me." As the bateaux approach the dueling pirates sitting on powder kegs, there is an explosion and the bateaux drop down a level to where the Disneyland attraction begins with "Dead men tell no tales" ringing in their ears and skeletal scenes abounding. The intention, according to Baxter, was to provide a moral to the story, "What good is all that treasure ... you can't spend it if you're dead."

The grotto scene ends with the talking skull that begins the Disneyland tour, only this skull issues instructions about disembarking in French and English and a bit of "pirate" thrown in. Having dropped back down to street level, there is no up ramp at the end, and guests can simply disembark though a labyrinthine passage back to Adventureland.

When designing Fantasyland, the Imagineers had to look at it in a special way, for Europeans were more familiar with the original versions of the stories and fairy tales than were most Americans. They were in fact giving the animated films a homecoming of sorts and recognizing that though they had been given a remake by Disney, they were still essentially European tales. *Snow White and the Seven Dwarfs* came from Germany, *Pinocchio* from Italy, *Peter Pan* and *Alice in Wonderland* from Britain, *Cinderella, Sleeping Beauty,* and *Beauty and the Beast* from France, and *The Little Mermaid* from Denmark. Therefore, the cast member characters should speak in their native language and shops and restaurants would retain their national origin. Pinocchio's themed shop would be called *La Bottega di Geppetto,* Cinderella's restaurant would be *Auberge de Cendrillon, Peter Pan's Flight* would retain its English name, and *La Château de la Belle au Bois Dormant* would replace Sleeping Beauty Castle.

Here more than in any other land, it was essential to minimize translations on every sign and menu, so Fantasyland was designed to "rely on dramatic visual symbols" to communicate to guests. Familiar movie icons would identify rides, shows, and shops to emphasize that Fantasyland was removed from reality. The illusion was continued with Alpine themed shops, Old Mills from Holland, an Italian Restaurant from *Lady and the Tramp* with a decidedly Pisa lean, and Alice's meandering labyrinth from an English country garden. Fantasyland was designed to give guests the impression that their fairy tale characters had returned home and that differences in culture, nationality, and language were unimportant and "could be set aside in the name of fun."

Entering Fantasyland from the Central Hub takes guests directly to *La Château de la Belle au Bois Dormant*. This castle is unique in the Disney Parks, for as Tony Baxter noted, "The fact that castles exist just down the road from Disneyland Paris challenged us to think twice about our design." Ideas ran the gauntlet, from redesigning existing Disney castles to installing a totally different kind of edifice instead of a castle. Eventually, the Imagineers settled on designing a new castle based on Mont Saint-Michel monastery, the castle as depicted in the movie *Sleeping Beauty* and the illustrations in the book *Les Très Riches Heures du Duc de Berry*. The castle stands fifty meters (160 feet) tall and is surrounded by sculpted trees in angular shapes as seen in the film. There is a dungeon beneath the castle, *La Tanière du Dragon* (Dragon's Den), where dwells an audio-animatronic beast, curled and sleeping. It awakens, growls, and with some smoke curling out of its mouth threatens to breathe fire on any who disturb it. It doesn't though; it just goes back to sleep.

Inside the castle are a number of establishments: *La Boutique du Château*, selling "holiday and Christmas merchandise year round;" *Merlin l'Enchanteur*, with "medieval figurines and gifts in crystal and pewter;" *La Confiserie des Trois Fées* (Three Fairies Confectionary) by Nestlé; and *La Chaumière Septs Nains* (Cottage of the Seven Dwarfs), where guests can purchase toys, games, and children's apparel. To the east of the castle stands *le Théâtre du Château*, where live stage entertainment is presented. The first show was *Le Livre Magique de Mickey* (Mickey's Magic Book) in 1992, considered by many as the best show ever produced in the park. The show stars Mickey Mouse in his sorcerer's apprentice garb and features him flipping through the pages of a huge pop-up book, bringing characters from Disney films, such as Snow White, Aurora and Cinderella, to life. The thirty-thousand-pound book was designed in the States by Animated Ideas Inc. and constructed in England by MWA Ltd. The pages are turned by a small vehicle on an elliptical track that allows the pages to open and close smoothly.

Directly ahead as guests leave the castle is *Le Carrousel de Lancelot*, a standard in most of the parks, with "eighty-six graceful galloping horses" accented with twenty-four-karat gold leaf. Astute observers will note that the horses in the inner ring are arranged by the colors of the rainbow. This is the first of the Disney park carousels to have two-seat chariots for guests who prefer not, or cannot, sit astride a horse. In keeping with the King Arthur and the Knights of the Round Table theme, the sword in the stone, known as Excalibur, is nearby for those who think they might have a chance to be crowned king of all England by extracting it from the rock.

To the east is a large building with a stone façade and a large window overhead through which the wicked queen peers. This is EDL's version of the Snow White and the Seven Dwarfs attraction. Interestingly enough, the name is simply *Blanche Neige et la Sept Nains*, without the words "Scary Adventures" as used in most of the other parks. The attraction is basically the same as the one in Disneyland with a slight variety in the ending, much like that in WDW.

Sharing the building is *Les Voyages de Pinocchio*, a copy inside and out of the attraction in Disneyland known as Pinocchio's Daring Journey. This version is slightly shorter in duration due to French building restrictions that required thick concrete walls between attractions. The use of holographic technology was first done here in the scene where bad boys looking into mirrors see themselves as donkeys. To complement the attraction is *La Bottega di Geppetto*, a "delightful woodcarver's shop with wooden dolls and marionettes," and nearby, in a cozy Alpine setting, is *Au Chalet de la Marionnette*, serving "fresh rotisseried (sic) chicken, hamburgers and sausages." Astute guests may notice that the exit (*sortie*) sign has Figaro the cat leaning against it giving a wink and a thumbs up. The rest of the story took place in Disneyland at the Village Haus Restaurant, where the exit sign was installed off center, but rather than move it and add to the costs, artists painted Figaro the cat pulling at the sign to shift it to its proper position.

Continuing north, guests will encounter one of the most popular attractions in any Disney Park, Peter Pan's Flight. This version is almost identical to the one in Disneyland. The exterior with its clock tower is also very similar. In anticipation of this popularity, the EDL version has four-person-capacity boats instead of the usual two or three (depending on the size of the guests). It is also longer, a full three minutes compared to two and a half minutes in the other parks. The story is told that while the attraction was being tested before opening, the system failed and the Imagineers in the boat were left suspended high above the floor with no means of getting down, as the emergency ladders had not yet been installed.

Keeping with the British theme of the area, Toad Hall Restaurant in located here, offering "authentic British fare, including fish and chips, roast beef sandwiches and English trifle." The original plan was for a Toad's Wild Ride attraction, but designers thought it would be fun for guests to be able to actually dine inside Toad Hall. The exterior is therefore inspired by the mansion as shown in the film *The Adventures of Ichabod and Mr. Toad* (1949), a Tudor style with twisted chimneys and brick walls. Inside, as guests make their way to the dining room, the restaurant is more like a walkthrough attraction. The foyer is decorated with antiques and wainscoted walls. Guests then wander through the library and into the kitchen where they place their orders and take their food to either the games room, the greenhouse, or the drawing room, all the while admiring Toad's memorable and heroic achievements.

Backing onto the Fantasyland Train Station is a small theater called Fantasy Festival Stage, one of the main entertainment venues for the park. The popular show *C'est Magique* (This is Magic) consists primarily of young cast members in costume doing songs and dances for each land in the park. Mickey appears in the Main Street, USA tribute and Goofy (as a cowboy), Chip 'n' Dale (as Indians), and Minnie (dancehall girl) appear in the Frontierland segment. The Adventureland portion features Goofy again and characters from *The Jungle Book*, with Donald Duck dancing with pirates. The Fantasyland finale features a multitude of Disney characters.

C'est Magique played for several seasons except for Christmas, when it was replaced by *Le Noël de Mickey*.

Completing the British section is an attraction unique to EDL, Alice's Curious Labyrinth, themed to the 1951 animated feature, *Alice in Wonderland*. The maze is made up of two parts, with the first starting with guests going into the White Rabbit's hole and encountering strange animals, various sizes of doors, signs with conflicting directions, and fountains spraying water. The smoking Caterpillar is come across, and guests can listen to his quotes before joining the Dodo in the Caucus Race and entering the Cheshire Catwalk Maze. The second part of the labyrinth is the Queen's Maze, during which the Queen or her soldier playing cards pops up from time to time shouting "Off with their heads." When guests reach the center of the maze, they find the Queen's castle where, from the top, they are rewarded with a view of

Fantasyland. Originally, there was a slide for children to go down from the castle, but it was removed for safety reasons.

Another part of the Alice in Wonderland area is a recreation of the Mad Hatter's Tea Party at March Hare Refreshments, where guests can sample or buy Unbirthday cakes (*Gâteau de non-anniversaire*). Lastly is Mad Hatter's Tea Cups, where guests whirl madly about on three rotating turntables. The EDL version is surrounded by gardens and has a petal-shaped glass roof in order to make it possible to run the attraction when it is raining; otherwise the saturated turntables do not spin. The teacups are the same design as those in TDL, and the Dormouse's teapot is outside of the ride.

Dumbo the Flying Elephant attraction is the only American story in Fantasyland. Work on the sixteen-elephant ride was completed a full year before it would be needed for EDL, so it was used instead to replace the aging thirty-five-year-old version in Disneyland, and another one was built for France. The EDL version is similar to Disneyland, with a central water feature, but Timothy Mouse has red and white stripes instead of rainbow colors on his balloon and Timothy does not hold a whip. This popular attraction allows guests to vary their height while in flight with a handle inside the Dumbo-shaped gondola.

To the east is the Old Mill from the Disney short of the same name. A tribute of sort to Holland, it is hosted by Chambourcy and features "creamy yogurt and light refreshments."

It's A Small World, presented by France Télécom, is situated in the northeast corner of Fantasyland. The EDL version of this doll extravaganza varies from other versions in that the clock face at the front of the attraction is rounded and more colorful that the angular designs on the other park façades. The attraction also featured an exclusive World Chorus Post-Show area, unlike any other version of the show. It closed in 2010 when sponsorship changed. Inside, much is similar, except for a large North American section absent from the other versions. Here we see such things as cacti dressed as cowboys, Old West scenes, and the Hollywood sign with ballroom dancers whirling beneath it. There is also a larger Middle East section where the songs are sung in Arabic. Throughout the ride, the song alternates between English, French, and German and was specially recorded for the EDL version with children from European choirs.

As guests move south they come to another large and long building containing shops and restaurants. Fantasia Gelati and Pizzeria Belle Notte are self-explanatory. *Auberge de Cendrillon* (Cinderella Inn) is an old French-style building that features "delicious cuisine fit for royalty, with an exquisite dessert menu." A pumpkin coach centerpiece sits amongst five Renaissance rooms filled with tapestries and murals featuring scenes from the 1950 movie. More shops are nearby with Sir Mickey's selling toys and games, *La Ménagerie du Royaume* (Royal Menagerie) featuring "cuddly toys, ceramics and glassware," and *Le Brave Petit Tailleur* (The Brave Little Tailor) with Disney hats and clothes.

Discoveryland was designed to combine fantasy with futurism, rather than use the Tomorrowland approach of other parks, a concept that often became more like Todayland before new ideas were even completed. With that in mind, the Imagineers went in a totally different direction and designed Discoveryland to reflect the visions of the past, particularly those held by Europeans such as Leonardo Da Vinci, H.G. Wells, and Jules Verne. They wanted to pay tribute to the contributions of these men and, by using more earth tones and less concrete, give it more of a brighter future appearance.

When guests enter Discoveryland, the first attraction they see is *Le Visionarium*. Similar to the Circle Vision in WDW and TDL, it also included 3-D special effects and audio-animatronics. Unlike the TDL version where the pre-show area was brightly lit, here guests wait in a dim library setting to watch a brief film about the history of the sponsor, Renault. The film was dropped when sponsorship changed in 2002. The feature film was titled *Un Voyage à Travers le Temps* (A Journey Through Time), and it transported viewers through thousands of centuries and over thousands of miles of European culture. The American portion of the film was severely reduced for the EDL version. *Le Visionarium* would run until 2004, when it was refurbished and replaced by Buzz Lightyear Laser Blast in 2006.

Orbitron was EDL's version of the Sky Jets, Rocket Jets, or Astro Orbiter found in the other parks. Imagineers saw the huge bronze spheres of the nineteenth century planetarium that comprised the attraction as a piece of art or a kinetic sculpture intended to draw people into the land. As in the other parks, guests piloted their spaceship around the center of the ride, but unlike the other parks, this version was at ground level rather than on a raised platform.

There were only two shops and two restaurants in Discoveryland on opening day. The shops were Constellations, with character clothing and merchandise, and Star Traders, next to Star Tours, where all manner of Star Wars items were available. The two restaurants were situated on either side of *Le Visionarium* and themed with European futurism. *Le Café des Visionnaires* was designed with flashy bronze and copper, much like the Orbitron, and featured a giant fresco with scenes from great European works of science fiction. *Café Hyperion*, a giant food court, whose exterior featured a docked thirty-foot Zeppelin awaiting take off, reminiscent of the Discovery Bay scene Tony Baxter had designed for an expansion of Disneyland that never happened. Inside was themed like a departure area for the airship. The café overlooks Videopolis, where "spectacular live stage shows, bands and live music" could be enjoyed.

A backstory had been provided for Videopolis as a former airship station. The airship, *Hyperion*, had a schedule including stops at some forty-nine destinations when suddenly her captain disappeared, leaving the airship waiting in vain to resume its scheduled flights. The area was therefore turned into a place where guests could eat and rest. The venue was originally designed to be similar to the Videopolis in Disneyland, where live music was played for the benefit of teenagers. It was soon discovered that the teens would rather go on the rides until the last minute. In addition, some of the diners at Café Hyperion complained that more kid-friendly entertainment should be considered for Videopolis instead of the *Rock Shock* show being performed. *Rock Shock* was a cutting-edge show with contemporary music enhanced with special effects, dancing, and costumes, a virtual ballet representing the Jules Verne novels.

In time, other Disney shows such as *Beauty and the Beast* and *Mulan* would replace *Rock Shock*. In between performances, rock videos were originally shown, but these were replaced by Disney and Pixar shorts.

Autopia, sponsored by Ford, is a popular import from Disneyland, taking up a large portion of Discoveryland. The attraction has a unique retro style, with cars rounded to a 1950s look and more toy-like in appearance.

The final two attractions are exact copies of those shown in the other parks. As in Anaheim, Orlando, and Tokyo, guests climb aboard a Starspeeder 3000 for the same version of Star Tours that debuted in Disneyland in 1987. Next door, at *Ciné Magique*, Michael Jackson would star in *Captain EO*, until 1997 when it was changed to *Honey, I Shrunk the Audience*.

That was just the beginning. In the Summer 1993, issue of *Disney News* a list of coming attractions was published. There was to be a ferris wheel with water bucket-shaped seats called *Les Pirouettes du Mieux Moulin* (The Spinning Mill) for Fantasyland; Legends of the Wild West was to mimic the Davy Crockett scene inside Disneyland's Fort Wilderness; a fourth railway station for Discoveryland; *Casey Jr., Le Petit Train du Cirque* would circle around *Le Pays des Contes de Fées* in a recreation of Casey Jr. ride around Storybook Land in Disneyland; Dream of the Future would expand Autopia into a four-lane mini highway; and a Temple of Peril-style roller coaster attraction for Adventureland with the name of Indiana Jones tentatively attached to it. The Imagineers were determined to stand by Walt Disney's promise that Disneyland "will never be completed as long as there is imagination left in the world." Only time would tell as to what was actually constructed.

Euro Disneyland, to all appearances, was a success. Bob Fitzpatrick called it "the most wonderful park we have ever created." Visitors, for the most part, gushed their praise, though a few grumbled about long lines and high prices. Those newspapers that complained "this is not France" missed the point; it was not supposed to be. Imagineers had gone out of their way to make EDL different from anything else Europe had seen.

Unfortunately, the magic of the Magic Kingdom wore off very quickly. As Michael Eisner later wrote, "In our initial euphoria, we didn't immediately recognize that we had other, serious problems."

Chapter Four
"The Tragic Kingdom"

It did not take long for tarnish to begin to appear on Disney's gleaming armor. The training had been too fast and intense, and some cast members began rebelling against being Disneyfied. The people were glad to have jobs, but they were not as invested in working for Disney as cast members in the States who had grown up in or close to the Disney way. Robert Anthony wrote in *Euro Disney: The First 100 Days* that many cast members were "acting like real people instead of Disney people ... you get the feeling that the whole thing was not yet under control."

In May 1992, less than a month after the grand opening, the *Hollywood Reporter* printed the story that three thousand workers had walked off the job at EDL. They cited low wages and poor working conditions for the mass walkout of some 25 percent of the total work force. This was followed by stories of declining attendance at the park and the possibility of the failure of the entire resort. Fitzpatrick spoke to the *Wall Street Journal* and called the story "pure fiction." He explained that only about one thousand had left and almost half of those had been asked to leave for a variety of reasons. But the damage was done. The market reacted to the gloom and doom story, and Disney stock took a tumble.

Fitzpatrick went into damage control mode and announced some attendance figures, against Disney's practice of only doing it annually. He claimed that in the first seven weeks, over 1.5 million guests had enjoyed EDL, which easily put it within the attendance projection of 11 million in the first year. He neglected to mention, and some analysts were quick to point out, that winter attendance would be considerably lower due primarily to inclement weather.

Regardless, Fitzpatrick announced special measures for long-term success. The expansion of a second gate, Disney-MGM Studio Europe, which had been scheduled to open in 1995 at a projected cost of $2.3 billion, was quietly put on hold. Prices for hotel rooms were lowered to encourage longer stays, and an advertising blitz aimed at repeat visitors from France was launched. Regardless, shares dropped on the Paris Bourse and the New York exchange.

In addition, government actions aimed at combating the recession were less than popular amongst the local farmers. One of these proposed cuts was to the European Community farm subsidies, a move that was part of American agricultural trade policies. "Euro Disneyland is the symbol of an American culture that has invaded our country," said Daniel Deswards, one of the leaders of the protesting farmers, according to the *LA Times*. "Now the Americans want to do the same thing to our agriculture."

Before dawn on June 28, some five hundred farmers protested against the nearest thing they had to America, Euro Disneyland. Three hundred tractors blocked the roads leading to the main entrance of the park, with the farmers knowing full well that reporters would turn out in droves to cover the story and give publicity to their cause.

They got the publicity they were after, and the term "Tragic Kingdom" surfaced once again in newspapers across France. Many guests who had attempted to drive to the park that day were turned away, including "several hundred families and busloads of schoolchildren." Others persevered and when they found they were unable to drive any further, left their cars or buses on the side of the road and walked to the park through angry crowds of farmers. The police who attended did not attempt to stop the protestors.

Disney officials strove to remain neutral. Disney spokesman Nicolas De Schonen stated, "It is a matter between the farmers and the French government" and declined further comment. French newspapers reported that "at least 70 school buses containing 2,000 children were prevented from reaching the site." Only those who arrived by train were permitted through the turnstiles. In a particularly touching interview featured by the French TV networks, a tearful child who had been denied access to the park did little to support the farmer's protest. "The tractors are mean!" she said.

In time the truth came out, and Disney announced that projections indicated that EDL would indeed incur a net loss by the end of their fiscal year. They tried to put a positive spin on the facts by noting that over the past three months some 3.6 million people had visited the park. Apparently more than had visited the other Disney parks in a comparable start-up period, including 30 percent above Tokyo Disneyland's initial attendance for the same time. Disney officials encouraged people to look to the future, as EDL was a "long term project."

Unfortunately, most shareholders were not interested in the long term and started selling their stocks, causing the stock value to plummet by 31% since opening day. Disney executives were still confident that the park would flourish in time. The bad press, and the fact that people were almost gleefully following the problems the park was having, was more hurtful to their pride than their enthusiasm for the enterprise.

The next step was an effort to increase the quality of experience for guests and to boost attendance before inclement weather set in. Cast member training was intensified and plans were put in place to decrease wait times for attractions. Marketing strategies were stepped up to increase the public's awareness of EDL, as tour operators, travel agents, and other like companies were targeted. The measures seemed to work; the crowds came and hotel occupancy was at 100% by August. In October, the beginning of the "low season," Newport Bay Club Hotel was temporarily closed, effectively taking 1,100 rooms off the schedule.

A few changes were made in the hierarchy as well. Robert Fitzpatrick was created Chairman of EDL, effective October 1. Philippe Bourguignon, a Frenchman who had been recruited by Euro Disney in 1988 and who was involved in the development of the EDL hotels, became Senior Vice-President. Michael Eisner saw the "value in having a French executive in the top job, who truly understood the culture." Former Disney Store executive, Steve Burke, was transferred to Paris to become the park's Executive Vice-President. The changes were seen as positive, and stock prices slowly began to rise.

Even before their appointments were officially announced, Fitzpatrick and Bourguignon went to work. Special events, aimed at drawing in more people, became more frequent. In early September, a ceremony was held to welcome the six millionth guest, who, much to Fitzpatrick's delight, was French. She was welcomed by Mickey Mouse and presented with a bouquet of flowers. A few days, later five thousand children "who had been unable to go away for summer vacation" were welcomed. A Euro Disney pavilion was set up in Seville, Spain as part of Expo '92, and here EDL Ambassador Sabine Marcon introduced the Expo mascot, Curro, to Mickey Mouse. Clint Eastwood and Kevin Costner, well known Western heroes in France, made special appearances in the park.

Despite the problems, Euro Disney still had the strong support of the

French government. This was underscored on October 12 when Prime Minister Pierre Beregovoy presented Michael Eisner with the honorary title of *Chevalier de la Légion d'Honneur* for his contribution to the French people. The same honor had been awarded Walt Disney in 1935. Beregovoy affirmed the "continued goodwill of the government," as the "projected economic advantages are being felt." The numbers spoke for themselves, as by this time almost seven million guests had visited EDL, of whom 36 percent were French. In their report "The Impact of Euro Disney on the Economy and Tourism After Six Months in Operation," the EDL executives went on to mention that most foreign visitors, 64 percent of guests, confirmed that they had come to France for the specific purpose of visiting the new park. They were estimated to have spent 6.8 billion francs in the resort and surrounding areas. The local economy was given a huge boost as well with the hiring of 12,596 employees, not including public works and construction workers. Even the housing shortage in the area had been given a boost with the construction of 1,800 homes.

The special events continued as 1,500 luminaries from the art world, entertainment industry, and political spectrum were invited to a pre-release screening of the newest Disney feature-length animated film, *Le Belle et La Bête (Beauty and the Beast)*. The first Disney store in France opened in November just west of Paris, and a prolonged and extensive media blitz was launched throughout France. Magazine ads, TV commercial spots, movie theater promotions coincided with the release of *Beauty and the Beast*, and radio announcements besieged the population at every turn. The 210 Metro stations, sixty movie theaters, and two major airports all sported advertisements for Euro Disneyland.

Regardless, there was still the Europe-wide recession, one fact of life in France that Disney could not fix and could not have prepared for. Eisner referred to the recession as "deep and sustained" and admitted that the prices set for admission, merchandise, food, and hotels "were ambitious." The collapse of the real estate market made it impossible for Disney to profit from any of the land they had purchased in order to pay down their debt. The value of foreign currency against the French franc also dropped, making it more expensive for foreign visitors.

It was also noted that despite their extensive research into French culture, Euro Disney misjudged a few important items. It was assumed that the French ate a light breakfast, so the hotels were not prepared for the demand for sit-down meals, resulting in long lineups for food. One of the major complaints was the lack of alcoholic beverages in the resort. A long-standing policy, initiated by Walt Disney himself, was that no alcohol be served in the parks. Michael Eisner supported the policy despite French cultural differences and suffered ridicule because of it. Jacques Chirac, the future president of France called, it "barbaric American puritanism," and the press turned it into American "insensitivity" to French culture.

As Christmas approached, Euro Disney began preparations for a Yuletide spectacular. The resort, including the park and hotels, was transformed into a Christmas wonderland with the erecting of massive Christmas trees, decorating of windows, and the donning of red and white Santa hats by cast members. Fantasyland hosted carolers and the stage show *Le Noël de Mickey*.

Reindeer were imported from Lapland to pull Santa's float in *Parade de Noël* down Main Street, and *la Cérémonie d'Illumination* brought millions of colored lights to life at the push of a button. The entire spectacle received nationwide publicity aimed at raising the number of French people visiting EDL, as rates were reduced and entertainment expanded.

Projected attendance for the special events was close to predictions. The colder weather had caused a decrease in visitors, as was expected, but Euro Disney officials took advantage of the slacker period to concentrate on training and take stock of the situation. Cast members were encouraged to work in other areas of the park and hotels to expand their experience and knowledge of the operation. After hours parties in the park for cast members helped boost morale. "Now we must create our own identity and a goal that goes beyond our day-to-day challenges," Bourguignon commented in an interview.

Two weeks into the new year of 1993, Fitzpatrick announced that he would be stepping down as chairman to start up an international consulting firm. He still intended to have a finger in the Disney pie as a consultant and member of the Euro Disney board of directors. Philippe Bourguignon would take his place on April 12, the first anniversary of the park's opening.

Before Fitzpatrick stepped down, he still had a few things to accomplish. The first was an agreement with Air France for joint promotions and package tours, including turning the Air France fleet into virtual flying billboards advertising EDL. Another was a promotional show, started at Hotel New York for the travel industry and expanded to include three months of tours to sixteen European cities. The show was made up of a multimedia program advertising EDL, as well as WDW and Disneyland, and character performances and entertainment.

It had been discovered that most Europeans made their reservations through travel agents, which meant a lower profit margin for Disney unless they could expand the market. Special price reductions on admittance were offered to Paris-area residents by as much as 33% in a promotion untried in the other Disney resorts. Star Nights, reduced entry for evening visitors, was introduced in June. The thought was that once guests had been to the park, they would want to return even if it cost more the next time.

Michael Eisner noted that though EDL was actually operating at a profit, they still had to face the "huge costs of servicing a $3 billion debt." A detailed analysis conducted in the winter of 1992 indicated that Euro Disney "was literally running out of money." The hope was that by the summer of 1993 the recession would have begun to diminish and both attendance and occupancy of the hotels would rise. To boost attendance, prices would remain low in all aspects of the park's operation, from admittance to merchandise, and a number of cast members had to be laid off.

In the meantime, Disney would have to deal with the banks. Disney analysts stated that financial restructuring was needed to avoid "losses of several hundred million dollars in 1994 and 1995." Restructuring would mean more bad press from the French media, which could lessen attendance at the park. Still, there seemed to be no other alternative. An investment firm, Lazard Frères, was hired to negotiate with the leading banks, while The Walt

Disney Company advanced Euro Disney enough money to cover operating costs for the six months they thought it would require for negotiations.

Despite all of the Big Thunder Mountain-like ups and downs and media forecasts of gloom and doom, EDL was still functioning on its first anniversary date of April 12, 1993. To celebrate the fact, the castle was bedecked with inflatable plastic forms to have it resemble a forty-three meter tall birthday cake complete with candy sticks, enormous strawberries, cherries, globs of whipped cream, and thick frosting. (The castle as birthday cake idea was used again on Cinderella Castle in WDW for that park's twenty-fifth anniversary in 1996.) A guest list of European celebrities was arranged for a Main Street Parade including politicians, singers, actors, and TV hosts. It was obvious that it was not as well received as the American star-studded celebrity bash on opening day when it was dubbed *La Parade des Célèbres Inconnus* (Parade of Unknown Celebrities).

In front of *La Château de la Belle au Bois Dormant* (which had been nicknamed *La Château Gâteau*), Roy Disney and Mickey Mouse extended their congratulations to cast members for their successes over the year. "The Park has integrated into Europe in a big way," Roy told them, "French culture stands unruffled." Philippe Bourguignon accepted the chairmanship from Bob Fitzpatrick, and Marsupilami, a Belgian character recently purchased by Disney from artist Franquin, made his first appearance. Pixie dust drifted in the air from the display of fireworks, and an unbirthday cake was sliced up and distributed, all of which was shown in unprecedented television coverage. The publicity generated by the event was priceless. Hundreds of articles were written about the celebration in magazines and newspapers, mostly complemented with a photo of the fireworks-framed *Château Gâteau*. Twenty babies born a year ago to the day, and thus sharing EDL's birthday, were invited to the park to become "godchildren" of Mickey Mouse.

All these events combined helped to improve EDL's image, especially since the media had done a complete about-face and now reported about the park more objectively. The Walt Disney Company was no longer viewed as the "monstrous, monolithic force feared by critics." Its early problems showed it to be just another complex corporation struggling to cope with the problems of the world. Within days of the first anniversary celebration, EDL welcomed its eleven millionth guest and became the "most frequented tourist destination in Europe."

Though Disney's image was thriving, its financial situation remained bleak. In an announcement on July 8, 1993, Disney executives let it be known that from the beginning of April to the end of June, there had been a loss of some 500 million francs (US$87 million), and the following quarter was expected to be the same. The recession was still running strong in Europe; spending on food, merchandise, and hotels remained flat in the resort. Tourists stayed away from France in droves due to devalued currencies in Spain, Italy, and the UK.

Bourguignon insisted that the company maintain its policy of being "prudent for the short term even if we ... remain confident in the long term."

Though plans for a second gate had been put on hold, this did not stop the Imagineers from "plussing" what they had already built. It was necessary to keep adding to the park to encourage people to come back and experience what was new and also to make it worthwhile for guests to stay overnight and spend a second or third day in EDL. The Imagineers also strove for unique rides to encourage people who had been to the American and Japanese parks to feel there was something different in Paris.

In March, just prior to the first anniversary celebration, the first new attraction opened in the castle. Called *La Galérie de la Belle au Bois Dormant*, it is located on the castle's mezzanine level and is a walkthrough of stain glass windows, tapestries, and picture boards telling the story, in French, of *la Belle au Bois Dormant*. This addition made the castle, unlike those in the other parks, fully accessible to guests, and that was just the beginning.

Legends of the Wild West opened in Frontierland in June between the Thunder Mesa Mercantile Building and The Lucky Nugget Saloon. The idea was similar to one previously used in Disneyland's Fort Wilderness. Here wax figures of Old West characters were placed in an upper-level setting inside Fort Comstock. Davy Crockett, Georgie Russell, and Buffalo Bill were there, along with a sheriff, a sleeping prisoner in jail, and a Forty-niner who had just struck gold. After the walkthrough, guests found themselves in a Native American village complete with Cheyenne inhabitants in ceremonial dress, tepees, and artifacts. There was a special path that guests could follow through the village. This area was later closed, but the tepees can still be seen, and an occasional puff of smoke will rise from each one, indicating it has not been totally abandoned.

Fantasyland's Old Mill food counter was expanded to include *Les Pirouettes de Vieux Moulin* (the Old Mill Ferris Wheel), based on the 1937 Silly Symphony short, *The Old Mill*. Designed for younger guests, the eight swinging water buckets lifted passengers up for an aerial view of the park before dropping down to skim the water below. Unfortunately, the charming ride backed up quickly with even the shortest of queues, and ceased operation.

Another Fantasyland attraction was inspired by Disneyland's Storybook Land. The concept of a canal boat ride and a second view from *Casey Jr. - le Petit Train du Cirque* were the same, but the layout and scenes were done quite differently. *Le Pays des Contes de Fées* differs from the Disneyland version in a number of ways. Guests clamber aboard from a revolving platform, are not accompanied by a cast member, and the boats are electric and guided on an underwater wire. There is no spiel from a cast member; instead the appropriate theme music is played as the boat passes the various scenes. Guests see miniature versions of the Seven Dwarfs' cottage, Hansel and Gretel's gingerbread house, Rapunzel's tower (originally a non-Disney version, as *Tangled* had not been released), The Old Mill, Eric's castle from *The Little Mermaid*, a Greek Temple and Mount Olympus from *Fantasia*, a scene from *The Sword in the Stone*, the village and castle from *Beauty and the Beast*, and the yellow brick road leading to the Emerald City from *The Wizard of Oz*.

Over in Discoveryland, *L'Astroport Interstellaires*, designed in a cooperative effort between Disney and IBM, was unveiled. After leaving Star Tours, guests would find themselves in this interactive showcase of futuristic technology with video games and Star Course, a big-screen game where players piloted vessels and avoided collisions with asteroids. Easier access to the land was also provided with the opening of a Discoveryland Railroad Station.

The largest new attraction was opened on July 30 in Adventureland. *Indiana Jones et le Temple du Péril* was to be different from all of the other Indiana Jones attractions. Here guests enter through a 1940s archeological dig site on their way to the Temple of Peril, a decomposing and weathered but once grand temple. Once there, they board rickety eight-person mine carts to a chorus of screams from the brave guests who ventured before them. The attraction is actually a roller coaster that makes its way, similar to the mine carts in the *Indiana Jones and the Temple of Doom* (1984) movie, in a circuitous route through the ruins, including a 360-degree loop. This was the first Disney park that dared turn people upside down. Until now, Disney had scorned typical amusement park roller coasters, but desperate times called for desperate measures, and a new thrill ride was necessary to take the pressure off the other extremely popular ride, Big Thunder Mountain Railroad. Further, the prefabricated Intanim coaster was bought from an outside source and justified as a cost-cutting measure. A few weeks after opening, the ride was shut down for inspection after the emergency brakes locked during a circuit, causing minor injuries to some of the guests.

Also unique to EDL was the celebration of European holidays with special events. Thus, festivities for France's Bastille Day and Germany's Oktoberfest were introduced, adapting the park more towards European tastes. European eating habits were also addressed. It had initially been thought that Europeans would prefer table-service restaurants, and so most of the eateries catered to that. It was soon discovered that like Americans, they had better things to do in the park at lunch time than sit and eat, and they tended to patronize the faster counter service establishments.

What was true for lunch, however, was not true for breakfast. The so-called "continental breakfast" of coffee and croissants was not acceptable to most guests who wanted a sit-down meal. Morning room service was expanded to meet this unexpected demand. Another miscue was the abundance of diverse menu selections aimed at the varied European tastes, when in fact, as happened in Tokyo Disneyland, guests were mainly craving American delights such as hamburgers, hot dogs, and barbecued ribs. As Michael Eisner later pointed out, it was like Disney opening a French restaurant in New York that served cheeseburgers.

Eisner's position that staunchly opposed the serving of alcohol in the parks also came under closer scrutiny. Initially, spirits were available in the hotels and at Festival Disney outside of the park but not inside the park. By June 1993, the position was reversed, and beer and wine sales were permitted in table service restaurants. The change made little difference to the financial situation but it did help to showcase French wines and showed Disney's respect for European cultural and dining differences.

Another similarity between TDL and EDL was the way Disney stocked its shops inside the park. The Japanese were more interested in upscale merchandise to take away as presents for those left at home. Disney decided that Europeans would feel the same way and have less interest in low-priced tourist junk. Under normal economic conditions this may have been true, but being in the grip of a recession caused guests to be more selective in what, if anything, they purchased in the park. As a result, efforts to clear out the original merchandise resulted in the shops taking on the appearance of a cut-rate shopping mall, as signs of *Soldes* (Clearance) appeared throughout.

These measures helped to placate disgruntled guests and bring more people into the parks, but more had to be done to placate unhappy cast members. To that end, Philippe Bourguignon created the post of Vice-President for Cast Members and appointed Michel Perchet of *Club Méditerranné* to hold the position. Labor unrest was stifled as cast members now had somewhere to air their grievances. French working practices replaced the American ones introduced before the park opened. The multitude of vice-presidents who often worked at odds with each other was reduced to one when Bourguignon appointed Steve Burke the Executive Vice-President of Euro Disney Resort, overseeing the park, hotels, and Festival Disney.

Again, the press took a negative view of the changes and called them acts of desperation rather than adjustments made to evolve from a park under construction to one in full operation mode. Some speculated that EDL would close down for the winter or, in some cases, for good.

Bourguignon replied to the criticism by stating, "One of our highest priorities will be to continue our effort to adapt to our European environment."

As was to be expected, the price cuts in hotels, admission, meals, and merchandise, while raising attendance by 8 percent and hotel occupancy by 10 percent, did little to increase profit margins. The Walt Disney Company stepped up and injected $175 million into an emergency fund to keep EDL afloat until the spring of 1994. Management fees were deferred until EDL actually made a profit. In October, *Business Week* ran a story describing how EDL was hoping to ease cash flow problems by eliminating 950 administrative positions.

The Economist noted that EDL had lost $960 million in the 1993 fiscal year and gave the ominous prediction that "Euro Disney could end up on the scrap heap." In fact, losses had only amounted to $308 million, but a one-time write off charge of $652 million had been added by executives in a financial maneuver to "disassociate themselves from the dismal performance of their predecessors and protect shareholders in the long term." This was easier said than done. A new sobriquet was applied to EDL by the *London Independent*, who labeled it "America's cultural Vietnam" when it pointed out that the company was losing $1 million a day. Eisner did little to improve the situation when he acknowledged in the company's late 1993 annual report that EDL was "our first real financial disappointment" and later musing that "Everything is possible today, including closure."

Meanwhile, the banks had not been sitting idle. They knew that if EDL failed, they would be left holding the $4 billion investment bag. If Euro Disney declared bankruptcy, it would be left to the banks to dispose of the assets or to run the park. Without the Disney name, the latter would be extremely difficult, and disposing of an animatronic dragon, over-sized tea cups, and a Wild West fort would be next to impossible.

An accounting firm, KPMG Peat Marwick, was retained and told to look into the prospects. The Disney hierarchy agreed to comply but insisted its own firm, Price Waterhouse, be privy to all that went on. Financial statements and figures could be interpreted a number of ways, and Eisner and Wells suspected that the European firm was looking for a way to prove that WDC actually ran the resort instead of the Euro Disney Company, which would then make it impossible for the latter to declare bankruptcy.

There were a lot of people invested in keeping EDL afloat and prosperous. The government of France saw the loss of some forty thousand jobs that were in some way connected to the park. Shareholders wanted to protect their investments. The banks did not want to get into the theme park business. It seemed apparent that with a little cooperation between the parties, something could be worked out.

How far apart were these interested parties? The banks wanted WDC to inject more capital and reduce fees. Disney wanted the banks to lower interest on what was owed and convert some of the debt to equity. The investors wanted more say in what was happening to the degree that they formed an association and demand representation during negotiations. The one thing they had in common was a desire to see EDL survive and flourish.

Negotiations dragged on until in February 1994, Euro Disney announced a loss 30% larger than the year before, citing $95 million in the last quarter of the year. An emergency meeting between the banks and Peat Marwick was arranged where the accountants confirmed that they could find no evidence that WDC was controlling EDL. They were able to confirm that the resort would need an infusion of some $2.5 billion if it was to survive. The March deadline set by Eisner was fast approaching. The banks were left with few options and agreed to discuss WDC's "Euro Disney Rescue Plan."

An agreement was reached on March 14 to restructure the resort's crippling debt and infuse it was the required capital. The plan involved millions of dollars in royalties, management fees, shares, investments, and asset conversions in a give-and-take arrangement between the banks, Disney, and the park's creditors. In the end it would cut the debt by half and pave the way for Disney to show a profit by September 1995. The banks in turn now had WDC more deeply invested in making the enterprise a success and less likely to declare bankruptcy. Michael Eisner wrote, "The worst is now behind us. At long last, we could focus all of our attention on simply making Euro Disney a great theme park."

To begin down that road, a new ad campaign was launched built around the huge success of Disney's latest hit animated feature *Aladdin*. Having topped $100 million in its first month in Europe, it was the obvious vehicle to carry the new Euro Disney image. Television spots, magazine, and newspaper ads showed Aladdin reveling in the celebration and excitement of the resort as he invited young and old to a magic vacation in Euro Disneyland. Special vacation packages were offered, prices lowered, children admitted free, and the resort advertised as a vacation destination that all could afford.

Near the Arabian Adventureland Bazaar, *Le Passage Enchanté d'Aladdin* was constructed with a series of showcase windows recreating nine scenes from the film, including "One Jump Ahead," "The Magic Lamp," "Cave of Wonders," "Prince Ali," and "Farewell." The shops *La Reine des Serpents – Cadeau Exotiques*, *L'Echoppe d'Aladdin* and *Le Chant des Tam-Tams* were converted into Agrabah Café Restaurant, leaving *Les Trésors de Schéhérazade* the only boutique left in Adventureland Bazaar.

Still, despite projections and endless optimism, the resort continued to lose money. Guest spending did not increase, nor did attendance or hotel occupancy. More needed to be done. As it happened, more was being done. For months, Disney executives had been in secret negotiations regarding the new $1.1 billion-share offering from Euro Disney. WDC would buy 49% and the rest would be offered at below-market rates. Unpurchased shares would then be picked up by the banks and offered to an as yet unnamed buyer who had offered to invest up to half a billion dollars in the park.

An announcement was made on June 1 that Saudi Arabian Prince Al-Waleed Bin Talal Bin Abdulaziz Al Saud (who preferred to be known as Prince Al-Waleed) was the unnamed billionaire Disney had been negotiating with. Not only would the Prince own between 13 and 25% of the shares, he also agreed to provide Euro Disney with a yearly $100 million towards a second convention center, which was hoped would help to breathe new life into the resort by filling hotel rooms. Finally, shareholders, Disney executives, creditors, and bankers could breathe a sigh of relief.

Another victory for Disney came on July 29 when former President George Bush, a friend of Eisner, invited French President François Mitterand to dinner at *L'Auberge de Cendrillion* next to *La Château de la Belle au Bois Dormant* in Fantasyland. Until that time, the president of France had refused all efforts to get him into the park. Now he was front and center with the press eagerly awaiting his appearance. After their meal the pair emerged, and it was obvious by Mitterand's stony expression that he was not pleased by the publicity. Bush gave him a nudge and said, "Smile. Come on, François, smile." The photo of the two men, smiling and waving in front of the castle, was on the front page of newspapers across France. Eisner later wrote about the incident, saying, "This image served as a powerful symbolic endorsement for the park."

A second symbolic endorsement was also required at this time. It was decided, after months of discussions, that the name of Euro Disneyland should be changed. Eisner had come to realize that while the name was initially chosen because "As Americans, we had believed that the word 'Euro' in front of Disney was glamorous and exciting. For Europeans, it turned out to be a term that they associated with business, currency and commerce." It was therefore decided to rename the resort Disneyland Paris to better identify it "not just with Walt's original creation but with one of the most romantic and exciting cities in the world."

Chapter Five
Disneyland Paris

THE NAME CHANGE DID NOT HAPPEN OVERNIGHT. The evolution was gradual, changing from Euro Disneyland to Euro Disneyland Paris at first, until the end of September 1994, and then Disneyland Paris after that. Disney executives knew that it would take more than a president's wave and a name change to turn the park's fortune around. It would take a new marketing strategy, aimed outside of Europe rather than solely at the European market. Many Americans saw Disneyland Paris (DLP) as a poor cousin to the U.S. parks, a failure due to mistakes in marketing. Jean-Marc Murro, the sales manager for DLP, wanted to change that. "We have to do something to change perspectives," he said, and invited three hundred American travel agents to visit the resort. He wanted them to see for themselves that DLP had the same charm and quality of the American parks, and enough differences that their clients could enjoy a visit there as much, if not more, than in the States.

More emphasis would be put on the peripherals of the resort, the expanded convention center (a 21,000 square foot annex was added in November), the hotels, and Festival Disney. The latter was described in the 1994 Disneyland Paris Guest Guidebook: "Just outside the Theme Park, Festival Disney comes alive to the rhythm of America. Restaurants, clubs, bars and shops are open every day and late into the evening for tasting culinary specialties, dancing to country and rock and roll music, discovering unique gifts and experiencing the legendary United States."

The main attraction at Festival Disney (renamed Disney Village in 1996) was Buffalo Bill's Wild West Show, performed twice a night and featuring Native American and cowboy performers as well as imported Canadian buffalo, Texas longhorn cattle, quarter horses, and French chickens. The show consisted of re-enactments of "buffalo stampedes and ride 'em cowboy rodeo games" as well as an Indian attack, stagecoach robbery, and the fabled Pony Express "faithful to Buffalo Bill's historic original concept." Even the dinner is themed to the show with a "mouthwatering barbeque dinner."

That it would still take time to turn the resort around was reflected in the announcement of a $353 million loss for the last fiscal year and the drop in visitors to 8.8 million, down just over 10% from the previous year. It was hoped that the results of Prince Al-Waleed's buy in would soon be felt. In the meantime, more "plussing" of the property was scheduled to draw in more people and get those numbers up.

On Main Street, the ground floor of Walt's – An American Restaurant was converted to Lily's Boutique in 1999, and with the exception of the fireplace, all of the Walt Disney-related decorations were removed.

Another establishment to have a number of reincarnations was *Café des Visionnaires*, a snack counter service restaurant located between Fantasyland and Discoveryland. It closed in 1993 to be replaced a year later by *L'Arcade des Visionnaires.* The building was renovated in 2002 to accommodate two institutions, the Annual Passport Office, including the Jules Verne mural, and a smaller version of *L'Arcade des Visionnaires* called Arcade Omega. The latter was in turn closed in late 2005 to make room for the backstage areas of Buzz Lightyear Laser Blast.

One of the earlier additions in Discoveryland was the walkthrough attraction *Les Mystères du Nautilus* (The Mysteries of Nautilus) an updated version of an old 1950s Disneyland attraction publicizing the Disney film *20,000 Leagues Under the Sea.* Opening on July 4, 1994, it allows guests to visit six of the rooms in the submarine seen in the film. These include the Ballast Compartment where Captain Nemo keeps many of his treasures, the Captain's Cabin, the Charts Room, the Diving Chamber, the Main Salon from where guests can watch the attack of a giant squid, and the Engine Room. The attraction was originally designed to be much larger, but financial problems led to it being scaled back, and additional rooms and an underwater restaurant were omitted. The squid attack scene was longer and more dramatic in the early years, but due to technical problems it was shortened.

A project that had been on the drawing board since the early design stages of the park was also under construction. First designed by Tony Baxter and show producer Tim Delaney, they strove for something different from the other parks and called it Discovery Mountain. It was part of the "future as seen from the past" concept that permeated Discoveryland and was based on Jules Verne's 1865 classic *From the Earth to the Moon.* Had money been no object, Discovery Mountain would have been built quite differently from what was eventually constructed. The original artist's concept paintings showed a transparent tube connecting Discovery Mountain to a giant circular window built into Videopolis for that purpose but never used. Inside would have been a unique ride, carrying guests in a Space Mountain-style ride to the moon, where they would tour craters and a Victorian-style moon base. The submarine *Nautilus* was also inside with a high-end restaurant called Vulcania inside Captain Nemo's salon. (Vulcania would later be part of Tokyo DisneySea's Mysterious Island complex.) Guests would have been able to access Star Tours, *Ciné Magique*, and a proposed but never built Journey to the Center of the Earth attraction from inside the mountain. A rickety elevator ride to take guests to the top of the mountain was also designed. It was not for the faint at heart, however, as it was designed to suddenly stop and drop back down at unexpected times. The concept was later used in the Tower of Terror attractions.

Financial problems necessitated scaling back the project. Imagineers' newer designs had the Columbiad, a huge cannon Verne theorized would be able to fire a projectile containing people to the moon. To duplicate the firing of the cannon, Imagineers "designed the world's first inclined catapult launch system" to replace the chain-lift system used in Space Mountain in other parks. The Discovery Mountain name was changed to Space Mountain after construction began in March 1993, though it retained the "from the Earth to the moon" concept in its full title, Space Mountain: *De la Terre à la Lune*, when it opened on June 1, 1995, next to the pool holding *Nautilus*. Though the initials DM remained on the vehicles, this Space Mountain was very different in appearance from the others around the world, as it is set in Jules Verne's time and was meant to simulate a flight from the earth to the moon, as the subtitle suggests. The most outstanding feature is the huge Columbiad Cannon that carries guests up a thirty-two degree slope before shooting them at the moon. The exterior does not have the gleaming white appearance of the earlier versions but instead a nineteenth-century plate and rivet exterior. It is also the only Space Mountain to feature three inversion loops to propel guests upside down in the darkness. Imagineers also added *la Voie Stellaire*, a walkway that guests could use to view the attraction before committing to riding it. It is the first roller coaster with a synchronized onboard audio track, written in a Victorian theme for this attraction by Steven Bramson.

The new attractions combined with the publicity and infusion of cash seemed to stabilize the park, and on July 25, 1995, it was announced that DLP had made its first quarterly profit of $35.3 million. By quarter's end in September, park attendance had climbed 21% from the previous year to 10.7 million and hotel occupancy was up to 68.5 percent. DLP finished the year with an after debt payments profit of $22.8 million, in direct contrast to the $366 million loss of the year before. Critics and cynics began to fear that France "had fallen under the evil spell of an American mouse."

Building on the success of Space Mountain, DLP continued with the space theme with a Space Festival. Videopolis became a showcase for space artifacts from European, American, and Russian spacecraft. A gathering of five hundred children from fourteen countries at Videopolis culminated in a satellite link-up with Mir, the Russian space station, and a conversation with the astronauts.

With the release of *Pocahontas* in theaters in 1995, she was added to the DLP parade and given her own stage show at the Chaparral Theater in Frontierland, replacing the Hill Billy Hoedown that had opened the year before. Chaparral Theater had been built in 1995 to help boost attraction capacity. Originally, the modest stage was a tiered stadium with wooden benches, exposed to the elements, and named Chaparral Stage. Its seating was roofed over in 1997 and the stage was covered the next year. Should Splash Mountain ever come to DLP, it is rumored that this would be the location for it. Plans for a Grizzly River Run attraction, as seen in Disney's California Adventure, had also been on the drawing board. In June 1996, Pocahontas Indian Village opened on the shores of Rivers of the Far West between Chaparral Theater and the River Rogue Keelboats. It was designed as a playground for younger children to run and climb on "swings, bridges and slides suspended between the open supports of tepees." The loading canal for the discontinued Indian Canoes attraction is on the shore behind Pocahontas' village.

The release of *The Hunchback of Notre Dame* in 1997 caused some modifications to the front of the castle in Fantasyland. A Carnival Castle theme overlay consisted of masks, jester hats, bells, and other frills, while the central plaza became Gargoyle Square, where a King of Fools contest was staged. The overlay remained until early 1998.

Les Pirouettes du Vieux Moulin, the old mill at the rear of Fantasyland, was opened in 1992 as a counter service window for ice cream, sandwiches, beverages, and other goodies could be purchased. A ferris wheel was added in 1993, but due to its low capacity it was closed in 2000. It was refurbished for the twentieth anniversary of DLP but never returned to its former glory.

When It's a Small World opened, it was sponsored by France Telecom, which had a World Chorus show in their pavilion at the exit from the attraction. Here guests could view miniature recreations of world-famous landmarks, some of whose windows had animated shorts of children from around the world. The shorts were produced in Montreuil by Walt Disney Animation France, S.A. and directed by Chris Bailey. The soundtrack of each movie was synchronized to the background music of the pavilion. The show was closed in August 2010 to make room for the interactive Princess meet-and-greet Disney Princesses, A Royal Invitation in the Princess Pavilion.

The Princesses were given a proper inaugural day ceremony on October 8, 2011, when the DLP ambassadors introduced four of the Princesses, Snow White, Aurora, Cinderella, and Tiana to the accompaniment of music from their films. Two young "princesses" were selected from the onlookers to pull the cover off of the Princess Pavilion to sign and declare the attraction officially open. In less than an hour, wait times had surpassed 120 minutes. Inside there was nothing recognizable from the France Telecom show, as the interior had been converted into an ornately-decorated queue area with castle-like stone walls, backlit stain glass windows depicting various Princesses' castles, and ornately-carved columns and statues. In time guests would be ushered into one of two themed alcoves, where one of the princesses would be waiting to sign autographs, have pictures taken, or just chat for a moment.

Though few major attractions have been added to DLP over the years, many of the older designs have been expanded, closed down, or converted. In Frontierland, the River Rogue Keelboats and the Indian Canoes nearby had been in service since opening day but over the years were dropped as attractions due to the number of cast members needed to operate them and their low capacity for guests. Over the years, the keelboats would be pressed into service on particularly busy days but by the turn of the century were withdrawn altogether, or at least so it was thought. In the summer of 2006, the boats and their loading facilities were completely refurbished when it was decided that more capacity was required on the Rivers of the Far West. The signs erected when the attraction closed down, "Smuggler's Cove– Danger! No trespassing!" were removed, but the keelboats were not relaunched until a full year later. It had been found that the pilots of the boats now required a French boating licence and cast members had to be trained to qualify for the licences. Finally, in July 2007, the keelboats began their first day of operation after seven years on the sidelines, making River Rouge Keelboats the only keelboat attraction remaining in any Disney park.

The keelboats were not the only boats on the river to have problems. The sidewheel steamer *Molly Brown's* engines overheated on May 16, 2005 as the boat was chugging around a corner at the far end of the Rivers of the Far West. With her engines and paint job damaged by smoke, she was dead in the water. The keelboats were sent out to rescue the passengers and carry them ashore. As *Mark Twain* was in the dry dock for refurbishing, this put an end to steamer travel on the river for some time, as *Mark Twain* was not ready for service until March 2006. In September, *Molly Brown* was put into the dry dock and would not emerge until April 2007. By 2010, *Molly Brown* was out of service again and needed to be totally rebuilt, not coming back to Thunder Mesa Riverboat Landing until March 25, 2011. No sooner was *Molly Brown* out than *Mark Twain* was back into the dry dock and has not operated since. Photos taken by fans and published in online blogs showed the venerable ship sadly in need of extensive repairs.

The Lucky Nugget Saloon's stage show, The Lucky Nugget Revue, starring saloon owner Miss Diamond Lil', was renamed a number of times over the years. It became Lilly's Follies from 1994 to 1996, Lilly's Anniversary Follies for DLP's fifth anniversary, and Rosie and the Rebels in 1998, after which it was discontinued. Today the Lucky Nugget is a character meet-and-greet.

The Woodcarver's Workshop at Cottonwood Creek Ranch, near Frontierland Depot, was a place where guests could buy carved figures of Indians, animals, or birds. The woodcarver left his post in 1995 and the shop is now used as Santa Claus' Post Office during the Christmas season.

While the ships were being neglected in Frontierland, particular attention has been paid to the castle. To mark the tenth anniversary of the park in 2002, an overlay was applied to the front of the castle with a golden scroll encircling a large number "10." For the fifteenth anniversary in 2007, the overlay consisted of Disney characters in gold on the spires and turrets, with Tinker Bell on the highest. A large illuminated "15" was placed on the front, and a Candlebration ceremony was held nightly on a temporary stage in Central Plaza, lasting until March 2009. Mickey's Magical Party replaced Candlebration as the themed celebration, and the castle was overlaid with Mickey and Friends plaques. With a different themed show planned for each year, a more permanent stage was required in Central Plaza. By 2011, the castle was repainted, restored, and festooned with multi-colored LED lights. The Disney Dreams nighttime spectacular required the Central Plaza Stage to be removed and water fountains installed in the moat as well as the upper window to become doors that reveal an LED star.

Le Théâtre du Château, which had presented *Le Livre Magique de Mickey*, in which a giant book on-stage would turn its pages to reveal new scenes, would also evolve over the years.

For a time, *The Magic Lamp Game Show* would alternate with the book, but by 1997, both came to an end to be replaced by *Winnie the Pooh and Friends, Too*. That show had a lengthy run but was moved to the Fantasy Festival Stage for a less-prominent and better-sheltered venue in 2005.

Le Théâtre du Château was then refurbished and became a meet-and-greet until 2009, when *Snow White: Happily Ever After* was presented for a brief time before it was converted back to a character meet-and-greet. In March 2011, most of the seating was removed with a few being left to provide general seating for parades.

In Discoveryland, the original version of *Space Mountain: De la Terre à la Lune* was closed in January 2005 to extend the theme of a voyage to the moon with *Mission 2*. The Space Mountain adventure was revamped and expanded upon rather than replace the old. The track remained unaltered, but the onboard sound was updated when it reopened in April. The new version takes guests further into space after the initial Columbiad blast-off, dodging meteorites, "corkscrewing twice past thundering comets and evading an exploding supernova." Another refurbishment took place over six months in 2015, when some improvements were made to the special effects.

Videopolis evolved from the original concept of a disco-era nightspot when the teens for whom it was designed were discovered to prefer the rides to the music. In time the only partying venues were special events on Hallowe'en and New Year's Eve. The rest of the time, music videos were played, and even they gave way to classic Disney cartoons. Eventually, a stage version of *Beauty and the Beast* took over the stage until 1996, when it was replaced by a series of shows such as *Mulan: La Légende*, *Minnie's Birthday Surprise*, *The Legend of the Lion King*, *Cinema Mickey*, *CineDisney*, and the latest incarnation, Jedi Training Academy, themed with characters and scenes from *Star Wars: The Force Awakens*. Two rooms beneath Videopolis, which had originally held a Space Exhibition, were turned into Arcade Alpha and Arcade Beta in 2004.

Buzz Lightyear Laser Blast replaced the Circle Vision *La Visionarium* show in 2006. The attraction is basically the same as Buzz Lightyear Astro Blasters in Disneyland. Guests board spaceship-like vehicles and shoot lasers at targets throughout the combination shooting gallery and dark ride.

Beginning in 2010, the Star Tours attractions in the Disney parks around the world were closed in anticipation of a new and updated version of the Star Wars story. *Star Wars: The Adventure Continues* takes place between *Revenge of the Sith* and *A New Hope* and opened first at Disney Hollywood Studios in Orlando, then Disneyland, and finally Tokyo Disneyland in 2013. The DLP version, however, was delayed with an announced closing date of early 2016 for the original version, which would not be reopened until 2017.

Captain EO, one of the original park attractions, closed in August 1998 to be replaced by *Honey, I Shrunk the Audience*. After the death of Michael Jackson in 2009, fans began petitioning for a return of *Captain EO* to the parks. In response, the attraction re-opened in Disneyland in February 2010 and in DLP in June. As in the other parks, the special effects used in the revival version were not as spectacular second time around, as the smoke and lasers effects had been removed for *Honey, I Shrunk the Audience* and not replaced. Discoveryland Theater is currently being used to publicize upcoming Disney/Marvel films such as *Ant Man* and *Star Wars: The Force Awakens*.

In 2000, over in Adventureland, a new twist and modified name was added to the thrill ride *Indiana Jones et le Temple du Peril: A l'Envers!* (upside down) when the mine carts were turned to face backwards. The change in direction also necessitated changes in the ride's lighting, as the scenery was not meant to be seen in reverse. Banking on some of the corners had to be adjusted as well. In addition, the cars had been modified for higher capacity to accommodate six guests instead of the original four. In December 2004, the attraction closed for a week and reopened with the cars facing forward again. Speculation has two reasons for the change. First, Space Mountain was about to close for refurbishment and upgrading to Space Mountain: Mission 2, and it was thought guests would prefer the forward facing ride as being similar to the popular Space Mountain experience. Secondly, it seemed that *Indiana Jones et le Temple du Peril* was a more popular attraction without the additional fear factor of the backwards ride.

After the Fantillusion parade closed in Tokyo Disneyland, arrangements were made by DLP to purchase it for their use. Unfortunately, the floats were left out in the elements while arrangements were being made to ship them to France and suffered some damage. The floats not bought by DLP are thought to have been destroyed. Due to budget limitations, only fifteen of the thirty-one floats in the TDL Fantillusion parade were shipped to Paris. Two of these were used for training purposes and later for spare parts. It took almost five weeks for the floats to travel in a cargo ship from Tokyo to Australia, through the Suez Canal, into the Mediterranean, and up to Le Havre. From there, they were trucked to DLP to be refurbished. Some of the floats, already damaged from being left outside in Japan, were further damaged in transit and required extensive repairs. Thousands of tiny light bulbs had to be replaced and entire electrical circuits converted to the European system.

The original cast member costumes used in Fantillusion were also shipped to France, but when they arrived it was discovered that the European cast members were invariably larger that their Japanese counterparts, so they were unusable and new costumes had to be made. Again, financial concerns over the price of new costumes caused some of the Villain floats not to be used, as the cast members could not be outfitted as required. The driver area of the floats also had to be enlarged to accommodate the larger Europeans.

Fantillusion had been scheduled to debut in DLP in 2002, when the Main Street Electrical Parade, which had been running since the park opened, was to cease operation. The problems with the floats and costumes made it necessary to retain the Electrical Parade until Fantillusion finally debuted in July 2003. When the parade premiered in TDL, it had thirty-one floats; the DLP version had only thirteen, and one of these was removed due to budget cuts and was only used on Halloween as the *The Nightmare Before Christmas* addition. The new parade continued through the summer with the added feature of having *Le Château de la Belle au Bois Dormant* coordinated with the parade and changing colors with the music. The parade returned for Christmas and continued to play in the summer and Christmas season until 2012.

Meanwhile, outside the park at Disney Village, formerly Festival Disney, the ambience and original design of architect Frank Gehry had been changed to accommodate more food counters. A Planet Hollywood restaurant was added in 1996 in front of the Buffalo Bill's Wild West Show building. A year later, an eight screen multiplex cinema complex was opened next to Planet Hollywood and was expanded in 2004 to include an IMAX theater. Some of the original restaurants were refurbished and re-themed, a McDonald's was added and Key West Seafood Restaurant was replaced by Rainforest Café in 1999, Los Angeles Bar and Grill became Café Mickey in 2002, and Rock 'n' Roll America, which had replaced Streets of America shop in 1994, became King Ludwig's Castle in 2003. To help accommodate guests who drove to the resort, an Art Deco-themed multi-story parking structure was opened in 2004.

Renovations began in the village in 2005 as some areas were beginning to look very tired. To light the village at night, colorfully-lit balloons replaced the oversized signs and neon lights. A new attraction appeared that year on the shores of Lake Disney in the form of *PanoraMagique*, a high-performing, helium-filled balloon ride. The six-minute ride takes thirty guests at a time one hundred meters (328 feet) straight up into the air for a 360-degree view of the surrounding area. The high speed winch can launch six flights per hour and it is touted as the "only system in the world to be certified and approved as an *Aéronef* (aircraft)."

More vegetation in the form of hedges, flowers, and trees were added in 2008, and terraces gave the restaurants and shops more visual appeal. As refurbishment continued, a beverage stand was added near the entrance and the tourist kiosk was given a new look. Starbucks coffee replaced the Buffalo Bill Trading Company in 2009.

Disney planners over-estimated the number of hotel rooms that would be required for guests to Disneyland Paris. Despite the elaborate theming that was done for each of the hotels, it would take many years of restructuring before occupancy reached what could be termed even close to full. The five hundred rooms of the Disneyland Hotel proved to be amongst the most popular, for even though they were more expensive, they allowed easy access to the park and, if your room was on the right side, a spectacular view. Until the Grand Californian was built in Disney's California Adventure, this was the only hotel that actually overlooked a Disney park.

As the hotels aged and renovations became necessary, it was decided that the rooms should be more Disneyfied. Beginning in 2010, major renovation work began on the hotels, some of which had been overdue for upgrading for some time, in order to improve quality standards and increase guest satisfaction. According to DLP's Digital Magazine, "The pedestrian passages and the lighting in and near the Disneyland, New York, Sequoia Lodge, Cheyenne, and Santa Fe hotels have been refurbished, while accessibility for people with a disability has been a strong criteria throughout these works." By 2015, half of the rooms had already been renovated, and it is expected the rest will be done by 2021.

Ranch Davy Crockett, originally Davy Crockett Campground, has had all of the original 1992 bungalows replaced over the years to the extent that the latest renovations are third generation buildings. Twelve of the bungalows are adapted for disabled people and the children's play area has been expanded. To pick up garbage, an environmentally-friendly, horse-drawn refuse cart was introduced.

There was cause for concern over in the hotel district in early September 1996, when a fire broke out in the thousand-room Sequoia Lodge. The fire was reported at 6:45 in the morning, forcing 1,500 guests to flee from their rooms, many in their pajamas. Some were already awake when the alarm sounded, preparing for the 8:00 opening at the park. The fire was extinguished within three hours. No one was seriously injured, though nine people were treated for smoke inhalation, two of whom were pregnant women who were hospitalized for observation. Much of the hotel's roof was destroyed and dozens of rooms damaged. Guests were given clothes from the resort's shops at Disney's expense and booked into rooms in other hotels.

In 2011 when Disney's Sequoia Lodge was renovated, the project went beyond replacing the old box televisions with flat screen TVs and into the realm of adding sedate touches of magic from the 1942 feature, *Bambi*. Retaining the National Parks theme of the hotel, the *Bambi* touches are sedate with additions in wallpaper borders and animation art on the walls. Even the new TV cabinets were designed to fit in with the theme, and green and gold tones give it an earthier look.

At Disney's Santa Fe Hotel next door, the theme now leans towards the Pixar-animated film *Cars*, with the original desert theme with trails and adobe-style pueblos changed and many of the details and props removed. The *Cars* theme is less subtle than in some of the other Disneyfied hotels, as the old Southwest is modernized to a Radiator Springs and Route 66 look with brighter color gradients. The frieze on the tops of the buildings that is reminiscent of the characters from the films is actually a safety rail required to bring the safety standards up to code. The greatest addition was the creation of the Golden Forest Lounge, a concierge service similar to that already installed in the Disneyland Hotel and Disney's Hotel New York.

The Newport Bay Club's New England resort theme is retained to a large degree, with new rooms taking on the appearance of the interior of an ocean liner cabin. The wooden façades were replaced with a material with a wood-like appearance that can better stand up to the Paris climate. The Yacht Club Restaurant was repositioned and a new Portland Restaurant added to increase dining capacity.

One would expect Frozen Summer Fun to be staged in Fantasyland. Instead, Frontierland's 1,500-seat Chaparral Theater and vicinity was transformed into Arendelle, the home of Anna and Elsa, the stars of Disney's animated feature, *Frozen* (known as *La Reine des Neiges* [*The Snow Queen*] in France). The thirty-five minute show is similar to that presented in WDW's Disney's Hollywood Studios the year before but with a distinct Parisian interpretation. The story goes that some of the cast (including Elsa) has been delayed by a snowstorm, so the audience has to take their places. While waiting for Elsa to appear, Anna leads the guests in a sing-a-long of hits from the film with help from Kristoff and Olaf (who only makes an appearance in this version). As the songs build towards a "Let it Go" finale, a huge screen appears, the music swells, and Elsa appears, singing her song amidst smoke and snow effects.

The rest of Cottonwood Creek Ranch (formerly the site of Critter Corral Petting Zoo and later Woody's Roundup Village meet and greet) has been transformed into Arendelle. The Marketplace has a Nordic-looking, floral-enhanced entrance leading into a photo-op location with Sven and Olaf. Nearby is the Royal Couturier, where little princesses can get a makeover, a stall where guests can purchase frozen treats, and the sole shop, Wandering Oaken's Trading Post (formerly the Woodcarver's Workshop) for *Frozen* merchandise.

Fearful of causing four-hour-long queues, it was decided not to have a meet-and-greet for the *Frozen* princesses, but instead guests can view them three times daily as they parade through the park in a horse-drawn carriage in Frozen: A Royal Welcome. They also appear in the Disney Magic on Parade! along with many of the other Disney characters and princesses.

In the wake of terrorist attacks in the French capital that killed 130 on the night of November 13, 2015, DLP issued the following statement on their website, "In light of the recent tragic events in France and in support of our community and the victims of these horrendous attacks, Disneyland Paris has decided not to open its theme parks on Saturday 14 November. Our thoughts and prayers go out to all of those affected by these horrible events."

News of the attack spread quickly, as many guests had returned to their rooms and were watching television when the reports started being broadcast, resulting in "pandemonium in the hotel lobby areas," wrote one reporter in Paris. "There were a lot of worried looking faces and it became clear that peoples' priorities had already turned to getting home." The Marne-la-Vallée train station was chaotic as people queued to buy tickets out of the area amongst the armed French soldiers, police, and security personnel patrolling the platforms.

Closure of the parks continued into the next day when the DLP website quoted Euro Disney president Tom Wolber as saying, "We mourn those lost to the horrific attacks in Paris. We pray for the injured and we hold them all in our hearts. As part of France's three-day national mourning period, Disneyland Paris will remain closed through Tuesday 17 November 2015 (included)."

The attacks happened as a large number of media arrived to partake in the Disney's Enchanted Christmas press event. With the park closure, the event was naturally canceled as well, but guests were invited to remain in the hotels and take advantage of the amenities provided there. Cast members were required to report to work as usual to help in serving hotel guests in the soon to be overtaxed shops and restaurants outside of the parks. Those who worked as characters wandered the hotels, often in groups, to help maintain spirits.

When the park reopened, attendance was down, with most of the guests being those who had decided to stay in the hotels during the closure. Trying to return to normal as quickly as possible, the park had all scheduled entertainment and attractions functioning. Security was stepped up as personnel and dogs noticeably increased in numbers and bag checks were done with scanners. Cast members were also scanned and subject to periodic locker checks. French soldiers continued to patrol the train station, and police presence was increased as Disney hired more security people for the hotels.

This was not the first time terrorist activities had been reported at DLP. After the Charlie Hebdo attack in early January 2015, a woman had shouted from a hotel window that she was Hayat Boumeddiene, who was wanted in connection with the attacks. Parts of the resort were evacuated as armed police moved in and arrested the woman. As it happened, the woman was not who she claimed, and the resort resumed normal operations.

Early in 2016, gangs of beggars and teenage pickpockets apparently supported by adult "minders" targeted the theme park. Police broke up a vast network that saw Roma criminals wearing Mickey Mouse ears outside DLP, as they allegedly earned £6,000 a day stealing from tourists. The ringleaders now face up to thirty years in prison for "theft in organised gangs, aggravated money laundering, human trafficking, direct incitement of minors to commit crimes, and neglect of minors under fifteen."

At the end of January 2016, in a widly-publicized event, a twenty-eight-year-old man and his female partner were arrested in the New York Hotel for attempting to bring two automatic handguns into the building. The guns were found during a routine x-ray machine security check. No one was injured and the park remained open. The man was also found in possession of a box of ammunition and a French-translated copy of the *Qur'an*, which due to the terrorist attacks the previous November raised concerns with the police. DLP had been the subject of numerous threats from radical Islamic groups in recent years. A dozen police officers surrounded the hotel as a car was towed away from the premises. The woman had initially left the scene when the man was arrested, and though a woman was arrested soon after the incident, it soon became clear she was not the suspect involved. The man's companion was detained a short time later. Paris newspapers reported that the man, a Paris restaurant worker, told them he was carrying the guns, as he feared for his safety. The subsequent police investigation found no connection to terrorists and the man's only police record was for a traffic violation. It was found that the man was in the process of moving and was storing some of his belongings at his mother's home. She did not want the guns in her house, so he decided to take them with him when he visited Disneyland with his girlfriend. The man was charged with acquiring and transporting arms and ammunition and faced fines and possible imprisonment if convicted. In early February, he was tried and sentenced to six months' house arrest at his mother's home in Meaux and banned from possessing firearms for five years.

In addition to terrorist threats, DLP was also under attack from the European Commission regarding accusations of "unfair and discriminatory pricing practices." As was reported in August 2015, German and British consumers had alleged that they had to pay considerably more than French and Belgian tourists for the same travel packages being offered online. Disney officials denied the accusations, saying that price differences were related to seasonality and booking practice demands. The Commission was not convinced and began an investigation in collaboration with *Le Conseil De Concurrence*, the French competition authority. The Commission considers the alleged breach to be a serious infringement of European Union rules, and DLP could face sanctions and fines. "European citizens face too many barriers to accessing goods and services online across borders," Margrethe Vestager, EU Commissioner in charge of competition policy, said. "With this sector inquiry my aim is to determine how widespread these barriers are and what effects they have on competition and consumers. If they are anti-competitive we will not hesitate to take enforcement action under EU antitrust rules." DLP is now required to provide detailed answers to a number of questions from the Commission or face fines. Disney was not the only American company being investigated; several Hollywood studios are being targeted as part of a wider crackdown on unfair treatment of consumers.

As if that was not problems enough, in August 2014, Disney officials reported to police that someone was using stolen credit and debit cards to buy a large number of tickets to the park online and then resell them to the public. A Disney spokesman told reporters that "the company has been working closely with the authorities to solve the case, and that it is very vigilant when it comes to fraudulent practices."

Two men were arrested in July 2015 at the entrance to the park as a result of the police investigation. The men are believed to have been selling as many as thirty tickets a day for the cut price of only thirty-five euros. Police believe the scam could have cost Disney as much as €600,000 (US$655,000) in lost revenue. Online purchases on DLP's website are now being monitored more closely, and security personnel have been alerted to watch for scalpers.

In January 2015, shareholders had approved a re-capitalization plan to raise one billion euros to revive the struggling theme park burdened by huge debt as well as falling visitor numbers. The shareholders voted in favor of a series of measures, including €420 million cash injection of fresh funds from the parent group, The Walt Disney Company.

Total park revenues increased to €592 million due to higher volumes and guest spending in both theme parks and hotels for the six months ending March 31, 2015. Tom Wolber commented, "We are pleased to announce an 11% growth in revenues for the first semester, reflecting improving performance across all our key indicators. Theme park attendance and hotel occupancy are up six and five percentage points, respectively, with growth in average spending per guest and per room. However, we have incurred higher costs, which reflect our commitment to the guest experience that significantly offset the improved resort performance." He went on to say that "we recently completed €1 billion in capital increases as part of a recapitalization and debt reduction plan." On November 18, 2015, five days after the Paris attacks, Kingdom Holding Co, owned by Saudi Prince Al-Waleed, announced a donation of €49.2 million euros into DLP.

Plans for DLP in 2016 included temporarily replacing Frozen Summer Fun at the Chaparral Theater with The Forest of Enchantment. In this presentation, Pocahontas, John Smith, Baloo, King Louie, Tarzan, Rapunzel, Flynn Rider, and Merida join together to pay tribute to nature and the forest. The show runs from February to May 2016, when the theater will close to be refurbished for the return of Frozen Summer Fun in June.

Disneyland Paris will also host its very first Disneyland Paris Half Marathon weekend in September, where runners of all ages will be able to take part in the first fairy-tale half marathon in the park. There will be multiple races to choose from, as well as a big "Race Party" on the eve of the half marathon.

Also, from March to May, guests can relax and "Swing into Spring," taking part in events like Goofy's Garden Party as well as celebrate the changes the season brings, with a multitude of experiences designed to awaken the senses.

Chief Operating Officer of Disneyland Paris, Daniel Delcourt, in an interview in late December, attributed the upswing in DLP's revenues to the efforts and involvement of cast members and much-delayed but finally-accomplished refurbishments throughout the park. He noted that guest satisfaction beat the previous year's results in nearly all areas. Delcourt is very hands on with the park and spends a great deal of time, inspired by Walt Disney himself, touring the parks and seeing what works and what doesn't. Attention to detail is a top priority. One of his first projects is the addition of more meet and greets in fixed locations so guests can find them more easily. In addition, "the means offered for maintenance will be more consistent going forward to better maintain the attractions after renovation." According to many fan blogs and websites, this is a radical and heartily-welcomed change from what had been done in the past and resulted in the hiring of a new subcontractor to handle cleaning of the parks and hotels.

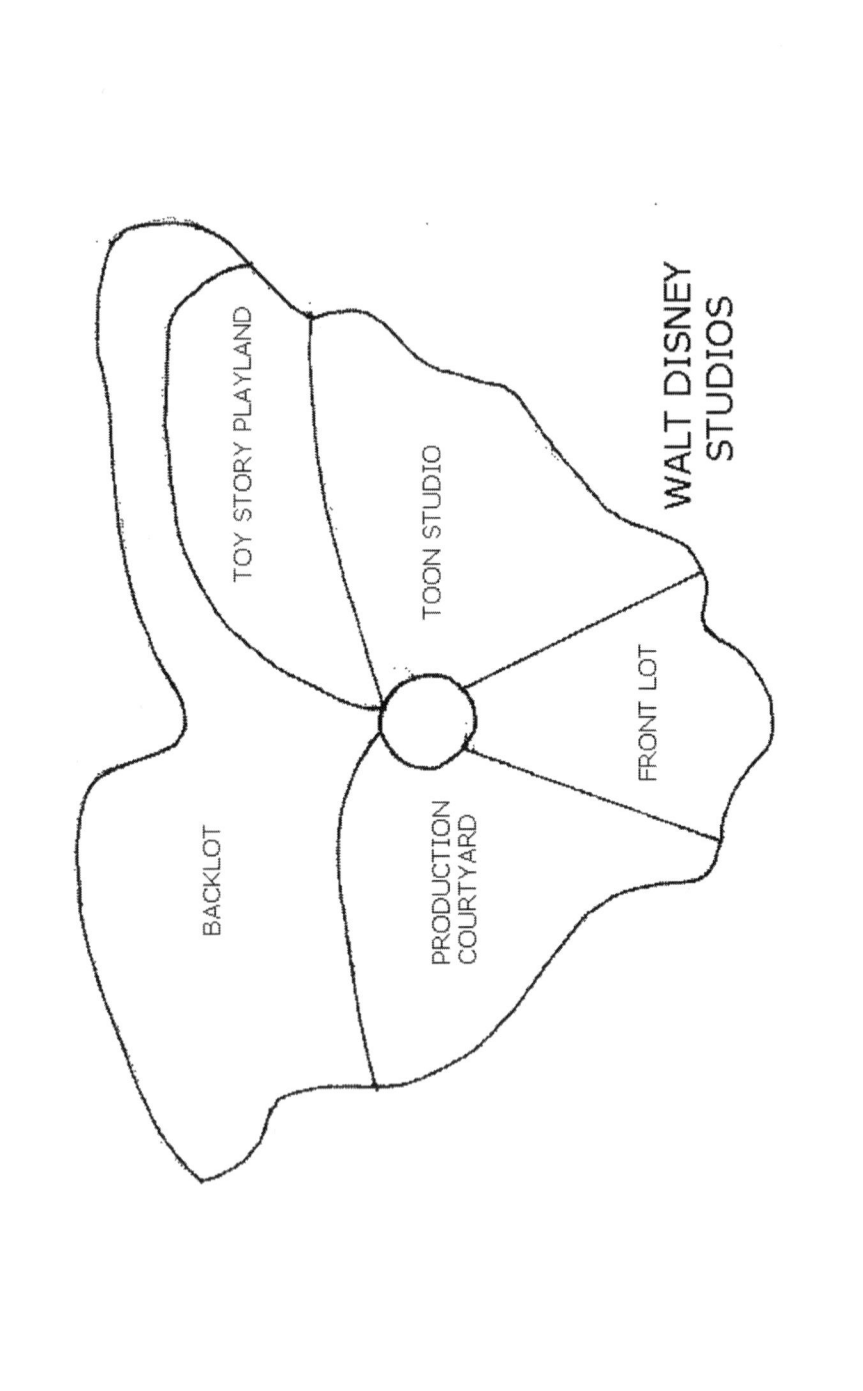

WALT DISNEY STUDIOS

- TOY STORY PLAYLAND
- TOON STUDIO
- FRONT LOT
- PRODUCTION COURTYARD
- BACKLOT

Chapter Six
Walt Disney Studios Park

Disney-MGM Studios Europe was on the drawing board at the same time as plans were being drawn up for Euro Disneyland. The success of the movie-themed park at Walt Disney World in Florida that opened in May 1989 convinced Michael Eisner and Team Disney that a similar park was a must for the Euro Disneyland site. In addition, the enthusiastic response to the Disney stock offering began to make the Disney executives wonder if perhaps they had not thought big enough. Accordingly, they raised the amount of their investments, made plans to increase the number of attractions initially planned, and moved the opening day of the proposed $2.3 billion second park from 1996 back to 1995, and even contemplated 1994.

In the months that followed, it soon became apparent that they had overemphasized success. In June 1992, after Euro Disneyland had opened to less-than-stellar attendance and debts began to mount, it was decided to postpone the opening of Disney-MGM Studio Europe until an unspecified date in the future.

Disney-MGM Studio Europe would remain in limbo for a number of years, always a possibility, always postponed but never forgotten. When Euro Disneyland was renamed Disneyland Paris, the prospective park's name was changed as well to Disney-MGM Studios Paris.

The Spring 2000 edition of *Disney Magazine* made the announcement that the park would indeed be built and gave the opening date as 2002. It was termed a combination production studio and theme park to be built on forty acres under creative directors and Imagineers Jan Sircus and Tom Morris. According to Morris, "We're not only going to show people how it's done, we're going to let them take part in the action."

With Disney-MGM Studios in WDW as the initial model, the French park would "take French sensibilities and the local climate into account." The entrance was to be through a "boulevard of dreams" sheltered from inclement weather, and the main attraction was to be *CinéMagique* celebrating one hundred years of American and European filmmaking. An as-yet-unnamed stunt show was being designed by Rémy Julienne, a well-known French stunt car driver who had coordinated action sequences in a number of James Bond films. Other attractions from WDW would include Catastrophe Canyon and Rock 'n' Roller Coaster. Two others, still on the drawing board, were *Armageddon*, a special effects show based on Touchstone's 1998 film of the same name, and a black light stage show called *Animagique*.

By 2001, the name of the second gate had been changed to Walt Disney Studios Paris (WDS) and a date more firmly set at Spring 2002. At the time, it was announced that the stunt show was to be called *Moteurs ... Action! Spectacle de Cascades* and was to be sponsored by Vauxhall. "The challenge," said John De Santis, Imagineering's Senior Vice-President, "has been creating stunts that not only are spectacular but that can be done again and again."

In order to give cast members a chance to hone their skills in the actual work environment, WDS began on-the-site training in mid-February. Eight days later, a soft opening was held on February 23 for cast members, shareholders, and their families, as well as members of the French Media Group NRJ (*énergie*).

The Grand Opening ceremony for WDS was more personal and low key than that held for TDS the year before and DCA in February. It was held on March 16, 2002 in the Production Courtyard and presented by the usual, though smaller, array of celebrities, dancers, fireworks, and Disney characters. A huge crystal-white curtain emblazoned with the WDS logo covered the three main entrances. Directly in front was a small stage where the dignitaries gathered. Roy E. Disney was there with his son, Roy Patrick, CEO Michael Eisner, CFO Tom Staggs, Paul Pressler (the Parks boss), WDI guru Marty Sklar, and executives from EuroDisney S.C.A., including the CEO Jay Rasulo. The sky was cloudless, this being the only one of the last three ceremonies without rain. Patty Disney, Roy's wife, called it "Walt weather."

Dancers clad in white, the women with black feather boas, cavorted to assorted Hollywood movie themes. Jay Rasulo was invited onto the stage, where he welcomed guests and commented on the development of the resort. Roy Disney was next, stating that with the opening of WDS the Disney Company was "coming home," as much early animation had begun in France and many of the films developed by his father and uncle had a European connection. He concluded with, "It is here that we find our roots and it is here that we find our future."

Michael Eisner stepped up onto the stage next, and after commenting on the weather, said, "We envisaged a place where people could take a true Disney vacation in Europe to immerse themselves in a deep Disney experience. Like Disneyland, this resort will never be completed as we continue to enrich it with new experiences." His speech was translated into French by the host as Roy and Jay Rasulo returned to the stage. Mickey, Minnie, Goofy, Donald, Pluto, and Chip 'n' Dale joined the human hosts along with a horde of children from the British-based NCH (National Children's Home) Action for Children Charity.

Rasulo gave the inaugural dedication in French followed by the English translation by Eisner. "To all who enter the studio of dreams, welcome. Walt Disney Studios is dedicated to our timeless fascination and affection for cinema and for television. Here we celebrate the art and the artistry of storytellers from Europe and around the world who create magic. May this special place stir our own memories of the past, and our dreams of the future."

Roy, Michael, and Jay were each handed a clapperboard by Goofy imprinted with the words Walt—Disney—Studios. In turn, each said a single word: Roy "Lights," Michael "Camera," and Jay "*Moteur* (action)." The white curtain fell as fireworks burst overhead, and the cast members behind the curtain urged the crowd through the gates and into the new park.

Opening day was a success, the only glitch being early that morning, when there was some confusion over security passes that resulted in some senior WDI personnel being left outside the gates. Guests and cast members had an enjoyable day under the warm sun, and the media departed to spread the good news.

Now, let's take the grand tour of Walt Disney Studios Park, as it was in 2002.

The new park was comprised of four "lands:" Front Lot, Animation Courtyard (later renamed Toon Studio), Production Courtyard, and Backlot.

The park's gates are unique to WDS, modeled in a Spanish Mission architectural style in warm peach colors reminiscent of California. The iron gates feature a small Mickey with an old-style movie camera, and the walkway leading to the gates is paved to represent searchlight beams emanating from a series of stars pointing the way.

Inside the gates, a Moorish-style courtyard is centered by Fantasia Fountain, with a bronze statue of Mickey in his Sorcerer's Apprentice garb surrounded by a parade of enchanted broomsticks. Occasionally, the randomizer program responsible for the wave action in the fountain also spurts water towards unsuspecting guests. The fountain is surrounded by palm trees and four symmetrical flower beds. One of the bronze broomsticks has escaped the fountain and is headed across the courtyard.

To the right side of the space, known as *Place de Frères Lumières*, is Guest Relations and Kodak's Studio Photo, set in a clock tower jutting out from the rest of the building. The courtyard is named in honor of the Lumière Brothers, French pioneers in film making, and designed in a Spanish Colonial Revival-style from Hollywood of the 1930s, loosely based on the original Disney Brothers Studio on Hyperion Avenue. On the left is WDS's largest store, called Walt Disney Studios Store for cinema and park-related merchandise. Stained glass and iron work are featured in the stunning entranceway. The interior walls are decorated with photos of the Disney brothers and animators in front of the original studio buildings. Towering over the area is the WDS version of the Earfful Tower, similar to the tower then at Disney-MGM Studios in Orlando. The Mickey ears atop the 163-foot (50 meter) tower are illuminated at night.

Disney Studio 1 is WDS's version of Main Street, known as Front Lot. Guests enter what appears to be a working soundstage. The entire area is under cover, and if it was an actual working soundstage, it would be the second largest in Europe. All the paraphernalia for making a movie is here. The numerous façades make it appear that the movie *Lights, Camera, Hollywood* is in production.

Six façades front the street on either side, with Shutterbugs, Glamor Girl Cosmetics, Alexandria Theater, Hollywood and Vine Five and Dime, The Gossip Column, and Last Chance Gas serving to front *Les Légendes d'Hollywood*. This is the only shop in Disney Studio 1 where one can purchase "all the accessories necessary to become a star." Control central for the daily parades is said to be located on the second story behind these storefronts.

On the opposite side of the soundstage is *Restaurant en Coulisse*, where guests have the opportunity to "dine behind the scenes" with burgers and pizza. The storefronts are Schwab's Pharmacy, The Brown Derby, Club Swankedero, The Gunga Din, The Hep Cat Club, and The Liki Tiki. On the upper floor, façades are neon signs for Cocoanut Grove and Carmen's

Veranda, the latter being an upstairs terrace for the restaurant with a view of Disney's Studio 1.

Leaving the soundstage and turning right, guests enter the Animation Courtyard and approach *Animagique*, a show about the classic Disney films. Donald Duck steals Mickey's keys to the animation vault and unwittingly unleashes scenes from Disney films such as *Pinocchio*, *Dumbo*, *The Jungle Book*, and *The Lion King*. This unique stage show utilizes black light stagecraft and Japanese Bunraku puppets in an "all-singing, all-dancing, mad, magical adventure." The Pinocchio segment was replaced by the Little Mermaid later in the year and the music energized.

Across the courtyard, under the massive Sorcerer's Apprentice hat is The Art of Disney Animation. The wait area has historic animation cameras and devices such as the multi-plane camera, the Zoetrope from 1834, and the Magic Lantern invented in Holland in 1659. In the Disney Classics Theater, guests can learn all about animation, from concept to finish art. This cinematic presentation enables guests to watch Disney characters from many eras take form. In the Drawn to Animation room, Disney animation techniques are taught by a Disney animator and Mushu, the dragon from *Mulan*. The final, and largest, room is where guests can try out the artistic techniques they learned in the previous shows at a series of interactive animation stations. Having been immersed in animation history, guests might want to purchase Disney art at The Disney Animation Gallery under the hat as they leave the building.

The final attraction in the Animation Courtyard is the only ride on this side of the park, Flying Carpets Over Agrabah, also known as *La Tapis Volants*. Similar in concept to the Dumbo ride in the other parks, this ride has a huge movie set backdrop of Agrabah and flying carpets, conjured up by Genie, instead of elephants. The ride lasts about ninety seconds, and the carpets seat four.

Leaving Animation Courtyard, guests wander into Production Courtyard and an area known as *La Terrasse*, where in the early days of WDS would be found half a dozen food trucks belonging to Studio Catering Co., "selling pizzas, hot dogs, salads and desserts." Guests could relax in this area with covered seating before venturing on. The famous Blaine Gibson bronze "Partners" statue of Walt Disney and Mickey Mouse would later be placed nearby.

To the left of Disney Studio 1 stands the Studio Theater building, an art deco-style structure with a large "2" on the façade indicating Studio 2. Inside the 1,100-seat theater, guests are treated to a show in which an actor interacts with a synchronized movie on the silver screen. *CinéMagique*, a half-hour tribute to motion pictures, unique to WDS, stars Martin Short and French actress Julie Delpy. This tribute to both American and European films begins with clips from a number of black and white films until the show is interrupted by a tourist on his cell phone, who begins interacting with the characters on the screen, often with hilarious results. The scenes range from an 1894 clip of *Workers leaving the Lumière Factory* to *Birth of a Nation* (1915), *Plane Crazy* (1928), *Gone With the Wind* (1939), *Casablanca* (1942), *To Catch a Thief* (1955), *The Good, The Bad and The Ugly* (1968), *Star Wars* (1977), *Trois hommes et un couffin* (1985), *The Three Musketeers* (1990), and *Monsters, Inc.* (2001), to name a few.

Next to the theater is the Television Production Tour at Walt Disney Television Studios, a rather long name for a tour of the Disney Channel Broadcasting Facility. After the tour, guests are introduced to Cyber Space Mountain, a simulator in which guests create their own customized roller coaster and take it for a test run.

The Disney Cinema Parade passes through this area daily with floats from Disney and Pixar films. The first float was originally in the DLP parade, The Wonderful World of Disney Parade. It was adapted to carry characters from more recent films and was followed by floats for *Pinocchio*, *The Lion King*, *101 Dalmatians*, *Mary Poppins*, *Toy Story*, and *Fun and Fancy Free*.

The parade ran until 2008.

The next major attraction is the Studio Tram Tour, a fifteen-minute ride adapted from a similar ride in Disney-MGM Studios Florida with a few extra additions. After boarding the tram, guests are taken behind the scenes at a movie studio. A video screen in each tram points out and explains (in English and French) what guests are seeing as they pass scenery, film props, special effects, and costumes. The height of the tour is the "accidental" diversion into the area known as Catastrophe Canyon, where the tram arrives in the midst of an action sequence involving an earthquake and the resulting fire and 58,300 gallons (265,000 litres) of water dumped onto the flaming set. The tram survives the canyon and enters the Star Cars garage, where vehicles from well-known movies are stored. The last scene is from the soon-to-be-released Touchstone film *Reign of Fire* (2002) and involves a tour of the dragon-caused conflagration of the city of London. The dragons are not seen but they are heard, and the heat from the fiery breath is felt as the tram progresses.

Next to the entrance to the Back Lot portion of WDS is the Backlot Express Restaurant, with "all the organized chaos of a film accessory shop," and the art deco-style Rendezvous des Stars buffeteria.

Across from the restaurant is the walkthrough attraction based on the 1998 Touchstone film *Armageddon – Les Effets Speciaux* (Special Effects). Guests enter the pre-show area in either Studio 7-A or 7-B, where they view a presentation and a short history of special effects. The props in the room were all actually used in the making of the film. Guests then learn that they will participate in a re-creation of the scene in the film where the Russian space station Mir is destroyed. Once inside the "space station," a series of catastrophic events occur, beginning with a meteorite shower which causes pipes to burst, lights to flicker, rocks flying across the room, and the ceiling about to collapse. A final meteor strike causes a final explosion, and the lights go out simulating the end of the station. *Armageddon – Les Effets Speciaux* claims uniqueness in that no other Disney attractions place the guests so close to explosive effects.

The fastest ride in DLP resort, and reportedly in all of France, is the enclosed steel roller coaster *Rock 'n' Roller Coaster Avec Aerosmith*. The ride is exactly the same as the prototype in Disney-MGM Studios which opened in 1999, though the story is different. Guests are taken through an

Aerosmith video instead of on the Los Angeles freeway. The name of the recording company where the entrance to the attraction is situation is *Tour de Force* instead of G-Force, as in Orlando. The six-carriage, twenty-four seat prototype vehicles are referred to as Soundtrackers and are purported to take guests through a new music experience. Unique to WDS is that each Soundtracker has its own theme soundtrack and lightshow. The circuit has two inversions and one corkscrew as guests blast through the "hi-amped world of rock music ... all set to the driving beat of Aerosmith" at an average speed of 50.4 kph (31.3 mph), taking a minute and a half to complete.

The final attraction at WDS in 2002 was the *Moteurs... Action! Stunt Show Spectacular*. In reverse to some of the other attractions, this one started life in WDS and was later cloned for Disney Hollywood Studio in 2005 and is expected to make an appearance at DCA in the future.

Guests view the show from bleachers set above the action. The pre-show is on a large screen showing an assortment of stunts being performed previous to speeding vehicles coming onto the Mediterranean village façade-encircled stage. Guests are treated to a forty-five minute extravaganza of stunts involving speeding cars, motorcycle stunts, gunshots, and explosions. The cars were created by Vauxhall and the attraction designed by Rémy Julienne, and the shows include comedic scenes, such as the appearance of Herbie the Love Bug between sequences.

It was not until the fifth anniversary of WDS that any significant additions were made to plus the park. One happened in 2006 in response to requests from guests for more family-oriented attractions. Monsters, Inc. Scream Academy began with two Child Detection Agency (CDA) figures and three interactive Scream Monitors placed between Disney Studio 1 and Studio 3, the *Animagique* building.

After a major financial restructuring for DLP, John Lasseter, the new creative director for WDI, made it known that he wanted to expand the Animation Courtyard with a new area inspired by the Mickey's Toontown idea in Disneyland and WDW. The new land, to be called Toon Studio, was announced on January 11, 2005, by Euro Disney SCA. In truth, it was an expansion and renaming of Animation Courtyard rather than a "new" land.

In June 2007, the Monster, Inc. meet-and-greet was expanded with a live character, usually Mike or Sully, posing for photos at select times. This was replaced by life-sized figures of two CDA monsters in safety gear and then a life-size photo set of Mike to allow photos at any time.

The entrance to the expanded Toon Studio, a concept created specifically for WDS, is between the Art of Animation building and Flying Carpets Over Agrabah. The area is themed as a toon backlot where animated characters work and produce the Disney and Pixar animated films. More expansion for this area was in the works.

Crush's Coaster, in Studio 5, next to Agrabah, is a spinning roller coaster attraction unique to WDS. Here Crush, the sea turtle from *Finding Nemo*, invites guests to climb aboard for a ride on a spinning turtle shell along the East Australian Current. Four guests at a time are seated on the turtle's back for a slow, relaxing ride down a waterway to be greeted by Nemo and some of Crush's offspring. As the turtles progress, the ride gets darker, and soon glowing denizens of the deep appear. All is peaceful and tranquil until the turtles enter a scene of floating mines and sunken submarines. Here Bruce the shark appears, and the pace of the ride quickens as the vehicles go up a lift. At the top, the turtles begin to turn and spin and accelerate as they move downward, dropping frequently as if is caught in the current. Sound effects and lighting techniques keep the attraction dark and guests disoriented until the ride ends in Sydney Harbour.

Across from Crush's Coaster is the Radiator Springs service station, featuring *Cars Quatre Roues Rallye* (Cars Race Rally), also opened in June 2007. Similar in concept to the Mad Hatter's Tea Party ride in the other parks and a bug's land in Disney California Adventure, the variable is that the guests are sitting in cars instead of teacups or bugs.

The next major addition was announced to the press on April 1, 2007: Hollywood Boulevard in Production Courtyard. The new area would encompass much of the land between Disney Studio 1 and the entrance to

Studio Tram Tour. The plan was for a studio lot concept designed by WDI with new street sets, a food court to replace *La Terrasse*, and a major new attraction. Construction continued throughout the summer as storefronts and movie façades were erected to simulate Hollywood in the 1950s. Though similar in many respects to the Hollywood Boulevards in WDW and DCA, the designs were altered, and the WDS version includes two buildings, Broadway Building Department Store and the First National Bank, that occur nowhere else. Speculation has it that should this area prove popular, then the entire Production Courtyard would be converted to a Hollywood Studio to complement the nearby Toon Studio.

On December 22, 2007, Hollywood Boulevard had its soft opening, along with the major attraction The Twilight Zone Tower of Terror. The Tower had been a long time coming. It was first designed at the same time as the Tower in TDL and slated to open in 1994 in Euro Disneyland. The financial difficulties previously mentioned put the Tower on hold, and the structure was erected in DCA instead and opened in 2004. Imagineers finally got the go-ahead in 2005 to build the tower in the center of WDS. Though the DCA and TDS versions are very similar, there are some differences, primarily in construction materials. Due to French construction standards, the Tower in WDS was built with concrete instead of steel.

The Twilight Zone Tower of Terror – A Jump Into the Fourth Dimension (known in French as *La Tour de la Terreur - Un Plongeon dans la Quatrième Dimension*) has a different host from the other versions with separate French and English narrations. While the WDW version has its vehicles in a continuous circular loop and a separate drop shaft, the DCA, TDL, and WDS Towers have independent drop shafts with vehicles that horizontally back into the shaft. The Twilight Zone theme is maintained as guests pass through the lobby, the library, the boiler room, and into the service elevator where their fate is sealed. The climb and drop sequences are similar to those experienced in DCA. The Tower was officially opened in January 2008.

Opened as the Television Production Tour in 2002, this studio tour in Production Courtyard had previously been replaced by the Disney Channel

Studio Tour. In March 2008, the *Stitch Live!* show was imported from Hong Kong Disneyland to occupy part of the same building. The theater was converted into Space Traffic Control, and once the computer connects with an alien spaceship, guests become interactive with Stitch, the little blue alien from Disney's *Lilo and Stitch* franchise. The attraction is similar to Turtle Talk with Crush in Disneyland.

The year-long celebration, Mickey's Magical Party, debuted on April 4, 2009, heralding new entertainment and attractions. Playhouse Disney Live on Stage with Disney Channel characters replaced the Disney Channel Studio Tour. Playhouse Disney originated from Disney Hollywood Studios and in France was presented in English, French, and Spanish. The show featured characters from the Disney Playhouse shows *Mickey Mouse Clubhouse*, *Little Einsteins*, and *Handy Manny*.

The Backlot Express Restaurant was renamed Disney Blockbuster Café and re-themed to such divergent films as *Pirates of the Caribbean* and *High School Musical*. A *Rendez-Vous avec Spider-Man* meet-and-greet was later set up nearby.

The Disney Stars 'n' Cars Parade from WDW was moved to WDS. Originally called Disney Stars and Motor Cars Parade at Disney's Hollywood Studios from 2001-2008, the parade was a procession of twelve vehicles with characters such as Mary Poppins, The Muppets, Mulan, Aladdin, and Disney Villains each in their own appropriately-themed car. The parade began near *Animagique* and traveled to *Place des Stars* in front of Playhouse Disney Theater, where it became a meet-and-greet and then returned to *Animagique*. A *Ratatouille* car was added in 2010, and in 2012, the meet-and-greet was dropped and it became just a parade. Disney's New Generation Festival replaced Mickey's Magical Party in March 2010.

Toy Story Playland opened in August 2010, at the same time as *Toy Story 3* opened in theaters in Europe. It is almost exactly the same as Toy Story Land in Hong Kong Disneyland (HKD) and opened almost a year previous to the Asian park. Advance information about the new area had been leaked in 2009, and at the time estimated to cost €70 million. The concept is that guests are entering Andy's backyard and therefore have to shrink to the size of toys. This is done using bamboo for blades of grass, giant replicas of characters such as Buzz Lightyear, Rex, and a large ball from the early Pixar short *Luxo, Jr.* Toy Story Playland is located behind Art of Disney Animation. Rumor has it that Toy Story Midway Mania, presently found in Disney Hollywood Studios, Tokyo DisneySea, and DCA, will make an appearance in Toon Studio.

The Green Army Men Meet and Play did not last long, but the other three attractions opening at Toy Story Playland were more successful.

Toy Soldiers Parachute Drop would later be copied and installed in Hong Kong Disneyland, but it first arrived in WDS. The parachute-style attraction opened on August 17 and is based on the scene from the *Toy Story* movie when green army men parachuted from the staircase to check out Andy's birthday presents. Here guests can "join the troops of green soldiers for a high flying adventure" in an eighty-foot drop in six-person parachutes.

Slinky Dog Zigzag Spin features the oldest toy in the park, complete with its original 1950s box. The queue is formed from Lincoln Logs at the start and winds through to the inside of the Slinky box. Aimed at the younger set, this roller coaster offers a continuous up-and-down ride on a gentle incline in a loop around a dog food bowl and Andy's baseball.

The last of the new attractions is another that was repeated in Hong Kong Disneyland, RC Racers. This steel shuttle roller coaster is nestled amongst mature trees that in this scaled-down land appear to be overgrown bushes. Based on the orange Hot Wheels toy car track, the ride lets guests "travel at dizzying speeds in Andy's favorite racing car" forwards and backwards on a semi-circular track to the maximum height of eighty feet (24 meters).

Included in the new land are Jessie's Snack Roundup, a food cart for a quick bite or drink and two new shops, Roundup Outfitters, and Barrel of Monkeys. The latter is located in a large Barrel of Monkeys lid, and the shelves inside are made from tinker toys and blocks.

Guests cannot actually visit Toontown in WDS but they can see it, as only one checkpoint by the studio security at the gate of the Toon Studios separates them from the town where the Toons live. The Toons, however, take every advantage of the proximity of their fans by making themselves available at the many meet-and-greet photo sets with interchangeable backdrops around Toon Plaza. Toon Studio Catering trucks are also in abundance, as well as shaded places to sit and relax

The New Generations Festival was also to include a new Monsters, Inc. show, but it was canceled late in its development, and the advertisements for it were transferred to the already existing Monsters, Inc. Scream Academy. Regardless, the new attractions and on-going shows seemed to be working their magic towards attendance. In 2009, attendance topped 2.6 million, but in 2010 it almost doubled to 4.5 million guests, increasing again in 2012 to over 4.8 million.

Construction on a revolutionary new attraction and restaurant themed around the 2007 feature film *Ratatouille* began in January 2012 and was formally announced in March 2013 at the annual Euro Disney SCA shareholders meeting. Robert Iger, President and CEO of The Walt Disney Company, officially inaugurated the attraction on June 21, 2014, and after a soft opening a week later was opened to the public on July 10. Rivaling the building size of Pirates of the Caribbean in DLP, the *Ratatouille* attraction is estimated to have cost around $270 million to complete.

Ratatouille: L'Aventure Totalement Toquée de Rémy (Remy's Totally Zany Adventure), a motion-based trackless dark ride, opened in a new Paris-themed area of the park in conjunction with a new restaurant following the *Ratatouille* theme. The exterior of the attraction is the front of Gusteau's restaurant, and the adjacent buildings form a Parisian plaza. Toon Plaza was renamed *Place de Rémy*, and it is the site of *Bistrot Chez Rémy* and the souvenir shop, *Chez Marianne*. The ratmobiles slide through the circuit on an LPS trackless ride technology similar to that used in Pooh's Hunny Pot Hunt in TDL and HKD's Mystic Manor.

Guests queue on the rooftops of Paris before boarding their ratmobiles on top of Gusteau's. According to the WDS brochure, guests will "shrink to rat-size, duck, dive and dodge your way past dozens of Disneylicious obstacles."

Rémy and his imaginative Chef Gusteau decide to concoct the famous Ratatouille dish just before Rémy and the guests fall through a swinging roof pane to land on the kitchen floor of the restaurant. A chase sequence follows, with Rémy leading the guests and other rats away from the cooks shown as the ratmobiles slide into 3-D domes. They pass through the cold room, under the hot oven, and eventually end up in the dining area, where they are seen by customers and cause a riot. Chef Skinner attempts to get rid of the rats and the guests as Linguini tries to help them escape into a nearby vent. The escape into the walls is challenged by Chef Skinner as he attempts to catch the rats or the guests through the vents. Finally, the guests make it safely to Rémy's kitchen, where they are cooking the Ratatouille. Guests bid farewell to the rat colony and Gusteau at Bistrot Chez Rémy restaurant.

Animagique closed in January and was replaced by *Mickey and the Magician* in July 2016. *Animagique* was shown an estimated 29,000 times and was viewed by some 17 million guests since its debut in 2002. The new show, created specifically for WDS, involves Mickey in his sorcerer's apprentice role and expands to include other Disney characters, with a touch of magic including the Genie from *Aladdin*, Cinderella's Fairy Godmother, Beauty and the Beast, and even mystic Rafiki from *The Lion King*.

Another major change in April was the appointment of Catherine Powell, former WDC Managing Director for Australia and New Zealand, as President of Euro Disney. Tom Wolber, whom she replaced, worked with her through the transition period until July, when he returned to the States to take up his position on operational responsibilities with Disney Cruise Line.

Plans for the future are rumored to include a re-theme of Toon Studio into Pixar Place, similar to an area in Disney Hollywood Studios in WDW. This is to include the addition of Toy Story Midway Mania and the possible removal or refurbishment of Flying Carpets over Agrabah.

PART III
HONG KONG DISNEYLAND

Chapter One
Penny's Bay

THE AREA THAT WAS RECLAIMED from the sea to form the land upon which Hong Kong Disneyland (HKD) would eventually be built was originally the location of a major ship builder called the Cheoy Lee Company. The company had started in Shanghai as a repair yard in 1870 and evolved to construct wooden commercial craft. Moving operations to Hong Kong in 1936 during the Sino-Japanese War, they specialized in power vessels designed to penetrate the Japanese blockade and outrun the Japanese patrol vessels. After the war, they diversified to produce teak sailboats and motor yachts. In 1964, Cheoy Lee Company moved to Penny's Bay, Lantau Island, where wooden-hulled vessels were phased out, and Cheoy Lee became one of the first shipyards to use fibreglass. Cheoy Lee was involved in the manufacture, repair, and maintenance of boats. In time the shipyards produced highly-sought-after yachts, and by the time they vacated Penny's Bay in 2001, they made everything from tugboats to ferries.

Reclamation work on Penny's Bay began on May 8, 2000. A conceptual study carried out by the Department of Earth Sciences, University of Hong Kong stated, "The reclamation methods and fill materials vary over the site with the different stages. The marine mud in the areas for seawall will be dredged. The mud in other areas will be largely left in place. Over seventy million cubic meters of fill material (including surcharging) will be placed in the reclamation area. The fill materials vary and can be marine sand from deeper sea deposits, river sand from Mainland China, decomposed igneous soil, construction waste, and public fill which will otherwise be disposed at strategic landfills or fill banks. The elevation of final ground surface after reclamation will be about 11 mPD. The bedrock around Penny's Bay is largely feldsparphyric rhyolite." (According to Wikipedia: mPD is a surveying term meaning 'metres above Principle Datum' and refers to height of 1.230 meters below average sea level.)

Environmentalists had concerns over whether reclamation would cause damage to some ancient structures at Penny's Bay. Antiquities officials believe that the area could have been used as a port or shelter for ships during the Ming dynasty. They soon found they had much more to worry about.

The government of China purchased the nineteen-hectare site on the north and eastern shores of Penny's Bay from Cheoy Lee for HK$1.48 billion (approximately US$191 million) and paid HK$22.7 million (US$2.9 million) in additional compensation, according to a May 2002 Public Works Subcommittee paper. The paper further stated that the land was for an "essential project with territory-wide significance."

What the government did not realize was that the manufacturing of boats and ships in the bay resulted in an accumulation of thirty thousand cubic meters of contaminated soil. The pollution was mainly due to years of using oils, heavy metals, dyes, and organic solvents brought about by shipbreaking activities and the disposal and burning of wastes on site.

The shipyard had not permitted the government access to the site to do an environmental impact study before purchase. Heavy metals, hydrocarbons, and dioxin also polluted the soil, which had to be excavated and transported to To Kau Wan on the north shore of Lantau Island. Here it was treated by "thermal desorption" and was sent to be incinerated at the Chemical Waste Treatment Centre on Tsing Yi Island.

Protests from Tsing Yi residents brought the process to a halt when they accused the government "of using them as guinea pigs by burning dioxin in their neighbourhood." An attempt was made on February 4, 2004 by the Civil Engineering Department (CED) to incinerate the deadly chemicals, but it was postponed when "Kwai Tsing district councillors, activists and residents blockaded the entrance to the centre."

At the next Kwai Tsing District Council meeting, Wing-tat Lee, a councilor and legislator, put forward a motion strongly opposing the disposal of the dioxin at the center.

By way of protest, seven guinea pigs and petitions were delivered to the council. The motion was passed by a margin of fifteen to eight.

Regardless, CED proceeded with their plan to dispose of ten tons of the waste at midnight of November 25. They then informed the council that the rest of the eighty tons would be destroyed, twenty tons at a time every seven weeks commencing January 4. They estimated each incineration could take up to four days depending on weather, air quality, and transport. All work would be done at night and would depend on the findings of an incineration testing report conducted by the Environmental Protection Department.

"This is not a consultation. They are just informing us that this is going to happen," Suet-ying Wong, a council member, said in the meeting. A repeat of the blockade carried out in February was called for by Councillor Pik-kin Lau, despite the fact that protestors had been removed by police and could expect the same to happen again. Councillor Wai-man Leung declared, "I don't care to sacrifice the lives of my family to impotent government officials.

If they think there is nothing wrong in burning the waste, let them spend a night at the entrance of the treatment centre during the incineration. I will agree with the burning if any of them dare to do so."

Kwok-kuen Yeung, CED deputy head, replied that as burning was the most effective way to dispose of the waste, they were going to proceed regardless of the protests. By the time the chemicals had been disposed of, costs had spiralled another HD$450 million.

Meanwhile, as all this was happening, the Walt Disney Company had been in negotiations with the government of China since the late 1990s to build a theme park in either Hong Kong or Shanghai. Hong Kong was favored by Disney due to its more open policy towards foreign trade. Unfortunately, this very openness also made it the least attractive of the two options, as most mainland Chinese required special permits to travel there, making it almost as difficult to get to Hong Kong as to travel abroad.

Though some Mandarin-dubbed Disney shorts had been shown in theaters in China previous to World War II, since the end of the war and the Communist takeover, the only Disney material one found were knock-offs produced by Chinese entrepreneurs with little regard to international copyright laws. Disney had offered free cartoons to state-run television stations in hopes of selling authorized products, but the plan went astray and only encouraged more and cheaper knock-offs.

When Hong Kong was ceded back to China from Great Britain in 1997, regulations were relaxed somewhat and Disney decided to go ahead with the Hong Kong option in cooperation with Hong Kong International Theme Parks. Imagineering Creative Director Doris Woodward explained that from the onset Disney "was going to be sensitive to local culture in our ideas and designs."

Problems soon arose when Disney bankrolled the film *Kundun*, a biography dealing with the life and writings of the fourteenth Dalai Lama which cast Tibetan Buddhist monks in a sympathetic light. China has long been criticized for its occupation of Tibet, human rights violations, and their refusal to permit Nepalese independence. Chinese leaders vehemently objected to the film even before it was released and threatened to curtail Disney's access to the Chinese market and the progress of negotiations for HKD. Disney went ahead regardless, though somewhat more circumspectly, with the result that several members of the production team were banned from entering China. *Kundun* was nominated for four Academy Awards but took in less than $6 million at the U.S. box office, primarily due to limited distribution. To assist in improving relations with China, Disney hired Henry Kissinger's consulting group and fired Michael Orvitz, one of its top executives who had approved *Kundun* after several trips to China.

Negotiations continued but still did not run smoothly, and the July 1, 1999 deadline originally agreed upon came and went without an agreement on financial arrangements being reached. The two parties did manage to agree on an extension of the deadline. Chief Executive Chee-hwa Tung, Hong Kong's government leader, explained, "The negotiation at times has been difficult because both parties want a good deal. Disney needs to be accountable to its shareholders and for Hong Kong government, we need to be able to strike a deal acceptable to the six and a half million people of Hong Kong."

Not only would reclaiming the land and construction of the park be expensive, but so would creating the infrastructure around the park. Penny's Bay is in a remote area of Landau Island, and though it was serviced by a new airport, Chep Lap Kok, it still required ferry terminals, roads, and other transportation facilities to allow site access to the park and the hotels that were expected to surround it. Tung noted that "much of this infrastructure would have been undertaken to develop north Lantau for tourism and recreational purposes anyway, even if a Disney theme park were not to be built. The government has a longstanding policy of investing in infrastructure to promote economic development."

Finally, on August 8, 1999, the Disney Company and government of Hong Kong Special Administrative Region (SAR) of the People's Republic of China announced their intention to build a resort in Hong Kong. By the end of November, the legislature had approved in excess of HD$22.45 billion in funding for Hong Kong Disneyland (HKD). This included HK$3.25 billion in cash injections and a HK$5.62 billion loan to the joint venture between Disney and the SAR. It was decided that the government would hold a 57% share while WDC had the remainder. Later, Hong Kong's share would decrease to fifty-three percent. It was not a unanimous decision, however; three Finance Committee members opposed the project. Emily Wai-hing Lau, Cyd Sau-Ian Ho, and Christine Kung-wai Loh cited fears "that the park would be exempt from environmental regulation, including the ban on fireworks." Environmentalists were angry that this happened before an environmental impact study had been completed.

A signing ceremony was held on December 10 as Disney executives and government officials gathered to finalize the agreement. The Commissioner for Tourism, Mike Rowse, and the Director of Civil Engineering, Yiu-ching Lo, "delivered the verdict on Disneyland's environmental impact."

The summer 2000 edition of *Disney Magazine* announced the new park but added that there was still much to be done as "right now most of the 315-acre project is under water ... the site must be reclaimed. This process of filling in a portion of the bay with compacted rock, dirt and sand will take a couple of years to complete."

Marty Sklar, vice chairman of creative development for WDC, remembered his first view of the HKD site from a boat in the harbor in his book, *Dream It! Do It!* "…it was all water, and we were warned not to drift to close to shore, because the small shipyard that was about to be displaced was not thrilled about the coming Disney park. Some of their boat repairmen were reputed to be excellent rifle marksmen."

Chairman and CEO of WDC, Michael Eisner, arrived in Tokyo in September 2001. While there, he attended a reception at the old government house with Hong Kong Chief Secretary, Donald Yam-kuen Tsang, chief executive of Hong Kong SAR, Chee-hwa Tung, and Antony Kam-chung Leung, Financial Secretary of Hong Kong. Eisner caused a bit of an uproar when he suggested that Disney was considering another Disneyland in mainland China.

Tsang promptly assured the reporters present that Eisner was talking about the future after the Hong Kong theme park was successfully up and running. Still, the headlines "Disney taking a Mickey" shook the backers of the project until lawmakers and tourism representatives urged Disney not to push the second theme park idea. In time Disney promised that there would not be a mainland park for at least eight years.

"Disney Promises Jungle Fever" was the headline for an article in *South China Morning Post* in October 2002. To stir up anticipation for the new theme park, Disney outlined its plans for the Adventureland portion by promising the world's largest Jungle Cruise attraction, including a twenty-five-meter-tall Banyan treehouse. There would also be a spaceport, Space Mountain, an Obitron ride, and a 2000-seat theater. Unlike the other Disneyland parks, there would only be four lands initially, the previously mentioned Adventureland, Tomorrowland, Fantasyland, and Main Street, USA, where the most expensive restaurant would serve dim sum. One of the performances that was being touted for Fantasyland was a live stage version of *Mulan*, and Disney was already searching the Hong Kong area for a woman to play the lead role.

With the land reclamation project completed, over four hundred guests and dignitaries gathered for the ground breaking ceremony on January 12, 2003. The backdrop was provided by the majestic Lantau Mountains and a mock-up of the still to be constructed Sleeping Beauty Castle. Amongst senior government officials and Disney executives were Chee-hwa Tung; Michael D. Eisner, Chairman and CEO of The Walt Disney Company; Robert A. Iger, President and Chief Operating Officer of The Walt Disney Company; and Jay Rasulo, former President of Walt Disney Parks and Resorts.

"This is an historic day for both The Walt Disney Company and Hong Kong," Michael Eisner said. "As we stand on this spectacular site, the promise of our partnership with the Hong Kong Government to bring a world-class Disney theme park resort destination to the people of Hong Kong has never been more clear. This project represents another important step forward as the company brings our classic Disney stories and characters to the most populous nation in the world."

Over the preceding eighteen months, the government had completed land reclamation, road work, support systems for the thousands of workers that would soon be on site, and the preliminary infrastructure that would support HKD. At the same time, Disney Imagineers in Glendale, California had been working on preliminary designs for the park and attractions. WDI was responsible for development from concept initiation to installation, including creative development, research, production, project management, and engineering.

Angus Cheng joined Walt Disney Imagineering as Director of Development for Hong Kong. He originally joined Disney in 1990 as development manager for Euro Disney Development and also worked on real estate development for the Disneyland Paris Resort until 1993. Cheng served as the central point of contact for Walt Disney Imagineering's HKD-based project team. In this role, he will serve as a liaison with both the Hong Kong SAR government and the Imagineering team in the United States.

Marketing of the park began in earnest in 2003. "We started regular programming on Hong Kong's TVB Jade," said Jennifer Chua, Director of Strategic Marketing for HKD, with live action and animated programs preceded by short documentaries on the history of Disney and the theme parks. It was their aim "to educate people on how Walt Disney first built the parks for his family, and the parks' progression, right up to the building of the one in Hong Kong." TV spots were also inserted in mainland channels in twenty selected cities, particularly in Guangdong province from where most guests were expected to come. The same was planned for Shanghai and Beijing.

Cognizant of the difficulties encountered with the French while working on the Euro Disneyland project, Disney was careful to avoid problems with Chinese culture, traditions, and customs. The ancient Chinese practice of creating harmony and good fortune by aligning man-made structures to their natural surroundings is known as *feng shui*. Disney strictly adhered to the rules of *feng shui* by hiring masters to make certain the park faced east to west, gates and other features were placed properly, and the walkway near the entrance curbed just right to be certain that good *qi* energy did not flow out and into the sea. In addition, two park structures, a water feature and a five-ton boulder, were built based on the advice of *feng shui* experts. Wing Chao, overseer of the master designs of the park, explained that the two hills towering over the site symbolize a green dragon and a white tiger. Working closely with *feng shui* masters, he noted, "We are surrounded by these two beautiful animals, so we are well protected."

Green hats are considered unlucky by the Chinese, so no green hats would be sold in the park. Water is synonymous with wealth and prosperity, fish signify abundance, so symbols of water and fish are used throughout. Even the hotels have koi ponds for good luck. The Hollywood Hotel's position had to be shifted a few degrees to "bring positive *chi*, which means energy," Wing Chao explained.

Local Hong Kong architectural firms had supported the design work and received it in preparation for construction. According to China's PR Newswire, "the site will have fifty-seven kilometers of pipeline, eleven kilometers of cable, 1,000 manholes, and two million cubic meters of topsoil created solely to support the extensive landscaping on the site."

Landscaping the site was mainly the bailiwick of Bill Evans, an Imagineer and Director of Landscape Architecture who had worked on the original Disneyland when it was first constructed in 1954-1955. Though he had retired in 1975, Evans had been called back to work on the landscape design of TDL as well as elements of the WDW resort in Florida. HKD was the culmination of the many years of experience of Evans and his protégées. Knowing that Hong Kong residents have an affinity to horticulture, Evans introduced a number of flowering trees previously unknown to the area and selected species known for their fragrance. Most of the plants used were native to southern China, but some were imported from Australia, New Zealand, Africa, and India.

Using trees to tell stories is multilayered in HDL. The *pohutukawa* tree Evans would plant in front of Sleeping Beauty Castle featured in New Zealand's Maori legend. They believed that by laying their deceased ones' ashes at the base of the tree, their soul would rise up "through the bright red blossoms to the afterlife."

The operation team for HKD was hired locally over a period of six months prior to opening to fill key management positions that would run the theme park. In addition, some five thousand cast members would be hired by the end of 2004. The deluge of applications was almost overwhelming. There were nine times more applications than front-line jobs available for the restaurants, hotels, and theme park. Multi-lingual candidates with winning personalities were given preference. The first five hundred people who had been successful in their interviews were soon sent to Orlando to learn "the Disney way" at Walt Disney World.

"We have never been more confident in Hong Kong or the potential success of Hong Kong Disneyland," said Bob Iger. "Hong Kong is an even stronger tourism market than it was back in 1999, when we first announced this project, and its potential for growth is outstanding."

A fanfare of trumpets marked the beginning of the ground breaking ceremony as Mickey, Minnie, and Goofy bounced onto the stage set before a mock-up of Sleeping Beauty Castle. Next was the traditional Chinese eye-dotting of the ceremonial dragon followed by the Lion Dance, with the cheerful Jackie Chan, Hong Kong's tourism ambassador, leading the way.

After the dignitaries had posed for the shovels-in-the-ground portion of the ceremony, the Grand Finale was staged featuring a multitude of dancers, singers, and, for good luck, Jiminy Cricket. Overhead and behind, fireworks and starburst banners fell from the castle towers as thirty-four Disney characters marched onto the stage to the tune of "Mickey's Magical Land."

A castle topping ceremony was held in the park on September 23, 2004, as a huge crane placed the tallest and final turret on Sleeping Beauty Castle, the park's centerpiece. Hong Kong Disneyland Group Managing Director Don Robinson, flanked on stage by Mickey, Minnie, Donald, Goofy, and Chip 'n' Dale, spoke at the ceremony, "Behind me rises our castle, the most memorable icon of our park. The castle emblem symbolizes the immersive world that guests enter inside every Disneyland around the world. Now, Hong Kong has its own Sleeping Beauty Castle." Marty Sklar later wrote that this was "the first and only time we have reused the design of Walt's Disneyland castle, and the look of its Main Street."

Singer and actor Jacky Cheung was selected as HKD's official spokesman in July 2004. Though virtually unknown in the West, Cheung was described by Robinson as "a household name in Hong Kong and across Asia." Cheung was involved in a number of large marketing events for Disney, including hosting the *Magical World of Disneyland* TV show. He filmed the music video for the multi-lingual song, "One," in HKD and recorded *Hong Kong Disneyland: The Grand Opening Celebration Album*.

Local geomancers were reportedly consulted to provide the most auspicious opening day. Highly regarded in China since at least the fourteenth century, geomancers identify and balance "earth radiations," the subtle energies believed to affect health and well-being. The date selected was to be September 12, 2005. A brightly-colored LED display board was set up in Central's Mass Transit Railway to help potential customers count down the days until the park opened.

With that done, a telephone call center was launched in February to sell tickets and reserve hotel rooms to complement the online booking site that had been in service since the previous July.

For the most part, the construction of HKD went smoothly and on schedule, despite the obvious disparity of a symbol of capitalist consumerism being constructed in a Communist country. The SARS (Severe Acute Respiratory Syndrome) outbreak caused a slowdown as many workers fell ill or failed to show up for work for fear of contamination. Construction costs plummeted, saving the owners HK$1 billion.

A few months before opening, the *Hong Kong Standard* ran a feature that reported Disney's plans to include shark's fin soup in the wedding banquets they planned to make available at the HKD hotels. Though the soup is considered a traditional Chinese delicacy and is seen to have cultural significance for the display of affluence and generosity, it is also a controversial environmental subject due to the method used to harvest the shark's fins. Local environmentalists were outraged at the announcement and fired off a letter to Michael Eisner stating that they "think this is a mistake of the highest order. No matter that such soup is perceived as prestigious by some consumers, from whom you simply wish to make money, shame on you." A reply from Esther Wong, Disney Public Relations Manager, was not long is coming, and she defended the practice by stating that HKD "takes environmental stewardship very seriously and we are equally sensitive to local cultures. It is customary for Chinese restaurants and 5-star hotels to serve shark fin soup in Hong Kong as the dish is considered as an integral part of Chinese banquets."

The response did little to assuage the environmentalists, who angrily reacted to the culture sensitivity reason Disney supplied for serving the soup, as it suggested that the Chinese people "are not also environmentally conscious and concerned about shark decline." In the June 10 issue of *The Standard*, it was reported that Disney was removing shark's fin soup from the wedding banquet menu. However, the soup would still be available on request and would be purchased only from "reliable and responsible suppliers." Further, the soup would be served only after customers had been informed about the threat to sharks, the environmental impact of killing the sharks, and the methods used to harvest the fins.

Environmentalists were still not pleased with the response and demanded the dish be withdrawn completely. The World Wildlife Fund (WWF) became involved when Hong Kong director Eric Bohm phoned the Disney Company in mid-June. He was informed that shark's fin soup would not be served in HKD and the fact that it was being served was a surprise to the American office. In response, WWF drafted a press release that asked, "In the context of Disney's commitment to youth and its public pronouncements of concern for the environment, this decision smacks of the grossest hypocrisy. Does Disney's environmentalism apply only in America? Outside America, do 'different cultures' make environmentally unsound practices acceptable?"

Other groups were demanding a complete boycott of Disney products and planning a protest to disrupt the opening day ceremonies for HKD planned for September. Disney's response was quick. On June 24, they announced that shark's fin soup would not be served at wedding banquets because they were not able to "identify an environmentally sustainable fishing source to ensure the fins sold were not products of large-scale butchering of sharks in open seas." Group Managing Director for HKD Don Robinson continued, "Striking the right balance between cultural sensitivities and conservation has always been our goal, and we believe this decision is consistent with our ongoing commitment to conservation and responsible consumption practices."

Behind the scenes, it was apparent why Disney did not press the shark's fin soup issue. A wedding inside the park or at the Disney hotels was a huge draw and was anticipated to bring in large crowds. Previous to opening day, over three hundred couples had already signed up for in-park weddings. Amongst these was a young woman who wanted desperately to be the park's first bride despite the fact that when she registered she did not yet have a boyfriend.

Labor protests, strikes over working conditions, and a threatened boycott by Daniel Wu Yin-cho, one of Hong Kong's biggest stars, after a problem with some American performers during a promotional shoot, all threatened the peace in the new Disneyland. A pre-opening show titled *Welcome to the Magic* fell flat when little-known singers and actors appeared on stage instead of the rumored celebrity appearances of Johnny Depp, Jennifer Lopez, and Zhang Zhiyi.

A man protesting "against lack of benefits for outsourced park workers" climbed to the top of Space Mountain on July 15 and unfurled a banner that read "No benefits for workers." The protestor remained on his perch for three hours as police attempted to coax him down. When he finally climbed back to earth, he was fired by the New World Development subsidiary that had been contracted to maintain the park's gardens.

By August, the first two Disneyland Hotels were finished. The luxurious

Hong Kong Disneyland Hotel boasted an 888-square-meter ballroom (eight rhymes with fortune in Cantonese), a Victorian maze, and four hundred rooms. It is smaller but very similar in appearance to the Grand Floridian in WDW. The Hollywood Hotel, a more affordable alternative, has a piano shaped pool and six hundred rooms. After passing a noise test for its fireworks display, HKD opened its website to give potential guests a virtual tour of the park.

At the end of the month, ten thousand welfare recipients were given a sneak peek at the park. As an indication of things to come, they had to endure activists at the gates protesting low wages and alleged abuses to workers at mainland plants making Disney merchandise.

It should be mentioned at this point that when activists wanted to protest against the Chinese government, whether it was due to abuses in factories or for whatever reason, they did not form picket lines in their native province on the mainland; instead, they went to Hong Kong. They selected HKD because it helped to garner international attention, not necessarily because they were the focus of their grievances; the primary reason was that Hong Kong had more liberal labor laws, thereby allowing protestors more freedom to air their grievances than they would on the mainland. When Hong Kong lawyer James To Kun-sun was interviewed by the *South China Morning Post*, on the subject he said, "When it comes to injustices committed in the mainland, many come to Hong Kong. Not just factory worker disputes, but business [and] trade disputes also are often brought down to Hong Kong, not because they are seeking a legal resolution here, but because it is a free place to express grievances. We have a relatively free flow of information." He went on to compare that to mainland China where such disputes are never heard about because state media glosses over stories about labor unrest in the country. Chinese authorities have a history of censoring content and reports of activity that could embarrass the ruling Communist Party.

The protests held at the entrance to HKD were conducted by Hong Kong-based Students and Scholars Against Corporate Misbehavior (SACOM) who alleged that WDC knew about abuses of the labor laws in the factories they dealt with and did nothing. In fact, Disney did what they could, considering that they were operating within a foreign and totalitarian country. WDC hired the non-profit group Verité to investigate the allegations leveled through the National Labor Committee, the American human rights lobby group. According to the National Labor Committee, "Disney and its various licensees . . . have conducted approximately twenty International Labor Standards (ILS) audits at these factories since 1998. These audits reflect instances of non-compliance followed by remediation."

Of the ten companies cited by SACOM as producing merchandise for Disney, five were investigated and their contracts with Disney terminated when they refused to address the deficiencies. The other five are being closely monitored, and Disney vows, "We will continue to work with those factories that are willing to allow us access to their facilities and workers and that are committed to improving working conditions."

A week and a day before opening, on September 4, 2005, a Hong Kong Disneyland Charity Day was held in conjunction with The Community Chest. It was seen both as an opportunity for the local community to visit the soon-to-be-opened park and also a chance for cast members to practice their newly learned skills "to ensure that Guests have a magical Disney experience." Tickets went on sale on June 28 and were sold out within three hours. All ticket sale proceeds would be donated to The Community Chest, and Cityline, Hong Kong's leading ticket sales agent, donated their services in handling online sales of tickets. "This will provide an opportunity for members of the public to preview the magic of Hong Kong Disneyland before the park celebrates its grand opening," Don Robinson said.

Before the park's opening presentation ceremony, a special Disney character breakfast was held at the Plaza Inn for HKD executives and Community Chest representatives. Don Robinson officiated and affirmed HKD's commitment to the local community. "The generosity of the people of Hong Kong is evident here today as the park is at full capacity, and on behalf of everyone who supported this initiative, I am delighted to present this donation of over HK$9.7 million to the city's largest charity organization, the

Community Chest. I am sure that the money raised from our ticket proceeds will be put to excellent use."

Some thirty thousand locals visited the park that day, and it was deemed a disaster. Before the guests even entered the park, protestors stood at the gates and harangued them about underpaid Disney merchandise factory workers on the mainland and expressed their concerns about how nightly fireworks displays would add to Hong Kong's already-polluted air.

The park was later criticized for overestimating daily capacity. Was it too many guests or not enough cast members? Either way, wait times for fast food stretched to forty-five minutes and waits for rides went to over two hours in some cases. Pressure was later put on HKD to lower capacity, but Disney insisted on keeping the limit, assenting only to extending park hours by an hour and offering discounts on weekends. This had little effect, as most guests stayed for the full nine hours.

Three days before opening day, officers from the Food and Environmental Department arrived to investigate alleged "unsatisfactory conditions at two food outlets." They were met at the gates by management, who insisted they remove their identity badges, caps, and epaulettes before entering the park to begin their work. Those that refused to "dress down" were refused entry.

Another small problem arose when some of the newly-hired cast members began complaining about human rights violations such as not being allowed to use their phones on breaks, or dye their hair, and only having fifteen minute breaks every four hours.

Despite all of the above, the park was completed on time, provided five thousand jobs while it was under construction, and was estimated to provide 36,000 jobs by the time HKD reached its full size. True, most of those jobs would be low-pay and low-skill positions, but Hong Kong SAR estimated that over the next forty years that would result in an economic boost of some $19 billion dollars. That represented eight times the original investment, but it is based on 5.6 million visitors in the first year and ten million within fifteen years.

"Hong Kong Disneyland will serve as an important gateway for bringing the magic of Disney to families across Asia," said Walt Disney Parks and Resorts President Jay Rasulo. Having aimed at all of Asia as a single market (with the exception of Japan that has its own Disneyland), the world's most populated region was also one of the most diverse in culture. Marketing strategy therefore had to aim at a broad selection of cuisine, as much of Asian culture is centered around meals. Entertainment had to be diverse as well, with park performances being in three languages, Mandarin, spoken by most mainland Chinese, Cantonese, the most popular dialect in Hong Kong, and English, which is the most common second language. The assumption is that about one-third of guests will be from the mainland, one-third from Hong Kong, and the rest from other Asian countries.

Though the "American" part of the park is still apparent and part of the ambience, such as Main Street, USA, Disney was careful to work within Communist Party lines. A partnership was formed with the seventy-million-member Communist Youth League, which made available a major market of Chinese young people. It became, according to Rasulo, "part of an overall brand-building process" to work with that League by presenting Disney characters in activities such as drawing, interactive games, and storytelling.

One day before the opening, there was a limited public attendance by invitation only, received through product suppliers and media handouts, another dry run for cast members to practice before the main event.

Finally, on Monday, September 12, 2005, the wait was over.

The sun was shining warmly as six hundred Hong Kong government officials, nine hundred members of the local and international press, hundreds of local businessmen, corporate management, and celebrities from stage and screen streamed into the park and took their seats. Singer, song-writer, and actor Jacky Cheung acted as master of ceremonies on the stage with Vice President Zeng Qinghong of the People's Republic of China, Hong Kong Chief Executive Donald Tsang, Disney CEO Michael Eisner, and Disney COO Robert Iger. Also present were the Disney Resort ambassadors: from Hong Kong Disneyland, Angela To; from Disneyland Paris, Elena Fumagalli; from Tokyo Disneyland Resort, Tomoko Nishikawa; from Walt Disney

World, Jeannie Amendola; and from Disneyland, Becky Phelps.

The guests were entertained by singers and dancers in traditional Chinese dress waving flags, pounding drums, and twirling parasols. After the entertainers had welcomed the dignitaries, a dotting the eye ceremony was done by Donald Tsang and Michael Eisner, which brought the lions to life when their eyes were dotted with brushes and red ink, after which the stage was filled with dancing dragons and lions performing acrobatics.

Michael Eisner spoke first, modeling his opening speech on ones he had made previously and quoting Walt Disney: "To all who come to this happy place, welcome. Many years ago, Walt Disney introduced the world to enchanted realms of fantasy and adventure, yesterday and tomorrow, in a magical place called Disneyland. Today that spirit of imagination and discovery comes to life in Hong Kong. Hong Kong Disneyland is dedicated to the young and the young at heart—with the hope that it will be a source of joy and inspiration, and an enduring symbol of the cooperation, friendship and understanding between the people of Hong Kong and the United States of America."

Donald Tsang remarked that the opening of HKD marked "a new chapter in tourism for Hong Kong. A chapter in which Hong Kong becomes a premium family-oriented destination . . . in the long term, it will bring in billions of dollars of economic benefit." He added, "We warmly and wholeheartedly welcome the Disney family to Hong Kong".

"This marks a new point of growth for Hong Kong's economy," Vice President Zeng Qinghong observed, "This partnership shows confidence in Hong Kong . . . I hope that foreign companies will continue to invest in Hong Kong."

After the four men cut hand-held red ribbons, Eisner declared HKD officially open at 1:00 PM. Dancers streamed out of Sleeping Beauty Castle followed by dozens of Disney characters. Fireworks burst over the castle as guests hurried off to enjoy the park.

The opening of Hong Kong Disneyland was to be one of Michael Eisner's last official acts for Disney. He resigned his executive position and his place as a member of the board of directors and severed all ties with the company on September 30. He was replaced by his long-time Chief Operating Officer, Robert Iger. The story behind his resignation can be found in the book *Saving Disney: The Roy E. Disney Story* by William Silvester.

FANTASYLAND

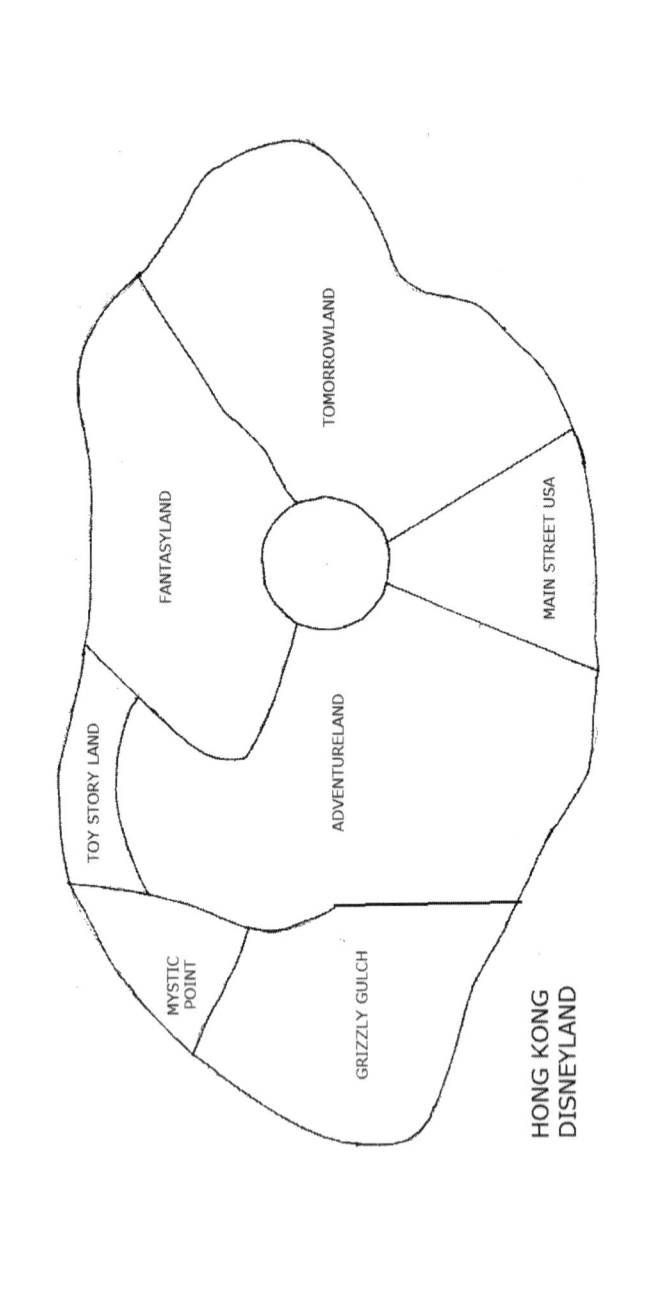

TOMORROWLAND

MAIN STREET USA

TOY STORY LAND

ADVENTURELAND

MYSTIC POINT

GRIZZLY GULCH

HONG KONG DISNEYLAND

Chapter Two
World's Smallest Disneyland

THE PRICE OF ADMISSION TO HKD when it first opened was comparable to other parks around the world at the time. Adults paid US$37.80 and children $26.90 during the week and about $5 more on weekends. In an effort to dissuade guests from buying knockoffs and pirated goods from shops around Hong Kong, merchandise in the park was reasonably priced.

Some businesses, such as Giordano, carried Disney lines of merchandise; Cathy Pacific Airline handed out in-flight Disney goodie bags, and the airport shops had sales "beyond expectations," with HKD logo emblazoned t-shirts being the biggest seller. Hong Kong Post office had issued a set of four stamps to commemorate the beginnings of the park in 2003 and another set and three souvenir sheets to commemorate the Grand Opening in 2005.

HKD is one of the easiest parks to access, at just twenty-five minutes from Central on Hong Kong's Mass Transit Railway (MTR). A special one-stop MTR line had been constructed to take guests to the park. With mouse ear-shaped windows, Mickey handgrips, and bronze statues of Disney characters inside the carriages, the HKD train starts the ambience before guests even arrive at the park. Disney has long been popular in Hong Kong, and visitors often arrive in homemade costumes or at least accessories or garments sporting favorite Disney characters.

Guests leaving the HKD Hotel travel north to the park promenade that connects the hotels, ferry pier, and public transport to the main entrance. Unique to HKD is a spectacular fountain directly in front of the ticket booths and turnstiles of the park's entrance. In the center of the water feature is a whale blowing water into the air upon which Mickey Mouse is surfing, surrounded by dancing fountains. Statues of various characters encircle the fountain, with Daisy Duck in a bathing suit poised to dive, Minnie on a seal balancing a beach ball, Goofy waterskiing, and Donald up the mast of a sinking boat. A medley of Disney tunes accompanies the show, and at night the fountain is bathed in colorful lights. *Feng shui* played a role in the placement of the character fountain, as it is meant to accrue the flow of wealth and guests.

Now, let's take a tour of Hong Kong Disneyland as it was on opening day.

There are three locomotives comprising the Hong Kong Disneyland Railroad, the first attraction guests see after passing through the turnstiles. *Walter E. Disney*, *Roy O. Disney*, and *Frank G. Wells* pull passenger cars named after locations that figure in Disney history, such as Anaheim, Burbank, California, Glendale, and Los Angeles. Those are painted pale green with a dark green trim, while a second line of passenger cars that are named after locales in Walt Disney's life, such as Chicago, Hollywood, Kansas City, Marceline, and Orlando are painted dark red with forest green trim. Each five-car train can carry 250 guests on a circumnavigation "Grand Circle Tour" of the park.

Unlike the other parks, the steam engine sounds made by the HKD railroad are pre-recorded, as the passenger cars are actually pulled by the tenders that run on diesel fuel rather than steam. The line has only two stations on its fifteen-minute run, Main Street and Fantasyland. The Main Street station is virtually identical to the station in Disneyland, though the sign is fancier and not as authentic-looking and shows an elevation of thirty-nine feet instead of Disneyland's 138 feet. The train first travels south on a three foot (914 mm) narrow gauge track on an elevated berm as guests listen to the pre-recorded narration of what they are seeing as they pass through Adventureland and Fantasyland, where the train stops at a station painted pink with baby blue trim, then continues on through Tomorrowland and back to the Main Street Station.

HKD does not have a Frontierland; instead, there is an oversized Adventureland.

Passing by the floral Mickey Mouse head and under the tracks, as in Disneyland, guests enter the Main Street, USA area, designed to resemble an early turn-of-the-century Midwestern U.S. town. The buildings are virtually identical to those in Disneyland, though early plans show a restaurant had been designated to fit under the train station and later scrapped. Another change was the horse-drawn streetcar tracks were drawn on the original plans but not laid down when the park was built. Only the Omnibus, Main Street Taxi, and Paddy Wagon are available for transport up Main Street. These vehicles can be boarded at the Town Square, where a bandstand had been placed instead of a flagpole, as in Disneyland, though benches and cannons are still placed about the area. Here Mickey and Donald can often be found for photos.

When Marty Sklar visited the park in May 2012, he noted how similar HKD was to Disneyland, and he was "taken aback for a moment as I walked" down Main Street. "It's an amazing feeling to be 7,241 miles from home and yet feel right at home in a foreign land."

To the south (left) of the entrance is City Hall, just like in Disneyland, for guest relations and information, with a fire hall beside it. On the north side of the town square is the Opera House featuring *The Disneyland Story: How Mickey Mouse Came to Hong Kong*, with "original artwork, rare film footage, and artefacts that take you on a journey from the creation of Mickey Mouse to the creation of Hong Kong Disneyland, with an exciting peek into the future!"

Moving up Main Street, guests can shop at the Emporium, Main Street Sweets, Town Square Photo, or Crystal Arts with the Arribas Brothers glass collectibles, noting exteriors all very much like the buildings in California. There were three restaurants on Main Street on opening day. First, on the right was the old-world-style Market House Bakery "featuring muffins, cookies, Chinese soft bun...fresh baked egg tarts and other delicious pastries," somewhat reminiscent of a Viennese bakery. At the end of the street on the right is Main Street Corner Café, a turn-of-the-century Victorian restaurant with table service, hosted by Lee Kum Kee and serving international fare from almost every region of China, as well as from Southeast Asia, Japan, and the West for lunch and dinner. On the left is Plaza Inn, whose interior mimics a classical Chinese eatery as if it had been designed by a wealthy American with a love of Chinese culture, serves Cantonese cuisine but has an exterior the same as the one in Disneyland. Unlike TDL, which started with Western food and slowly evolved to Japanese cuisine, HKD began by serving primarily Asian food.

As in the other Disneyland parks, HKD pays tribute to people who have had an important impact of the planning and development of the theme park in the form of a window on Main Street. The first four to be put in place were for Michael Eisner, Robert Iger, Jay Rasulo, and Wing Chao. Thereafter, a plethora of windows were dedicated, primarily to Imagineers such as Tom Fitzgerald and Marty Sklar and executive producers like Lori Coltrin, Skip Lange, Kelly Forde, and Tim Delaney. Harper Goff has a window about the River View Café in Adventureland.

The main difference between HKD's Main Street and other Disney parks is that the streets are paved with red brick-like pavers, while in Disneyland only the sidewalks have them. The red, white, and blue buntings decorating the buildings are also absent. Some of the buildings have different names, the Penny Arcade is called Carriage House but uses the same arched façade, and most of the color schemes have also been changed. Perhaps the most striking difference is the lush, green, nearby Lantua Island hills that form a striking backdrop to the park, and as long as they remain undeveloped they will not intrude on the magic of Disney.

The hub in the center of the park is designed, as in the others, to be an area from which guests can select and go to the land of their choice. The one here has a fountain in the center and the usual gardens, lamp standards, and fences next to a huge compass rose in front of Sleeping Beauty Castle.

The Adventureland in HKD is the largest of all the Disney theme parks and is a combination of that land and Frontierland from the American parks. Whereas in Disneyland the Jungle Cruise is behind Main Street, in HKD there is a huge African-style building housing the *Festival of the Lion King* show. The performance is billed as "a colorful pageant of music and dance inspired by and celebrating Disney's animated classic *The Lion King*." It is similar to the show in WDW's Animal Kingdom, but this is a condensed retelling of the story rather than the Animal Kingdom's abstract version. The show is in English with extra performers repeating some lines in Cantonese. During the early months of the park, it was one of only five fast pass attractions.

Nearby is an outdoor area with open-sided huts and palm trees leading to the Lion King show. Moving west through that, guests will find the Tahitian Terrace restaurant, offering "freshly prepared BBQ, noodle and wok dishes from the South Asia and Guangdong regions." Nearby is Professor Potter's Trading post, the only shop in Adventureland, where guests will "be delighted to find souvenirs for every safari."

Ahead, on the banks of Rivers of Adventure, are rafts to Tarzan's Treehouse. The Hong Kong version is on an island on the shore of a jungle river, so it has to be accessed by rafts similar to, but larger and sturdier than, the Tom Sawyer rafts in Disneyland. Only HKD and Disneyland have

Tarzan's home; the other parks with a treehouse have the original Swiss Family Robinson version.

Once off the raft, guests climb a wooden staircase made from salvaged shipwreck items and sway across a suspension bridge to enter the attraction. As in Disneyland, the treehouse has a number of vignettes showing scenes from the 1999 film, *Tarzan*, including the threatening leopard, Sabor, kindly great ape, Kala, and baby Tarzan hanging from a tree limb. In the study, Tarzan poses as Jane sketches, and in the laboratory, a magic lantern show projects scenes from Tarzan's life. The hands-on kitchen allows guests to try out various musical pots, pans, and whirligigs.

The tree is nineteen meters (sixty-two feet) tall with ten thousand leaves on 717 branches. To see the spectacular views from the top, guests must climb 157 steps. The Disneyland version is twenty-one meters (seventy feet) tall with six thousand leaves on 450 branches. Counts vary depending on the source.

Tarzan's Treehouse is the only part of the island guests can visit; the remainder of the island is restricted for viewing from the Jungle Cruise boats, much like the Disneyland *Mark Twain* cruise around Tom Sawyer's Island, with Disneyland Jungle Cruise sites.

The Jungle River Cruise boats are docked on the north side of the Rivers of Adventure. The boarding dock is next to a small boathouse that is not as elaborate as in the other parks. The boats are about the same size but not as colorful. The line is divided into three queues depending on your preferred language, Cantonese, Mandarin, or English.

The boats navigate a wider river than in the other Jungle Cruises, and the route is an eight-minute voyage around the island rather than through a labyrinthine waterway. The boats chug east to pass Tarzan's Treehouse and then encounter a baby Indian elephant playing in the water with its mother, another elephant showering, and a bull elephant that attempts to squirt the boat.

The waterway narrows as the boat passes ancient Cambodian ruins partially covered by jungle foliage and guarded by giant spiders and cobras.

Crocodiles and piranha hungrily eye guests as the boats pass and emerge into Africa, where curious gorillas are exploring a safari camp as a nearby radio plays "Trashing the Camp" from the *Tarzan* film. The African veldt, replete with a multitude of animals, comes into view followed by a pool of unruly hippos and a rhinoceros with a safari trapped up a tree.

The boat's skipper warns guests that they are about to enter head-hunter country and attempts to sneak by a village. The boat narrowly escapes a barrage of spears and poisoned darts and floats into even greater peril in a narrow, rocky canyon with two rock formations resembling carved faces. These are the water god and fire god, and they are constantly battling one another, as the fire god sets the river on fire and the water god spits water to put it out, enveloping the canyon in a cloud of steam. Somehow, the boatload of guests manages to escape and returns safely to the boathouse dock.

Just west of the Jungle River Cruise boathouse is the Liki Tiki attraction. Unique to HKD, this area is particularly busy on hot days, as it gives guests a chance to "cool off to the beat of jungle rhythms and splashes of water." Guests are invited to enter a circle of wooden statues, "a sacred gathering of towering totems and stand beneath the weathered, wooden faces of a primeval culture." Through a cooling mist comes spurts of water as "those mischievous tiki gods are known to pump water at all who enter when they least expect it!" For those who want to join in with the drumming, there is an area across from the Liki Tikis where they can pound their own boisterous beats on tribal drums.

Jungle Puppet Carnival is a street show where cast members pull huge rod puppets on frames and wheels along Adventureland paths at random hours throughout the day. It was discontinued in 2009. Another roaming attraction guests might encounter is the animatronic, eight-foot-tall, green segnosaurus, Lucky the Dinosaur. The animatronic beast pulls a cart covered with flowers and is accompanied by Chandler the Dinosaur Handler. Lucky had appeared in a number of Disney parks in the States until he was sent to HKD for the grand opening. The Imagineers created Lucky as the first free-moving, audio-animatronic figure to be able to have limited conversations with guests. His flower cart conceals his power source and computer.

There is one other place to eat in Adventureland, River View Café, a tropical-outpost-style building located across from the Jungle River Cruise boathouse. This table service restaurant features "a set menu and a la carte choices inspired by China's regions" and has gorgeous views of the Rivers of Adventure.

Returning to the hub, guests can now enter Fantasyland through Sleeping Beauty Castle. Off to the right is Snow White Grotto, much like in Disneyland and TDL. The castle is nearly identical to the one in Disneyland. The rooftops are a darker shade of blue and the walls are a natural white with pink accents and cornices, giving it a more medieval and less fairy tale appearance.

There are no attractions inside the castle, and directly ahead, as in Disneyland, is the carousel. This one is Cinderella Carousel, built by Chance Rides of Wichita Kansas. The medievally-decorated carousel has horses and Columbia chariots for guests to ride, unlike King Arthur Carousel in Disneyland that has only horses. In front of the carousel is a sword in a stone, as in Disneyland. The structures inside the castle are similar to those in Disneyland but do not contain the same things. Peter Pan's Flight, Snow White's Scary Adventures, and other classic dark rides are not offered in Hong Kong.

To the south of the carousel is the Royal Banquet Hall, unique to HKD, where Snow White's Scary Adventure is located in Disneyland. This restaurant is a European medieval festival tent-themed structure, where guests can "eat like a prince or princess" and choose from grill, sushi, dim sum, or kettle. Inside is an "ornate gothic dining hall, filled with soaring archways, vaulted cathedral ceilings, marble columns, wrought iron chandeliers, elegant woodwork, colorful murals and intricate tapestries."

Next door is *Mickey's PhilharMagic*, where guests can watch a "magical 3-D adventure starring Maestro Mickey Mouse." This show is in a cottage-like concert hall, with an entrance displaying posters of classic Disney characters. 3-D glasses are handed out as guests enter the 492-seat theater and take a seat before the red velvet curtain. Donald Duck is seen asleep as the lights dim and Mickey appears to awaken him. Mickey goes offstage, leaving Donald to prepare the orchestra. Donald comes across Mickey's sorcerer's hat and a wand and "schemes to work a little magic." As expected, things go awry, and Donald conjures a dream world of 3-D Disney animated sequences. The show is the same as the one presented in TDL and WDW, where it first appeared, except that it is in Cantonese.

There are two shops in this area, Storybook Shop, next to Royal Banquet Hall, with "tiaras, jewelry, and dolls . . . something for every young royal," and Merlin's Treasures, a quaint cottage adjacent to *Mickey's PhilharMagic,* "where wizards of every age can discover spell-binding souvenirs and . . . magical merchandise."

On the opposite side of the castle, where Disneyland has Peter Pan, Mr. Toad, and Alice in Wonderland, HKD has The Many Adventures of Winnie the Pooh, the only dark ride in Fantasyland. Guests "glide and bounce" through scenes from A.A. Milne's Hundred Acre Woods in a six-seater Hunny Pot, meeting Winnie the Pooh, Piglet, and the other characters from the stories. This song-filled story book wonderland includes scenes like A Blustery Day in Hundred Acre Wood, Bounce with Tigger, Heffalumps and Woozles, A Rainy Place, and a Party For Pooh. After the ride, photos taken by Heffabee in the Heffalumps and Woozles scene are available for purchase at Pooh Corner. Similar to the one in WDW's Magic Kingdom, this is Fantasyland's most-visited attraction, and on busy days often has two-hour wait times and frequently runs out of fast passes.

At the west end of the land, near the Fantasyland train station, is the Dumbo the Flying Elephant aerial ride. This attraction is the same as the one in Disneyland, with the water feature beneath it.

To the north is Fantasy Gardens, where guests can have photos taken with Mickey, Winnie the Pooh, and whatever Disney character happens to be available. The area contains five themed gazebos "nestled among a peaceful garden," where guests are encouraged to stroll "past colorful flowers, lacy trees and wondrous topiaries" to the accompaniment of classic Disney music. The Heart Gazebo is a Victorian structure where Daisy, Donald, or Marie from *The Aristocats* will be on hand. The Hundred Acre Wood Gazebo is styled after Owl's and Kanga's houses and features Winnie the Pooh, Eeyore, or Tigger. Toon Fair Gazebo is in a festive circus tent style where Mickey and Minnie hang out. Pagoda Gazebo is styled as the name suggests, and guests can meet Mulan or Mushu there. Lastly, Crown Gazebo is a royal octagonal structure where Goofy, Chip 'n' Dale, Pluto, or Donald Duck are likely to be found. Each gazebo has a professional photographer on hand to capture meet-and-greets with the Disney stars.

Mad Hatter Tea Cups is located to the northwest and is basically the same as the one in Disneyland, with the exception of a roof over top making it appear more like a carousel. Each of the eighteen teacups holds four guests on three separate turntables which are mounted on a single large turntable. The speed and craziness of each cup can be controlled with a steering wheel in the center of the cup. There is a sign at the entrance advising people of the capacity of the tea cups and a suggestion to watch children and a caution that states, "You should be sober and in good health to ride."

Just east of the teacups is Clopin's Festival of Foods, inspired by the Festival of Foods scene in *The Hunchback of Notre Dame* (1996). Four show kitchens offer "curries, dim sum, sushi and tempura, and chicken and beef favorites."

The first venue to be constructed outside the berm was the Storybook Theater for *The Golden Mickeys*. This musical stage show is presented as an awards ceremony, with Disney characters as nominees for awards in heroism, romance, friendship, adventure, and villainy. It was first performed in September 2003 on the Disney Cruise Line ship *Disney Wonder*. The HKD version is narrated in Cantonese with Chinese and English subtitles, and the songs are all in English.

A dance performance of the title song begins the show as cast members prepare costumes and take photos of the celebrities as they arrive. Footage of Disney characters arriving is shown on screens beside the main stage.

Interviews are conducted by host Bebe, who talks to Mickey, Minnie, Goofy, Donald, and Pluto between song and dance routines. In addition to martial arts, fireworks, puppetry, and aerial acrobatics, other costumed characters from *Toy Story*, *The Hunchback of Notre Dame*, *Tarzan*, *Mulan*, *Lilo and Stitch*, and *Beauty and the Beast* also perform.

Similar to Disneyland in Anaheim when it first opened, there was not a lot in Tomorrowland in 2005. The land's décor has an emphasis on metallic trim dominated by purple and blue, and most of it is unique to HKD. Entering from the hub, guests pass between two restaurants; the Comet Café is on the left, a quick serve restaurant with "freshly prepared BBQ, wok and noodle specialties, served in an interstellar setting" from the Jiang Nan Region; on the right is the Starliner Diner, "featuring out of this world burgers, chicken, salads and desserts." These buildings are unique to HKD; the Comet Café has a dark blue, sky blue, and orange roof and covering for outside seating, and the Starliner Diner's façade is shaped like a starship on a gantry. The Starliner is reputed to have the fastest service in the park, with 1,750 meals possible in an hour.

The first attraction encountered is the Obitron, based on Disneyland's Astro Jets attraction. Every Disney park has a version of this ride, and pilots are able to control how high they fly and "initiate sound effects by pressing buttons inside." The HKD Obitron has saucer-shaped vehicles seating up to four passengers in an effort to expand capacity, unlike the other parks, which could only seat two in their rocket-shaped pods. The Obitron itself is designed as "a constellation of planets inspired by centuries-old astronomical designs."

To the west is Space Mountain, which at first glance looks exactly like the one in Disneyland. In fact, it is, with the exception of the spires on top which are straight and pointed, while the ones at HKD look more like ship's masts. Space Mountain is described as "an indoor, rollercoaster-type attraction designed for adventurous cosmonauts" (note the Russian term instead of the American "astronaut"). It is more like the refurbished version in Disneyland finished in 2005 rather than the original one opened in 1977.

The Space Station built in Disneyland and TDL is absent, replaced by a dark queue decorated with neon-colored planets and star patterns. There are a few variations in the show elements like a hyper-speed tunnel, and the boarding area is smaller than in most theme parks and sports overhead glowing planetoids. There is also onboard audio, and the projections are similar to those used in Disneyland's Ghost Galaxy during Hallowe'en, which, incidentally, originated in HKD.

There are only two shops in Tomorrowland. Space Traders, near Space Mountain, where guests can purchase "an out-of-this-world selection of interstellar merchandise," and Star Command Supplies, adjacent to Buzz Lightyear Astro Blasters, where there is everything from "space-age toys to Disney character themed souvenirs." Walking east towards the next attraction, guests pass by the under construction Autopia tracks, just outside the northern berm.

Buzz Lightyear Astro Blasters is another of the more popular attractions in HKD. Here guests can "Fire lasers to defeat Zurg in this shooting-gallery attraction that puts you in the center of a thrilling space battle." The attraction is at various stages of development in various Disney parks depending on the technology available when it was installed. Being one of the newest, the HKD version is one of the more advanced. Though the name changes in other parks, the attraction itself is basically the same. It is a combination dark ride and shooting gallery on an omnimover system in which guests "maneuver an XP-38 space cruiser through the shadowy Gamma Quadrant and fire lasers from an onboard cannon to stop Zurg and score points."

Returning to the hub, guests may arrive just in time for the fireworks over Sleeping Beauty Castle. The nightly fireworks show, *Disney in the Stars*, is similar to the *Fantasy in the Sky* show at other Disney theme parks, wherein pyrotechnics and music from Disney classic films are coordinated. Guests have blogged that they prefer the HKD show over the U.S. versions "due to its soundtrack and more engaging set of bursts. There are spinners on the face of the Castle and a wider spread of near-level fireworks." The show was part of the park's inaugural ceremony.

At first, Disney was reluctant to release attendance figures, particularly after reports in the press began to speculate that those figures might not be as high as expected. Finally, on November 24, Disney announced that HKD had surpassed one million guests in its first two months. But local negative publicity had its effect on attendance, and to boost the number of people going to the park, HKD offered a $50 discount to ticket buyers with Hong Kong identification cards in the month before Christmas.

The park was off to a slow start, but there was much more to come.

Chapter Three
"The Happiest Land of Fortune"

THE SMALL SIZE OF HONG KONG DISNEYLAND was cited as one of the main reasons for low attendance figures. Many guests felt they could see it all in one day and felt no need to return. In fact, the new and smaller park reflected Disney's new strategy: instead of trying to build a large and extensive park all at once, management decided to open the park in phases, a lesson learned in Paris. It would soon become obvious how well that plan worked.

Business Week quoted Hong Kong Disneyland Managing Director Andrew Kam as saying that expansion was vital to the park's success. HKD has plenty of room to grow, as only half of the available land was being utilized. "Expansion is part of the strategy to make this park work for Hong Kong,"

Kam told reporters and remarked that the SAR government and the Disney Company were "very much interested in growing the business," as new attractions "will drive our future growth."

A month after the grand opening of HKD, a forty-eight-year-old former security guard for the park climbed to the top of Space Mountain and threatened to slash his own throat to protest his dismissal. He was wearing a white t-shirt with the words "reveal the truth" and "SOS" written in red paint. According to spokeswoman Esther Wong, speaking to the press, the guard had been fired for violating park rules, including using obscene language on the job. Police and fire-fighters attended the scene and spent two hours talking to the man before he would come down.

There had also apparently been some sixty complaints from cast members to trade union representatives about Disney abusing labor laws regarding long hours and short rest times in just one month since the park opened. However, Ricky Chan of the Labor Department contradicted those statements and said that Disney had not violated any labor laws and had in fact discussed the problems with the unions and made improvements.

The New Year did not begin well. On the face of it, it seemed a good idea to boost attendance by offering Hong Kong residents two-day tickets for the price of one. The idea did work. Attendance was increased, unfortunately by more than was expected. Chinese New Year was one of the "golden weeks" that the government of the People's Republic of China mandated for the people. It was a semi-annual, seven-day national holiday, and it appears many people though it would be a good time to visit this new park they had heard so much about.

It did not take long before an overabundance of people arrived at the turnstiles, already having tickets they bought online and wanting to enter the park. The park filled quickly and even before the afternoon came, it was full to capacity. Cast members closed the gates. Complaints began at once, as the waiting people had valid tickets; they had already paid and yet they were being refused entry. Some attempted to force their way in by climbing over the gates. They hurled abuse at the cast members and rattled and banged on the entrances. The magic of HKD was wearing thin, and for the rest of "golden week," the crowds were noticeably thinner. It was a public relations disaster.

Bill Ernest, Executive Vice-President and managing director of Hong Kong Disneyland who had a wealth of experience with theme parks, hotels, and cruise ships, offered an emotional apology and promised to have a better understanding of Chinese culture. Management took a lesson from the debacle and revised their ticketing policy by designating "special days" near Chinese holidays when only date-specific tickets would be accepted. In June it was announced that summer passes would be released in an effort to boost attendance.

It was not until July 13 that a significant increase was seen in attendance, as the first part of the expansion plans were completed and opened to the public. Three new, and hopefully appealing, attractions should draw people in.

All three were in the underdeveloped area of Tomorrowland. *Stitch Encounter*, an interactive show, was a combination of digital puppetry and real-time animation. Guests can have conversations with Stitch, aka Experiment 626 from the *Lilo and Stitch* movies and TV shows, in any one of the usual three languages. Located in Space Traffic Control, next to Space Mountain, it is similar to the *Stitch Alive!* show at Walt Disney Studios in Disneyland Paris.

The second new attraction was Autopia, unusual in that this was the first Disney park to not have an Autopia on opening day, though it was under construction. It differs from the other versions in that the cars are electric and have an onboard audio system. Sponsored by Honda Motors, the "highways of tomorrow" run through lush tropical jungles on the outside of the berm on the north side of the park beside Space Mountain.

UFO Zone was the third of the new attractions. This outdoor aquatic attraction is unique to HKD and is located between the Autopia entrance and Space Mountain in what had originally been an open rest area. The idea is similar to the Liki Tikis in Adventureland, designed to cool guests off by squirting "water ray guns" at alien invaders.

Adding an extra bonus to Summer Passes helped to boost attendance as sixty thousand passes were sold from July 1. Still, the attendance goal was not reached, as by the time the first anniversary rolled around, only five million of the anticipated 5.6 million guests had entered the park. It was suggested that this was mainly due to fewer than expected guests from mainland China.

The date of the first anniversary, September 12, 2006, was marred by rain and protestors agitating against alleged sweatshop practices for Disney merchandise. HKD launched an annual pass scheme at the end of September and held its first Hallowe'en celebration throughout the month of October.

Still, low attendance numbers plagued management. The press announcement on September 28 that WDC was thinking about building another Disneyland in Seoul, South Korea did little to bolster the public's or the government's faith in the success of HKD, as another Asian Disney park would only add more competition. In a bid to entice more people to the park, ticket prices for Hong Kong residents were cut by HK$50 for the month of November. Finally, as the year ended, Disney announced plans for more additions to the park over the next two years.

The *South China Morning Post* managed to get a hold of some confidential documents that confirmed that the park had registered a HK$1.6 billion deficit in its first two years of operation. Attendance for the second year had amounted to only 4.17 million guests, a figure that incited local legislators invested in HKD. *Business Week* reported that "Disney agreed to waive management and royalties for two years after the joint venture failed to meet performance targets."

With no major construction projects scheduled to be completed in 2007, the park looked for other new attractions to entice guests. One such was the Pirate Invasion of Adventureland, slated to run from May 4 through June 30. Though HKD does not have a Pirates of the Caribbean attraction like most of the other parks, the Pirate takeover was extensive with entertainment, guests interacting with the roaming pirates, and decorations fitting a pirate lair. Jack

Sparrow's Boot Camp became the place where guests could learn to be scurvy pirates, Pirates Procession was where they could learn swashbuckling dances, and pirate treasure could be won by "cracking the secret code throughout Pirateland in Treasure Hunt" or in the Tiki Toss Game. Special menus were offered at the restaurants where one could order Captain Hook's Butcher's Cut or Jack's Treasure Pot. Even Mickey, Goofy, and Pluto were recruited by the pirates to dress in buccaneer costumes and pose for pictures.

So popular was the Pirate Takeover by Captain Jack Sparrow and crew that it was extended until the end of August and Adventureland was temporarily renamed Pirateland. A new comedy performance called *Pirates Swab the Deck* was "filled with watery antics" and often ended with pirates and guests getting wet.

Naturally all of this pirating was accompanied by over one thousand related merchandise items: "from plush toys and pins to souvenirs and stationery, these colorful keepsakes will make true collector items or gifts for friends and family."

The summer of 2007 was unusually hot, even for Hong Kong, and park management decided that perhaps that was contributing to the low attendance. To remedy that, more water-related affairs were introduced. Making its dazzling debut is Mickey's Water Works Parade, "a brand new, vibrantly waterful, parade," exclusive to HKD "to keep guests wet and cool all summer long." It also accomplished the dual task of "keeping the landscape at Hong Kong Disneyland lush and beautiful. Using a variety of sprinklers, hoses and spouts, the gang are ready to water the plants and the guests." Bonaqua-mineralized water sponsored the new afternoon parade of "brand new floats" and "100 energetic performers including thirty Disney characters to perform water filled antics to an original musical score. Guests can join in the 'splashtastic' extravaganza or keep dry at the designated dry zones as indicated in the Times Guide." The Main Street Water Brigade also got into the act of keeping guests cool, when three comedic firefighters surprised "guests several times a day with splashy performances."

The entire keeping cool through water promotion was under the banner of "Mickey's Summer Blast" and was introduced in a special ceremony at the forecourt of Sleeping Beauty Castle. Bill Ernest and Jasmine Law, the HKD ambassador for 2007, were joined by members of the popular Taiwanese band, Fahrenheit, who were doing nightly performances, before "immersing themselves in the wet, wild and animated entertainment and attractions that guests can enjoy from now till the end of the summer." In keeping with the Summer Blast theme, Stitch and his pals held an electrifying beach party at the forecourt of Sleeping Beauty Castle. Meanwhile, Mickey and Minnie, in Hawaiian garb, held meet-and-greets in the town square gazebo, and the Dapper Dans barbershop quartet, on loan from Disneyland, spent a year serenading in the park.

Animation Academy was the first new attraction on Main Street. Situated next to the Opera House on the north side of the town square, its intent is to "inspire creativity in guests and allow imaginations to soar." The venue is restricted to sixty-six guests at a time who sit in a studio setting as a Disney artist, using a projecting system, teaches them how to draw Disney characters. The attraction is similar to the Animation Academies in other theme parks, having first opened at WDW's DisneyQuest in 1998.

By 2008 attendance had started to creep up. An 8 percent attendance growth was registered, bringing the total up to 4.5 million, still well below the anticipated 5.6 million, and the average was 12,300 guests per day. Ocean Park, a marine mammal amusement park in southern Hong Kong, ranked sixteenth in global rankings of the most visited theme parks, while HKD was only twenty-first. HKD management hoped to turn those figures around when they introduced more attractions, starting in Fantasyland on April 28 with the opening of It's a Small World.

The façade for It's a Small World is a carbon copy of the one in WDW's Magic Kingdom, though sharp-eyed Disneyphiles will notice that a Chinese opera singer, exclusive to HKD, has been added to the clock tower parade of multinational figures. The interior has only a few variations. As this attraction was being built at the same time as the one in Disneyland was being refurbished, Imagineers took advantage of the changes being made in

Anaheim to do the same thing in HKD. Characters from the Disney movies were being added to the Small World entourage, thirty-eight in all, still in the original Mary Blair style. The Asia sequence was expanded, a Middle East room added, and a new scene was put in the North America section. The last room was enhanced with fiber-optic lighting effects not used in any other Small World. The finale song was recorded in the three languages for HKD, with Cantonese, Mandarin, Korean, and Tagalog (Philippines) versions being recorded especially for this ride. It's a Small World is located outside the tracks in Fantasyland next to the theater with the Golden Mickey's show.

The Disneyland Story presenting *How Mickey Mouse Came to Hong Kong* in the Opera House at Town Square was removed to accommodate the Art of Animation. Here guests "Discover how animated movies are made at this exhibit that includes a stunning Toy Story Zoetrope and rare artifacts."

Turtle Talk With Crush made a brief appearance on Main Street but only ran from May 31 to August 10, when it was sent to TDL for installation there. Apparently it was felt that Stitch Encounter had enough interaction for guests. Another short-lived attraction was Mickey's House, a meet-and-greet near the hub which opened in January but closed in August, though it would come and go over the ensuing years.

Muppet Mobile Lab was tested at Disney California Adventure and WDW before arriving in HKD. Designed by Disney Imagineering, it is described as "a free-moving, audio-animatronic entertainment attraction." Attached to a Segway platform and looking like a small rocket ship, this science lab is piloted through the park by Muppet characters Dr. Bunsen Honeydew and Beaker, his assistant. Controlled remotely by puppeteers, the Muppet can interact with guests and deploy flashing lights, spray jets, confetti cannons, and moving signs. The attraction is equipped with microphones, speakers, and cameras to allow the puppeteers to see the guests and interact with them. The same basic technology is used for Turtle Talk With Crush, Stitch Encounter, and Lucky the Dinosaur. The attraction won a Thea Award for Outstanding Achievement in 2009.

In addition to the new attractions, a number of food carts had been placed at strategic positions around the park since opening day. In the Main Street area, an ice cream cart was positioned between Market House Bakery and Main Street Corner Café. Two carts, one selling coffee, the other popcorn, ice cream, and cotton candy, faced each other across the hub. Two others were set up in Adventureland, one by the Liki Tikis selling "jumbo sausage, squid tentacles and fish balls," and a second peddling "tropical frozen treats" near Tahitian Terrace. Tomorrowland had a single cart selling popcorn and cotton candy near Space Mountain, and Fantasyland had one with chicken legs and cotton candy near Dumbo.

Experiencing a financial downturn in 2009, and unable to reach an agreement with the SAR about funding expansion, Disney decided it was time to raise admission, despite the government requesting justification for the move. Rates went up to HK$350 for adults and HK$250 for children under eleven. Unexpectedly, in March, all creative and design work for future expansion projects was halted, and thirty Imagineers were laid off, leaving only a skeleton team of ten to carry on. A similar situation developed in the States due to a market downturn.

Negotiations broke down due to Hong Kong SAR being reluctant to invest more money into something that did not seem to be working. Disney insisted that in order to make it work, the park must be expanded. The press and industry experts began to speculate that HKD might just be the first Disney park to shut down due to lack of interest. Both sides were anxious to resolve the dilemma. Disney realized that their reputation as a successful theme park operator was in jeopardy, and the SAR had to uphold their credibility as a steward of public investment.

Disney and the government got back together to try and solve the problem, and on June 30, Donald Tsang, Chief Executive of Hong Kong, let it be known that the Executive Council had approved further expansion of HKD. Three more lands were given the go-ahead to be built on the south side of the park, outside the berm. The Legislative Council approved the expansion on July 10 after overwhelming approval of the Finance Committee. It was to be the most ambitious project of expansion since the park opened, involving three new lands, thirty attractions, restaurants and, shops and higher capacity, all based on two shareholders agreeing to invest HK$3.63 billion.

The official ground breaking ceremony was held on December 13. Jay Rasulo, Chairman of WD Parks and Resorts, and John Tsang attended with assorted representatives from Disney and the SAR. An HKD press release proclaimed that "the expansion will bring the total number of attractions, entertainment and interactive experiences at the Park to more than 100, create 3,700 jobs during the construction phase and 600 new full-time jobs after expansion." Work on the expansion would "begin immediately on the primary infrastructure and road work that will support the construction of the three themed areas.

"Two of the three themed areas, Grizzly Gulch and Mystic Point, will be exclusive to HKD for the first five years after their respective openings. The third, Toy Story Land, will be exclusive within Asia for the first five years after opening."

Despite this exciting news, all was still not well within the company; the first three years of operation showed a net loss of HK$4.4 billion up to October 2009. To help cut back losses and control operating costs, HKD cut paid sick leave for cast members in January 2010. The hope was that between then and the opening of the new attractions in 2011, the fifth anniversary, celebrations would be enough of a draw to boost attendance.

Main Street was the scene of the Park's fifth anniversary photo op when four thousand people were treated to a private party and breakfast in Tomorrowland. Bill Ernest, President and Managing Director, presented a gift from the Walt Disney Company of one million Hong Kong dollars as a scholarship grant to the Vocational Training Council of Hong Kong. The scholarships would benefit students in the hospitality, tourism, design, and entertainment fields.

To celebrate the Year of the Tiger, "a relaxing holiday experience will be waiting for Guests at Hong Kong Disneyland, the Happiest Land of Fortune ... with decorations in colors that symbolize good luck."

Half an hour before the official park opening in the morning, guests were allowed to wander about Main Street, make purchases in the shops or grab a bite to eat. A rope cordoned off the rest of the park. Then, a few minutes before opening, four princesses, Belle, Snow White, Aurora, and Cinderella came out of the castle and walked to the hub. Waiting for them was a family who had been previously selected. After an announcement in the three park languages and a brief countdown, a child cut a ribbon and the park was open. It was a simple ceremony but much loved by guests as the multitude of cameras attest.

The all new Jumpin' Jam stage show featuring Disney characters, drummers, and dancers took place on a 360-degree stage in front of Sleeping Beauty Castle, allowing guests to view the show from any vantage point. The popular Celebration in the Street led by maestro Mickey Mouse returned to Main Street in February. The parade included golden dragons, Chinese drummers, and an elaborate display of giant puppets. Minnie presented a beautiful fan dance, and Goofy appeared as Disney's God of Fortune. Main Street had been transformed from a quiet shopping area to the place to go for live entertainment, "with traditional and modern Chinese New Year themed performers including Drummers and Lion Dancers spreading joy and happiness all around."

The Lucky Trail promised to bring more luck to guests as it featured "Eight Disney Character figurines made with over eighteen types of flowers symbolizing Happiness, Wealth, Longevity, Romance, Success in Studies, Harmony, Achievement, and Prosperity." The *Disney in the Stars* fireworks show was temporarily replaced by *Disney's Nightmare in the Sky* for a month and a half before Hallowe'en.

The celebrations and promise of more to come seemed to have been a successful strategy for HKD, as attendance rose to 5.2 million, the highest registered to date, though still short of the original goal of 5.6 million. HKD was finally able to surpass Ocean Park for the first time.

The celebration of HKD's fifth year shifted into high gear in January 2011 as *Celebration in the Air*, designed by, Steve Davidson, producer of *World of Color* at Disneyland Resort's DCA, replaced *Disney on Parade*, the long running opening day feature.

Sleeping Beauty Castle was transformed into Tinker Bell's Dusted Castle with golden pixie dust that "sparkled and shimmered in the sun and was illuminated by night." To complement that, Tinker Bell made her HKD debut "in her own magical garden newly built in Fantasyland."

Lightning McQueen Live! debuted in HKD on May 30 in advance of the movie premiere of Disney/Pixar's *Cars 2*. Essentially a meet-and-greet with the *Cars* star, the story goes that McQueen has stopped by the park on his way to the first ever World Grand Prix. "The Cars stars will be awaiting Guests at four international photo locations, including Japan's luxurious Ginza, the beautiful Italian coast and the Euro-chic streets of London and Paris. Guests may also grab a Secret Agent Passport and track the characters as they collect exclusive passport stamps from each location." Guests can then "try some delicious grab-and-go snacks, ranging from Roasted English Honey Sausage, Sushi Roll, French Mini Puff Skewer and delicious Tiramisu." *Lightning McQueen Live!* replaced *High School Musical Live!*

Toy Story Land opened on November 18, 2011, the first new themed land since the park opened in 2005. It was marketed as "Asia Exclusive," as TDL did not have one and the only other was Toy Story Playland in WDS in France. Located on the west side of the park, a new access route had to be built between Adventureland and Fantasyland. This entailed digging through the berm and under the railway tracks. The idea of the land was to create the illusion of guests shrinking down to toy size, so bamboo was used to simulate giant blades of grass surrounding the area. Once inside the new land, people became toy sized or toys became people sized, whatever way you want to look at it, so characters from the Toy Story movies are larger than in the films.

Entering Andy's backyard, the first thing guests see is Barrel of Fun, a big blue barrel of monkeys, where guests can meet their favorite toys from the Toy Story movies. Woody and Jessie are the ones most likely to be there.

After leaving the Barrel of Fun, the next obvious attraction is RC Racer, a copy of the steel shuttle roller coaster already in operation at WDS in France.

The concept is that Andy had been playing with his remote controlled car, RC, but now that he has gone away, RC keeps on running. Guests climb into a twenty passenger vehicle and "experience RC's astounding driving abilities as you careen up and down a steep twenty-seven meter-tall, half-pipe roadway."

Across the road is Slinky Dog Zigzag Spin, another import from WDS, where Slinky "chases his tail around a giant food bowl." The tamest ride in the park, it is a circuitous powered gentle up-and-down roller coaster providing sensations similar to the Dumbo ride.

There were two places for refreshments in Toy Story Land, Jessie's Snack Roundup for "frozen yogurt, Mickey cookie, pizza cone" and Frozen Lollipops Cart. These were situated between Slinky Dog and the final attraction, Toy Soldier Parachute Drop.

Again, the idea came from a similar attraction in Toy Story Playland in WDS, Paris, where it had opened over a year earlier. This parachute jump-style ride simulates Andy putting his soldiers through parachute drills, and with Andy gone to do other things it is the guests' turn to train. The area is themed with a World War II jeep and an open supply warehouse filled with military material. Once inside the six person jump vehicle, guests float up a twenty-five meter parachute jump tower for a sweeping view of Toy Story Land and the areas still under construction to the east before suddenly dropping down and then back up in "a series of exhilarating aerial exercises."

One of the HKD Railroad trains derailed on November 2, and a local reporter suspected a cover-up. A Disney spokesperson denied that, saying "the train was out of service at the time and no injuries were sustained," so "they didn't feel the need to publicize the incident." The spokesman went on to say that the problem was not due to equipment failure: "the accident was due to the driver not providing enough space for the train to switch tracks, leading to six wheels veering off course." The driver was suspended, and park officials and the Hong Kong Electrical and Mechanical Services Department would be investigating.

Attendance figures for the year seemed to prove that Disney had been right in thinking that expanding the park would bring in more people. The original projected figure of 5.6 million was finally surpassed in 2011 with a total of 5.9 million guests through the turnstiles. Investors could breathe a sigh of relief, but the Imagineers knew they could not rest on their laurels; they had just begun to expand and more was needed.

Negotiations continued with the Hong Kong government in January 2012 for another HK$5 billion over the next year for a shopping complex and more hotels. The reclaimed land was available and ready to be built upon as the Phase 2 Extension. A Phase 3 was also being considered.

Meanwhile, construction continued on the next land, Grizzly Gulch, located on the southeast side of the park with access from Adventureland, not far from the Rafts to Tarzan's Treehouse. A new bridge had to be constructed to allow the train to pass overhead, with a popcorn car on the other side to entice guests through. The centerpiece of that area was Big Grizzly Mountain, standing eighty-eight feet (twenty-seven meters) tall, and being built by twenty painters and thirty sculptors working eight hours a day for fourteen months using a special, softer kind of cement. The realistic-looking rocks, wooden logs, and bricks were constructed from 3,859 tons of concrete which had all been designed through several stages of sketches, models, and computer scans to make them look authentic. Design teams had previously visited Yellowstone National Park and the Sierra Nevada Mountains in California for inspiration. By May, two hundred people had been hired to run Grizzly Gulch.

The Grand Opening Ceremony of the new area was attended by the usual dignitaries, including the guests of honor: the Honourable Chun-Ying Leung, Chief Executive of the Hong Kong Special Administrative Region, and Tom Staggs, Chairman of Walt Disney Parks and Resorts. Staggs pointed out that Grizzly Gulch was "the first themed area of its kind at any of our parks around the world."

Grizzly Gulch was themed as a California gold rush-era town built at the foot of Big Grizzly Mountain. It was founded on August 8, 1888, a string of lucky numbers, by gold-seeking prospectors. "Accidently constructed atop a bed of active geysers, the town was literally sinking and financially underwater." For those who enjoy getting wet on a hot day, the town has a water tower, and "those brave enough to get close can expect a light rain from the tiny holes in the tank," and Lucky Springs Geyser, which, if it erupts when you are making a wish will make your wish come true, unless you are wishing not to get wet. "There's a little friendly competition between a blacksmith shop and a dry goods store" who shoot water back and forth at each other and invite guests to join in. The rest of the town is made up of the Grizzly Gulch Jailhouse, where guests can have their picture taken for a wanted poster, and Grizzly Gulch Assay Office, where the Lucky Nugget, "the largest piece of gold ever unearthed in the gulch," is situated. "Grizzly Gulch has been lovingly renamed Geyser Gulch by the locals." The outstanding top of the mountain was modeled after Grizzly Peak in Disney's California Adventure Park in Anaheim. The Lucky Nugget Saloon is the lone restaurant in the land, with "fish and chips, salads and desserts," and the only place to shop is at the Bear Necessities.

The main attraction is Big Grizzly Mountain Runaway Mine Cars, a Vekoma roller coaster with 3,600 feet (1100 meters) of track. To make sure everything was working as planned, Big Grizzly Mountain Runaway Mine Cars began soft openings in June and officially opened on July 14 with the rest of Grizzly Gulch. Like Expedition Everest in Disney's Animal Kingdom in WDW, it has a backwards section in it and has a number of similarities to Big Thunder Mountain in Disneyland and Grizzly Peak in Disney's California Adventure.

Guests enter the *Big Grizzly Mountain Mining Company* building and board one of several twenty-four seater trains. The train heads for lucky tunnel "8," but a grizzly bear sends it careening down unlucky tunnel "4" instead. Chugging up a hill until it almost reaches the top, the train suddenly switches into reverse as a lift cable breaks and it speeds backwards into another mine shaft. Two bears set off an explosion with TNT to launch the car onto still another track and through a number of turns and twists circumnavigating almost all of Grizzly Gulch before returning to the station.

The new attractions probably had a great deal to do with the attendance numbers for 2012, as they passed the 5.6 million projected figure and the previous year's record with a new attendance record of 6.7 million. That February it was announced that the Resort had "its first-ever net profit since opening in September 2005, reporting a net profit of HK$109 million for the year ending 29 September 2012, attributing the results to record revenues driven by timely expansion, strong sales and marketing strategies and effective cost management." In March 2013, HKD raised ticket prices by slightly over 17%, hoping that the new attractions that opened the previous year and the new land scheduled for that year would convince guests that paying more was worthwhile.

The opening of Mystic Point marked the final chapter in the expansion project, which was completed one year ahead of schedule, and when added to Toy Story Land and Grizzly Gulch effectively increased the size of Hong Kong Disneyland by 25%. When the announcement was made in April 2013, Andrew Kam, Managing Director of HKD Resort, said, "We are delighted by our guests' continued response to Toy Story Land and Grizzly Gulch, and Mystic Point is sure to be just as powerful." Since April, the Park had put on a series of preview days for more than thirty thousand guests, including cast members and families, trade partners, business partners, media, bloggers, and celebrities.

A problem developed when the Palm trees lining the avenue leading to the entrance started dying. Coconut leaf beetles were suspected as the culprit, but tree experts said the trees had also been attacked by the more invasive red palm weevils.

Officiating at the next grand opening on May 17, 2013 were the Honorable John Tsang and Bill Ernest, President and Managing Director, Asia Walt Disney Parks and Resorts. "Today we mark the completion of Hong Kong Disneyland's current expansion project on a high note with the opening of Mystic Point. This one-of-a-kind themed area has never been seen in any of our Disney parks worldwide," said Bill Ernest. "For the first time, guests can immerse themselves in a unique adventure of theatrical wonders that combines traditional storytelling with innovative technology and special effects."

According to the HKD Press Release, the story of Mystic Point is set in 1909 and "follows the adventures of eccentric explorer and art collector Lord Henry Mystic, who invites guests to board the Mystic Magneto-Electric Carriage for a tour of his private museum located within his Victorian manor. When Lord Henry's companion, his monkey Albert, mischievously opens a newly acquired magical music box, the enchanted Music Dust within is released and, accompanied by a haunting tune created by renowned composer Danny Elfman, a mysterious journey begins."

The mystery of Mystic Point extended its reach to select overseas markets. Publicity activities were carried out in various markets, including Indonesia, Philippines, Malaysia, Thailand, Taiwan, Singapore, and India. HKD also collaborated with a number of prominent TV programs in Mainland China.

"We are confident that Mystic Point, along with Toy Story Land and Grizzly Gulch, will be the key drivers of growth for our Resort." As Walt Disney is often quoted as saying, "Disneyland will never be completed as long as there is imagination left in the world." "The same applies to Hong Kong Disneyland, which will continue to grow, contribute to Hong Kong's economy and create countless magical experiences for guests of all ages and origins," affirmed Andrew Kam.

The iconic Mystic Manor is located in the centre of Mystic Point, which is placed between Toy Story Land and Grizzly Gulch. The Manor features one of the most sophisticated ride systems ever built by Disney, has the Explorer's Club Restaurant next door, with international cuisines ranging from Korean and Japanese to Halal food, and The Archive Shop, where guests can purchase exclusive novelty items and collectibles. Nearby is the Mystic Point Freight Depot, where Lord Henry's grandnephews share stories from their adventures with Lord Henry and introduce special guests from "their far-away homes, each of these cultural representatives adds to the Mystic Point collection of priceless artifacts by demonstrating a beautiful dance from their country of origin."

Across from the Manor is Garden of Wonders where "there's more than meets the eye," as guests "roam a well-manicured garden of three ornate exhibits from around the globe and discover something fascinating in their curious arrangements when glimpsed through a special viewing station." Three statues, a firebird, a carp, and a Chinese unicorn transform into one sculpture, the bas-relief reveals a "celestial being from Mesopotamian mythology," and the mosaic lets guests see Neptune, the Roman god of the sea, spring to life when viewed through the strategically-positioned oculus.

Sometimes erroneously likened to Disneyland's Haunted Mansion, Mystic Manor "has a lighthearted, fantasy-based theme with no references to ghosts or the afterlife, due to differences in traditional Chinese culture." The mansion's design was inspired by the Bradbury Mansion, since demolished, in Los Angeles. The trackless ride system in similar to that utilized in Pooh's Hunny Hunt, and the musical score is by Danny Elfman. Some similarities include a changing portrait of Medusa and bust heads that turn to follow guests around the room. There is also a nod to Disneyland's Enchanted Tiki Room, with several figures featured in the tribal arts room.

Mystic Manor was built as a museum for the growing collection of art and artifacts gathered by members of Lord Henry's team, the Society of Explorers and Adventurers (S.E.A.). Guests are invited to tour the establishment and view the eclectic collection aboard the Mystic Magneto-Electric Carriage. "Edge your way through a labyrinth of rooms overflowing with photographs, drawings and rarities chronicling the thrilling global expeditions of Lord Henry and Albert, and, following a brief slideshow introduction, proceed to the museum's workroom for the start of your tour."

Guests climb into the trackless Mystic Magneto-Electric Carriage and glide off to the first stop, the cataloguing room, where Albert paws at the "enigmatic Balinese music box . . . unexpectedly causing the box to open . . . a haunting melody is heard and a stream of glittering dust drifts throughout the room and museum, miraculously imparting life to whatever it touches."

Guests follow the magical music dust through Mystic Manor as it magically brings the artifacts to life in the eight galleries of the Manor.

The first is Musical Instruments, where "a musical menagerie of exotic instruments" play. Next is Mediterranean Antiquities, where guests watch the eruption of Mount Vesuvius and see a woman transform into Medusa. The Solarium features a carnivorous plant. In the Slavic-Nordic Chamber, guests encounter Stribog, the Slavic god of winter, who blankets "a pleasant spring scene with frost and ice." Next is Arms and Armor, where guests narrowly avoid a blasting cannon and a crossbow bolt while listening to armor sing. The Egyptian Antiquities room features "a swarm of creepy-crawly bugs fleeing an ancient sarcophagus." Lava flows from the mouth of a Tiki idol in the Tribal Arts room as guests avoid "the clutches of a tribe of angry warrior idols." In the last room, The Chinese Salon, guests encounter the mythical Monkey King.

In November 2013, it was announced that Mystic Manor had been honored with the coveted Thea Award for Outstanding Achievement – Attraction. Mystic Manor was recognized for its excellence in original storyline, special effects, Audio-Animatronics technology, musical score, and the trackless, wire-guided ride vehicles. The Themed Entertainment Association (TEA) noted that "Mystic Manor exemplifies the seamless integration of the latest technology with true state-of-the-art storytelling."

"HKD is honored to have received this prestigious award from the Themed Entertainment Association, which represents all our peers across the industry," said Andrew Kam, Managing Director of HKD. "We are especially proud of the inspired creativity of our talented Imagineers and their spirit of innovation as HKDL continues to bring the best of Disney storytelling to our Guests."

A month after the official opening of Mystic Point and in celebration of the soon to be released *Monster University*, HKD offered guests a taste of campus life at Monsters U from June 1 to the end of August. Guests could register for personalized student cards, meet Mike and Sulley, purchase Monsters U merchandise, and snack on "monsterized" summer menus and beverages as they "experience some monster-style campus fun."

The Monsters University Administration Building was located on Main

Street and available to be explored. Once guests have their personalized student cards from Town Square Photo, they can use them to log into the HKD website and have their Monsters University Graduate Certificate printed. Monster-style menus were offered at restaurants throughout the park and included such tantalizing treats as "the blinking Mike Cotton Candy, the scarily cute Mike Bun, and over ten thirst quenchers, including the fun-filled Staring Mike, Sulley's Rainbow and the fruity Blink Blink Eye, to name just a few."

Early in 2014, HKD was able to report that for the 2013 fiscal year the Resort "generated HK$4,896 million in revenue, up 15% from the previous year, while net profit more than doubled to HK$242 million." The Resort also broke attendance records with "an all-time high of 7.4 million guests. The results are attributed to expansion efforts, strong marketing, effective management strategies and positive tourism growth during the fiscal year," according to a HKD press release. "Overall hotel occupancy was at a new high of 94% for fiscal 2013, while guest spending broke records with a 6% year-over-year increase."

Plans for a new hotel were also announced, adding 750 rooms to the existing inventory, "pending all necessary project approvals." The Press release continued: "The new hotel will increase the total number of hotel rooms in the Resort by 75% to 1,750. The total investment of $4.263 billion will be funded by a combination of operating cash of HKD, cash equity injection from The Walt Disney Company along with a partial conversion of the existing Hong Kong Special Administrative Region Government term loan to equity on a dollar-for-dollar basis, and new term loans from WDC and the SAR.

"In fiscal 2013, additional spending in Hong Kong by HKD visitors generated HK$11.6 billion of value added to Hong Kong, which is equivalent to around 0.58% of Hong Kong's GDP. A total of 33,200 jobs (in terms of man-years) were created, primarily benefiting frontline workers as well as the travel and hospitality industry. Construction of the new hotel will create additional job opportunities and another 600-700 full-time equivalent jobs in HKD after the new hotel commences operation.

"HKD has also redoubled community outreach efforts . . . over 100,000 underprivileged community members were welcomed to the park during the fiscal year, while close to 8,500 hours of skills and services were contributed through the Disney VoluntEARS program, among other outreach programs that directly benefited society.

"Since opening, HKDL has received 271 awards in recognition of its design, technical achievements, distinctive guest services, commitment to the community and environment and high family appeal. HKDL received a total of sixty-one awards during the fiscal year, including Best Theme Attraction at the Twenty-Fourth Annual TTG Travel Awards, the Pacific Asia Travel Association Gold Award 2013 in the Marketing Industry category, the Best Theme Park of the Year from China Travel and Meetings Industry Awards, the Fourth Asia's Best Employer Brand Award presented by the Employer Branding Institute, and the 2013 Randstad Award for Best Workplace Culture in Hong Kong."

New initiatives for 2014 included a brand new nighttime parade spectacular called *Disney Paint the Night*. Touted as HKD's "newest chapter after the completion of its three-part expansion project," *Disney Paint the Night* replaced the Main Street Electrical Parade. HKD is the first Disney park with a fully LED parade, featuring seven new floats and over 740,000 lights with "the scintillating power of Tinker Bell's pixie dust." Tinker Bell, Ariel, Belle, Buzz Lightyear, Woody, and many other characters are featured, including Sulley and Mike, who appear in an HKD parade for the first time, continuing the Monsters U theme of the previous year. The team working on the spectacular spent over two years developing the interactive parade. Guests can make some parade costumes change colors in real time when they wave their "Mickey Magic Paint Brush" as Disney Characters and dancers get close. The magical brushes can also be used to animate hidden "Magical Art" pieces and "watch as the artwork comes to life right before your eyes." A nearly exact copy of *Disney's Paint the Night* was also used in Disneyland for the sixtieth anniversary celebrations.

Another event exclusive to HKD is Disney's Haunted Hallowe'en, a frightening walkthrough attraction with ghosts and specters around every corner (though no blood or gore), as well as Phantom Food and Creepy Keepsakes.

Ticket prices went up another 16.2% in November, but that did not stop HKD from reaching a new attendance record at 7.6 million visitors. The resort also posted a record HK$336 million net profit for the last financial year, up 36%.

Work began on the 750-room Disney Explorers Lodge in January 2015, with a scheduled opening date in early 2017. When completed, the hotel would feature Polynesian, Asian, African, and South American sections as well as a themed outdoor pool and restaurant.

The tenth anniversary year of the HKD Resort in 2015 promised "new entertainment and shows that bring interactive and immersive guest experiences to a new level." A glittering ceremony in the forecourt of Sleeping Beauty castle was headed by Walt Disney Parks and Resorts Chairman Bob Chapek. The *Happily Ever After* celebration to follow would last a year with an amazing array of entertainment.

One of the most popular shows at HKD was *The Golden Mickeys*, celebrated as "being the longest-running Broadway-style show in Hong Kong." After more than nineteen thousand performances before over sixteen million guests over a period of ten years, the show closed on July 26. A new show, *Mickey and the Wondrous Book*, took its place in Disney's Storybook Theater in the northwest corner of Fantasyland in November. Set in a magical library, Mickey and Goofy discover a fantastic book that brings stories to life. When Mickey opens the book, Olaf, the snowman from *Frozen*, falls out, and when Mickey attempts to get him back into the book, the mouse is drawn in as well. Setting off with Goofy, they travel through six stories, *Jungle Book*, *The Little Mermaid*, *Tangled*, *Brave*, *Aladdin*, and *The Princess and the Frog* before finally arriving at *Frozen*. The twenty-five-minute show includes twenty-two original costume designs and concludes with the song *Happily Ever After*, the Tenth Anniversary theme song for HKD.

More Disney films are featured in the *Disney in the Stars* fireworks show, which includes "cutting-edge technology, lighting effects and state-of-the-art video projection shown on Sleeping Beauty Castle." The projections vary in different locations to encourage people to view the show a number of times from different areas. The show has scenes from *Snow White and the Seven Dwarfs*, *Peter Pan*, *Pinocchio*, *Aladdin*, *The Little Mermaid*, *The Princess and the Frog*, *Tangled*, *Finding Nemo*, *Cars*, *Big Hero 6*, *Brave*, and *Inside Out*.

The annual Hallowe'en attraction featured an outdoor theme, Dare to Get Lost in Ghost Town, with ghostly lands in Mystic Point, Grizzly Gulch, and Adventureland. Ghosts returned to the gold mining town of Grizzly Gulch to settle a feud, Mystic Point featured dancing ghosts trying to lure guests into the Cycle of Spirits time warp, and Jungle River Cruise was transformed into a perilous voyage through a creepy rain forest of danger including a quest for a cursed trio of emeralds.

The popular *Disney Sparkling Christmas* returned in mid-November when Queen Elsa and Princess Anna lit up the Christmas tree adorning Main Street, USA.

There were also a pair of new attractions, Fairy Tale Forest, opening on December 17, and Frozen Village. In the former, guests wander through "a winding, living storybook realm" that uses creative landscaping to feature miniature scenes from a number of princess films such as *Snow White and the Seven Dwarfs*, *Beauty and the Beast*, *Cinderella*, *Tangled*, and *The Little Mermaid*. The forest is also the home to Tinker Bell in a themed area, similar to one in Disneyland, where she greets guests in Pixie Hollow.

"We've spent over two years building Fairy Tale Forest from its conceptual design," said Kelly Willis, WDI's Director of Creative Development and Show Quality. "It's an intricately designed maze set in a beautiful garden setting, presenting spectacles of five cherished princesses in every corner. This attraction is bound to give guests more chances to snap photos of these classic Disney fairy tales."

Before going to Frozen Village, guests are encouraged to visit Elsa, Anna, and Kristoff outside the Royal Banquet Hall near Sleeping Beauty Castle, then join the processional of costumed characters and guests in the castle forecourt before going to Animation Academy on Main Street to learn to draw Olaf. Having done all that, guests can proceed to Frozen Village, which is accessed between Adventureland and Grizzly Gulch.

Frozen Village is in what Disney calls a "Black Box Space," which is "a flexible event venue that can cater to different scales of entertainment and shows. By incorporating world-class theatrical equipment, the venue offers amazing potential for conceiving and delivering immersive experiences." The fifteen-thousand-square-foot area can be used for any special events, whether small or large scale or spanning one day to a whole season.

Frozen Village contains a castle-like venue covered in snow. Oaken's Trading Post for food, including Olaf mini waffles and cupcakes, is near the entrance to the left, and Oaken's Trading Post for merchandise on the right. (Fans snap up 530 costumes each week, seventy per cent of them are Elsa's dress.) Further inside, guests can have a photo-op with Sven in one spot and Olaf in another, make a wish at the Fountain, hop on a toboggan for a downhill ride on Olaf's Ice Slide, or just play in the snow. The Crown Jewel Theater presents a *Frozen Festival Show* with characters, songs, and more snow.

Frozen items make up between 8 and 11% of all Disney merchandise and contributed to a growth of 3% in per capita merchandise spending in the 2015 fiscal year from the previous year. "We've never seen demand for our products like we've seen for Frozen," said Jim Greene, director of merchandise at HKD.

Hong Kong Disneyland is generally a happy place, but arguments and real life do happen. In September, a couple was having an argument in Mandarin just outside of Sleeping Beauty Castle. Before long, the altercation started getting very loud and began frightening other guests. As the yelling escalated, the pair became more erratic until the women abruptly turned away from the man, ran, and jumped into the castle's moat. Standing in the waist deep water, she continued yelling at her partner, who had gone onto the bridge and was repeatedly shouting "come back" at her.

Unable to convince the woman to come out of the water, the man jumped into the shallow water after her and tried to drag her to shore. She resisted his attempts, refusing to leave the moat until cast members arrived and assisted them both out of the water. A park spokesperson later confirmed that neither had suffered any injuries but would not say if they had been escorted from the park. A witness suggested that they had jumped into the moat because it was so hot that day.

There was another incident earlier in July that, according to an article in *Apple Daily*, was not that out of the ordinary, at least for mainland Chinese tourists. A woman was spotted airing her undergarments on a railing near Town Square by a man searching for a spot to watch the parade. Reportedly, he watched her "draping five pieces of soggy clothing, including her bra and undies, on the iron railing. A few security guards approached the tourist and asked her to pack up her lingerie. She removed the garments from the railings for a short while, but placed them out to dry again as soon as the parade started. Security once again asked her to remove her belongings, and she flashed them a 'death glare' before reluctantly collecting her things and leaving," the report said. It was noted by the man who reported her that "the woman's behavior reflected poorly upon the theme park as well as the somewhat tarnished reputation of mainland travelers in Hong Kong." Response to the article was even more critical, as readers commented, "If you can tolerate them peeing everywhere you can tolerate this" and "Just wait till the Disneyland in Shanghai opens, and 'indulge' in this kind of behavior there."

"With the launch of the year-long tenth anniversary celebration and Christmas offerings, the resort will increase marketing and sales efforts in twenty countries and cities in Asia," said HKD Managing Director Andrew Kam. "These efforts will further expand our markets and contribute to the city's ability to attract tourists from across the globe."

In their annual business review, HKD announced its fifth consecutive record-breaking year, and the resort also welcomed its 50 millionth guest.

Along with expanding the markets it serves, HKD has several projects slated for the future. According to David Lightbody, the park's Director of

Entertainment, The Iron Man Experience is scheduled to open in late 2016 inside a Marvel-themed area in Tomorrowland. This will be the first Marvel-themed attraction in a Disney park with a re-creation of the iconic Stark Tower and a storyline where guests will fight alongside Iron Man in an epic adventure across Hong Kong in a Star Tours-style simulator. In addition, Stark Expo will showcase the inventions of Howard and Tony Stark, with the Iron Wing, a large Iron Man suit that allows guests to experience being in Stark-armor, as the main attraction. The overall area will also feature a Marvel-themed merchandise store and a character-greeting experience where guests can take photos. HKD is also expected to add a Star Wars special program in the summer.

2015 was not a good year for HKD, following a drop in visitors from the mainland. The decline was blamed on a waning of visitors from all parts of Asia, a problem felt all over Hong Kong and not just in the Disney Park. The Chief Secretary for Administration of SARS was quoted as saying "many people are concerned that calls for political reform have led to a growth in radicalism, divided the public and caused stagnation." The unrest had certainly led to an economic downturn for Hong Kong, mainly due to a drop in tourists wishing to avoid the unpleasantness. Hoping to heal divisions, the government launched an "Appreciate Hong Kong" scheme that provides free entry to museums, amusement parks, and other perks. Handouts under the campaign included free entry to museums in January, ten thousand free tickets to Ocean Park for low-income families, and thirteen thousand free tickets to Hong Kong Disneyland for students with special needs.

The park welcomed only 6.8 million guests, compared to 7.5 million the year before. Revenues dropped from US$705 million (HK$5.47 billion) to $659 million (HK$5.11 billion). Despite the numbers, HKD officials stated that the figures still represent the second highest annual revenue and third highest attendance in the park's history. Guest spending was also on the increase, and hotel occupancy was almost 80 percent, though the previous year saw closer to 93 percent.

By March 2016, the situation had not improved, and when another 9%

decrease was noted, Andrew Kam resigned after eight years of service, citing personal reasons. Samuel Lau was promoted to Managing Director by Walt Disney Parks and Resorts. "Mr. Kam led the HKD team in accomplishing a series of major expansion works and drove the performance of the park to new records. We wish him every success in his future endeavours," Hong Kong's Financial Secretary Tsang said.

Despite the downturn, plans are still ongoing to expand the park. "HKD's two shareholders, WDC and the Hong Kong Government are also in discussions on the resort's Phase 2 development. Hong Kong Disneyland was also built with the space for a second park directly across from the entrance to the current park. Disney has not yet announced that the second park is in development. Land is also available for additional hotels other than the current and one being built, but the common thought is that the second park will be built before a fourth hotel. Looking ahead, the resort will continue to strengthen its position as a leading entertainment destination in Asia, a regional employer of choice, and a pioneer in the theme park industry," says a HKD press release.

PART IV
SHANGHAI DISNEYLAND

Chapter One
Pudong

THE SITE OF SHANGHAI DISNEYLAND is in the eastern portion of the Pudong district in the city of Shanghai, just west of the Shanghai Pudong International Airport and the Yangtze River. The name means "East Bank" and refers to its location from Shanghai on the east bank of the Huangpu River which flows through central Shanghai. In the twentieth century it was a flat, underdeveloped area consisting mainly of farmland and a few wharfs and warehouses along the banks of the Huangpu River. Pudong had been established as a county in 1958 but a few years later was split up between neighboring counties, only to be re-established and joined with Chuansha County in 1992. A year later, the Chinese government set up a "special economic zone," thereby creating the Pudong New Area.

The western part of Pudong developed rapidly after that, as a number of high-profile buildings such as the Shanghai Tower, the Shanghai Stock Exchange, the Oriental Pearl Tower, and the Shanghai World Financial Center were constructed. In addition, Shanghai Expo and Century Park were developed, along with the Pudong International Airport and Jiuduansha Wetland Nature Reserve.

From an underdeveloped area, Pudong has become the most populous district of Shanghai, with over five million people, approximately one quarter of Shanghai's total population as recorded in the 2010 census. As a popular immigration destination, Pudong had an over 58 percent population increase in the first decade of the twenty-first century. All this contributed to making Pudong the ideal site for the next Disneyland.

However, it would be a long and sometimes rocky road from the first introduction of the Disney product in China to the opening of Shanghai Disneyland. Disney first arrived in China in the 1930s, when Mickey Mouse cartoons, dubbed in Cantonese, became popular with moviegoers. By the mid-1930s, most theaters showed a Mickey Mouse cartoon before the main feature. In 1938, Disney introduced the first full-length Technicolor animated feature film, *Snow White and the Seven Dwarfs*, to the Chinese market. Over four hundred thousand Chinese saw Disney's first animated feature during the first six months of its debut at the Metropol in Nanking.

The Chinese in the major cities such as Shanghai, Peking, and Nanking soon had little time for movies. The Second Sino-Japanese War began in 1937 as Japan invaded China, attacking Shanghai in the same year. That war became part of the global conflict when Japan attacked Pearl Harbor in 1941. Previous to that, Walt Disney had become involved in the United China Relief effort and headed the Campaign for Young China, according to a September 1941 letter in *Life* magazine. The Campaign was involved with "organizing the sale of stamps from China among American schoolchildren.

Disney is now starting a new type of club to aid Chinese children called 'Esteemed Grandparents' which has already won the support of Herbert H. Lehman, Mrs. Sarah Delano Roosevelt, Dr. Albert Einstein. Senator Hiram Bingham, Dr. Franz Boas and others."

As the United States became more involved in the Pacific War, military and naval components requested Disney-designed insignia for their units. One of the most famous of these was designed by Disney artist Roy Williams in the spring of 1942 for Claire Chennault of the 1st American Volunteer Group of the Chinese Air Force, known as the Flying Tigers. The insignia consisted of a winged tiger flying through a large V, which members of the unit applied to the fuselage of their aircraft. A second insignia was designed in November 1943 for Military Government Specialists: TNGS, featuring Chinese characters and a lion's head.

After the war, the turmoil in the country made it impossible for Disney to introduce any of their products, and once the People's Republic of China was established in 1949, Disney was banned from the country.

The Communist Party adopted Mickey as their poster mouse in its health campaign against rats as both rodents are referred to as *laoshu*. Much to Disney's chagrin, before long, posters of *Mi Laoshu*, as Mickey was known in China, began appearing with all sorts of violence being directed towards him, not as anti-Mickey or anti-Disney or even anti-American, but simply because he was the best-known rodent in China

It would take almost fifteen years before Disney comic books were again available in China. The Sino-American Publishing Co. in Hong Kong launched Disney Comics Magazine in the Chinese, Malay, and Thai languages. A letter that Walt Disney wrote to the company in November 1963 was reprinted in the first issue: "Here at the studio, we look upon this latest addition to the family of Disney Magazines as a means of establishing even closer ties of friendship with our neighbors overseas."

Little progress was made by Disney over the ensuing years to establish a foothold in the Chinese market. The historic meeting between President Richard Nixon and Chairman Zedong Mao in February 1972 led to an easing of tensions between the two countries, and after a brief meeting with Mao in Beijing, Nixon also traveled to Hangzhou and Shanghai. The Shanghai Communiqué that was issued while Nixon was in China briefly stated, amongst other things, the wish that economic and cultural contacts between the two countries be extended. Little was done beyond that wish.

Ronald Reagan was the second president to visit the People's Republic of China. He met with China's president, Li Xiannian, in 1984 to discuss the status of Taiwan. A year later, Xiannian visited Canada and then touched down at Andrews Air Force Base in Maryland. He and his wife, Madame Jiamei Lin, met Ronald Reagan at the White House, where he proclaimed that he was visiting the US to "deepen mutual understanding, enhance our bilateral relations, increase the friendship between our two peoples, and safeguard world peace."

Shortly afterwards, the Chinese President flew to Chicago and then Los Angeles and on Sunday, July 28, was met at the entrance to Disneyland by Mickey and Minnie Mouse. The Chinese delegates and their security officers were escorted into the park and signed the guest book in front of the floral Mickey to the accompaniment of a fourteen-piece band. They then climbed into an antique-replica car for a ride down Main Street. The sixty or so government officials were cheered and applauded by Disneyland visitors lining the street.

Their next stop was in Tomorrowland's Circle Vision Theater for a special, private screening of the 360-degree film *American Journeys*, with its panoramic views of the United States. Later, Xiannian's wife and some members of her entourage were treated to a viewing of another Circle Vision film, *Wonders of China*, which had been flown in from EPCOT just for the occasion.

President and Chief Operating Officer for the Walt Disney Company, Frank Wells, took advantage of the opportunity to speak to Xiannian "in the most general terms" about expanding Disney operations in China. The Chinese Press Officer, Huming Li, later told an Associated Press reporter, "In China, we don't have such a thing for the moment. We are interested in such an entertainment place."

It's a Small World was a favorite of the Chinese First Lady when she viewed it accompanied by Melissa Tyler, Disneyland's 1985 ambassador. The attraction featured a Chinese panda bear and Chinese acrobats, and its rendition of the Great Wall of China had been refurbished shortly before the tour. "The interpreter was explaining the message of It's a Small World, and I think she enjoyed that," Tyler commented afterwards. President Xiannian expressed his praise for it as well, but he seemed to prefer the Jungle Cruise, "particularly when an animated elephant nearly sprayed the tour boat with water," Tyler explained with a smile.

According to the *LA Times*, there were a couple of minor incidents with overzealous Americans. One involved a lady from Pennsylvania who "begged onlookers to step aside" as Xiannian sat down for a cruise through It's a Small World: "I only have one frame left in my camera. Please, can you let me get a picture? OK, now which one is he?"

A nurse from Los Angeles tried for three hours to get close enough to Xiannian to tell him "how welcome he is in America. This way, both his country and our country can work together for peace in the world." Finally, as he climbed out of the Jungle Cruise boat, she grasped his shoulder and called out, "Welcome, sir." Seconds later, she was smiling and saying "I touched him. I touched him," as Secret Service Agents hustled her away.

The visit seemed to have paid off, for less than a year later, in 1986, WDC was permitted back into China with a regular television broadcast of shorts, albeit tightly monitored by the national media supervision system. Disney officials announced the deal at a news conference in Peking (now Beijing), stating that Mickey Mouse and Donald Duck will make their debuts on Chinese television in a weekly half-hour cartoon series on the China Central Television Network (CCTV).

Disney's Buena Vista International subsidiary licensed the state-owned Chinese network to air 104 episodes of the "Mickey and Donald" cartoon series over two years. In exchange for the shows, Disney was to receive two minutes of advertising time per half hour, which it envisioned selling to major international companies interested in marketing goods in China. The CCTV network translated and dubbed the Disney cartoons into Mandarin. Frank Wells told a reporter that WDC hoped to use the TV show for "development of a number of profitable and interrelated businesses. We are exploring the potential for motion picture distribution and moving forward to establish the Chinese manufacture and distribution of Disney-character merchandise, publications and other consumer products."

Michael Eisner, WDC Chairman and Chief Executive Officer, added, "This marks the first time a major U.S. studio has been invited to broadcast a TV show of this magnitude on Chinese television." Eisner also stated that he expected that the series would create a significant demand for such Disney products as clothing, toys, gifts, books, and magazines. Disney officials declined to put a dollar value on the TV advertising time or on the eventual demand for Disney goods that may be created in the vast Chinese market. CBS had previously received commercial air time in exchange for permitting Chinese television to air a collage of documentaries and features.

Disney's strategy was successful for the most part, as their characters became popular with the Chinese consumer. The 1980s and 1990s produced a generation of young Chinese whose collective memories "include childhood TV time dominated by Mickey Mouse, Donald Duck, and Winnie the Pooh. Mickey acted as a cultural ambassador, winning the hearts of billions of Chinese with his kindness, optimism, and good humor." *Mickey Mouse Magazine* was first published in China in 1993 and remains in circulation today.

The shows also planted the germ of an idea in the head of the mayor of Shanghai that one day he would like to see a Disneyland-style park in his city. In July 1990, Mayor Rongji Zhu visited Disneyland in California with four other Chinese mayors and returned home determined to make the idea a reality. In time Zhu rose through the ranks to become premier of China from 1998 to 2003. According to Michael Rowse, the Hong Kong government official who played a central role in negotiating the establishment of Hong Kong Disneyland, Zhu was a consistent champion of the project.

Unfortunately, the popularity of the Disney characters also touched off a deluge of pirated videos and knockoffs of merchandise. It has been estimated that theft of American copyrighted films by Chinese companies on video or cable company showings has resulted in an $800 million profit for the bootleggers. But Disney fought back and in 1994 brought a suit against Beijing Publishing Press, the first major copyright case involving a foreign party in China.

Disney had previously licensed Maxwell Company to use Disney characters in Chinese language publications. However, the license specifically stated that the characters "may not be assigned by the Licensee to any third party in any manner or by means of any legal procedure." Maxwell ignored that provision and assigned its rights to an affiliate of Beijing Publishing Press known as Beijing Children's Publishing Press. Children's Press then submitted the contract to Beijing Municipal Copyright Authority for approval, but it was denied due to lack of permission from WDC. Beijing Press went ahead anyway under the proviso from Maxwell that they would be responsible for "any disputes that may arise." The result was the publication and subsequent sale of the book *Collection of Disney Morale Tales*. Disney sued.

The case went before Chief Judge Chi Su, who decided that since the signing of the Sino-U.S. Memorandum of Understanding became effective on March 17, 1992, U.S. subjects had the protection of Chinese law. As the commercial use of the cartoon characters had not been authorized by Disney, doing so was an infringement of their copyright. Maxwell's assigning of those rights was an infringement of Disney's rights and also fraud on the Children's Press. Therefore, the contract was void as a matter of law. No further action was taken, as Maxwell had already declared bankruptcy, but a precedent had been set.

Other filmmakers took heart at the decision. American films to be shown in China first had to be submitted to China Film, who would permit or veto the showing of the title. Many filmmakers did not even bother to submit their films due to the likelihood of them being refused. Disney, MGM, and Columbia Tristar were amongst the few who tried, as they felt their films met the criteria of being "sincere" towards China and supportive of Sino-American relationships.

In 1994, Disney forged a partnership with Beijing TV that created *Dragon Club*. Though it started out modestly, within ten years it had expanded to air on more than 450 stations across China reaching an estimated 60 million households. Winnie the Pooh figures prominently in CCTV's flagship kids show, *The Big Windmill*, and on CCTV's new children's channel. According to Andy Bird, President of Disney International, Disney-branded segments reached more than 380 million households, making the company "the number one provider of Western programming to China."

Bob Iger, a name that would loom large in Disney history, was president of ABC-TV in 1994 when he arrived to inaugurate *Dragon Club*. He had been to China previously in 1979 when he worked for ABC Sports, and later recalled, "I stayed in a hotel, I swear, this is the complete truth, my mattress was filled with straw. No one spoke English, I spoke no Chinese. It was almost a joke, but a great adventure."

After the Disney Channel debuted in Taiwan in March 1995, Disney opened Mickey's Corner "merchandise displays" in eighty retail outlets around mainland China to give Asians the same advantage that people enjoyed at the Hong Kong and Tokyo Disneylands. As for building a Disneyland somewhere in mainland China, WDC would say little more than to acknowledge the possibility. A spokesman for Disney, John Dreyer, said, "It's so far down the road at this point, I wouldn't even want to put a timetable on it."

Beijing had finally permitted Disney movies to be shown in Chinese theaters beginning with *The Lion King* in 1996, which grossed around $4 million. Two others, *The Rock* from Hollywood Pictures and Pixar's *Toy Story*, followed and added to the revenue generated from the sale of seventy thousand Disney movie video tapes and 1.3 million audio soundtracks.

As previously related in the chapters dealing with Hong Kong Disneyland, problems arose when Disney bankrolled the film *Kundun*. Chinese leaders vehemently objected to the film even before it was released and threatened to curtail Disney's access to the Chinese market. Despite that, Disney released the film in 1997, which did not do very well due to limited distribution, and then hired Henry Kissinger's consulting group to smooth over the backlash.

The next attempt at the Chinese market was Disney's version of the old Chinese legend of Fa Mulan. WDC hoped to smooth over relations with the Chinese government after the *Kundun* incident and replicate their success with *The Lion King* as China's highest grossing Western film. The Chinese, however, were in no hurry to accept Disney back into their good graces, and when it finally allowed *Mulan* to be shown, it was to be a limited release and only after the Chinese New Year, to enable Chinese films to dominate the lucrative holiday market.

When it was finally released, *Mulan* did not do well, even though it was dubbed into Cantonese and Mandarin. The late release date, piracy, and the fact that it was too different from the original legend all contributed to the lowest returns for a Western film since the first import, *The Fugitive*, released in 1994.

The situation deteriorated further in May 1999 when, during a NATO bombing raid of Belgrade in Yugoslavia, U.S. guided bombs hit the embassy of the People's Republic of China. The intention had apparently been to bomb a nearby Yugoslav government building, but they had accidently hit the Chinese Embassy, killing three Chinese reporters. The Chinese government saw it as a deliberate and "barbarian act," and despite President Clinton's apology permitted its citizens to attack U.S. embassies in Chinese cities, including Shanghai, for four days before airing the apology on Chinese television. Though the riots stopped, the Chinese government introduced a total ban on U.S. films which lasted for a number of months.

By the turn of the century and into the early 2000s, tensions cooled and Disney films and characters once again climbed in popularity. More Disney animated shows such as *Goof Troop*, *Aladdin*, and *Winnie the Pooh* began appearing on Chinese television. *Mickey Mouse Magazine* subscribers topped 180,000, and there were now 157 Mickey's Corner retail outlets in China.

The next step was to set up operations in China to make Chinese films for Chinese audiences. The first of these to go into production was *The Secret of the Magic Gourd*, shot in Shanghai with a Chinese director and crew, based on a Chinese story. WDC partnered with Centro to make the live action, CGI movie in cooperation with China Movie Co. Ltd.

To further penetrate the China market, the *LA Times* reported that "Disney has considered remaking some of its classics oriented towards Chinese audience. One proposal was to make *Snow White and the Seven Dwarfs* as an action film shot in China with monks instead of dwarfs."

The earliest indication that the general public had that Disney was planning to build another Chinese Disneyland came in July 2002. It was reported that WDC had signed a framework agreement with the Shanghai Government that included plans to create a joint venture to build a theme park. Bill Ernest, President and Managing Director of HKD, originally denied rumors of the new park. The Hong Kong SAR was understandably troubled when they heard the news and they immediately demanded an inquiry. Disney was prepared, and while refusing to acknowledge such a deal, they insisted the while another park might be possible, HKD would remain the flagship park.

With the success Disney had with *The Lion King* on Broadway, which started in 1997 and has since become the highest grossing Broadway production of all time, it was decided to take the show to Shanghai in 2006. The award-winning musical would open at Shanghai's Grand Theatre on July 18 and play for one hundred performances. Special support was provided from the China Culture Development Fund and Wenhui-Xinmin United Press Group. The production was brought from Australia to Shanghai in two specially-commissioned 747 air freighters.

The Secret of the Magic Gourd was released in 2007 and quickly became "the most successful locally produced children's movie for the past five years culminating in winning Best Children's Film at the sixteenth Golden Rooster Film Awards." The same year was also successful for *Pirates of the Caribbean: At World's End* and Disney Pixar's *Ratatouille*. When the former was released in China, some censorship problems were encountered. The official news agency, Xinhua, reported that censors had halved actor Chow You-Fat's screen time because his scenes were "vilifying and defacing the Chinese."

By this time, Shanghai's mayor, Zheng Han, on behalf of the city, had applied to the Chinese Central Government to build a Disneyland. At the First Session of the Eleventh National People's Congress, Han confided to reporters that "We have applied to the National Development and Reform Commission, but so far we haven't received any document of approval." Though the location of the park had not been confirmed, Han said that he thought "the best choice is Pudong," but it was necessary that "any big-scale project of this kind has to get Central Government approval." Earlier media reports had said the Shanghai government preferred it to be built on the city's island county Chongming.

It was reported in December 2007 that construction of the new Shanghai Disneyland could begin after Expo 2010 was finished. This led to speculation that the site of Expo 2010, in the Nanpu Bridge area of Pudong along both banks of the Huangpu River, would be the site of the new park, building on the infrastructure used for the exposition. The site covered 5.2 square kilometers, and Shanghai spent over $48 billion preparing the site. Land along the river was cleared for 2.6 kilometers, and some eighteen thousand families were relocated. The Jiang Nan Shipyard, which employed ten thousand workers, and 240 other factories were also moved. Though it was never intended as the site of Shanghai Disneyland (SDL), the opening of six new subway lines and the addition of thousands of taxis to the area would eventually make access to SDL's construction site in Shanghai much easier. In addition, the 1.7 million volunteers trained by Shanghai to staff the expo could one day provide a convenient pool for Disney to draw cast members from.

The Shanghai Oriental Art Center became the site of the first *Disney Live!* tour shows in Asia on May 27, 2008. It was aimed at introducing Chinese audiences to the classic Disney characters. *Disney Live! Three Classic Fairy Tales* featured Belle, Cinderella, and Snow White.

The *South China Morning Post* ran an article on January 12, 2009, stating, "The Walt Disney Company and Shanghai's municipal government have completed negotiations on building the first Disneyland theme park in mainland China, and have submitted a joint proposal to the central government for approval." Sources close to the negotiations said that the National Development and Reform Commission had "verbally approved" the proposal.

After decades of negotiations, the global economic downturn was credited for encouraging both sides to take a more flexible stance in order to reach an accord. Disney wanted a 43% stake in the park, leaving the rest to a municipal joint venture holding company. The park was expected to cost US$3.59 billion, and it was thought it could open by 2014.

Disney was working in conjunction with the Shanghai Shendi (Group) Co. Ltd. (SSC). This totally state-owned venture investment holding company consisted of three sponsors, Shanghai Lujiazui (Group) Co., Ltd., Shanghai Radio, Film and Television Development Co., Ltd., and Jinjiang International Group Holding Company. They were all involved in project investment, construction, and operation through two full subsidiaries: Shanghai Shendi Tourism and Resort Development Co., Ltd. and Shanghai Shendi Construction Co., Ltd. Disney holds 43% of shares of the owner companies, and Shanghai Shendi Group holds 57%. The management company, responsible for creating, developing and operating the resort on behalf of the owner companies, is owned 70% by Disney and 30% by Shanghai Shendi.

An official announcement was not expected to be made until after the Beijing Olympics, but *Wen Wei Po* newspaper in Hong Kong offered an exclusive report. The paper said that the park would be located on ten square kilometers, eight times the size of HKD, near Chuansha Town, Pudong, about a twenty minute drive from Pudong International Airport. The Shanghai government would provide the land, finance construction, and own a majority stake in the park. Disney would handle management and get a percentage of operational income and royalties. The newspaper went on to say that the park would open "at the earliest possible time," possibly as early as in 2012, when about one-third of the park would be completed. An unnamed "expert involved in the appraisal of the project" was quoted as saying, "Considering inflation, the budget to build the park, excluding the land cost, should rise to about 40 billion yuan (US$5.7 billion), from the earlier estimate of 30 billion yuan."

Despite all the speculation and "expert" opinions, the Shanghai government still did not make the official announcement. Mayor Zheng Han attended the twenty-first session of the International Business Leaders Advisory Council on November 1, 2009 and gave guarded replies to reporter's questions regarding SDL. "Shanghai Municipal Government will, in the near future, convene a special press conference to release the latest information and to answer your questions," was all he would say on the subject. It wasn't until November 4 that the Shanghai Municipal Government Press Office made the following statement: "Shanghai Disneyland project application report has been approved by the relevant state departments. Estimated total investment of 24.4 billion yuan."

It was unclear what convinced China to finally approve the deal after years of on-again, off-again talks. "The prospect of creating tens of thousands of jobs at a tough economic moment might have played a role," said Orville Schell, Director of the Asia Society's Center on U.S.-China Relations. "It's a signal that now they will tolerate a certain kind of Western investment."

Needless to say, there was a dramatic increase in land value around the site as soon as the announcement was made. According to a statement posted on the website of the Shanghai Urban Planning, Land and Resources Administration Bureau, "Less than two hours after the decision was publicized, a 56,570-square-meter land parcel in Chuansha designated for residential development was sold to a real estate developer from Xiamen, eastern China's Fujian Province, for 1.19 billion yuan (US$174 million)." The starting price had been 326.8 million yuan, and the Xiamen developer had outbid seventeen companies who competed for the land only three kilometers from the SDL site. Industry analysts speculated that the limited supply of land in Chuansha might account for the record price. "In the short term, we expect housing prices in the area to remain rather stable as they're already very high." Over the past few years, housing prices had jumped from two thousand or three thousand yuan to over thirteen thousand yuan per square meter.

The arrival of a Disney park in the area was seen mostly as a positive thing, particularly in regards to retail and transportation lines. A realtor for Colliers International said, "The park will draw a large number of tourists, from both home and abroad, who will spend not only in the park and the vicinity but also in other prime retail areas across the city." There were predictions from industry analysts that due to the growing demand for cast members, transportation drivers, and construction workers there would be a dramatic increase in the number of shops and restaurants in the vicinity.

One of the main reasons WDC had selected Shanghai for its next park was that the transportation network was already established and could be easily expanded, making it easier to move people and goods into the area. With around 300 million potential guests within two hours of the site, that was essential.

Now that approval had been given, WDC and Shanghai could move forward towards the final agreement and start preliminary development work. The initial phase of the project would include a Disneyland theme park with characteristics tailored to the Shanghai region and other amenities consistent with worldwide Disney resorts. With Beijing's approval for the Magic Kingdom part of the development secured, the next step was for WDC to negotiate with Shanghai on construction plans. That was merely a matter of process, though details on what attractions would be installed still needed to be worked out. Shanghai preferred a combination of classic and new rides, with the latter reflecting Chinese history, stories, and culture.

Not everyone was enthusiastic about the new park. Many families were being relocated, and they were not necessarily happy about it. One resident at Zhaohang village, Guoyao Min, expected to see the ancestral house he had lived in for fifty years demolished. "Our family has been living here for many generations. I really have no idea how we'll be resettled in another place," Min told reporters. A brick kiln factory in the area was looking at closing down, as they could no longer afford the rapidly-rising rent. The workers were concerned about the difficulties of finding new jobs. Some local residents had been looking forward to the park for some time and had almost reached the point where they doubted it would ever happen. Now they were just waiting to receive their relocation packages to decide whether or not this was a good thing for them.

Even the other theme parks already in Shanghai, such as Jin Jiang Action Park and Shanghai Happy Valley, knew they would be affected but tried to remain philosophical. Zhineng Cui, general manager of Jin Jiang Action Park, stated, "We take the Shanghai Disneyland not as a competitor, but as a foreign counterpart that will inspire us to provide better services." Kelei Ren, chairman of the company running Happy Valley, was optimistic in that "As a home-grown theme park, we have more products based on the Chinese culture and cater to Chinese visitors and we cost less." It was generally conceded that Disney's arrival would pose threats to the existing theme parks, but it was also felt that the new park would attract more tourists, which would benefit all of the parks.

Government officials announced that construction work would begin in the spring with a scheduled opening date sometime in 2015. Preparatory work had started in April, with 3 billion yuan already being spent building roads and drainage systems, as well as sightseeing and traffic structures. A ten-kilometer waterway was being dug that would eventually enclose the site. A three-meter wall was erected between the projected park area and the remaining Chinese villages, and everything within, trees, shops, houses, had all been leveled. Two elevated roads connecting S1 and S2 highways were slated to be finished by spring, along with a Metro link that was expected to expand the system by some eighty kilometers. Convoys of trucks now sped up village roads, passing villagers on their bicycles.

The final agreement was completed on January 18, 2011, and government officials confirmed that the park would open in 2015. Speculation was that eventually the resort would contain three parks, a Magic Kingdom, one modeled after EPCOT, and an Animal Kingdom-style area.

TREASURE COVE

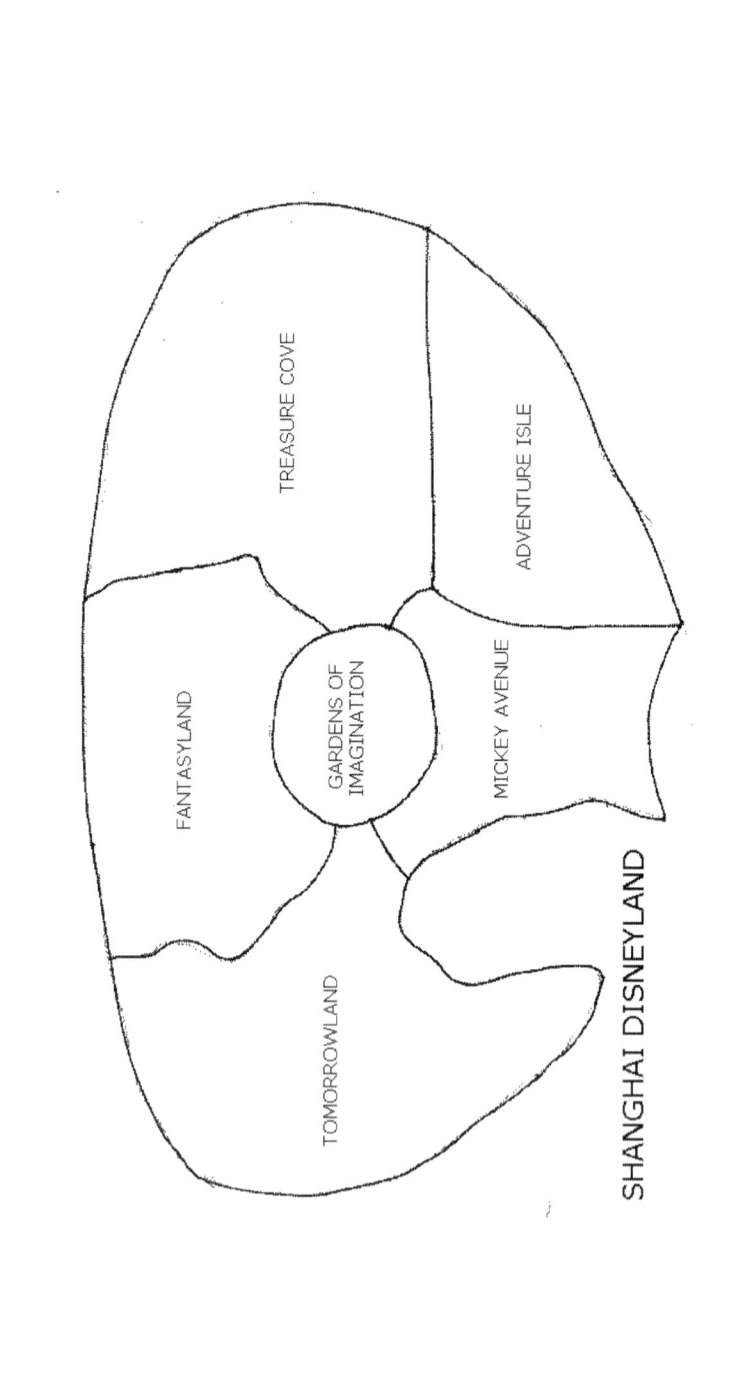

ADVENTURE ISLE

FANTASYLAND

GARDENS OF IMAGINATION

MICKEY AVENUE

TOMORROWLAND

SHANGHAI DISNEYLAND

Chapter Two
"Authentically Disney and Distinctly Chinese"

THE GROUND BREAKING CEREMONY was held in grand Disney style. On April 8, 2011, dignitaries from the Walt Disney Company and Shanghai Shendi Group gathered on the future site of Shanghai Disneyland. Paying homage to the people and culture of China, the preamble to the ceremony included traditional Chinese drum music, a female soloist singing in Mandarin, a fifty-voice Shanghai children's choir, and Mickey Mouse dressed in a traditional Chinese costume.

Following the entertainment, Robert Iger, President and CEO of The Walt Disney Company, made a few remarks: "Today marks a significant milestone in the history of The Walt Disney Company. Our Shanghai resort will be a world-class family vacation destination that combines classic Disney characters and storytelling with the uniqueness and beauty of China. Working with our Chinese partners, the Shanghai Disney Resort will be both authentically Disney and distinctly Chinese."

Thomas O. Staggs, Chairman of Walt Disney Parks and Resorts, confirmed those words and added, "We are hard at work designing Shanghai Disneyland, which when complete will be a special place where guests of all ages will discover a world of imagination, creativity, adventure and thrills."

Iger and Staggs were joined on stage by Shanghai Party Secretary Zhengsheng Yu and Shanghai Mayor Zheng Han to officially break ground on the project. Twelve dignitaries stood in a line, shovels in hand, before a long rectangular box filled with soil from the site. On cue, they lifted a bit of dirt on their shovels as music filled the air. Once they were off the stage, more singers and dancers appeared, followed by a parade of Disney characters led by Mickey, Minnie, Goofy, Pluto, and Chip 'n' Dale resplendent in red and gold Chinese-themed costumes. A choir of young people wearing Mickey Mouse ears sang "When You Wish Upon a Star" as more characters danced out onto the stage. The Disney princesses, Buzz Lightyear, Woody, and Jessie appeared in their familiar costumes.

In the *Disney Parks Blog*, Tom Skaggs wrote, "This is truly a defining moment in our company's history. Shanghai Disneyland will be the name of the theme park itself, but the property will also have two themed hotels, a venue for retail, dining and entertainment, a wonderful sparkling lagoon and some outdoor recreation areas."

As the year progressed, WDC kept those interested in the park up to date on plans. At the 2011 D23 Expo in August, Bob Weis, Executive Vice President, Creative, Walt Disney Imagineering, described the new castle: "The Enchanted Storybook Castle is going to be the largest and most immersive castle at any Disney park around the world and it will be the first of our castles not dedicated to a specific princess because it represents all of them." The multi-level castle would be open to exploration of a Once Upon a Time

Adventure, contain a Bibbidi Bobbidi Boutique for those desiring a princess makeover, and have a place where guests can meet their favorite princess. "Also, for the first time, the castle will be part of a boat ride attraction that will be one of the anchor experiences of Fantasyland."

The site formation work was completed by Shendi Construction Company within a year. Working in partnership with Disney and deploying "cutting-edge technologies for soil remediation and stabilization," the construction company "created new records for the scale, efficiency and quality of the work completed." Site formation work for the theme park and guest parking lot were finished on time and "to the highest local and global standards."

According to the newspaper, *Shanghai Daily*, "Construction crews have almost finished grading the uneven land to prepare it for the large-scale construction in the next step. To reduce subsidence and create a safe amusement park, the builders have adopted a so-called vacuum-preloading method on the 1.68-square-kilometer plot. They divided the area into four parts and inserted pipes into the land to draw ground water," with the result meeting "the standard of an airport runway." According to the builders, "The land will not sink by more than one centimeter for at least fifty years." The report went on the state that "about 98% of the necessary soil has been removed to form the river around the theme park, and 84% of the soil of the future inner lake has been removed."

Another ceremony was held at the build site on April 26, 2012. The Shanghai Shendi Construction Company handed over two key parcels of land to one of the owners of SDL, Shanghai International Theme Park Company Limited. In addition to representatives of WDC and SSG, the ceremony was attended by people from the Administrative Commission of the Shanghai International Tourism and Resort Zone. Bill Ernest, President and Managing Director (Asia), Walt Disney Parks and Resorts, was also present and said, "With great respect and appreciation, we acknowledge the efforts of our partner, Shendi, to prepare the build site over the past year, as well as the strong support from government. Their work will ensure that the resort development continues to move forward on schedule."

The next major phase of the project, resort construction, could now begin with a "highly talented and experienced team of Chinese and international Imagineers working in close cooperation with leading local design institutes and construction companies." A few more details about what the resort would consist of were also made available. In addition to the theme park and hotels, there would be "recreational facilities, a lake and associated parking and transportation hubs."

Now that the construction of the new park was underway, Disney began looking for Imagineers and cast members to staff it. The first recruitment drive focused on technical and creative people to fill over one hundred highly skilled positions in project and construction management, project integration, engineering design, information technology, procurement, and finance. Disney was looking for people who fit the criteria of "education, experience and a passion for excellence." Those selected would then be immersed in Disney culture and trained in a wide range of skills and service.

By mid-November, the first steel column of the Project Administration Building had been installed on the site. This would be the workplace of some thousand Imagineers, the creative specialists who worked on designing and building the resort. Completion of the building was expected in the first quarter of the next year, at the same time as the development of the resort entered a key phase of construction.

The end of April saw the completion of construction and the opening to traffic of the Tanghuang Road and Hangcheng Road, the eastern and southern border roads of SDL. There were eleven road-related projects underway, totaling ninety kilometers, for which the Pudong government was responsible. Of these, the Shenjiang elevated road, the main entrance road, and a bus hub would be completed by the end of June at a cost of 9.4 billion yuan.

By June, 492 households and 133 businesses had been relocated to make room for the roads. The former residents had been offered relocation packages and given plenty of time to move. The value of their new properties, often with larger homes than before, would rise in value substantially once the park opened.

"Authentically Disney and Distinctly Chinese"

Shanghai Disney Resorts creative head, Bob Weis, was on a lunch break with three Chinese Imagineers in Anaheim when they talked to a reporter from *China Daily*. Weis told him that designers from California visited China on numerous occasions to discuss progress and improvements with their colleagues and to experience Chinese culture. This was in July, and the final designs for the main castle had still not been finalized. A giant wall was covered with concept drawings, plans, and drafts in the hopes of getting input from other Imagineers and random visitors. The Shanghai castle was going to be the largest castle built in a Disney park. It would be the home of all the princesses, from Snow White to *Frozen's* Elsa and Anna, not just Sleeping Beauty or Cinderella, as in the other parks. SDL would also contain numerous Chinese elements to differentiate it from the other Disney parks. These will mainly involve souvenirs, performances, and festival celebrations.

Reports in the Chinese media indicated the mainland Chinese were especially interested in the development of the park in Shanghai, and it appeared likely attendance might easily trump that of Hong Kong Disneyland. The reason being that "the only mainlanders allowed to visit Hong Kong as individual tourists are the 270 million permanent residents of fifty-one 'advanced' cities. Others have to visit as members of tour groups."

Xuan Yu, a Beijing born and raised but Los Angeles based-Imagineer, was charged with "organizing creative design focus groups and immersive trips across China." She explained that their ideas were gathered through questionnaires and interviews with thousands of people in many cities across China. She wanted to find out what people wanted. "One key thing we have found is that they all want to take away from their Shanghai Disney Resort experience a collective memory that can be shared among family members throughout their entire lives," she said. Many of the designs had been completed, but many were still being modified, improved, and refined as more ideas were sought and more feedback analyzed.

One source of ideas was explored by John Sorenson and Joseph Parinella, design supervisors at the Shanghai Disneyland Landscape Department, when they took a design team of twenty people to visit Shanghai Chenshan

Botanical Garden in September. The team members were from a number of countries, Singapore, Great Britain, Hong Kong, and the U.S. amongst them. Their plan was to incorporate the characteristics of a botanical garden into SDL, so they consulted with researchers at the garden regarding technology for plant landscape construction and plant materials. In addition, they visited Quarry Garden and Aquatic Garden, where they were interested in ground cover, greenhouse, and aquatic plants.

By the end of December, work was underway on the Disneyland Hotel, which was located to the west of the park, surrounded by trees. It was being constructed in the shape of a flat "8," a number meaning prosperity, success, and wealth in China. The hotel would be seven floors high and cover almost 45,000 meters. An innovative technique was to be used on the glass wall by using hollow glass with a less than 20% light reflectivity, which would limit light pollution for drivers on the Hulu freeway to the west of the hotel.

As the 2013 Chinese Spring Festival approached, construction work on SDL continued on schedule. The Resort's Show Production Center (SPC) was scheduled to be operational in the second quarter, when it would become the heart of show production for SDL. *China Daily* reported, "Here the park's most complex and high technology show elements would be assembled, programmed and tested, before being permanently installed within the park. This was Disney's first on-site show production facility in Asia, and would provide a world-class centralized location where Disney Imagineers will oversee the creation of the technology and magic."

To celebrate, the Chinese Spring Festival executives and VoluntEARS from the resort visited the construction workers and brought them New Year gifts and greetings. Before the workers went home to visit their families for the Chinese New Year holiday, they were each given special Disney gifts as a token of thanks for their work over the past year. Even Mickey Mouse made a surprise visit for the first time since ground-breaking in 2011 to meet the workers and allow photo-ops for those who wanted a picture with the world's most famous mouse. Disney management felt it was important that they "continue to share special moments and milestones on a regular basis with the workers and their families, introducing them to Disney characters and stories through film nights, character visits, town halls with Disney resort leadership and many other special activities, while ensuring they enjoy high quality living conditions and a safe working environment."

What appeared to be a celebration in early March was actually Disney collecting technical data. Over several days, displays of fireworks lit up the night over the SDL construction site. Disney received a number of complaints from residents who feared it would increase the troubling amount of pollution already in the area. A spokesman assured the complainers that they were just running tests to collect data to enable them to keep their future displays below polluting levels. A local expert stepped in to assure residents that while the fireworks might increase pollution, it would not be enough to raise health concerns.

Meanwhile, in Burbank, at the Annual Meeting of Shareholders of the Walt Disney Company, Robert Iger, revealed the first image model of SDL. In doing so, he reiterated his "authentically Disney and distinctively Chinese" slogan when he pointed out that "There will be entertainment and show elements that will be very Chinese in nature, performed by Chinese, and designed, directed and created by artists from China." The image provided the first public look at the unique Enchanted Storybook Castle, centered in a beautiful eleven-acre green space. The extent of the resort was also revealed as including a theme park, a 46,000-square-meter retail, dining, and entertainment venue, two themed hotels, recreational facilities, a lake, and parking and transportation areas.

The latter was to be particularly extensive, as it was expected to have to serve millions of guests every year. The west gate transportation hub was being built to comprise five bus terminals, taxi and car parking lots, six lounges, and a restroom facility, covering 77,492 square meters. The government invited tenders in May for construction of the hub, with a 182 million yuan (US$22.54 million) budget. The Metro Line 11 extension was still in progress, and it was revealed that the last portion of the run would be underground so that guests would enter the park from a subterranean passage lit but skylights. Trees, shrubs, and an artificial lake will surround it.

More information about Enchanted Storybook Castle was released on May 24 as construction workers sunk the first piles into the ground as the basis to the castle's foundation. The castle was designed to be the largest and tallest in any Disney theme park and would also include a boat ride "that goes through a secret underground chamber in which fountains of light will dance in shimmering pools and surround visitors with magic, music and color."

At the end of May, Mike Crawford, General Manager of SDL, announced in a press release that "Shanghai Disney Resort has been devoted to seeking new technology and business solutions which reduce our impact on environment, save resources, and promote sustainable technology, and to support all kinds of cooperation with our local partners." To back up this claim, he pointed to an agreement that The Shanghai Disney Resort Management Company announced to adopt a leading new environmental technology that would supply the resort with heating, cooling, and compressed air, thereby increasing the overall energy efficiency of the resort by three times and ensuring the resort's efficient and environmentally-friendly operations. The utilities will be co-generated by a Combined Cooling and Heating Plant (CCHP) to be built and operated on the resort site by the Shanghai International Tourism and Resort Zone New Energy Company Limited. CCHP is a grid-tied, gas-fired power plant that co-generates cooling and heating via engine waste heat and produces compressed air by self-generated electricity. The CCHP project would supply hot water and chilled water for space heating and cooling, domestic hot water, and all compressed air needs for the Shanghai Disney Resort's daily operation. The project is designed, constructed, and operated by Shanghai International Tourism and Resort Zone New Energy Company Limited and will become operational in time to support the resort's opening, still scheduled for the end of 2015.

The concrete pour for the two Disney themed hotels on the resort site began on September 12. The two hotels, one a deluxe and the other a value hotel, will provide 1,220 rooms within the resort and will have a unique theme as well as easy access to dining, shopping, and recreational opportunities.

Mickey Mouse returned to the construction site with Goofy to greet construction workers for the Mid-Autumn Festival. Many workers were not able to go home for the three-day festival, so WDC and VoluntEARS from the resort presented workers with Disney-themed moon cakes, served food from a barbecue, and hosted a series of fun and interactive activities. Seven workers were recognized for their "outstanding contribution to the construction" of the park and named "Model Workers," with the presentation of certificates from senior management.

By mid-October, another milestone in the construction of SDL was reached with the installation of the first steel column marking the beginning of the vertical construction stage.

Most of the piling work, involving the installation of over 23,000 concrete piles, was complete, and work now shifted to substructure construction of buildings and infrastructure. An estimated 72,000 metric tons of structural steel was to be needed to build the key elements of the park. Management from WDC and SSG were present for the occasion and witnessed the installation of an eighteen-meter steel column, which "is part of the structure for some of the world's most advanced ride and show systems." Howard Brown, Senior Vice President and Project Development Executive of Shanghai Disney Resort, said, "Safety and quality remain the top priorities in building the resort, and we are committed to using the most advanced technology, the most efficient practices and the most environmentally friendly techniques in the development of this world-class tourism destination."

Rumors started swirling through the media as Empire Industries announced that their Dynamic Structures business unit had been awarded an $18 billion contract to build a new attraction. It was suspected that a top-secret version of Disneyland's *Soarin' Over California* was in the works for SDL, with the name *Soarin' Over the Horizon*, featuring landscapes and famous places around the world. For the first time the name Mickey Avenue was heard as a replacement for Main Street, USA as the main entrance into the park. The eleven-acre hub would be called Gardens of Imagination, and other lands included Tomorrowland, Fantasyland, Toy Story Land, Treasure Cove, and Adventure Isle. It was suggested that SDL's version of Toy Story Land would not have the Green Army Men Parachute Drop found in HKD but instead have something called a Round-up attraction, about which nothing was known. Treasure Cove and Adventure Isle would replace Adventureland and Frontierland. Attractions in Tomorrowland were rumored to include the Astro Orbiter, Buzz Lightyear, and a new Tron coaster. Fantasyland was said to have a new style Tea Cups ride, a bigger and better Peter Pan's Flight attraction, but they would do without It's a Small World. A River Rapids ride was thought to be slated for Adventure Isle as well as a Lost World Dinosaurs area. Garden of the Twelve Friends is believed to be slated for a location inside the central hub in front of the castle. Here will be twelve mosaic murals depicting the twelve signs of the Chinese zodiac using Disney characters. Mike Crawford referred to it as "the perfect symbol of how we are designing with the Chinese guest in mind, but with a link to Disney characters and storytelling."

Even though the park was far from finished, expansion plans were already in the works. On December 21, it was announced that the resort, known officially as The Shanghai International Tourism and Resorts Zone, would receive another four square kilometers, since the municipal government approved Disney's expansion plans.

Two days later, the first topping out of a building was celebrated when concrete was poured into the last section of the roof structure of an as yet unnamed building near the central lake of the resort. "The building will host a variety of dining and entertainment options for guests while offering stunning views of both the lake and Shanghai Disneyland's Enchanted Storybook Castle," an official with the resort said.

The usual Chinese New Year celebration for the site workers took place at the site, with greetings and gifts before the statutory holiday began, and workers took the opportunity to go home for a visit. As usual, management and VoluntEARS arrived to recognize outstanding workers and provide entertainment. 2014 saw the first appearance of Minnie on the site since the 2011 ground breaking.

By the end of January, the first of the hotels had been topped out. SDL and partner leadership teams poured the last concrete onto the roof section of the hotel, marking the milestone. The seven-floor hotel was slated to have eight hundred rooms and would provide a splendid view of the lake. The week before, the first vertical steel was installed for SDL's mountain which, when completed, would be the second tallest structure in the park after the castle and the highest mountain in Pudong New Area. Though not given a name at the time, the mountain would eventually become the site of the Roarin' Rapids attraction.

Details of the land that would come to be known as Treasure Cove were released in mid-March. The first of the six themed lands was to be dedicated to the characters and stories inspired by the series of *Pirates of the Caribbean* films. The announcement coincided with the completion of key structural work on the attraction. Unique to SDL will be a high-tech boat ride called *Pirates of the Caribbean: Battle for the Sunken Treasure*. The attraction's state-of-the-art technology, designed by Disney Imagineers working collaboratively with local talent, will take guests on an adventure with Captain Jack Sparrow and Davy Jones.

The second recruitment drive began in mid-April as SDL launched its 2014 China Campus Roadshow Program by visiting several universities and colleges in the Shanghai area. The program would later move to other regions including Anhui, Henan, and Zhejiang. Management teams from the resort explain the unique career opportunities available to the students throughout the park. This program was a precursor to the "resort's mass graduate recruitment campaign to be launched in the second half of this year, when the resort will recruit several thousand graduates to fill positions in a wide range of disciplines to support the resort's operations, such as food and beverage, merchandise, park operations and hotel operations," Mike Crawford explained. "We are seeking to attract local talent from Shanghai and across China who are interested in the tourism and service industry and who are driven by a passion for excellence to join us in creating a world-class family vacation destination in China."

In addition, the Entertainment team presented information sessions to performing art colleges in Shanghai to support the upcoming talent auditions slated for the second half of the year. "The shows and performances in Shanghai Disney Resort will provide a unique platform to integrate Chinese creative and performing talent into our world-class Disney productions," said Laurie Jordan, Vice President of Entertainment and Costuming, Shanghai Disney Resort. "We look forward to recruiting top Chinese talent, both onstage and behind the scenes, to help bring our exciting entertainment program to life."

By this time, SDL already employed over seven hundred local cast members and Imagineers working on the development and operation of the resort. SDL expected to expand quickly in the next year and a half to support the start of operations still expected to be in late 2015.

Disney apparently rethought its strategy over the year and decided they needed to expand the park beyond its original capacity. Robert Iger had noted that "Since we first broke ground in Shanghai we've been very impressed with the growth of China's economy, especially the rapid expansion of the middle class and the significant increase in travel and tourism. Our accelerated expansion, including additional attractions and entertainment, will allow us to welcome more guests for a spectacular Disney experience on opening day." In order to do that, they made an agreement with Shanghai Shendi Group for increased investments of around 5.5 billion yuan (US$800 million) to be used for more attractions and additional entertainment and anything else required to increase capacity. Disney knew that there was an income qualified population of some 330 million people within a three hour travel radius of SDL. "From 2012 to 2015, the Chinese travel market is projected to grow 34%," according to Phocuswright, a Global Travel Market Research Company. "The number of upper-middle class and affluent households in China is expected to grow 18% annually between 2012 and 2022." Disney optimistically projected ten million visitors-a-year when the resort opened, compared to HKD which had only reached 7.5 million in 2014. The new figure was more realistic when compared to Tokyo Disneyland Resort's 2014 figure of over 17 million. They had to wonder, however, if they were not about to make the same mistake they had made for Euro Disneyland and over build.

With its elegant art nouveau style and a touch of Disney, Shanghai Disneyland Hotel would be the signature hotel of SDL. The other hotel was to be Toy Story Hotel, with décor inspired by the Disney/Pixar films of the same name.

Nearby Disneytown was also under construction as SDL's equivalent to Downtown Disney in the California park. Here guests will find "world-class entertainment" at the 1,200-seat, art deco Walt Disney Grand Theatre in Broadway Plaza, soon to host the world's first Mandarin version of *The Lion King*. Casting for the show was scheduled to begin in the summer, with a focus on recruiting and developing local talent. The Marketplace will be "filled with specialty shops with Disney merchandise, musicians and entertainers." Next to the Marketplace will be Spice Alley, "offering a variety of popular Asian cuisines in a casual, yet romantic environment . . . and the intimate streets and festive lights encourage leisurely after dinner strolling." There will be stylish boutiques on Broadway Boulevard with "an exciting array of popular labels and trendsetting products."

In the central lake area, guests will be offered "an opportunity to commune with nature, surrounded by peaceful greenery and a beautiful lake." The area will also include a walking path and various gardens, "which present guests with awe-inspiring natural views and beautiful sunsets."

By July, the China Campus Roadshow Program, mentioned earlier, had gathered over two hundred local students from fourteen universities and colleges to participate in an international summer internship program in Orlando, Florida. During the two month long internship, students would work in a number of areas, including food and beverage, merchandise, and park operations at Walt Disney World. "By living and working at Walt Disney World Resort, students will take courses of study as they gain academic training at Walt Disney World Resort and learn directly from some of the most talented entertainment and guest service professionals in the industry." When they completed the program, the students would be selected for the talent pool to be a cast member in support of SDL's opening. According to an August news report, only around 150 of the students completed the program and were offered positions with SDL.

Recruitment and training was becoming a key focus, as it was noted that the 888th local cast member had been hired. In addition to new cast members, SDL resort also received a new general manager in early August. Philippe Gas had held key leadership positions in many parts of the world including human resources in thirteen countries in the Asia-Pacific area. He also served as president for Euro Disney working with the French government to negotiate land deals. As Gas moved to Shanghai, Tom Wolber, President of Shanghai Disneyland, was appointed President of Euro Disney, trading jobs with his successor. Wolber had been in Paris before when he helped open EDL in 1992 and also had over twenty years of experience at Disney Cruise Line, where he saw the launching of *Disney Dream* and *Disney Fantasy*, Walt Disney World, Disney Vacation Club, and Walt Disney World Resort and Transportation Operations.

To further advertise their new resort, SDL participated in its first Shanghai Tourism Festival's grand opening parade in mid-September. The festival is a major annual event in the city, so SDL gathered a team of Chinese and foreign experts to "design and create a specially decorated float blending authentic Disney features with distinctly Chinese elements to bring Disney magic to the people of Shanghai and to millions of TV viewers across China." The brightly-colored Shanghai Disney Resort "Happy Dream" float was described as having "a shimmering Disney castle" as its centerpiece, "surrounded by jewel tones and a flowing, red Chinese paper-cut 'ribbon' embedded with hidden Mickey patterns." Not wanting to waste the opportunity on just one parade, SDL would then join in the festival's roadshows and travel throughout the district to visit numerous local communities.

The resort's thirty-five-kilovolt substation was powered up on August 19 with the support of the State Grid Shanghai Municipal Electric Power

Company. The substation was designed to provide power for the resort and parking facilities with "an advanced digital collection system which allows for remote monitoring of all associated equipment. The resort's operation team will be able to track the power consumption information, and use this data to analyze the theme park's electricity load and power quality and efficiently manage facility operations and maintenance," Howard Brown, Project Development Executive, Walt Disney Imagineering Shanghai stated. "We are devoted to seeking new technology, which reduces our impact on the environment, saves resources, and promotes sustainable technology, while supporting technology transfer and localization."

The use of other technology earned SDL a prestigious professional honor recognizing the innovative design and technology practices that have been used in the development of Enchanted Storybook Castle. "The American Institute of Architects presented its Technology in Architectural Practice Award to Walt Disney Imagineering for its successful implementation of Building Information Modeling (BIM), the process of generating and managing digital representations of structures and facilities," Howard Brown explained. "The Enchanted Storybook Castle is designed with retail, dining, operations and theatrical spaces, and a ride system running through it which marries traditional architectural detailing with modern building technology. BIM enabled collaboration using web-based social collaboration, video-telepresence and cloud-based computing which brought together dozens of team members on opposite sides of the globe, and allowed them to reach key project milestones ensuring a successful delivery of Shanghai Disney Resort."

As the size and scope of Shanghai Disneyland Resort expanded, people were beginning to wonder if perhaps Disney had not overreached itself. It was feared that this going to be another financial fiasco beset with the troubles that plagued Euro Disneyland in its early years. Bob Iger was asked that question in an interview from Vanity Fair New Establishment Summit in San Francisco, to which he replied, "Euro Disney's troubles date back a couple of decades and had to do with a financial structure of that business almost at inception. They took on a lot of debt. Their pricing models were off, and they ended up in an economy that was very, very bumpy over the years. The Shanghai park won't have the debt overhang that hurt Disneyland Paris from the start, and will benefit from a larger local population base and stronger economy."

In December, the mountain feature mentioned earlier was successfully topped out. Its height was not disclosed, but it was said to be the second tallest structure in the park, after the castle, and the highest mountain in Pudong New District. The key element of each Disney experience is the physical landscape of any particular land, whether majestic mountains or tropical landscape, with matching rockwork and horticulture. The new mountain was designed and constructed by an international team of Imagineers "working hand-in-hand with local contractors to transfer unique Disney techniques in design, rockwork and themed finishing expertise to local artisans to bring the best of Disney to the people of China."

Late in December, Bob Iger announced, as he delivered WDC's earnings for its first fiscal quarter, that while the park was expected to be completed by the end of 2015, opening day would likely not be until the spring of 2016, though an exact date was not mentioned. Iger explained that the delay was due to the expansions to increase capacity and the benefits of opening closer to the Chinese New Year celebrations. "Even with that expansion, we will complete major construction by the end of this calendar year. We are planning a spectacular grand opening in the spring of 2016, which we believe is the optimal time to showcase the full grandeur of this world-class destination."

While this was probably true, further investigation reveals that this was only part of the reason. The British newspaper *The Daily Mail*, in their November 25 edition, reported on what they called "the leaning towers of Shanghai." Two fifteen-story condominium blocks were built in Chuansha two years ago to provide accommodations for the people who had been relocated due to the clearing of the land for the theme park. When first built, the buildings had a gap between them, "but residents who live in the high-rise apartments . . . say the original narrow gap between the buildings has disappeared and they are now touching." The tilting of the buildings was first noticed when a resident had gone up on the roof for a smoke and saw the crumbling concrete on the edge of the building. She left the structure "as fast as I could expecting it to fall down any minute, and called the emergency services. But they refused to do anything, told me to speak to the property management company. They insisted it is safe, but I don't trust them. Now some residents were afraid to go into their homes for fear the buildings would collapse." The head of the engineering department at the Xintuan Real Estate Company that maintains the properties and is responsible for them denied there was a problem. He said, "Only some decorative parts on the eaves were broken and residents can live in the blocks without any worries at all." His remarks did little to address the concerns of the people, who were promised they could settle in "model" relocation homes.

According to Screamscape.com, "The Ultimate Guide to Theme Parks," the author wrote, "From what I've heard, and I've heard this over the years from other industry professionals, building anything major in China can be a bit tricky, and is the primary cause of the delay problems. Chinese contractors can be a bit shady at times, and are known to sometimes cut a corner or two when they think no one is watching to either save a buck or meet a promised timetable. Fortunately, Disney management is watching and they have no patience for shenanigans like this, and caught onto a few things early on that were not built to their satisfaction and had them rebuilt the right way." The author of the blog also mentioned that he had spoken to "someone who knows a bit about the business and who has traveled to see many of these new Chinese theme parks." That unnamed person told him that "in addition to having a different set of construction standards in China compared to what we have in the U.S., the attitude towards the amusement park industry is also very different in China compared to the rest of the world. For most in China, working at a theme park is just about the job . . . they have no passion for the industry . . . they are simply assigned a job to do and do it." It has also been rumored that the Seven Dwarfs Mine Train attraction being constructed in

Fantasyland did not meet Disney's high standards and had to be completely rebuilt.

Despite the problems, average apartment prices in the Chuansha area climbed to 28,331 yuan (US$4,534) per square meter by the end of 2014. According to information from Dooioo Property, a Shanghai-based realty services provider, that was about a 25% year-on-year growth, and 70% higher than that of 2011 when construction started.

Another construction project behind schedule was the Disney Store in Shanghai. The 5,000-square-meter (54,000 square feet) store, advertised as being the biggest Disney store in the world, was still scheduled to open in 2015. The store was being built to accommodate a Disney themed indoor plaza as well as state of the art retail space where customers can interact with characters from the Disney, Pixar, Star Wars, and Marvel universes.

Chapter Three
Unveiling the Magic

As the New Year dawned, all was not going well. Following Bob Iger's announcement in December, Shanghai Mayor Xiong Yang admitted that while the park would be "basically" finished within the year, the exact opening day was still under discussion. *South China Daily* confirmed that there "might be some difficulty with a 2015 opening." Regardless, Shanghai Construction Group Co. Ltd. still maintained that the first phase of the theme park would be completed by the end of January.

Those in charge were making it increasingly difficult for curious people to see what was going on inside the site. Though some report there was little to be seen, security was very tight. Security staff sporting black flak jackets had been known to stop people from taking pictures from across the street from the main gate, though there was little that could be done to deter photographers who use the encircling roads or remote control drones.

To show citizens that the park was indeed progressing, aerial photographs of the resort's themed hotels and the Adventure Isle attraction, Pirates of the Caribbean: Battle for the Sunken Treasure, were released. The topping out of the 420-room Shanghai Disneyland Hotel, one year after construction began, was celebrated as a lead up to the Chinese Spring Festival in February.

At the same time, work was continuing elsewhere, as the resort's horticultural team was planting the unique trees and shrubs they had selected from across China and other parts of the world. The plants were carefully chosen to grow in various parts of the resort to reflect the different themes within the park. A particularly noticeable addition was an eighteen-meter-tall Chinese Chestnut Oak from Zhejiang transplanted in Treasure Cove. It is expected to grow to thirty meters over the years to become the tallest tree in the Pirate-themed land. The jungle-like area will eventually contain "over one thousand meticulously selected trees, and countless bushes and ground cover plants to create an immersive environment" for the Pirates of the Caribbean.

Details regarding The Garden of Twelve Friends were released as part of the Chinese New Year celebrations. The garden was introduced as "a whimsical area of the theme park that recasts twelve beloved Disney and Disney/Pixar characters as members of the Chinese zodiac" by Philippe Gas, Shanghai Disney Resort General Manager. It was intended that the Garden of Twelve Friends would enable guests to experience a blend of Disney storytelling "with traditional Chinese elements and pays homage to the central role of the Chinese zodiac in daily life in China."

Twelve Disney characters were selected to "accurately symbolize each element of the Chinese zodiac, while retaining their own distinctive traits." As 2015 was the Year of the Sheep, amongst the first selected were lambs featured in the *Jolly Holiday* segment from the 1964 mega-hit, *Mary Poppins*. Aladdin's friend Abu was to represent the Year of the Monkey, while for the

Year of the Rooster, Allan-a-Dale, the minstrel from *Robin Hood* was selected. The others decided upon were: Mickey's pal, Pluto, for the Year of the Dog; Hamm, the piggy bank from *Toy Story*, for the Year of the Pig; Remy, the rat who wanted to be a cook, from *Ratatouille* for the Year of the Rat; Babe the Blue Ox from the 1958 featurette, *Paul Bunyan*, for the Year of the Ox; Tigger, the exuberant friend of Winnie the Pooh, for the Year of the Tiger; Thumper, the cottontail companion of the young Prince in *Bambi*, for the Year of the Rabbit; Mushu, the pint-sized dragon from *Mulan*, for the Year of the Dragon; *The Jungle Book's* wily python, Kaa, for the Year of the Snake; and Flynn Ryder's horse Maximus from *Tangled* for the Year of the Horse.

In addition to the colorful glass mosaic vignettes of the zodiac characters done by local artists and craftsmen, the garden walls would be decorated with flowering vines. The interior would be a serene classic Chinese garden resplendent with cherry blossoms, where guests could pause and relax between visiting the various lands.

In April, according to the Shanghai International Tourism Resort Zone Management Committee, twenty-four roads, bridges, rivers, lakes, parks, and train stations were assigned names respecting both the local Chinese culture and offering a touch of Disney fantasy. The east entrance would henceforth be known as Disney Boulevard, the west entrance, Sunshine Boulevard, and the south entrance, Avenue of the Stars. The train station would be known as Disney Station, and the central lake was named Wishing Star Lake, with nearby bridges named Rainbow Bridge and Clouds Bridge. Other street names would be Inspiration and Wonderful Way.

One of the stipulations Disney had for constructing a Disneyland in Shanghai was government protection for its copyrights. In March, Guoqiang Lu, director of Shanghai Intellectual Property Administration, said that efforts by the Chinese government "will involve massive work on intellectual property rights protection, including its patents, trademarks and copyrights, as well as other related business logos." Until 2014, Chinese law had been very lax towards protecting foreign copyrights, so piracy and knock-offs were rampant. Since protective measures had been put into effect and Shanghai

Customs began a special campaign against infringements of Disney products, "fourteen trademark and copyright violations were recorded till the end of December, and 69,400 commodities worth nearly 1.35 million yuan were confiscated. That was 104.1% jump from the previous year."

Pre-opening development was ongoing, as SDL announced a multi-year strategic alliance with Mengniu Dairy Group as the official supplier of dairy products to the resort. The alliance ensured a wide variety of milk, yogurt, and ice cream products. The arrangement would also give Mengniu a variety of locations throughout the park, with an ice cream shop and ice cream carts.

Another strategic alliance was entered into with Pictureworks (Shanghai) Limited, who would become the official imaging service provider for the resort. Guests would have access to Pictureworks by using Disney PhotoPass, a state-of-the-art imaging operation at many picturesque locations and platforms throughout the park.

Shanghai Disneyland's first Disney ambassador, Jennie Xu, made her first public appearance with Disney VoluntEARS in an Earth Day celebration. Previously, Jennie was a Learning and Development Specialist for Shanghai Disney Resort, with five years with Disney. She led a series of environmental-themed classes at Gonglu Primary School near the resort. Over four hundred students learned about recycling and other environmental skills in a program that would become part of the SDL VoluntEARS program.

Other behind-the-scenes research was being done to decide ticket prices. Shanghai Tourism Administration revealed to *China Daily* that "special discount tickets will be given to fortunate groups of guests on the opening of Shanghai Disney Resort in 2016." Yang Jinsong, director of the administration, informed the reporter that Disney was studying the market to assist them in deciding on the discounts and that they were primarily enjoyed by seniors, youth, and special groups.

Bob Iger was back in Shanghai again to help celebrate the topping out of the iconic Enchanted Storybook Castle as the last golden finial was placed atop the highest of the castle's eight towers. "The finial . . . is topped with a golden peony, the flower of China, placed atop a cascade of Disney stars shooting out toward the heavens from the central spire. This finial joins another larger golden finial, installed recently on a separate tower of the castle which includes other unique Chinese elements including traditional Chinese cloud patterns, peonies and lotuses. This finial also features Magnolia flowers, representing Shanghai, and a Disney crown symbolizing Disney's princesses." Enchanted Storybook Castle is apparently some two hundred feet taller than WDW's Cinderella Castle.

More information about the centerpiece of the park was also revealed when it was made known that not only would the castle provide immersive attractions, dining, shopping, and spectacular entertainment, but "a magnificent winding staircase in the middle of the castle will lead guests on a 'Once Upon a Time Adventure,' providing an unparalleled and memorable experience unique to Shanghai Disneyland."

All this could have been lost were it not for the prompt action of personnel on the scene. On October 13, 2015, a fire broke out in the castle, supposedly due to welding being done in the area. Fortunately, it was extinguished within two minutes and no one was injured or damage done to the structure. The fire is under investigation, and management is also trying to trace the person who released photos of the fire onto social media. Apparently, this was a breach of rules, as all SDL employees had been previously warned not to take pictures on site.

As work on the resort continued, Disney stepped up its recruitment program so that by May they had over one thousand employees, with several thousand more still to be hired before opening. Several job fairs had been held which targeted university graduates for management vacancies in the entertainment, hotel service, catering, and sales fields. As an additional incentive, staff was offered a free pass to every Disneyland around the world, excepting Tokyo.

Disney participated in the annual Shanghai Tourism Festival by unveiling the design for the *Igniting the Dream* parade float to be used in the park. The train like float pulled six cars showcasing the six themed lands of SDL accompanied by singing cast members, dancers, and ridden on by Disney characters. After the festival, the train will go on a roadshow to further advertise the upcoming park.

Disney was carefully watching the response of Shanghai citizens when the doors were opened on the largest Disney Store in the world in the popular Lujiazui area of Pudong, Shanghai. "The magic was unleashed with a sprinkle of pixie dust at exactly 1:14pm or 1314 hours on May 20th, which represents a highly popular social media code among young people as a time to openly express love and long-term commitment to each other." Like every Disney event, there was an opening ceremony with Mickey and Minnie on hand as a select group of potential shoppers turned the key to unlock the magic inside.

The first Disney store in China is larger than its counterparts, the World of Disney stores at Walt Disney World Resort in Orlando and Downtown Disney in Anaheim. Paul Candland, President The Walt Disney Company, Asia-Pacific region, explained that the "Disney Store plays a critical role in how millions around the world experience our brand and allow kids, young adults and families to have a unique fun and immersive experience while shopping for their favorite Disney, Pixar, Marvel and Star Wars products."

An hour after the official opening, the Shanghai Disney Store had to close its doors, as too many people were already inside. Hundreds of potential shoppers were lined up for more than a mile, down the street and across a bridge. Those who had been there since 5:30 that morning got in, but others further down the line had to wait as much as three hours or more for a chance to enter the store and buy something. Security held up "Closed for Today" signs so no more people would join the lineup, and then set up a queue system for those already waiting. Signs were set up along the road at 60, 90, or 120 minute marks to let people know how much longer they had to wait from that point.

Once inside the doors, customers found over two thousand items of Disney merchandise ranging in price from twenty yuan to one thousand yuan. The enchanted store covered five thousand square meters (54,000 square feet) full of merchandise. There was a nineteen-foot Disney Magic Castle in the center where hourly shows were performed. A Mickey Mouse flowerbed adorned an outdoor plaza. An area dedicated to the Marvel characters featured a hand-sculpted, eight-foot-tall Hulk, as well as Iron Man, Captain America, and Thor. There was a balloon area featuring one-of-a-kind hot-air balloons in the shape of Mickey, Minnie, Pluto, Donald, and Chip 'n' Dale. A twelve foot tree concealed Disney characters, a gateway paid homage to Monsters University, and a crystal chandelier invited young adult females to where Tinker Bell sprinkled her pixie dust. Even the roof was Mickey shaped and adorned with over eight thousand LED lights that could be seen from any of the nearby tourist spots. That was just opening day.

All through the next week, security kept putting out the wait times signs. Only fifty shoppers were allowed in the store at a time on the weekend, twice that during the week. If the response to the opening of the Disney store was any reflection on what would happen when the theme park opened, Disney had little to worry about in making attendance quotas.

The two hotels were almost finished. The Shanghai Disneyland Hotel and Toy Story Hotel, with 420 and 800 rooms respectively, are "conveniently located next to Shanghai Disneyland" and are certain to "keep the Disney magic alive from day into night." Guests entering through the *porte cochere* of the Shanghai Disneyland Hotel will pass bronze statutes of Mickey and Minnie as well as meeting characters from many of the Disney classics, while those in Toy Story Hotel are greeted by Woody and Buzz Lightyear.

Shanghai Disneyland Hotel will have a fountain with a large glass peony blossom with classic Disney fairies as a unique centerpiece. The flower will be one of the largest sculpted, solid glass flowers in all of China.

Both hotels will have Disney-themed menus at their respective restaurants. The buffet at Lumiere's Kitchen features dining with the characters while fine dining and views can be enjoyed at the Aurora Restaurant. The Toy Story Hotel's Sunnyside Café has the extra attraction of *Toy Story*-themed Chinese-style kites from Weifang in Shandong Province flying over the diners. Facilities at the hotels will include gift shops with an array of Disney merchandise, King Triton Pool, Mickey Mouse Playhouse, Family Activity Centers, and a Hakuna Matata Oasis. There will also be complimentary shuttles from Toy Story Hotel to the park and a water taxi service across the lake for Shanghai Disneyland Hotel customers.

Next door to Toy Story Hotel is the site of Disneytown, the Shanghai equivalent of Downtown Disney in Anaheim, Disney Springs at Walt Disney World, Disney Village in Disneyland Paris, and Ikspiari in Tokyo Disneyland. The first tenants in this 46,000-square-meter area were announced in June and are expected to include both local and international brand names. Spread out over the five districts of Lakeshore, Marketplace, Spice Alley, Broadway Plaza, and Broadway Boulevard, some of the restaurants will be The Cheesecake Factory, Shanghai Min, Food Republic, Hatsune, Blue Frog, Breadtalk, Chow Tai Fook, and Crystal Jade. Retail options will have names like I.T., BAPE Store, and LEGO Store, to name a few of several dozen expected.

Festive lights and intimate streets are designed to encourage after-dinner strolls or browsing down Broadway Boulevard past stylish boutiques. The area will also feature trendsetting galleries with imported collectibles and designer goods in a sophisticated setting.

In the center of Disneytown will be the Marketplace where many specialty shops will be located, including World of Disney Store, Marketplace specialty shops, and Spoonful of Sugar confectionery. On weekends and holidays, there will be Disney-themed entertainment.

The three-thousand-square-meter World Of Disney store, the first of its name in Asia, is located in a railroad roundhouse and offers an array of "unique Disney apparel, toys, stationery, collectibles, and gifts, including exclusive items found only at Shanghai Disney Resort." Video walls and digital screens are placed strategically around the store, as well as an interactive Magic Mirror and an eight-foot projected globe hanging from the ceiling featuring scenes from Disney films.

Adjacent to World of Disney will be specialty shops such as Dstreet, with its urban trends, Dtech, for creating personalized electronic accessories on demand, and TrenD, a stylish boutique with Disney fashions. Mary Poppins-themed Spoonful of Sugar confectionery has a show kitchen where guests can watch tasty treats being prepared. Nearby is Spice Alley, with a variety of Asian cuisines and international food situated along narrow cobblestone streets and small courtyards reminiscent of bygone days.

Guests will walk to Walt Disney Grand Theater along a floral-inspired paving pattern that comes to life at night with sparkling lights. The theater in Broadway Plaza will have a Mandarin performance of *The Lion King*. Some of the storefronts will have *Shikumen*-style architectural features common in Shanghai's old lane houses.

At Lakeshore, guests can enjoy fine dining along the waterfront in a "picturesque collection of restaurants and shops inspired by current lifestyle trends" or dine in the expansive second-story seafood restaurant. Not far away is Wishing Star Lake surrounded by forty hectares of beautiful gardens and a 2.5-kilometer walking path.

In mid-July, Bob Iger chose the Shanghai Expo Center for his presentation to unveil highly-anticipated details about the new Disney theme park. Iger revealed a huge scale model of the resort and displays highlighting key components of the attractions, hotels, entertainment, and dining options. Also on hand were Imagineer and SDL show producer Bob Weis, Disney COO Tom Staggs, and Walt Disney Parks and Resorts Chairman Bob Chapek,

"We are building something truly special here in Shanghai that not only showcases the best of Disney's storytelling but also celebrates and incorporates China's incredibly rich heritage to create a one-of-a-kind destination that will delight and entertain the people of China for generations to come," Iger told the media during the presentation. "We are taking everything we've learned from our six decades of exceeding expectations, along with our relentless innovation and famous creativity to create a truly magical place that is both authentically Disney and distinctly Chinese."

* * *

The following tour of Shanghai Disneyland is as the park was expected to be when Bob Iger released the information in July 2015, as gleaned from subsequent information from Shanghai Disneyland Resort and press releases to the end of 2015 and early 2016. The actual attractions, shops, and restaurants that are in the park on opening day in June 2016 may be slightly different. Most of the quotes are from the Official SDL website.

Just before guests enter the park, they will see the Steamboat Mickey fountain as a tribute to Mickey's first appearance in *Steamboat Willie* (1928), though the Mickey here is a more modern version.

The entrance to SDL is typically Disneyland, as guests pass through the turnstiles and into a large open space looked down upon by a floral Mickey face. Unlike most Disney parks, there is no train station here, though the clock tower building over the entry portal through which guests pass has the appearance of a train station. Just inside the entrance is Mickey Avenue, the first Disney park main street that is represented as the home of Mickey Mouse and his friends and not as a Main Street, USA. Mickey Avenue is made up of four neighborhoods, Celebration Square, Park Place, The Market District, and the Theater District. The buildings have a whimsical appearance, but not cartoonish like those in some of the other park's Toontowns.

Avenue M Arcade is themed after the Carthay Circle Theater and will feature the largest selection of gifts and collectibles inside the theme park, with items exclusively designed for Shanghai Disney Resort. The façade pays tribute to the famous Disney characters represented on mosaic panels as universal virtues; Hospitality is Mickey Mouse; Minnie and Figaro as Compassion; Optimism with Goofy; Worldly as Donald Duck; Friendliness for Daisy Duck; Generosity with Pluto and Fifi; and Friendship with Chip 'n' Dale. The checkout area is themed as the First Bank of Scrooge McDuck.

There will naturally be a number of places where guests can find something to eat. Mickey and Pals Market Café is a counter service restaurant with Chinese and international menus in four themed dining rooms. Designed like an open-air market, there is Mickey's Gallery, Daisy's Café, The Three Caballeros, and in a nod to *Lady and the Tramp*, Tony's. The agricultural heritage of Mickey Avenue is celebrated with a mural showing scenes of Mickey and Friends engaged in agrarian pursuits. French bakery and café-inspired graphics draw guests to Rémy's Patisserie for a variety of pastries, muffins, breads, and desserts. The Queen Anne style of Sweethearts Confectionery decorate the candy store run by Minnie Mouse where murals tell the story of the courtship of Minnie and Mickey and the décor is inspired by Minnie's polka dot dress. There is also an outdoor snack area, Chip 'n' Dale's Treehouse, a Haus of Waffles, and a gelato shop, Il Paperino, themed to Donald Duck.

Similar to the other parks, Mickey Avenue will have its own band playing along the street where "the zany musicians of the Shanghai Disneyland Band will bring a fun and silly underscore to Mickey's happy neighborhood." The band will play traditional instruments expected with a marching band as well as Chinese instruments, whistles, and kazoos.

After leaving Mickey Avenue, guests head towards Gardens of Imagination, another area unique to SDL. At the entrance is Storytellers Statue, a bronze rendering of Walt Disney and Mickey Mouse as they supposedly appeared when Walt first went to California in 1923. In truth, it should perhaps have been Oswald the Lucky Rabbit with Walt, as Mickey did not arrive until 1928. The same statue is also situated on Buena Vista Street in Disney California Adventure.

Gardens of Imagination is unique to SDL as the first garden-designed land in a Disney theme park. The area caters to the love that the Chinese have for gardens and includes terraced areas to allow guests to view shows performed before the castle, and at night it becomes an excellent viewing area for the fireworks show "Ignite the Dream, a Nighttime Spectacular of Magic and Light." Gardens of Imagination was created especially for SDL to celebrate both the joys of imagination and the wonders of nature. The area also acts as the "hub" of the park, as guests can go from here to the other lands. Bridges and trails crisscross the area, and Disney characters are likely to be encountered as one strolls through the gardens. There are seven individual gardens. Garden of the Twelve Friends was mentioned earlier with the lunar year-themed characters, and at Melody Garden guests can practice balance and harmony with Donald or Chip 'n' Dale "in the fun-filled Tai Chi with Character." There is also the Garden of the Magic Feather, Woodland Garden, Romance Garden, Storybook Castle Garden, and Fantasia Garden. At night, the gardens will be filled with music and twinkling lights "as if Tinker Bell and her fairy friends are sprinkling enchanted pixie dust in every garden."

Mickey's Storybook Express, the daytime parade, passes through the gardens as it traverses the longest parade route of any Disney park. The parade is headed by a whimsical locomotive followed by themed train cars featuring music and characters from the Disney films.

If one isn't into gardens, there are other attractions here. The Fantasia Carousel, as the name suggests, is themed to the 1940 Disney release, *Fantasia*, and the horses are distinctly different from the usual Disney-park-style medieval mounts. The carousel was created by Chinese artisans and features "sixty-two magnificent, flying horses, Papa, Mama and Baby horses, and two chariots, painted in seventy-two optimistic colors." Dumbo the Flying Elephant is here as well, one of the few rides that is present in every Disney Park. The sixteen elephants offer a good view of the park that guests have yet to visit.

"The restless, creative spirit of China's wandering poets, as well as the diverse and beautiful landscapes that inspired them" is honored by the Wandering Moon Teahouse. This is another restaurant unique to SDL, particularly with its Chinese architecture and quick-serve Chinese food.

Standing in the center of Gardens of Imagination, Tomorrowland is to the left, instead of the right as in most Disney parks. "With imaginative design, cutting-edge materials and programmable spaces, it blends the best of mankind, nature and technology" and puts forth the same themes as the original Disneyland, "hope, optimism and potential of the future."

After entering Tomorrowland, the first attraction guests see is Jet Packs. The concept is similar to the Astro Jets and Orbitron ride found in other parks, but in this rendition guests are strapped into individual Jet Packs with legs dangling. As the ride progresses, it spins faster and faster and guests can control the altitude, but the higher a jet pack goes the more it tilts forward.

The TRON Lightcycle Power Run was inspired by the 1980s film *TRON* and its sequel *TRON: Legacy* (2010). Guests mount individual, two-wheeled Lightcycles and are "launched across a canopied section of track, the Upload Conduit, before diving high-speed into a mysterious game world of lights, projection and sound effects." Even waiting in line is an attraction in itself, as guests "listen to the evocative soundtrack and watch the Lightcycle trains twist and turn all around them, all under a color-shifting canopy. Covered in a translucent material, it reveals the pulsing glow of Lightcycle trains as they zip through the attraction." The canopy is edged in a dramatic, blue-green color-changing ribbon that "rolls across, over and around the Tron Plaza, like the tail of a dragon." According to the backstory, Sam Flynn has chosen Shanghai as the location for a "permanent portal between Earth and his computer world of *TRON*."

Next, guests can go to infinity and beyond in the target shooting adventure, Buzz Lightyear Planet Rescue. Though the same concept as the Buzz Lightyear attractions in other parks is used, here the technology is more advanced in the special effects and targeting systems. The attraction features "cosmic visuals, animated targets, LED screens and real-time feedback from the targeting system." The shooting gallery features more than one hundred targets with real-time feedback, outnumbering all of the other Lightyear attractions worldwide. The backstory has also been modified, as Lightyear and his Space Rangers try to prevent the evil Emperor Zurg from invading the Little Green Men's home planet. Now, SDL's Tomorrowland is Buzz Lightyear's "Earth-bound Star Command station for the recruitment and mounting of planet-saving missions."

In one of the two theaters slated for Tomorrowland is Stitch Encounter, a replica of the same attraction that is in Hong Kong, Paris, and Tokyo. Here again, Experiment 636, aka Stitch, from the *Lilo and Stitch* movies and TV series, "engages in unrehearsed conversations, plays games, makes jokes and takes guests for a spin around the galaxy."

Early concept drawings and maps of SDL showed a People Mover twisting its way around Tomorrowland, but that mode of transportation was dropped in favor of more popular attractions based on the recently acquired franchises of Star Wars and Marvel.

Near the entrance to Tomorrowland, guests can step into Star Wars Launch Bay and "meet heroes and villains of the saga, visit iconic intergalactic set-pieces, view props and memorabilia from the most recent Episode, and be immersed in the Skywalker story through a state-of-the-art cinematic experience." Having explored the Star Wars universe, they can then enter the Marvel Universe and meet the Marvel heroes and see their super-powered technology. There will be a "multimedia mission briefing on the thrilling world of Marvel" and lessons on drawing some of the Marvel characters "just like a real comic book artist." Similar versions can be seen in Disneyland and Disney Hollywood Studios.

On the upper concourse of Tomorrowland, guests will find Stargazer Grill and some of the best views from anywhere in the park while munching on Chinese or Western food. Stargazer Grill is the largest restaurant in SDL and is described as having "a rippled sculptural design and a mix of futuristic comfortable seating positions. Natural light, sleek technology and the gracefully curved ceiling will create an understated sophistication, while glass orbs of light twinkle from the ceiling like stars in the sky." On the lower level is a stage where bands, dancers, and artists perform encircled by a winding ramp to the upper concourse and TRON plaza.

Leaving Tomorrowland and returning to the Garden of Imagination, guests can then proceed to Fantasyland, the largest of the SDL lands.

As in all of the Disney parks, the entrance to Fantasyland is through a fabled castle. SDL's Enchanted Storybook Castle is unique in that it is the largest, tallest (196.8 feet), and most complex of the Disney castles and it is dedicated to all of the Disney princesses. In addition, it contains shopping, dining, entertainment, meet-and-greets, and a "magnificent winding staircase in the middle of the castle will lead guests on a Once Upon a Time Adventure." The castle overlooks a storybook village and an enchanted forest. At night, the sky above Enchanted Storybook Castle "will be painted in dazzling light, with music, special effects and fireworks" touted as a special "kiss good night" for guests at the resort.

In the Royal Banquet Hall, everyone is treated like royalty, provided you make a reservation to this table service restaurant complete with wandering characters. Princesses are available for photos in Storybook Court at the Enchanted Storybook Castle

Voyage on the Crystal Grotto is an "enchanting excursion that travels the waters of Fantasyland. Fanciful fountains and sculptures line the water's edge, celebrating classic tales of magic and imagination." The attraction could be called a cross between the Jungle Cruise and Storybook Land boat rides in that it has the life-sized vignettes of Jungle Cruise and the fantasy aspect of Storybook Land. Guests climb into the boats in the center of Fantasyland for the cruise. A scene from *Beauty and the Beast* is the first vignette seen, followed by *Aladdin*, *Mulan*, *Fantasia* (the *Sorcerer's Apprentice* segment), *Tangled*, and *The Little Mermaid*. In the finale, the boat cruises underneath the castle and into the Crystal Grotto, "a secret, underground chamber in which fountains of light will leap and dance in shimmering pools, surrounding guests with magic, music and color," and ends back at the loading dock.

The stage in front of the Enchanted Castle will be the site for daytime shows, presenting moments from the stories of the Disney princesses in dance and song. The Evergreen Playhouse will present *Frozen: A Sing-Along Celebration*, where guests can "join their *Frozen* friends and the villagers of Arendelle for a fun and frosty interactive showcase, packed with a flurry of stories, songs and sing-alongs." The show is hosted by two Festival Guides from Arendelle who will introduce the musical numbers.

After the quiet, serene cruise through the Crystal Grotto, guests can line up for some excitement on Seven Dwarfs Mine Train, similar to the one recently opened in WDW's Magic Kingdom. Guests board a train of mine cars in this family-friendly coaster where each car "is mounted in a cradle-like pivot that allows it to swing back and forth as the track turns." The coaster visits the Seven Dwarfs' diamond mine where the Dwarfs are singing and working, then winds "through rolling hills, with views of pools and waterfalls as they leave the mine and dash on toward the cottage of the Seven Dwarfs."

Most Disney parks have an attraction dedicated to Winnie the Pooh, and SDL is no different. Their version is the Hunny Pot Spin, a family attraction where guests ride inside whirling honey pots. Similar to the teacup ride in Disneyland, the honey pot spins according to the whim of the guests inside turning the wheel. The pots appear to be dripping honey and spin "beneath a canopy strung with honey-dripping hives, friendly bees hum the Winnie the Pooh song to accompany the twirling guests."

Unique to SDL is the Alice in Wonderland Maze attraction, which is themed to Tim Burton's live action version rather than the animated classic. Guests wind their way through the "delightfully whimsical world of Wonderland" and encounter the White Rabbit, the Cheshire Cat, and the Red Queen, as well as other characters in this maze of "sculpted hedges, stone garden walls, giant flowers, and whimsical sculptures."

Peter Pan's Flight is another perennial favorite in all the Disney parks, but SDL has a special twist to the old attraction. The ride has a newly developed inverted coaster ride system, debuting at SDL with this attraction. Soaring through Neverland in a pirate ship, guests come "closer to the action and face to face with the characters, as they are engulfed in Pixie Dust."

Evergreen Playhouse is to be the scene of *Frozen: A Sing-along Celebration*, "a fun and frosty interactive showcase, packed with a flurry of stories, songs and sing-alongs" with the cast of *Frozen*. The entertainment is introduced by "two amusing and engaging Festival Guides" who encourage guests to sing along with *Frozen* tunes.

As darkness falls, the park prepares for *Ignite the Dream: A Nighttime Spectacular of Magic and Light*. Mickey Mouse hosts this extravaganza of "stunning projections, lasers, fountains, inflatables and pyrotechnic effects." The finale of "painting" on, around, and above the castle transforms the structure "into an amazing new world."

For those who require some refreshment after all that singing, there is the Tangled Tree Tavern in the Fantasyland Forest, modeled after the

Snuggly Duckling Pub in *Tangled*. In this tavern, "full of rich details and an atmosphere befitting the boisterous ruffians and thugs in the film," guests are served a hearty meal in a lush woodland setting.

Leaving Fantasyland, guests now enter the first pirate-themed land in a Disney park, Treasure Cove, wherein they can join in the swashbuckling adventures of Captain Jack Sparrow and Davy Jones. Originally designed for Hong Kong Disneyland, the idea was disapproved by the SAR government, possibly because of the less-than-flattering depiction of the Chinese pirates in *Pirates of the Caribbean: At World's End*, and shelved by Disney until a more suitable park presented itself. Treasure Cove took seven years to design and is themed on the *Pirates of the* Caribbean movie franchise, in reverse of the other theme parks in which the movies are inspired by the *Pirates of the Caribbean* attractions.

One writer noted that while the attraction was under construction, the designers brought in water from all of the other Pirates of the Caribbean attractions (Disneyland, WDW, DLP, and TDL) and poured it into the Treasure Cove pond.

The plan for Treasure Cove was revamped and re-created to suit Shanghai Disneyland, where it became a "home to a wild, colorful crew of scoundrels, always on the hunt for fun, action, adventure and danger ... a raucous collision of color, sights and songs, blending cultures and countries with pirate frivolity, mayhem and personality." Treasure Cove is set in a seventeenth-century Caribbean fortress where piracy was a thriving enterprise indulged in by a "band of seafaring rogues who chased legendary treasures, fought monsters and battled each other, always with a humorous glint in their eyes."

Treasure Cove is divided into various neighborhoods, The Entry, Shipwreck Shore, Fort Snobbish, Landlubber Landing, and the Village, each having its own personality and distinctive charm. There is a mixture of architectural styles, two giant ships docked alongside, a water play area, and pirate-themed restaurants.

The Imagineers have taken the Pirates of the Caribbean attraction and stepped it up to another level with Pirates of the Caribbean: Battle for the

Sunken Treasure. The basic premise is the same, an indoor boat ride through the domain of scurvy pirates, but instead of cruising through a Caribbean town under attack by pirates, guests follow Captain Jack Sparrow "on, over and under the sea" as he sets out to steal the treasure of Davy Jones. Along the way, guests will encounter more pirates, lovely mermaids, and a fierce kraken. Advances in audio-animatronics and robotic technology make this version the most life-like in all the parks. "The ride will take guests down to the ocean depths, through the bellies of pirate ships, and straight into the heart of a ferocious naval battle, all the while braving the nautical twists, spins and turns of a pirate adventure." The ride system was specially designed for SDL, and state-of-the-art technology allows the boast to "spin, move and react smartly to their position, triggering action and synchronized music as they travel through breathtaking scenes and lively battles."

Adjacent to the Pirates of the Caribbean attraction is the 1,200-person capacity El Teatro Fandango, with the elaborate stage production *Eye of the Storm: Captain Jack's Stunt Spectacular*, premiering in SDL. Taking an idea from WDW's *Indiana Jones Stunt Spectacular*, this show features "fantastic stunts and swordfights, spectacular scenery, and stunning visual effects." Captain Jack and his rowdy pirates cavort about the stage "with plenty of swashbuckling . . . light-hearted humor, a raging storm and a remarkable finale, as Jack fights off a Royal Admiral in a whirlwind adventure."

Across the way in Pirate Cove, guests can relive their paddling experiences from Disneyland's Davy Crockett Explorer Canoes or HKD's Beaver Brothers Canoes. This version of Explorer Canoes is the way the pirates did it, but the guest propulsion system is the same. On the journey, the canoe captain points out various landmarks about the Caribbean Island at a leisurely pace until onshore pirates launch an attack with water cannons.

For those who enjoy getting wet, they have Shipwreck Shore to cavort about in. The water park is located in the remains of a French galleon, wrecked in a storm and tossed upon the beach. The interactive zone allows children and other pirates to "spray, splash, squirt and even climb amid random bursts of water, sound effects and animated elements."

A Pirate's Life for You! is a game where guests compete to become Captain Jack Sparrow's first mate, meet the fabled captain, and have photos taken.

As pirates get hungry too, the area provides one of the largest restaurants in the park, Barbossa's Bounty, in the form of a "lively, aromatic, colorfully ramshackle 'grog shop'" reflecting the personality of owner, Captain Hector Barbossa. In addition to pirate chefs showing off their skills in a demonstration kitchen, there are a number of themed dining rooms, including one reminiscent of Disneyland's Blue Bayou where guests can dine inside the Pirates of the Caribbean attraction.

Leaving Treasure Cove, guests now enter the first Adventure Isle in a Disney theme park where guests become immersed in "a newly discovered lost world brimming with mystery and hidden treasure." This land was designed specifically for SDL from the ground up with original characters and a new backstory. "The history of Adventure Isle combines lore and Disney imagination, beginning with the Arbori people, whose thriving civilization was founded on this island several thousand years ago. As the story goes, the island was discovered by a group of international explorers known as the League of Adventurers. Every corner of Adventure Isle offers guests of all ages the chance to unravel ancient mysteries, reconnect with a land lost in time and create cherished memories."

One of the major attractions in Adventure Isle will be Roaring Rapids, "a white-knuckle adventure through the heart of Adventure Isle." Similar in style to Grizzly River Rapids in DCA, guests ride a raft along a raging river, down a mountain, and into a dark cavern "where the undiscovered secrets of an ancient tribal legend and the reptilian creature Q'aráq are revealed." According to legend, the sporadic rumbling of the mountain is the roar of a mysterious reptilian being that dwells in the mountain.

Camp Discovery is located at the base of Roaring Mountain, and here guests of all ages can "prove themselves as true adventurers and blaze their own trails ... explore waterfalls, ruins and dig sites in search of ancient tribal relics." The exploration of ancient legends and natural wonders leads them past waterfalls and tribal ruins viewed from "an elevated ropes course created specifically for this land."

Storyhouse Stage will present an original production of *Tarzan: Call of the Jungle*, a high-energy musical retelling the story of Tarzan being raised by great apes to become Lord of the Jungle. The production is based on the Disney film, *Tarzan* (1999), and features Phil Collins' iconic score as well as "a fusion of theatrics, Chinese acrobatics and a rock concert."

Arbori natives are responsible for the "enticing tribal rhythms of fantasy and nature" coming from the Stone of the Sun and Moon. The nearby tribal lodge Happy Circle is also a meet-and-greet where characters from *The Lion King* (1994) and *The Jungle Book* (1967) are likely to be encountered.

Soaring Over the Horizon is SDL's answer to *Soarin' Over California* shown in Disney's California Adventure. *Soaring Over the Horizon* begins in "an ancient observatory nestled in the cloud forest, guests will soar and explore spectacular scenic wonders, with special segments for guests of Shanghai Disneyland overlooking Shanghai and The Great Wall of China." The attraction offers a walkthrough experience as well as the filmed aerial tour.

If all that excitement has made guests hungry, they can dine at the festive, art-filled Tribal Table, the ancient gathering place of the Arbori villagers. "Sights, sounds and smells will whet the appetite as guests enjoy the action of live cooking with fiery woks and rotisseries. The murals, artifacts and illustrations will dazzle visitors with scenes from a rich native culture."

***

Opening day for SDL was finally announced on June 16, 2016 after more than a decade of negotiating, designing, planning, and construction. Challenges were many over the years, not least of which were the cultural and political barriers that had to be surmounted when dealing with such a massive project in a communist country. The delay, however, took the opening from the heady days of a bustling economy into an economic slowdown. The effect on the opening can only be surmised before the numbers roll in, but it has been suggested that the optimistic numbers earlier forecast might be lower due to the middle class' lack of confidence in the economy and their uncertainty about the advisability of pricey vacations.

On the positive side, the recent success of Disney's feature films on the big screen have firmly established the Disney name in Chinese minds. The 2015 films, *Avengers: Age of Ultron*, *Ant Man*, and *Cinderella* combined to contribute a healthy $500 million to Disney coffers. Another $100 million from *Star Wars: The Force Awakens* was added in sales by the end of January, according to Forbes.

Little has been left undone in educating the Chinese citizens about the upcoming theme park, but risks still remain. Shanghai Disneyland Resort will not be unique in the country, as many real estate developers have added entertainment projects to their developments for decades. A conservative estimate of the number of parks vying for the average wage earner's leisure-time dollars is around 850, having risen by 40% since 2006. Not only have regional parks gone up, but other international American-based giants such as Universal (in Beijing) and Dream Works (in Shanghai) have stepped into the lucrative market. According to consulting firm Aecom, the Chinese-operated Chimelong Ocean Kingdom in Hengqin and Songcheng Park in Hangzhou rank among the most attended in the world.

As happens in the Hong Kong Disneyland Resort, peak periods tend to center around the few national holidays the government offers. To keep attendance up and customers content, wait times for the major attractions have to be reduced. Disney does this by adding street performances, parades, games, and robots to distract guests as they wait. Even these do not always work, due to the Chinese propensity for "line-cutting." The International Association of Amusement Parks & Attractions published an article in *InPark Magazine* in 2010 which describes the various techniques used to get ahead "such as 'constant walking,' moving forward while pretending there's no line, or using a kid as an 'advance man' to snake through the queue, bypassing the waiting throngs." The remedy to this practice seems to be narrower-enclosed lines, making it more difficult to perform the tactics.

Disney seems to have learned from past mistakes with SDL. When EDL opened, the lack of French food and alcoholic beverages was a complaint; SDL has addressed the problem with local food at competitive prices. EDL had far too many hotel rooms, leaving many empty and not bringing in revenue; Shanghai has only two Disney-run hotels. HKD was too small and could be done in a day; SDL is three times larger.

There were other concerns as well. The Air Quality Index (AQI) was monitored closely by the Shanghai fire department, who decreed that there would be no fireworks, by Disney or anyone else, if the AQI went over 201. Had the park been built in any other large city in China, particularly Beijing, this would have been a major problem, but in Shanghai the air was not as toxic. Still, it was not to be dismissed lightly, as air quality had deteriorated and was worse in 2015 than in previous years. There had been eight days with pollution registering in excess of three hundred, compared to only four the year before. Clear days, those with one hundred or less, dropped to 71% from 77%. The city was working to combat the problem by creating more green areas and banning polluting factories and vehicles. A smog fee was introduced aimed at cutting pollution levels, and limits were placed on dust emissions from construction sites. Disney, in turn, pledged to use more environmentally-friendly fireworks as they worked closely with the government to adhere to all local regulations.

In response to Disney's efforts to cooperate with the government, the city of Shanghai has kept its word to clamp down on Disney pirates. A Shenzhen-based hotel chain that was using the Disney name on five of its properties received a heavy fine of $15,000. Though they did not use Disney characters, their advertising declared the hotels a "Disney branch," and thus received the fine.

With an expected ten million guests a year, it is anticipated that a strain will be put on Shanghai's authorities to keep control of the crowds. An incident at a 2014 New Year's Eve party resulted in the deaths of thirty-six people when poor crowd management caused a stampede on the Bund. Emergency plans are in place for public security issues such as crowd control procedures, rapid transit and shuttle services, and extreme weather. The Shanghai International Tourism and Resort Zone Administration Committee spokesman assured the press that "We have a general contingency plan in place, which centers on the control of big crowds ... we will carry out emergency drills based on what is actually needed to ensure good management."

Shanghai began to institute a policy of demolishing illegal buildings that had sprung up around the park as it was being constructed. According to news reports, some 120,000 square meters of buildings, including homes, had been pulled down over a two month period in early 2016. Some of the structures had been built to house workers as the park was being built and later used for storage or offices. In time, officials decided they had come to pose a fire risk and had to be vacated and removed. Occupants were informed of the plan to remove the buildings, and those refusing to leave had their power and water cut off to facilitate their departure. Drones patroled the area around Pudong to make certain no new buildings were being erected. The demolitions were also done due to safety concerns, as people were building under high voltage lines and more than one worker had been electrocuted as a result.

With the buildings gone, trees were planted and a green space provided for "the public to relax and exercise," officials stated. An area of one square kilometer near SDL's east gate was designated by Chuansha New Town's urban administrative director, for "environmental improvement." Easier access to the area was also on the table with more subway trains being added to Line 11 and the extension of traffic hours.

Recruiting continued well into 2016 as more cast members, administrators, and staff were still required. Those seeking jobs were lining up for as long as five or six hours in hopes of finding employment in the resort.

The price of tickets was finally announced, as Disney worked with China's top online vendors to create an efficient ticketing system for the expected high demand. According to the SDL website, tickets are offered both for regular and peak period prices. "Special pricing discounts will be provided to many of our guests, including children, seniors and our guests with disabilities. Infants receive free admission. A two-day ticket will be available at a 5% discount." Tickets went on sale March 28. With the tiered pricing, SDL hoped to manage "the extraordinary demand we anticipate for our park in order to deliver a world-class experience for our guests." The tickets for opening day were sold out on the official ticketing website within hours after going on sale, and scalpers started charging ten times the price of admission.

Epilogue

DISNEY THEME PARKS ARE THRIVING all over the world, though as described above, some decidedly more so than others. It is probably dependent upon whether or not Shanghai Disneyland thrives, and the world's economic stability, as to when or where the next Disneyland will be constructed. There are always rumors circulating from countries eager to cash in on the Disney name, but as of this date there appear to be no firm plans to build another Disney theme park. Undoubtedly, one day in the future another park will be announced, for Disney CEO Robert Iger has frequently said that international expansion is one of the Walt Disney Company's three strategic priorities.

Over the years, whenever someone tries to secretly buy up a large parcel of land anywhere in the world, rumors begin to fly that Disney is going to build another theme park on that location. After all, Walt quietly bought orange groves in Anaheim and swampland in Orlando before building his successful parks in those areas. It stands to reason, therefore, that Disney would do the same again, and as themes parks are springing up in Asia and Europe, it could also happen elsewhere. Most of those rumors were based more on wishful thinking than fact. Some went beyond rumor, such as Disney's America, planned for Virginia but shelved after a groundswell of protests caused Michael Eisner to rethink the plan. Port Disney, also known as DisneySea, was planned for Long Beach as mentioned in the Tokyo DisneySea chapter above, but proved to be too expensive for the time and place.

The *LA Times* noted that Disney had talked about potential parks in a number of locales, including "Australia, India and Latin America."

AUSTRALIA

There were rumors when Disney was negotiating with China that they were also considering Australia's Gold Coast as a promising site for the next theme park. According to an article in *The Gold Coast Bulletin* quoting developer Gordon McAlister, "The president of Disney theme parks absolutely loved the plan. We were so far down the line, we had all the impressions drawn up, the site mapped out, the land optioned. We had the state and federal governments on our side." Executives, including the theme park president, visited the Gold Coast numerous times, checking out the site and making plans.

McAlister said that despite the strong backing of then premier of Queensland, Rob Borbidge, and present and past prime ministers, including Bob Hawke, the plan came from humble beginnings. Borbidge said the deal was well advanced to build a Disney park on land originally bought for a failed World Expo bid. "It had got to the stage where there were proposals before Disney and proposals before the government," he said. "Part of what would have been required was a pretty significant contribution from the state government. In those days the government had plenty of money and plenty of reserves and our feeling at the time was that it was worth pursuing." The government was voted out in the next election, and Borbidge never did find out what happened to end the deal.

"We got to the last meeting in Burbank, California, when Michael Eisner stepped in and said 'No, I want to go to China.' That was it, he was the boss. He wanted Disney dollars in China, he was looking at Disney as a whole corporation, not just a theme park. And that's how Hong Kong got a Disneyland instead."

A few years later, in 2014, the *Sydney Morning Herald* ran a story about a project that "was so secret it was discussed in whispers with a special code name inside the state government, and flew under the radar." Talks were purportedly held in 2007 and 2008 regarding prime waterfront real estate around White Bay and Glebe Island for a project to be called Disney Wharf at Sydney Harbour. Under the code name "Project Lester," the vision was not only for classic Disney elements but "also themed hotels, a marina and ferry wharf, two new light-rail stations, a retail space, an entertainment quarter and a residential development." Glebe Island's concrete waste was to feature topiary Disney characters in a Fantasia Gardens setting, and the old power station at White Bay was envisioned as a "design studio and arts centre". Not far away, a "'high-energy NY theatre-style district" was to be developed. Disney Village on the north end of White Bay would have upscale residences, a hospitality school, Disney university, a yacht club, and a Disney town centre with "prime waterfront office space."

The theme park was slated to have *Finding Nemo* (2003) themed attractions as well as Dumbo and Peter Pan rides, Disney characters for meet-and-greets, and the obligatory shops and eateries such as Goofy Candy Store and Princess Boutique.

Though the idea was designed to refresh Sydney's tourism offerings and draw patrons from "all over Australia and the world," the state government had mixed feelings about the project. The Labour administration saw it as a political as well as a financial challenge and suspected that it "wouldn't have gone down at all well" with neighboring boroughs. Amongst the few enthusiastic supporters of the plan were Ian Macdonald, State Development Minister, Premier Morris Iemma, and Treasurer Michael Costa, who were involved in high-level talks with WDC.

However, according to *Sydney Morning Herald*, "their interest waned as the scale of infrastructure investment expected by Disney became apparent." Disney had put forward a starting cost of $500 million just for the road and rail changes required for what had become to be seen as a "development proposal dressed up as fun park." The legislators saw it as a fabulous proposal, but they wanted something more interesting than "million dollar apartments." In time they found they were having difficulty getting written and detailed proposals from Disney, which fostered doubts about the feasibility of the project and whether or not it would even work.

Though Disney will admit that they are always looking to expand the company and that they have had talks with many divergent entities, they would not confirm or deny the existence of Project Lester. The land for the Sydney proposal remains "a concrete expanse, housing a temporary exhibition centre and a cruise passenger terminal."

PHILIPPINES

The Philippines became a possible Disneyland site when *The Disney Examiner* reported that Walt Disney International Chairman Andy Bird had met with Philippine President Benigno Aquino III during the US-ASEAN Summit in California in February 2016. Had WDC or the Philippine government quashed rumors at this time, it probably would never have developed into anything, but the Philippine Government offered "no comment" and Disney said they were discussing "potential investment opportunities," so rumors began.

There appeared to be some basis for hope, as three years earlier a Pampanga representative had put a Disneyland Philippines proposal to WDC, and there were speculations that Disney was ready to invest $350 million in the idea. Reportedly, Jim Filippatos, Vice-President for Global Public Policy, had said, "Disney finds the Philippines a great location for entertainment and amusement goers." A report from OKD2 claimed that WDC was looking at buying land on Laguna, Batangas, Bulacan, and Pampanga areas and that the park was slated to open in the summer of 2018.

Though most financiers scoffed at the idea of a Disneyland Philippines due to the country's small market and limited infrastructure, an HKD director pointed out that the Philippines was an important market. A large percentage of visitors from outside of China come from the islands. In addition, many performers, composers, and singers in HKD originated in the Philippines, so there appeared to be a large entertainment base to draw from.

In March 2016, *Disney Examiner* put an end to the rumors by stating that the entire Disneyland Philippines story had been the result of a hoax article reportedly from the website of OKD2.com. A spokesperson from Walt Disney Parks and Resorts wrote a statement for *Disney Examiner*, reiterating, "While the Philippines is an attractive market, we have no plans for the region at this time."

INDIA

Another huge, underdeveloped market for Disney is India. According to an article in *The Hindu* in November 2014, an official from the State of Hyderabad tourism department stated, "The talks with Disneyland Park representatives are at a preliminary stage now. Once the terms are finalised, Telangana will have its own Disneyland with all its splendour." The officials had met with a Disney team in New Delhi a few weeks previous to discuss building an amusement park on the outskirts of Hyderabad in the southern Indian state of Telangana. Disney representatives had been assured about "the availability of ready-to-use manpower and technical expertise to meet their operational standards" during the preliminary presentation. They were also brought up to date on incentives the government had to offer, particularly in the tourism sector.

It seems that WDC had some interest in the project, particularly in certain areas along the Krishna River in the "vicinity of Nagarjuna Sagar in the neighbouring Nalgonda district." Significant plots of land suitable for a theme park had been identified as possible sites in the Ranga Reddy and Nalgonda districts. *The Hindu* reported that the Andhra Pradesh government was in the initial stages of talks about a Disneyland similar to the one in Paris amongst other initiatives.

In addition to Disneyland, there would be other theme parks and convention centers as well as promotions for water sports, cruising, beach tourism, and spiritual tourism in Tirupati, Vijayawada, and Visakhapatnam. The future of a Disneyland in India is still undecided.

LAOS

Early in January 2016, the Laos government's state-run *Vientiane Times* ran an article that appeared to announce the building of a Disneyland in Thakek the capital of Khammouanne, a rural province of southern Laos. "Excavation work to prepare land for construction for Disney Laos will begin next month," the newspaper's front cover proclaimed. The report went on to state that the $5 billion project would be in three phases, with Disneyland Laos to be in the last phase within the next seven to ten years. Investors from Laos, Malaysia, and Thailand were all said to be involved in the massive project. Reaction was mostly positive, with thirty thousand likes being promptly registered on the Laotian state-run Facebook page. Not everyone was excited about the prospect. One woman stated, "We do not need Disney. We are already a Mickey Mouse country."

The first thing to invite skepticism of the project was the location. Thakek is over ten hours away from the capital of Laos, Vientiane, on roads which are usually washed out during the rainy season. Also, it seemed strange that Disney would choose Laos instead of neighboring Thailand, which has over ten times the population.

At first financiers put the rumors down to an attempt at land speculation, as even the rumor of a Disney theme park would send land prices soaring. Eventually, the true source of the misunderstanding was put down to the use of the name "Disneyland" as generic for theme park in the Lao language. To put an end to the speculation, Disney sent an email to the Thai media website

Khaosod, stating, "While Laos is an attractive market, we have no plans for the region at this time."

SOUTH KOREA

In February 2005, the *LA Times* printed an article stating that WDC executives had spent the previous several months in negotiations with government officials from South Korea regarding a possible Disneyland in Seoul. The proposal was for a smaller version of the Hong Kong theme park, already the smallest Disneyland in the world. Sources cautioned that the talks were only preliminary and no final commitments had been made. Jay Rasulo admitted that South Korea was "a potentially attractive market" but denied the rumor that WDC had bought an eight-hundred-acre site near the South Korean capital.

Observers suspected that Disney was using the Korean talks as leverage to get better deals from the Chinese government during its negotiations for the Shanghai site and the Hong Kong park due to open in a few months. A similar strategy had been used in Europe when French and Spanish negotiators had been pitted against each other for the most lucrative deals. Frank Stanek, now working for Universal Studios, said such a practice would be a "logical extension of their historical practice."

South Korea was a largely untouched market where WDC had only recently made inroads into the book market and started broadcasting the Disney Channel. The country's 50 million population and affluent middle class made it a tempting prospect. The world's fourteenth-busiest theme park, Lotte World, run by the Lotte retail chain, is in Seoul. Frank Stanek once commented that "Korea has enough population and economic wealth to sustain a theme park." One major problem would be the tumultuous political climate and the instability of relations with North Korea making the area unattractive to international travelers. Another is the probability of upsetting Disney's partners in Japan and China by adding even more competition to an already straining theme park market. Based on attendance figures released by the Themed Entertainment Association (TEA), in 2016, ten of the world's top twenty theme parks are in China, Japan, and Korea, one is in France, and the rest of the twenty are in the United States.

The announcement of another Disneyland in Seoul, South Korea during Disney's negotiations with Hong Kong SAR was later put down to an ill-conceived attempt to speed up negotiations for Tokyo DisneySea with a hint of going elsewhere.

JAPAN

A recent mayoral election in the city of Ginowan on the Japanese island of Okinawa sparked rumors about a Disney park replacing the soon to be vacated U.S. Marine Corps Air Station Futenma. One of the candidates, Sakima Atsushi, wanted to have a Disney resort constructed on the land once the Marines vacated and apparently had support from Tokyo. Chief Cabinet Secretary Suga Yoshihide supported the mayor and his efforts towards a Disney park on a site of the base. The controversial site could also be used for a new airstrip, a preference of Teruya Kantoku of the Japanese Parliament's lower house who considered the Disney idea to be no more than a "populist, vote-winning gesture." All involved are against the construction of a new United States military base on the island.

An Oriental Land Company representative was quoted as saying they were "considering a pertinent proposal by the city of Ginowan" but would not comment on whether the political backing from Tokyo had any influence over future plans. It is also more likely that a Disney Vacation Club Resort such as Aulani on Hawaii would evolve rather than a full-sized theme park.

BRAZIL

Word leaked out in February 2010 that Disney was planning to build a theme park at Curitiba, the capital city of Paraná state in southern Brazil. Unnamed sources stated that Curitiba had been chosen because of "its excellent infrastructure, its strategic location and its international airport."

Construction was slated to begin in August 2011 and expected to last for five years as twenty-five square kilometers of land were serviced and developed. The Disney resort would consist of a theme park, a zoo, water park, shopping center, and hotel complex.

José Carioca, a suave Brazilian parrot who made his debut in *Saludos Amigos* (1942) appearing with Donald Duck, would have a special area.

Disney already has a strong presence in Latin America with several Disney-owned TV channels, radio stations, a complex for dubbing Disney movies into Portuguese, and numerous publications.

As the announced dates have long passed, it is apparent that the Curitiba project was little more than a rumor but one that rears its head every now and again as other infrastructure and construction projects take place. The announcement that the 2014 World Cup was to be held in Curitiba and the awarding of the 2016 Olympic Games to Rio de Janeiro give the hint of possibility to the speculation.

ZIMBABWE

Walter Mzembi, Minister of Tourism for the African nation of Zimbabwe, reportedly revealed to the United Nations Tourism Organization that his country "was to take on Disney with a proposed $300 million theme park in Victoria Falls." According to a report from the *Daily Mail*, despite being crippled by ten years of internal strife, the plan was for shopping malls, exhibition facilities, and casinos around a three-hundred-acre theme park.

Mzembi wanted to get away from the stereotypical view of Zimbabwean tourism as "old people in safari suits," and "attract the youthful market into this destination." The main response to the park, dubbed Disneyland-by-Zambezi by some, was to call the idea "bizarre," as Zimbabwe had far more pressing matters to concern itself with than a theme park. Political analyst Clifford Mashiri told South West Radio Africa that the plan was just a tactic to divert attention from the country's problems of lack of such basics as water and electricity in many areas.

"The reason people visit the falls is because it's unspoiled and natural . . . not because they want to buy candy-floss and be immersed in an American style theme park," reporter and Africa travel expert Lisa Grainger wrote. "It would be like building a casino beside the pyramids."

Work has begun on a $150 million upgrade of Victoria Falls airport that includes a new terminal building, control tower, and runway, a step in the right direction to increase tourism, but a very long way from ground breaking for an African Disneyland.

Perhaps subsequent editions of *Building Magic: Disney's Overseas Theme Parks* will tell the whole story behind the rumors, and some of the above mentioned will actually become Disneyland.

Bibliography

BOOKS

Anton-Clavé, Salvador – *The Global Theme Park Industry* – Oxford University Press – 2007

Bailey, Adrian – *Walt Disney's World of Fantasy* – Everest House – 1982

Beard, Richard R. – *Walt Disney's EPCOT Center: Creating the New World of Tomorrow* – Harry N. Abrams, Inc. – 1982

Benoliel, Michael– *Negotiation Excellence: Successful Deal Making*– World Scientific Publishing– 2011

Bestor, Theodore C.– *Tsukiji: The Fish Market at the Center of the World*– University of California Press – 2004

Birnbaum, Steve– *Birnbaum Guide to Disneyland* – various years

Birnbaum, Steve– *Birnbaum Guide to Walt Disney World* – various years

Bright, Randy – *Disneyland Inside Story* – Harry N. Abrams, Inc. – 1987

Broggie, Michael – *Walt Disney's Railroad Story* – The Donning Company – 2006

Cameron, George D. – *International Business Law: Cases and Materials* – Van Rye Publishing – 2015

Clarke, Alan, and Wei, Chen – *International Hospitality Management* – Routledge – 2007

Cotter, Bill – *The Wonderful World of Disney Television: A Complete History* – Hyperion – 1997

Eisner, Michael – *Work in Progress: Risking Failure, Surviving Success* – Hyperion – 1998

Finch, Christopher – *The Art of Walt Disney from Mickey Mouse to the Magic Kingdoms* – Harry N. Abrams, Inc. – 1999

Finnie, Shaun – *The Disneylands That Never Were* – Lulu.com – 2006

Flower, Joe – *Prince of the Magic Kingdom* – John Wiley & Sons – 1991

France, Van Arsdale – *Window on Main Street* – Laughter Publications – 1991

Fung, Anthony Y.H. (Ed.) – *Asian Popular Culture: The Global (Dis)continuity* – Routledge – 2013

Gordon, Bruce and Mumford, David – *Disneyland: The Nickel Tour* – Camphor Tree – 1995

Gordon, Bruce and O'Day, Tim – *Disneyland: Then, Now and Forever* – Disney Editions – 2005

Grant, John – *Encyclopedia of Walt Disney's Animated Characters: From Mickey Mouse to Hercules* – Hyperion – 1998

Greene, Katherine and Greene, Richard – *The Man Behind the Magic: The Story of Walt Disney* – Viking Press – 1991

Grover, Ron – *The Disney Touch* – Business One Irwin – 1991

Heikkila, Eric John and Pizarro-O'Byrne, Rafael – *Southern California and the World* – Greenwood Publishing – 2002

Hollis, Richard and Sibley, Brian – *The Disney Studio Story* – Justin Knowles – 1988

Imagineers, The – *Walt Disney Imagineering: A Behind the Dreams Look at Making the Magic Real* – Hyperion – 1996

Imagineers, The – *The Imagineering Field Guide to Disney Hollywood Studios at Walt Disney World* – Disney Editions – 2010

Imagineers, The – *The Imagineering Field Guide to EPCOT at Walt Disney World* – Disney Editions – 2010

Imagineers, The – *The Imagineering Field Guide to Disney's Animal Kingdom at Walt Disney World* – Disney Editions – 2007

Imagineers, The – *The Imagineering Field Guide to the Magic Kingdom at Walt Disney World* – Disney Editions – 2009

Imagineers, The – *The Imagineering Field Guide to Disneyland* – Disney Editions – 2008

Jing, Jun – *Feeding China's Little Emperors: Food, Children and Social Change* – Stanford University Press – 2000

Kano, Yasuhisa – *The True Story of Tokyo Disneyland* – Tokyo – 1986

Koenig, David – *Mouse Tales: A Behind-the-Ears Look at Disneyland* – Bonaventure Press – 1994

Koenig, David – *Mouse Under Glass: Secrets of Disney Animation and Theme Parks* – Bonaventure Press – 2001

Koren, Leonad – *Success Stories: How 11 of Japan's Most Interesting Businesses Came to Be* – Chronicle Books – 1990

Kurtii, Jeff – *Since the World Began: Walt Disney World The First 25 Years* – Hyperion – 1996

Kurtti, Jeff – *Walt Disney's Imagineering Legends and the Genesis of the Disney Theme Park* – Disney Editions – 2008

Lainsbury, Andrew – *Once Upon an American Dream: The Story of Euro Disneyland* – University of Kansas Press – 2000

Littaye, Alain and Ghez, Didier – *Disneyland Paris From Sketch to Reality* – Neverland Editions – 2012

Maltin, Leonard – *The Disney Films* (4th edition) – Disney Editions – 2000

Medley, Travis – *Travelers Series Guide to Tokyo Disneyland and Tokyo DisneySea* – Createspace – various years

Miller, Diane Disney – *The Story of Walt Disney* – Dell – 1959

Misawa, Mitsura – *Cases On International Business And Finance In Japanese Corporations* – Hong Kong University Press – 2007

Monaham, Torin – *Globalization, Technological Change and Public Education* – Routledge – 2013

O`Day, Tim – *Disneyland: Celebrating 45 Years of Magic* – Disney Editions – 2000

O'Day, Tim and Santoli, Lorraine – *Disneyland Resort: Magical Memories for a Lifetime* – Disney Editions – 2002

Raz, Aviad E. – *Riding the Black Ship: Japan and Tokyo Disneyland* –Harvard University Press – 1999

Sehlinger, Bob – *The Unofficial Guide to Disneyland* – Simon & Schuster – various years

Sehlinger, Bob – *The Unofficial Guide to Walt Disney World* – Simon & Schuster – various years

Silvester, William – *Saving Disney: The Roy E. Disney Story* – Theme Park Press – 2015

Simons, Henrietta Gorzenska, Editor – *Polish Americans in California, Volume II* – National Center for Urban Ethnic Affairs & Polish American Historical Association –1995

Sinyard, Neil – *The Best of Disney* – W.H. Smith – 1988

Sklar, Marty – *Dream It! Do It!* – Disney Editions – 2013

Smith, Dave – *Disney A to Z: The Official Encyclopedia* (3rd Edition) – Disney Editions – 2006

Smith, Dave – *The Quotable Walt Disney* – Disney Editions – 2001

Smith, Dave and Clark, Steven – *Disney: The First 100 Years* – Hyperion – 1999

Stewart, James B. – *Disney War* – Simon & Schuster – 2005

Surrell, Jason – *Pirates of the Caribbean: From the Magic Kingdom to the Movies* – Disney Editions – 2005

Surrell, Jason – *The Haunted Mansion: From the Magic Kingdom to the Movies* – Disney Editions – 2003

Surrell, Jason – *The Disney Mountains: Imagineering at Its Peak* – Disney Editions – 2007

Taylor, John – *Storming the Magic Kingdom* – Alfred A. Knopf – 1987

Thomas, Bob – *Walt Disney: An American Original* – Pocket Books – 1980

Thomas, Bob – *Building a Company: Roy O. Disney and the Creation of an Entertainment Empire* – Hyperion – 1998

Thomas, Bob – *Disney's Art of Animation: From Mickey Mouse to Beauty and the Beast* – Hyperion – 1991

Ungson, Gerardo R. and Wong, Yim-Yu – *Global Strategic Management* – M.E. Sharp Inc. – 2008

Unknown – *Tokyo Disneyland's Diary* – Oriental Land Company – 1994

Unknown – *Walt Disney's Pirates of the Caribbean*

Veness, Simon and Susan – *Brit Guide: Disneyland Paris and Paris Attractions* – various years

MAGAZINE ARTICLES

Bonin, Liane – *Tragic Kingdom* – Detour Magazine – April 1998

Castro, Janet – *Mickey Mouse Goes to Paris* – Time – December 1985

Corliss, Richard – *Voila! Disney Invades Europe* – Time – April 1992

Decarlo, Angela Rocco – *Mickey and L'Affaire Française* – Disney News – Spring 1990

De Roos, Robert – *The Magic World of Walt Disney* – National Geographic – August 1963

Epstein, Jeffrey – *Fab Five* – Disney Magazine – Spring 2005

Fisher, David – *Can you Say Ka-boom in French?* – Disney Magazine – Winter 2001-2002

Fisher, David – *Hello, Hong Kong* – Disney Magazine – Summer 2000

Fisher, David – *Opening Scene* – Disney Magazine – Spring 2000

Fisher, David – *Tokyo DisneySea* – Disney Magazine – Fall 2001

Flanagan, Tom – *Cultural Exchange* – Disney Magazine – Spring 2004

Flans, Robin – *Splash Mountain Rises Again…and Again* – Disney News – Fall 1992

Harmon, Ryan – *E-Ticket Architecture* – Disney News – Fall 1992

Harmon, Ryan A. – *The Ultimate in Euro Disneyland Trivia - Part 1* – Disney News – Summer 1993

Harmon, Ryan A. –*Euro Disneyland Trivia – Part Deux* – Disney News – Fall 1993

Henderson, Jim – *Euro Disney: Oui or Non?* – Travel and Leisure – August 1992

Huey, John – *Eisner Explains Everything* – Fortune – April 1995

Janzon, Jack E. (ed.) – *Art of the Pirates of the Caribbean* – The "E" Ticket – Summer 2007

Kurtti, Jeff – *vive la difference!* – Disney News – Fall 1990

Lee, Jean and Kawamura, Steve – *Tokyo Disneyland Undercover* – Disney News – Summer 1993

Noceti, Steve – *Pan Galactic Pizza Port* – Disney News – Summer 1989

Okey, Anne K. – *Bienvenue, Euro Disney Resort!* – Disney News – Summer 1992

Okey, Anne – *Faites Vos Réservations!* – Disney News – Winter 1990

Okey, Anne K. – *Getting Dressed For Success* – Disney News – Winter 1991

Okey, Anne K. – *Hai, Mickey* – Disney News – Summer 1992

Okey, Anne – *It's Just a Matter of Time* – Disney News – Summer 1991

Okey, Anne K. – *Mickey's Home Across the Sea* – Disney News – Winter 1988

Okey, Anne K. – *Now Accepting Applications* – Disney News – Fall 1991

Okey, Anne K. – *Que Le Spectacle Commence!* – Disney News – Spring 1992

Ono, Kosei – *Disney and the Japanese: Maintaining a Dream Over Half a Century* – Look Japan – 1983

Oppenheimer, Lisa – *Vive la Différence* – Disney Magazine – Winter 2002-2003

Persons, Dan – *A World of Differences* – Disney Magazine – Spring 2000

Shinozaki, Fran – *The Nighttime Spectacular "Disney's Fantillusion" at Tokyo Disneyland* – The Disney Magazine – Winter 1995

Smith, Shanna – *Where the Buffalo Roam* – The Disney Magazine – Fall 1995

Stiepock, Lisa, ed. – *Disney Traveler: Master Plan* – Disney Magazine – Spring 2003

Toy, Stewart – *An American in Paris* – Business Week – March 1990

Toy, Stewart – *Euro Disney's Prince Charming* – Business Week – June 1994

Tully, Shawn – *The Real Estate Coup at Euro Disneyland* – Fortune – April 1986

Van Maanen, John – *Displacing Disney: Some Notes on the Flow of Culture* – Qualitative Sociology – 1992

Ward, Mark E. – *Bon Anniversaire, Disneyland Paris* – Disney Magazine – Fall 1997

Wiley, Kim Wright – *Cinéma Fantastique* – Disney Magazine – Spring 2002

NEWSPAPERS AND PERIODICALS

Asia Times Online

Business Week

Chicago Tribune

The China Post

The Gold Coast Bulletin

The Hindu

InPark Magazine

International Business Times

The Japan Times

LA Times

Manila Times

New York Post

New York Times

Orange County Register

Orlando Sentinel

Port Disney News – 1991

Sankei News

Shanghai Daily

South China Morning Post

Spokane Chronicle

Sydney Morning Herald

The Hong Kong Standard

Vientiane Times

Wall Street Journal

Washington Post

WEBSITES

CNN – www.cnn.com/2011/WORLD/asiapcf/04/15/japan.quake.disneyland/

D23 – https://d23.com

Designing Disney – https://www.designingdisney.com

Disneyland Paris Resort – http://www.disneylandparis.com

Disneyland Paris News – http://disneylandparis-news.com

Disney Parks Blog – http://disneyparks.disney.go.com

Disney Ambassadors – http://www.tuttodisneyland.com/forum/index.php?topic=3610.0;wap2

Frank Stanek – http://theaawards2013.blogspot.ca/2013/01/frank-stanek-to-keynote-case-studies.html
https://www.youtube.com/watch?v=eYU6JPhotIg

Grand Openings – https://www.youtube.com

Hong Kong Disneyland – https://www.hongkongdisneyland.com

Insight: The Voice of the American Chamber of Commerce in Shanghai – http://insight.amcham-shanghai.org/disney-history-in-china/

Jim Hill Media – http://jimhillmedia.com

Laughing Place – http://www.laughingplace.com

Oriental Land Company – http://www.olc.co.jp/en/50th/01.html
http://www.olc.co.jp/en/tdr/history.html

Shanghai Disneyland Resort – https://www.shanghaidisneyresort.com.cn/en/

Tokyo Disneyland Resort – https://www.tokyodisneyresort.jp

Videos of attractions in various parks – https://www.youtube.com

Walt Disney Company – https://thewaltdisneycompany.com/

OTHERS

Anthony, Robert – *Euro Disney: The First 100 Days* – Harvard Business School Case Study – 1993

Burgoyne, Lyn – *Walt Disney Company's Euro Disneyland Venture* – Master's Paper – University of Illinois at Urbana-Champaign – 1995

Corporate Social Responsibility and Environmental Management (CSREM) journal published by John Wiley and ERP Environment.

Disneyland Paris Resort Guidebooks and Guide Maps – various years

Disneyland Paris Press Releases

Hong Kong Disneyland Resort Guide Maps – various years

Hong Kong Disneyland Press Releases

Jiao, J.J. – Preliminary conceptual study in impact of land reclamation on ground water flow and contaminant migration in Penny's Bay – Department of Earth Sciences, University of Hong Kong

OKD2

Shanghai Disneyland Press Releases

Tales From the Laughing Place Magazine –various issues

Tokyo Disneyland Resort Guidebooks and Guide maps – various years

Tokyo Disneyland Information Packet – 1983

Tokyo DisneySea Resort Guide maps – various years

The Disney Team: Creating Tomorrow's Dream – 1995

Walt Disney Productions Annual Reports – various years

Yale Global Online – a publication of the MacMillan Center

Index

20,000 Leagues Under the Sea, 82, 126, 221
A Journey Through Time, 198
A Pirate's Life for You, 384
A Table is Waiting, 115
Abe, Shinzo, 39
Abu's Bazaar, 122
Adventure Isle, 155, 189, 190, 354, 365, 385
Adventureland, 14, 33, 43, 45, 46, 47, 48, 49, 50, 51, 52, 54, 57, 67, 80, 81, 83, 155, 174, 177, 188, 190, 191, 195, 200, 213, 217, 229, 267, 285, 286, 287, 289, 290, 300, 301, 302, 305, 309, 311, 321, 322, 355
Adventureland Bazaar, 50, 188, 217
Agrabah, 83, 122, 217, 247, 251, 258
Air Station Futenma, 398
Akiyama, Yoshi, 74
Aladdin, 67, 83, 121, 122, 123, 188, 217, 254, 257, 320, 337, 366, 380
Alice in Wonderland, 39, 95, 192, 196, 291, 381
Alice's Curious Labyrinth, 177, 196
Alice's Wonderland Party, 83

Allen, Bob, 29, 30
Aloha Mickey, 81
Alpine Haus, 58
ambassadors, 39, 225, 279
American Journeys, 62, 332
American Waterfront, 105, 110, 111, 113, 117, 130
Anaheim, (see Disneyland) 12, 25, 32, 51, 52, 79, 87, 88, 116, 120, 200, 284, 293, 304, 312, 349, 370, 372, 392
Animagique, 243, 246, 251, 254, 257
Animal Kingdom, 287, 312, 344, 404
Animation Courtyard, 245, 246, 247, 251
animē, 9
Anna and Elsa's, 95
AquaSphere, 110
Aquatopia, 116, 117
Arabian Coast, 105, 110, 121, 122, 123, 130
Arboretum, 179
Arbori, 385, 386
Arcade Omega, 221
Archive Shop, 315
Ariel's Greeting Grotto, 125
Ariel's Playground, 124
Armageddon – Les Effets Speciaux, 249
Arribas Brothers, 46, 286
Atencio, X, 58
attendance, 17, 20, 65, 68, 71, 72, 73, 76, 77, 80, 81, 86, 100, 107, 121, 127, 131, 139, 159, 203, 204, 205, 208, 209, 215, 218, 223, 235, 238, 242, 256, 279, 295, 298, 299, 300, 301, 302, 303, 307, 308, 313, 317, 319, 324, 349, 371, 387, 398
Australia, 230, 257, 270, 338, 392, 394
Autopia, 9, 60, 199, 200, 294, 300
Avenue M Arcade, 375
awards, 293, 318
Backlot, 245, 249, 254
Bailly-Romainvilliers, 148
Bambi, 9, 138, 233, 366
Barbossa's Bounty, 385
Barcelona, 138, 142, 144
Barnacle Bill's, 112
Barrel of Monkeys, 255
Basque, 143
Baxter, Tony, 71, 154, 155, 156, 157, 163, 164, 184, 188, 190, 191, 192, 199, 222
Be Magical, 112
Bear Country, 79
Beauty and the Beast, 95, 192, 199, 207, 212, 228, 257, 293, 321, 380
Beaver Brother's Explorer Canoes, 79
Belly of the Earth, 189
Beregovoy, Pierre, 206

Bernard, Jean-Rene, 148, 154
Bibbidi Bobbidi Boutique, 347
Big Grizzly Mountain, 311, 312
Big Hero 6, 320
Big Thunder Mountain, 71, 72, 94, 154, 155, 166, 167, 182, 183, 186, 187, 209, 213, 312
Bigle, Armand, 139
Bixby Brothers, 180, 181
black ship, 14
Blackbeard's Portrait Deck, 51
Blowfish Balloon Race, 124
Blue Bayou Restaurant, 50, 51
Blue Lagoon Restaurant, 190
Boardwalk Candy Palace, 180
Boetto, Joe, 147
Bonanza Outfitters, 186
Boot Hill Cemetery, 185
Bourguignon, Philippe, 205, 208, 210, 211, 214, 215
Brave, 197, 320
Brawling Sea, 189
Brazil, 399
Brer Rabbit, 77
Bridgestone Tire, 33
Bright, Randy, 98, 402
Broadway Boulevard, 358, 372
Brown, Debbie, 29
Brown Derby, 246
Brown, Howard, 354, 369
Brown, Molly, 183, 226
Buffalo Bill's Wild West Show, 164, 220, 231
Burbank, 9, 17, 23, 128, 284, 352, 393
Burke, Steve, 205, 215
Buzz Lightyear Laser Blast, 198, 221, 228
Buzz Lightyear Planet Rescue, 378
Buzz Lightyear's Astro Blasters, 88
Cable Car Bake Shop, 181
Café des Visionnaires, 199, 221
Café Hyperion, 165, 199
Café Mickey, 231
Café Orleans, 51
CalArts, 158
Camp Davy Crockett, 164
Camp Discovery, 385
Campaign for Young China, 330
Cape Cod, 112, 113, 114, 116, 130
Captain EO, 61, 86, 156, 159, 200, 229
Captain Hook, 56, 177, 190, 302

Captain Hook's Gallery, 56
Captain Jack Sparrow, 302, 356, 382, 383, 384
Captain's Chest, 190
Caravan Carousel, 123
Carousel of Progress, 63
Carr, Tom, 29
Cars, 233, 249, 252, 254, 308, 312, 320
Cars Race Rally, 252
Casbah Food Court, 122
Casey Jr, 200, 212
Casey's Corner, 165, 182
Cast Members, 26, 34, 214, 313, 323, 357
Castle Rock Ridge, 55
Catastrophe Canyon, 242, 249
Cayo, Ron, 18, 19, 23
Celebration Square, 375
Center Street, 45, 46, 47
Center Street Coffeehouse, 46
Central Hub, 182, 192
Cérémonie d'Illumination, 208
C'est Magique, 195, 196
Chamber of Planets, 113
Chan, Jackie, 271, 299
Chao, Wing, 162, 269, 270, 286
Chaparral Stage, 224
Chapek, Bob, 319, 374
Cheesecake Factory, 372
Cheng, Angus, 268
Cheoy Lee Company, 262
Chessy, 147, 174
Cheung, Jacky, 272, 279
Chevalier de la Légion d'Honneur, 206
Cheyenne Hotel, 163
China Campus Roadshow, 356, 359
China Voyager Restaurant, 80
Chinese New Year, 299, 308, 336, 351, 355, 362, 366
Chip 'n' Dale, 76, 84, 91, 195, 244, 271, 292, 371, 375, 376
Chirac, Jacques, 145, 146, 149, 207
Christmas Fantasy, 86
Cinderella Castle, 40, 45, 46, 55, 59, 68, 70, 90, 96, 125, 157, 209, 369
Cinderella's Castle Mystery Tour, 89
Cinderella's Fairy Tale Hall,, 89
Cinderella's Golden Carousel, 58
Cinderellabration, 81
Cine Magique, 159
Cinema, 45, 228, 248
Circlevision, 62, 81

Cirque du Soleil, 129
Citrus House, 46
City Hall, 85, 179, 285
Coats, Claude, 62, 63, 185
Cobb, Chuck, 141
Coca-Cola, 33, 61, 154
Colombe, Michael, 148
Colonel Hathi's Pizza Outpost, 189
Columbia, 105, 115, 116, 290, 335
Columbiad, 222, 228
Communist, 148, 160, 264, 272, 276, 278, 330
Community Chest, 276, 277
Confectionary, 45, 193
Cora, Jim, 26, 27, 28, 29, 30, 31, 34, 42, 43, 141, 142, 143, 158
Cosmic Encounter, 73
Cottage of the Seven Dwarfs, 193
Cottonwood Creek Ranch, 187, 227, 234
Country Bear Jamboree, 33, 80
Country Bear Theater, 53
Crawford, Mike, 352, 355, 356
Critter Country, 77, 79, 80, 187
Crush's Coaster, 251, 252
Crystal Palace, 47
Crystal Wishes Journey, 112, 131
cultural Chernobyl, 150
Curious Giraffe, 188
Cycle of Spirits, 321
Daisy's Snack Wagon, 85
Dapper Dan's Haircuts, 181
Davis, Marc, 184
Davy Crockett and the River Pirates, 187
Davy Crockett Explorer Canoes, 54, 384
Davy Jones, 356, 382, 383
De Schonen, Nicolas, 204
Degelmann, Thor, 165, 169, 170
Delaney, Tim, 222, 286
Delcourt, Daniel, 239
Diet, 2, 3, 11
Dinghy Drinks, 85
Discovery Arcade, 179
Discovery Mountain, 125, 126, 222, 223
Discoveryland, 156, 159, 165, 177, 180, 197, 198, 199, 200, 212, 213, 221, 222, 228, 229
Disney & Co, 46, 81, 182
Disney Blockbuster Café, 254
Disney Boulevard, 367
Disney Classics on Parade, 72, 75

Disney Clothiers Ltd, 180
Disney Club, 168
Disney Comics, 331
Disney Cruise Line, 257, 293, 359
Disney Dreams On Parade, 90
Disney, Edna, 138
Disney Explorers Lodge, 319
Disney in the Stars, 295, 308, 320
Disney Magic on Parade, 234
Disney Paint the Night, 318
Disney Resort Cruiser, 128
Disney, Roy. E. 105, 106, 128, 136, 137, 165, 171, 173, 205, 237, 238, 271, 392
Disney, Roy O., 9, 13, 19, 35, 107, 108, 137, 167, 175, 210, 243, 244, 280, 284, 330
Disney Sparkling Christmas, 321
Disney Stars 'n' Cars Parade, 254
Disney Store, 168, 205, 363, 370, 372
Disney Village, 220, 231, 372, 393
Disney's America, 392
Disneyana Collectibles, 180
Disneyland (see Anaheim), 5, 6, 10, 12, 13, 14, 17, 18, 24, 25, 26, 27, 28, 29, 30, 32,
    33, 34, 36, 39, 41, 43, 44, 45, 47, 48, 51, 53, 54, 55, 56, 57, 58, 59, 60, 61, 62, 63,
    65, 67, 70, 71, 73, 77, 78, 79, 84, 85, 86, 87, 88, 90, 93, 97, 104, 115, 118, 119,
    120, 124, 126, 131, 139, 140, 143, 150, 153, 154, 157, 159, 162, 176, 177, 178,
    179, 181, 182, 183, 186, 187, 189, 190, 191, 192, 194, 196, 199, 200, 208, 211,
    212, 221, 228, 229, 244, 251, 253, 270, 272, 279, 285, 286, 287, 288, 290, 291,
    292, 293, 294, 303, 304, 308, 312, 313, 314, 315, 319, 321, 322, 331, 332, 377,
    379, 381, 382, 383, 384, 385
Disneyland Hotel, 91, 94, 100, 105, 128, 163, 165, 166, 176, 232, 233, 275, 350, 358,
    365, 371, 372
Disneyland Paris (DLP), 83, 91, 95, 120, 125, 139, 142, 143, 144, 145, 146, 148, 154,
    157, 158, 159, 160, 165, 174, 182, 190, 192, 203, 205, 207, 209, 211, 219, 220,
    230, 232, 233, 235, 237, 238, 239, 242, 243, 256, 257, 269, 279, 298, 300, 308,
    310, 359, 361, 372, 378, 396
Disneyland Paris Half Marathon, 239
Disney-MGM Studio, 28, 98, 99, 160, 161, 162, 171, 203, 241, 242 246, 248, 250
DisneySea Electric Railway, 113
DisneySea Symphony, 112
Disneytown, 358, 372
Disney, Walt, 9, 10, 12, 14, 19, 26, 28, 30, 39, 40, 46, 56, 66, 99, 100, 103, 108, 128,
    138, 157, 158, 162, 174, 175, 178, 200, 206, 207, 219, 239, 248, 272, 279, 284,
    314, 331, 376, 392
Donald Duck, 36, 39, 43, 84, 85, 91, 121, 137, 140, 195, 244, 246, 271, 284, 285, 291,
    292, 293, 306, 333, 334, 371, 375, 376, 399
Donovan, Chris, 29, 145
Dorsey, Don, 67
Downtown Disney, 87, 358, 370, 372
Dragon's Den, 193

Dream It! Do It!, 13, 20, 267
DreamLights, 67
Duffy, 111, 116, 130
Dumbo, 57, 60, 121, 196, 247, 292, 305, 309, 377, 393
Earfful Tower, 246
earthquake, 31, 91, 92, 93, 94, 128, 129, 184, 185, 186, 249
Eastside Café, 46
Eastwood, Clint, 182, 206
Edminster, David, 117, 126
Edo, Hideo, 2, 3, 5, 32
Edo River, 2, 3, 32
Eisner, Michael, 98, 99, 100, 101, 104, 106, 107, 140, 141, 143, 144, 145, 146, 148, 149, 154, 156, 157, 158, 160, 161, 162, 163, 165, 171, 173, 175, 178, 201, 205, 206, 207, 209, 214, 215, 216, 217, 218, 241, 243, 244, 267, 268, 273, 279, 280, 286, 333, 392, 393
Electrical Parade, 67, 81, 82, 230, 318
Elfman, Danny, 314, 315
Emporio, 111
Emporium, 43, 181, 286
Enchanted Spices, 189
Enchanted Storybook Castle, 347, 352, 355, 360, 368, 369, 380
Enchanted Tiki Room, 47, 189, 315
EPCOT, 14, 19, 20, 28, 35, 44, 61, 63, 98, 116, 139, 332
Ernest, Bill, 299, 303, 307, 313, 338, 348
Espace, 166, 167
Eureka Mining Supplies and Assay Office, 186
Euro Disneyland (EDL), 145, 146, 150, 153, 154, 157, 158, 163, 167, 168, 169, 171, 173, 174, 175, 176, 177, 178, 179, 181, 182, 183, 186, 187, 188, 191, 194, 196, 197, 198, 201, 203, 204, 205, 206, 208, 209, 210, 211, 213, 214, 215, 216, 217, 359, 388
Evergreen Playhouse, 381, 382
Expedition Eats, 118
Explorer's Club, 189, 315
Fabius, Laurent, 144, 145
Fairy Tale Forest, 321
Fantasia, 69, 138, 166, 197, 212, 245, 377, 380, 393
Fantasy in the Sky, 65, 295
Fantasyland, 14, 27, 43, 53, 55, 57, 58, 59, 60, 84, 87, 95, 123, 154, 155, 166, 171, 174, 177, 190, 192, 195, 196, 197, 200, 207, 212, 218, 221, 224, 234, 267, 284, 290, 291, 292, 303, 304, 305, 308, 309, 320, 347, 354, 363, 379, 380, 382
Fantillusion, 82, 83, 230
feng shui, 269
Ferrante, Orlando, 18
Festival Disney, 164, 214, 215, 220, 231
Fiesta Tropical, 83
Figaro, 112, 194, 375
Finding Dory, 131

Finding Nemo, 67, 131, 251, 320, 393
fireworks, 65, 174, 210, 243, 244, 266, 271, 275, 277, 293, 295, 308, 320, 351, 376, 380, 388
fishermen, 2, 5, 6, 7, 10
Fitzpatrick, Robert, 148, 150, 151, 158, 161, 170, 175, 200, 203, 205, 208, 210
Florida, 10, 20, 31, 44, 51, 53, 59, 63, 71, 79, 141, 159, 161, 162, 178, 241, 249, 270, 359
Flounder's Flying Fish Coaster, 123
Flying Carpets, 247, 251, 258
Flying Mickey Friendship Tour', 72
Fort Sam Clemens, 55
Fort Snobbish, 383
Fort Wilderness, 55, 200, 211
Fortress Explorations, 113
Four Corners Food Faire, 59
France, 139, 140, 141, 142, 143, 144, 145, 146, 150, 151, 154, 159, 161, 165, 166, 169, 170, 174, 175, 177, 178, 192, 196, 197, 200, 203, 204, 206, 207, 208, 211, 213, 216, 218, 223, 225, 230, 234, 235, 244, 250, 253, 309, 398
France, Van Arsdale, 26, 27, 28, 29, 30
French government, 144, 148, 149, 153, 160, 162, 204, 206, 359
French Market Restaurant, 47
Front Lot, 245, 246
Frontierland, 14, 52, 154, 155, 174, 177, 182, 184, 185, 187, 188, 195, 211, 224, 225, 227, 234, 285, 287, 355
Frozen, 95, 132, 234, 239, 309, 320, 321, 322, 349, 381, 382
Frozen Festival Show, 322
Fuente del Oro (Source of Gold) Restaurant, 186
Fuji Photo, 33, 59
Fukuda, Takeo, 39
Gadget's Go Coaster, 84
Galleria Disney, 111
Garden of the Magic Feather, 377
Garden of Twelve Friends, 366
Garden of Wonders, 315
Gardens of Imagination, 354, 376, 377
Gargoyle Square, 224
Gas, Philippe, 246, 359, 366
Gehry, Frank, 164, 231
Gibson, Blaine, 64, 181, 247
Golden Forest Lounge, 233
Golden Galleon, 51
Golden Horseshoe, 53, 183
Golden Island Revue, 81
Golden Mickeys, 293, 320
Goofy, 36, 39, 59, 84, 91, 118, 195, 239, 244, 271, 284, 292, 293, 302, 307, 320, 346, 353, 375, 393
Goofy's Bounce House, 84

Grand Canyon Suite, 176
Grand Circuit Raceway, 33, 60, 84, 95
Grand Theatre, 338, 358
Grandma Sara's Kitchen, 79, 80
Grim Grinning Ghosts, 58, 185
Grizzly Gulch, 306, 311, 312, 313, 314, 321, 322
Grizzly Gulch Assay Office, 312
Grizzly Peak, 312
Grumbach, Antione, 163
Hallowe'en, 75, 76, 228, 294, 301, 308, 319, 320
Hanger Stage, 121
Harrington's Fine China and Porcelains, 180
Harrison Hightower III, 114
Haunted Mansion, 42, 47, 56, 57, 58, 67, 77, 80, 183, 185, 315
Hench, John, 18, 55, 157
Hill Billy Hoedown, 224
Hollywood Boulevard, 252
Hollywood Hotel, 270, 275
Honey, I Shrunk the Audience, 86, 200, 229
Hong Kong, 91, 253, 254, 255, 261, 262, 264, 265, 266, 267, 268, 269, 270, 271, 272, 273, 274, 275, 276, 277, 278, 279, 280, 283, 284, 285, 287, 290, 295, 298, 299, 301, 302, 303, 304, 305, 306, 307, 310, 311, 313, 314, 318, 320, 322, 323, 324, 325, 331, 334, 336, 338, 340, 349, 350, 378, 382, 387, 393, 397, 398,
Hong Kong Disneyland (HKD), 254, 256, 261, 265, 266, 267, 268, 269, 270, 272, 273, 274, 275, 276, 277, 278, 280, 283, 284, 285, 286, 287, 288, 289, 290, 291, 293, 294, 295, 298, 299, 300, 301, 302, 303, 304, 305, 306, 308, 310, 313, 314, 316, 317, 318, 319, 320, 322, 323, 324, 325,338, 340, 354, 358, 384, 388, 395
Honshu Paper, 2
Hoop-De-Do-Revue, 81
Hoot and Holler Hideout, 80
Hotel Cheyenne, 168
Hotel MiraCosta, 110, 131
Hotel Santa Fe., 163
Huey, Dewey and Louie's Good Time Café, 85
Hungry Bear Restaurant, 54
Hyperion, 167, 199, 245, 402, 403, 404, 405, 407, 408
Hyperion airship, 167
Iger, Robert, 256, 268, 286, 335, 346
Ignite the Dream, 376, 382
Ikspiari, 87, 106, 372
Imagineers, 31, 35, 51, 62, 74, 78, 79, 84, 98, 100, 105, 123, 125, 126, 127, 155, 165, 178, 188, 190, 192, 193, 195, 198, 201, 211, 222, 242, 252, 268, 286, 290, 304, 305, 310, 317, 348, 349, 351, 356, 357, 361, 383
IMAX, 231
India, 270, 314, 392, 395, 396
Indian Canoes, 183, 187, 224, 225
Indiana Jones, 118, 120, 200, 213, 229, 384

Inside Out, 320
Iron Man Experience, 324
Isigny-sur-mer, 173
It's a Small World, 13, 40, 59, 93, 121, 155, 166, 177, 225, 303, 304, 332, 355
Jackson, Michael, 61, 150, 156, 185, 200, 229
Japan Airlines, 33, 89, 114
Jasmine's Flying Carpets, 121
Jedi Training Academy, 228
Jessie's Snack Roundup, 255, 309
Jet Packs, 377
Jiminy Cricket, 271
Jolly Trolley, 85
José Carioca, 399
Journey to the Center of the Earth, 126, 222
Jumpin' Jellyfish, 124
Jungle Cruise, 9, 32, 42, 48, 49, 50, 188, 267, 287, 288, 332, 380
Junior Woodchucks, 94
Kagami, Toshio, 91, 101, 104, 106, 107, 108, 128
Kam, Andrew, 267, 298, 313, 314, 316, 323, 325
Kamisawa, Noburu,, 12, 25
Kaspar, Steve, 29
Kawasaki, Chiharu, 3, 4, 5, 9, 10, 17, 18, 22, 75
Keisei, 3, 4, 5, 11, 17, 21, 22
Keisei Electric, 3, 4, 21
King Ludwig's Castle, 231
King Triton's Concert, 124
Kirk, Steve, 74, 104, 105, 106
Kundun, 265, 336
La Galérie de la Belle au Bois Dormant, 211
La Parade des Célèbres Inconnus, 210
La Petite Parfumerie, 50
Lady and the Tramp, 192, 375
Lafitte's Pirate Chest, 50
Landlubber Landing, 383
Lanzisero, Joe, 78
Laos, 396, 397
Last Chance Café, 183
Le Carrousel de Lancelot, 193
Le Château de la Belle au Bois Dormant, 174, 175, 231
Le Gourmet, 50
Le Livre Magique de Mickey, 193, 227
Le Pays des Contes de Fées, 200, 212
Le Visionarium, 198
Legend of Mythica, 127, 129
Legends of the Wild West, 200, 211
LEGO Store, 372
Leonardo Da Vinci, 113, 198

Les Légendes d'Hollywood, 246
Levy, Bill, 137
Liberty Arcade, 179, 181
Liberty Court, 181
Liberty Square, 14, 57
Lido Isle, 112
Lights, Camera, Hollywood, 246
Lilo and Stitch, 48, 95, 253, 293, 300, 379
locomotives, 49, 174, 177, 284, 377
Los Angeles, 10, 30, 117, 140, 145, 178, 231, 250, 284, 315, 331, 332, 350
Lost River Cookhouse, 118
Lost River Delta, 105, 110, 111, 112, 115, 117, 120, 121, 123, 131, 132
Lucas, George, 156
Lucky Nugget Café, 72, 95
Lucky Nugget Revue, 183, 226
Lucky Nugget Saloon, 183, 211, 226, 312
Lucky Springs Geyser, 311
Lunching Pad, 62
Mad Hatter, 59, 116, 124, 196, 252, 292
Madame Leota, 58, 185
Magellan's Lounge, 113
Magic Carpet 'Round the World, 33, 62
Magic Eye Theater, 61
Magic Journeys, 42, 61
Magic Kingdom, 14, 28, 32, 34, 51, 53, 55, 57, 59, 95, 123, 145, 157, 163, 171, 176, 178, 201, 291, 303, 342, 343, 381
Magic Lamp Game Show, 227
Magic Lamp Theater, 122
Magic Shop, 45
Maihama, 11, 72, 88, 97, 98, 101, 128
Main Street, 14, 26, 41, 43, 44, 45, 46, 57, 67, 111, 115, 154, 155, 156, 157, 159, 165, 175, 176, 177, 178, 179, 180, 181, 195, 208, 210, 221, 230, 246, 267, 272, 278, 284, 285, 286, 287, 302, 303, 304, 305, 307, 318, 321, 331, 354, 375
Main Street Transportation Co., 180
Maleficent, 69, 82
Malmuth, David, 100
Mama's Biscotti Bakery, 111
Mandarin, 264, 278, 288, 304, 322, 333, 337, 345, 358, 373
Mao, Zedong, 331
MAPO, 27
March Hare Refreshments, 196
Marcon, Sabine, 167, 173, 175, 206
Mark Twain, 42, 54, 55, 183, 226, 288
Market District, 375
Market House Deli, 180
Market Street, 180
Marketplace, 122, 234, 358, 372

Marne-la-Vallée, 142, 143, 144, 147, 174, 235
Marsupilami, 210
Marvel, 229, 324, 363, 370, 371, 379
Mary Poppins, 62, 248, 254, 366, 373
Matsushita, Konosuke, 63, 89
Matsushita Electric, 63, 89
Matterhorn, 9, 26
McDuck's Department Store, 114
Meaux, 174, 237
Mediterranean Harbor, 105, 107, 110, 111, 112, 113, 127, 129, 130, 131
Meet the World, 62, 63, 65, 73, 89
Melody Garden, 376
Menken, Alan, 122
Mermaid Lagoon, 105, 110, 121, 123, 124, 125
Mermaid Memories, 123
Mermaid Treasures, 124
Metro, 72, 99, 143, 144, 207, 343, 352
Mickey and Friends Greeting Trails, 117, 130
Mickey and Pals Market Café, 375
Mickey and the Wondrous Book, 320
Mickey Avenue, 354, 374, 375, 376
Mickey Kids, 8
Mickey Magic Paint Brush, 319
Mickey Mouse, 8, 32, 36, 40, 42, 43, 45, 59, 60, 72, 73, 76, 88, 91, 137, 139, 140, 145, 146, 150, 159, 160, 167, 173, 175, 193, 206, 210, 236, 248, 254, 284, 285, 291, 304, 307, 329, 333, 334, 337, 345, 346, 351, 353, 371, 372, 375, 376, 382, 396
Mickey's Gallery,, 375
Mickey's Magic Book, 193
Mickey's Magical Party, 227, 253
Mickey's Storybook Express, 377
Mickey's Trailer,, 84
MicroAdventure, 86
Mile Long Bar, 54
Miller, Ron, 28, 36, 39, 140
Mineral King, 13, 14
Ministry, 11, 23
Minnie Mouse, 48, 59, 75, 85, 93, 107, 108, 118, 195, 228, 244, 271, 284, 292, 293, 303, 307, 331, 346, 355, 370, 371, 375
Minnie's House, 85
Mir, 224, 249
Mitsubishi, 17
Mitsui, 3, 11, 19, 21, 22, 29, 30
Mitsui Real Estate, 11, 21, 22
Mitterand, Francois, 175, 218
Monorail, 98, 106
Monsters University Administration Building, 317
Monsters, Inc. Ride and Go Seek, 89

Monsters, Inc. Scream Academy, 250, 256
Moteurs... Action! Stunt Show Spectacular, 250
Mount Prometheus, 105, 108, 113, 125
Movie Premiere Showcase, 83
Mulan, 199, 228, 247, 254, 268, 292, 293, 336, 337, 366, 380
Mumford, David, 123, 403
Mysterious Island, 104, 105, 110, 111, 123, 125, 127, 222
Mystic Magneto-Electric Carriage, 314, 315
Mystic Point, 306, 313, 314, 317, 320
Mystic Point Freight Depot, 315
Mystic Rhythms, 121
Nara Dreamland, 9
Nautilus, 82, 125, 221, 222, 223
Nautilus Galley, 125
New Century Clock Shop, 33, 46
New Generations Festival, 256
New Orleans, 47, 50, 51, 57
New York, 13, 91, 113, 114, 115, 138, 149, 150, 156, 163, 164, 178, 179, 203, 208, 214, 232, 233, 236
New York World's Fair, 13
Newport Bay Club, 164, 205, 233
Nixon, Richard, 331
Northern Isle, 189
Numata, Takeshi, 24
Nunis, Dick, 17, 27, 28, 29, 30, 140, 141, 143, 144, 145
Okuyama, Yasuo, 25
OLC, (see Oriental Land), 4, 7, 9, 10, 11, 15, 17, 18, 19, 20, 21, 22, 23, 24, 26, 27, 29, 31, 33, 34, 35, 39, 41, 44, 62, 66, 70, 72, 73, 74, 77, 86, 88, 91, 93, 96, 98, 99, 100, 101, 102, 103, 104, 105, 106, 107, 108, 114, 128, 129, 130, 131, 132
Old Mill, 197, 212
Omnibus, 47, 180, 285
Once Upon a Time Adventure, 369, 380
Opera House, 179, 285, 303, 304
Orbitron, 159, 198, 199, 377
Oriental Land, (see OLC), 3, 5, 6, 11, 12, 17, 18, 21, 27, 30, 66, 88, 91, 97, 98, 132, 139, 398
Orlando, 18, 98, 140, 159, 162, 171, 200, 229, 246, 250, 271, 284, 359, 370, 392
Palazzo Canals, 112
Pan Galactic Pizza Port, 74, 411
PanoraMagique, 231
Parade de Noël, 208
Park Place, 375
Partners, 46, 248
Party Gras Parade, 76
Pasilla, Jim, 29
Peat Marwick, 216
Pecos Bill Café, 53

Penfield, Bob, 32
Penny Arcade, 45, 287
Penny's Bay, 262, 263, 265, 417
Perry, Admiral Matthew, 14, 64
Peter Pan's Flight, 55, 56, 177, 192, 194, 290, 355, 381
Phantom Manor, 155, 167, 183
Philippines, 304, 314, 394, 395
Pinocchio, 36, 60, 69, 138, 167, 192, 194, 247, 248, 320
Pinocchio's Daring Journey, 60, 194
Pirate Cove, 384
Pirates Beach, 190
Pirates of the Caribbean, 42, 51, 52, 63, 104, 121, 155, 160, 166, 167, 177, 184, 190, 254, 256, 301, 338, 356, 365, 366, 382, 383, 384, 385
Place de Frères Lumières, 245
Playhouse Disney Live on Stage, 253
Plaza, 46, 47, 52, 62, 67, 68, 110, 180, 181, 227, 256, 277, 286, 358, 372, 373, 378
Plaza Garden Restaurant, 181
Plaza Inn, 181, 277, 286
Plaza Terrace, 46
Pleasant, Cynthia, 39
Pleasure Island Candies, 59
Pocahantas, 83
Pocahontas Indian Village, 224
Pogue, Ron, 31, 36, 42
Polynesian Terrace, 48, 81
Polynesian Terrace Restaurant, 48
Pooh's Hunny Hunt, 87, 117, 315
Port Discovery, 110, 114, 116, 117, 131
Port Disney, 100, 104, 105, 115, 392
Powell, Catherine, 257
Power House and the Gag Factory, 85
Predock, Antione, 163
Price, Vincent. 184, 216
Primeval World, 54, 177
Prince Al-Waleed, 218, 221, 238
Princess Pavilion, 225
Production Courtyard, 243, 245, 247, 252, 253
Pudong, 328, 329, 339, 340, 349, 356, 361, 370, 389
Pueblo Trading Post, 187
Queen Mary, 100, 105, 115
Queen of Serpents, 188
Rackety's Racoon Saloon, 80
Rafferty, Kevin, 74
Raft's to Tarzan's Treehouse, 311
Raging Spirits, 114, 120
Railroad Station, 213
Rainforest Café, 231

Rasulo, Jay, 243, 244, 268, 278, 286, 306, 397
Ratatouille, 254, 256, 257, 338, 366
Ravenswood, Henry, 184, 186
Raz, Aviad E., 14, 63, 64, 70, 100
RC Racers, 255
Reagan, Ronald, 331
Red Cross, 93
Reign of Fire, 249
Reihm, Julie, 39
Rémy's Patisserie, 375
Remy's Totally Zany Adventure, 256
Renaissance, 113, 197
Restaurant en Coulisse, 246
Restaurant Hakuna Matata, 189
Restaurant Hokusai, 46
Riding the Black Ship, 14, 50, 63, 70
Rimenbranze, 113
Ristorante di Canaletto,, 112
River Rogue Keelboats, 186, 224, 225
Rivers of America, 54, 55, 79, 95, 177, 182
Rivers of the Far West, 177, 182, 186, 187, 224, 226
Roaring Rapids, 385
Robin Hood, 366
Robinson, Don, 155, 189, 271, 272, 274, 277, 288
Rock 'n' Roll America,, 231
Rock 'n' Roller Coaster Avec Aerosmith, 250
Rock Shock, 199
Roger Rabbit, 81, 84, 85, 86
Royal Banquet Hall, 290, 291, 321, 380
Royal Couturier, 234
Royal Menagerie, 197
Royal Street Veranda, 51
Runaway Mine Cars, 312
Ryman, Herb, 55, 62
Sailing Day Buffet, 115
Santa Claus' Post Office, 227
Schweitzer Falls, 50
Scuttle's Scooters, 123
Sebastian's Calypso Kitchen, 124
Secret of the Magic Gourd, 338
Seisen International School, 40
Sequoia Lodge, 163, 232, 233
Seven Dwarfs Mine Train, 363, 381
Shanghai Disneyland (SDL), 5, 262, 264, 269, 323, 328, 329, 330, 331, 334, 337, 338, 339, 340, 341, 342, 343, 345, 346, 347, 349, 350, 352, 354, 355, 356, 357, 358, 359, 360, 361, 362, 363, 365, 366, 367, 368, 369, 370, 371, 372, 373, 374, 375, 376, 378, 383, 386, 387, 388, 389, 391, 397

Shanghai Shendi Tourism, 340
Shapiro, Joe, 145, 146
shareholders, 102, 103, 205, 215, 218, 238, 243, 256, 265, 306, 325
shark's fin soup, 272, 273, 274
Sherman Brothers, 62, 64
Shinto, 30, 91, 106
Shipwreck Shore, 383, 384
Shiyanagi, Satoko, 107
Shootin' Gallery, 54, 71, 185
shoplifting, 94
Show Production Center, 351
Showbase 2000, 75, 98
Silhouette Studio, 46
Silver Spur Steakhouse, 183
Sindbad's Storybook Voyage, 121
Sklar, Marty, 13, 20, 47, 51, 62, 98, 105, 156, 164, 166, 171, 243, 267, 272, 285, 286
Skywatcher Souvenirs, 117
Skyway, 60, 87
Sleeping Beauty, 9, 155, 157, 164, 167, 168, 175, 178, 192, 193, 268, 270, 271, 272, 280, 287, 290, 295, 303, 307, 308, 319, 320, 321, 322, 349
Slinky Dog Zigzag Spin, 255, 309
Slue Foot Sue's Diamond Horseshoe, 53
Small World Restaurant, 59
Smuggler's Cove, 186
Smuggler's Cove, 226
Snow White and the Seven Dwarfs, 8, 137, 138, 192, 194, 320, 321, 329, 337
Snow White's Adventure, 55, 56
Snow White's Grotto, 53, 56
Snuggly Duckling, 382
Soaring Over the Horizon, 354, 386
Society of Explorers and Adventurers, 315
Song of the South, 8, 77
Sotto, Ed, 156, 163
South Korea, 301, 397, 398
Space Mountain, 33, 42, 61, 62, 75, 88, 90, 222, 223, 228, 229, 248, 267, 274, 294, 298, 300, 305
Space Place Food Port, 61
Space Traffic Control, 253, 300
SpacePort, 61
Spain, 138, 140, 141, 142, 143, 144, 206, 211
Spice Alley, 358, 372, 373
Splash Mountain, 77, 78, 79, 80, 154, 224
Spruce Goose, 100
Spyglass Hill, 190
Stanek, Frank, 12, 13, 14, 19, 20, 21, 40, 397
Staggs, Thomas, 225, 259, 270, 271, 296, 379
Star Cars garage, 249

INDEX

Star Course, 212
Star Tours, 73, 74, 75, 89, 96, 117, 154, 156, 168, 177, 198, 200, 212, 222, 229, 324
Star Traders, 198
Star Wars Launch Bay, 379
Starcade, 61
Stargazer Grill, 379
Starjets, 33, 61
Stark Tower, 324
Starspeeder, 73, 200
Steamboat Willie, 137, 374
Steinberg, Mickey, 164, 165, 170, 171
Stern, Bob, 162, 163, 164, 166
Stitch Encounter, 300, 304, 378
Stormrider, 117, 131
Storybook Land, 200, 212, 380
Storybook Store, 45, 179
Storyhouse Stage, 386
Storytellers Statue, 376
Studio 1, 246, 248, 251, 252
Studio 5, 251
Studio Tram Tour, 248, 252
Sunshine Boulevard, 367
Surrell, Jason, 71
Sweethearts Confectionery, 375
Swiss Family Robinson Treehouse, 90, 189
Takahashi, Masatomo, 5, 6, 10, 22, 23, 30, 31, 33, 39, 40, 67, 73, 98, 103, 106
Tangled, 67, 212, 320, 321, 367, 380, 382
Taran, 69
Tatum, Donn, 9, 18
Teddy Roosevelt Lounge, 116
Television Production Tour, 248, 253
Temple du Péril, 120, 213
Temple of the Crystal Skull, 118
Terasaki, Yaeko, 39
Terravators, 126
terrorist, 174, 235, 236, 237
Tezuka, Osamu, 9
The AristoCats, 56
The Art of Disney Animation, 247
The Black Cauldron, 68, 69
The Brave Little Tailor, 197
The Coffee Grinder, 180
The Emperor's New Groove, 120
The Eternal Sea, 61
The Glass Slipper, 68
The Hub, 45, 46, 47, 53
The Island at the Top of the World,, 167

The Jungle Book, 62, 189, 195, 247, 367, 386
The Legend of Mythica, 112
The Lion King, 247, 248, 257, 287, 336, 338, 358, 373, 386
The Little Mermaid, 124, 160, 168, 192, 212, 320, 321, 380
The Princess and the Frog, 320
The Spinning Mill, 200
The Sword in the Stone, 212
The Toy Chest, 181
Theater District, 375
Theater Orleans, 50
Themed Entertainment Association, 127, 316, 398
Thomas, Jim, 105, 346, 408
Three Caballeros, 375
Three Men and a Baby, 144
Thunder Mesa, 183, 184, 185, 186, 211, 226
Thunder Mesa Riverboat Landing, 183, 226
tickets, 42, 49, 59, 68, 89, 166, 179, 276, 277, 283, 295, 301, 313, 368, 390
Tigger, 87, 179, 291, 292, 366
Tiki Tropic Shop, 50
Timothy Mouse, 196
Tinker Bell, 82, 227, 308, 319, 321, 371, 377
Tinkerbell Toy Shop, 59
Tivoli Gardens, 158
Toad Hall Restaurant, 195
Toad's Wild Ride, 63, 195
Toho Studios, 64
Tokyo DisneySea (TDS), 72, 86, 88, 95, 101, 103, 105, 106, 107, 108, 110, 111. 116, 119, 120, 121, 123,125,126, 128, 130, 131, 222, 243, 253, 255, 392, 398
Tom Sawyer Island, 54
Tom Sawyer Treehouse, 55
Tomorrowland, 14, 27, 43, 45, 46, 60, 61, 62, 67, 73, 74, 75, 81, 84, 86, 87, 89, 95, 116, 156, 197, 267, 285, 293, 294, 300, 305, 307, 324, 332, 354, 377, 378, 379
Tomorrowland Terrace, 61, 81
Tony Solaroni, 74
Toon Studio, 245, 251, 252, 255, 256, 258
Toontone Treats, 85
Toontown, 84, 85, 94, 251, 255
Tower of Terror, 114, 115, 222, 252, 253
Town Square, 178, 179, 180, 181, 285, 286, 304, 317, 323
Toy Soldier Parachute Drop, 255, 310
Toy Story, 67, 114, 248, 254, 255, 258, 293, 304, 306, 309, 310, 313, 314, 336, 354, 358, 366, 371, 372
Toy Story Land, 254, 306, 309, 310, 313, 314, 354
Toyville Trolley Park, 114
Trader Sam's Jungle Boutique, 189
Tragic Kingdom, 204
trains, 32, 54, 71, 88, 92, 142, 186, 310, 312, 378, 389

Treasure Cove, 354, 356, 366, 382, 383, 385
Treasure Island, 8, 139, 155, 190
Treasures of Scheherazade, 188
Triton's Kingdom, 123
TRON Lightcycle Power Run, 378
Troubadour Tavern, 56
Tsang, Donald, 267, 279, 280, 306, 313, 325
Tsing Yi Island, 263
Tsukiji, 7
Tumbleweed, 71
Turley, Tom, 81
Turtle Talk With Crush, 116, 304
TV, 9, 39, 43, 84, 99, 114, 159, 168, 173, 204, 207, 210, 233, 269, 272, 300, 314, 333, 334, 335, 360, 379, 399
Undersea Observatory, 116
Uptown Boutique, 45
Urayasu, 1, 2, 3, 5, 6, 7, 10, 17, 18, 19, 30, 33, 36, 65, 72, 92, 97, 98
Valentina's Sweets, 111
Venetian Goldolas, 112
Venturi, Bob, 164
Verne, Jules, 82, 125, 126, 156, 198, 199, 221, 222, 223
Videopolis, 165, 166, 167, 199, 222, 223, 228
Visionarium, 81, 159, 198, 228
VoluntEARS, 318, 351, 353, 355, 368
Voyage on the Crystal Grotto, 380
Vulcania, 125, 222
Vulcania Restaurant, 125
Walker, Card, 9, 17, 19, 20, 23, 30, 39, 40, 46, 139
Walt Disney Imagineering, 13, 27, 31, 106, 154, 268, 347, 360
Walt Disney Presents, 8
Walt Disney Company (WDC), 98, 102, 103, 106, 107, 150, 160, 216, 217, 218, 257, 266, 267, 276, 301, 318, 325, 333, 334, 336, 337, 338, 342, 347, 348, 353, 354, 394, 395, 396, 397
Walt Disney Imagineering (WDI), 27, 117, 243, 245, 251, 252, 268, 321
Walt Disney Productions, 8, 14, 17, 18, 19, 21, 30, 34, 39, 137
Walt Disney Studio Park (WDS), 243, 244, 245, 246, 247, 248, 249, 250, 251, 252, 253, 254, 255, 257, 309, 310
Walt Disney World (see WDW), 10, 12, 13, 14, 17, 20, 27, 28, 31, 32, 34, 39, 47, 63, 99, 141, 159, 241, 271, 279, 359, 370, 372
Walt's-An American Restaurant, 181, 221
Wandering Oaken's Trading Post, 234
Waterfront, 112, 115
Watson, Ray, 39
WDW (see Walt Disney World), 14, 34, 39, 46, 51, 56, 57, 58, 59, 61, 62, 63, 68, 70, 71, 73, 77, 78, 79, 82, 86, 88, 90, 95, 123, 126, 157, 162, 169, 171, 177, 181, 184, 187, 190, 194, 198, 208, 209, 234, 242, 251, 252, 253, 254, 258, 270, 275, 291, 303, 304, 312, 381, 383

WED Enterprises, 12, 13, 21, 27, 63, 64, 154
Weis, Bob, 347, 349, 374
Wells, Frank, 100, 104, 140, 141, 145, 146, 157, 163, 164, 165, 216, 284, 332, 333
Wells, H.G., 82, 156, 198
Westcot, 104
Western River Expedition, 184
Western River Railroad, 33, 48, 49, 54, 72
Westernland, 33, 43, 47, 49, 52, 53, 54, 55, 56, 57, 58, 67, 71, 77, 79, 154, 182
Whirlpool, 124
Wilderness Island, 187
Williams, Roy, 319
Willis, Kelly, 321
Wilson, Mandy, 39, 146, 161, 162
Winnie the Pooh, 59, 87, 227, 291, 292, 334, 335, 337, 366, 381
Wishing Star Lake, 367, 373
Wolber, Tom, 235, 238, 257, 359
Wonderful People and Their World, 12
Wonderful World of Disney Parade, 248
Wonders of China, 332
Wong, Esther, 264, 273, 298
Woodcarver's Workshop, 187, 227, 234
Woodward, Doris, 265
Woody's Roundup Village, 234
World Bazaar, 32, 39, 40, 41, 43, 44, 45, 46, 47, 57, 81, 83, 86, 111, 139
World Of Disney store, 373
World War II, 2, 5, 8, 20, 64, 131, 264, 310
Yacht Club Restaurant, 234
Yazu Park, 4
Zambini Brothers Ristorante, 111
Zed, 129
Zimbabwe, 399, 400
Zzyxx, 74, 82

About the Author

William Silvester is a free lance author with a love of things Disney. In addition to hundreds of articles he has also written Handbook of Disney on Stamps, The Adventures of Young Walt Disney and Saving Disney: The Roy E. Disney Story, available on Amazon.com.

For more information go to williamsilvester.weebly.com.

Printed in Great Britain
by Amazon